Contemporary Pakistan

Contemporary Pakistan

Political Processes, Conflicts and Crises

Veena Kukreja

SAGE Publications
New Delhi/Thousand Oaks/London

First published in 2003 by

Sage Publications India Pvt Ltd
M-32 Market, Greater Kailash-I
New Delhi 110048

Sage Publications Inc
2455 Teller Road
Thousand Oaks, California 91320

Sage Publications Ltd
6 Bonhill Street
London EC2A 4PU

Published by Tejeshwar Singh for Sage Publications India Pvt Ltd, typeset at Instill Technologies in 10 pt Egyptian 505BT and printed at Chaman Enterprises, Delhi.

Library of Congress Cataloging-in-Publication Data

Kukreja, Veena, 1960–
    Contemporary Pakistan: political processes, conflicts and crises/Veena Kukreja.
        p. cm.
    Includes bibliographical references and index.
        1. Pakistan—Politics and government. 2. Civil-military relations—Pakistan. 3. Political stability—Pakistan. 4. Authoritarianism—Pakistan. 5. Democracy—Pakistan. I. Title.

JQ629.A91 K85   954.904–dc21   2002   2002073420

ISBN: 0-7619-9682-6 (US-Hb)   81-7829-146-0 (India-Hb)
            0-7619-9683-4 (US-Pb)   81-7829-147-9 (India-Pb)

Sage Production Team: K. Shankarnarayan, Shahnaz Habib, Mathew P. J. and Santosh Rawat

Contents

List of Tables

List of Abbreviations

AIML	All India Muslim League
ANP	Awami National Party (formerly the NAP)
APC	All Party Conference
APMSO	All Pakistan Muhajir Student Organization
ARD	Alliance for the Restoration of Democracy
ATA	Anti-Terrorism Act, 1997
BCCI	Bank of Credit and Commerce International
BDs	Basic Democracies
BNA	Baluch National Alliance
BNM	Baluchistan National Movement
BNP	Baluchistan National Party
BPLF	Baluchistan People's Liberation Front
CA	Constituent Assembly
CENTO	Central Treaty Organization (formerly Baghdad Pact)
CGS	Chief of General Staff
CIA	Central Intelligence Agency (US)
C-in-C	Commander-in-Chief
CII	Council of Islamic Ideology
CJCSC	Chairman of the Joint Chief of Staff Committee
CMLA	Chief Martial Law Administrator
COAS	Chief of Army Staff
COP	Combined Opposition Parties
CSP	Civil Service of Pakistan
DCC	Defence Committee of the Cabinet
DG	Director General
EBDO	Elective Bodies (Disqualification) Order 1959
FATA	Federally Administrated Tribal Areas
FIA	Federal Investigation Agency

FMS	Foreign Military Sales
FSF	Federal Security Force
GDA	Grand Democratic Alliance
GHQ	General Head Quarter
GST	General Sales Tax
HuM	Harkat-ul-Mujahideen
IB	Intelligence Bureau
ICOs	Indian Commissioned Officers
IDA	Islamic Democratic Alliance
IJI	Islami Jamhoori Ittehad
IMF	International Monetary Fund
ISI	Inter-Services Intelligence
ISID	The Inter-Services Intelligence Directorate
JCO	Junior Commissioned Officer
JeM	Jaish-e-Mohammad
JI	Jamaat-i-Islami
JCSC	Joint Chiefs of Staff Committee
JUI	Jamiatul Ulama-i-Islam
JUP	Jamiatul Ulama-i-Pakistan
JWP	Jamhoori Watan Party
KCOs	King's Commissioned Officers
LeT	Lashkar-e-Toiba
MI	Military Intelligence
ML	Muslim League
MNA	Member of the National Assembly
MPA	Member of the Provincial Assembly
MQM	Muttahida Quami Movement (formerly Muhajir Quami Movement)
MRD	Movement for the Restoration of Democracy
NAP	National Awami Party
NDP	National Democratic Party
NGO	Non-Governmental Organization
NLC	National Logistics Cell
NWFP	North-West Frontier Province
PCO	Provisional Constitutional Order, 1981
PDA	Pakistani Democratic Alliance
PIA	Pakistan International Airlines
PIF	Pakistan Islamic Front
PML	Pakistan Muslim League (formerly AIML)
PNA	Pakistan National Alliance

PNCB	Pakistan Narcotic Control Board
PPP	Pakistan People's Party
PRODA	Public Representative Offices (Disqualification) Act
RAW	Research and Analysis Wing (Indian Intelligence Organization)
RCO	Revival of Constitutional Order, 1985
SAARC	South Asian Association for Regional Cooperation
SAMs	Surface-to-Air Missiles
SBNF	Sindhi-Baluchi National Front
SBPF	Sindhi-Baluchi-Pakhtun Front
SCOs	Senior Commissioned Officers
SEATO	South East Asia Treaty Organization
SNA	Sindh National Alliance
TJP	Tehrik-i-Jafaria Pakistan (formerly TNFJ)
TNFJ	Tehrik-i-Nifaz-i-Fiqah-i-Jafaria
UF	United Front, 1954
ULFA	United Liberation Front of Assam
USMAAG	United States Military Assistance Advisory Group
VCO	Viceroy's Commissioned Officer

Acknowledgements

Several individuals and institutions provided vital assistance during the preparation of this study. A number of friends and colleagues in the scholarly community took a keen interest in my work. I have gained much from exchange with a number of colleagues and friends. My greatest intellectual debt is to Professor M. P. Singh, my colleague and former teacher who helped me in innumerable ways, for his invaluable comments, academic discussions and relevant material. He has scrutinized the manuscript and spurred me on with his questions and criticisms and balanced it with unflinching faith and encouragement.

Data collection for this study proved to be a Herculean task in which many people generously devoted their energy and time. Special thanks are due to my Pakistani friends for sending me some of the most recent articles and other materials on Pakistan published there. I would like to express my appreciation to the staff of the Pakistan High Commission for providing required material.

I wish to thank the Institute for Defence Studies and Analysis Library, New Delhi; the Indian Council for World Affairs Library, the Indian Institute of Public Administration Library, the Jawaharlal Nehru University Library, the Delhi University Central Library, the Ratan Tata Library, the Ministry of External Affairs Library, the Ministry of Defence, Historical Division, the Teen Murti Library, and the United Service Institution of India Library for the assistance rendered to me in the collection of material for this study. I would like to express my sincere thanks and appreciation to my friend Ms. Amita Narang, Senior Library Assistant of IDSA, for tirelessly and competently helping me with relevant books and journals.

I also wish to express gratitude to my colleagues in the Department of Political Science, University of Delhi, especially Professor Manoranjan Mohanty, Professor Subrata Mukherjee, and Professor Neera Chandhoke, for their support and cooperation. Mr. Nand Lal deserves thanks for his meticulous and conscientious typing.

I would like to place on record my gratitude to my publishers and Ms Omita Goyal of Sage Publications for the encouragement and support they gave me.

Long years of research and writing a book would have been impossible without the understanding and support of my family. My mother as ever has offered me unflagging support, without her sensibility and understanding, whose confidence in me is a constant source of reassurance, it would be difficult to justify the burden of an academic career. The display of concern and interest of many friends—Suman, Neelam, Alka, Sunita and Anjana, boosted my morale and alleviated the inevitable strains that accompany scholarship. My sister Meena helped me in various ways with painstaking care during the preparation of this study, and my nephew Kshitij kept me in good humour—this book is affectionately dedicated to them.

The responsibility for inadvertent mistakes, error in interpretation, emphasis, methodology or otherwise are, of course entirely mine.

Delhi University
30 March 2001   **Veena Kukreja**

Introduction

Since its creation in 1947, Pakistan has undergone a tumultuous process of nation-building, struggling to create sufficient consensus and the political institutions necessary for stable polity. The struggle to establish a parliamentary democracy in a federal setting has been handicapped by inter-ethnic strife, social strains, fragmented elite, praetorian rule, and the influences of external powers, both regional and global. Since independence, 'the men on horseback' have four times administrated governments by martial law, seeking to gain legitimacy through the so-called 'civilianization' and 'democratization' of the military regimes. In other words, Pakistan's traumatic and uncertain political history exemplifies a struggle between the forces of authoritarianism and constitutionalism, or a conflict between state and the civil society. Contemporary Pakistan is facing conflicts between the forces of authoritarianism and ethnicity. Simultaneously, today's Pakistan is inflicted with frequent onslaughts of military rule, a rising wave of terrorism and militancy, and a so-called *Jihadi* culture, resulting in increasing sectarian violence and a sinking economy.

Pakistan in the 53rd year of its existence as an independent nation, has entered the most difficult time it has ever faced in its history. Drugs, weapons and terrorism, originally meant for export, are now threatening to destroy Pakistan's own society and polity. In Pakistan, non-state actors possess money power, weapons and a certain mindset that is threatening society and has gone beyond the control of government to dictate how, when, and where these would be used and against whom. Today Pakistan is unable to contain the forces of anarchy it has unleashed.

The use of *Jihad* and gun culture as tools of state policy to acquire strategic depth in Afghanistan and Jammu and Kashmir, has boomeranged on Pakistan. *Madrassas* as 'schools of hate' that were created to wage the proxy war in Afghanistan and later in Kashmir, have no doubt served Pakistan's short-term interests. But in the long-term they have created rabid/fanatical fundamentalists who are ultimately likely to wreck and ruin Pakistan. The steep increase in violent Shia-Sunni sectarian clashes exemplifies this point. By sponsoring terrorism, Pakistan has let loose hydra-headed monsters, either in the form of drugs, arms proliferation or the *Jihadi* culture, that have torn the fragile weave of its society and polity. This is the cost Pakistan is paying for waging proxy war against India.

For 25 years, out of the 53 years of its existence, the military has been the final arbiter of Pakistan's destiny. Dominated by Punjabis and representing landed and industrial interests, the military regards its dominance of Pakistani politics not only as a right but as a duty based on the need to safeguard the territorial integrity of the country in the face of lingering ethnic, linguistic and religious fissures. Praetorian interventions in the name of order and stability have been justified by an alleged commitment to improve the economy, although the economic performance during these military regimes has been of less significance in determining their survival than have the persistent problems of sub-national identities, organizational ineptitude, socio-economic disparities and crises of governance.

The interplay of regional and international factors with the socio-economic dynamics underlying political processes reveals a fascinating example of state formation in Pakistan. At the time of its creation, Pakistan had no well-developed party organization, and is still struggling to establish a strong grass-roots party based system of parliamentary democracy. The Muslim League government in the early years of young Pakistan was not able to effectively integrate its provinces or distribute resources fairly between the dominant Punjab and the subordinate provinces of East Pakistan, the North-West Frontier Province and Baluchistan and Sindh, as well as between the diverse linguistic groups within them. However, state-building in the difficult circumstances of the early years entrenched the centre and the bureaucratic-military elite at the expense of the political institutions and processes. The institutional dominance of predominantly Punjabi civil and military bureaucracies within the state structure has curbed participatory politics and aggravated regional grievances. The representative government, which may have provided a better balance between the provinces and linguistic groups has been under suspension.

To make matters worse, the ruling Punjabi-*Muhajir* (Muslim migrants from India) political group, which came into power in the country, stressed on Islam and the Islamic state to conceal and curb the reality of the country being a microcosm of the ethnic communities that inhabited it. Paradoxically, the ruling coterie attempted to project ethnic divide as unlawful and subversive to national unity and integrity.

The military's pre-eminent position in Pakistan's politics and society is the crystallization of the importance it has enjoyed from the beginning. In an antagonistic regional security environment (hostile relations with India and Afghanistan), a strong apparatus of state security was given precedence over the need to create participatory political institutions and processes. Strong defence posture led to high defence allocations. Almost 60 per cent of the country's total revenue was spent on defence, with little left over for the social sector. Having failed to make even the most nominal investment in human capital, Pakistan's development prospects look somewhat bleak at a time when the international economic environment has limited the prospects of fresh infusions of external assistance.

On the other hand, Western efforts to uphold Pakistan's strategic defence in the wake of Soviet military intervention in Afghanistan in 1979 had only led to an intensification of its internal socio-economic and political dilemmas. The military and economic support lent by the military regime of General Zia-ul-Haq to the Afghan resistance movement, and the presence of some three million Afghan refugees on Pakistani soil, have generated a parallel arms and drug economy which has fractured Pakistan's social fabric. The proliferation of arms as a result of Pakistan becoming a 'frontline state' during the Afghanistan operation has led to the arming of various ethnic groups within Pakistan itself. Since the 1980s, continuous battles between the security forces and the disaffected youth in rural Sindh, violent conflicts between Sindhis and Urdu speaking *Muhajirs* in Hyderabad and Karachi—a city ruled by armed narcotics barons and their moles in the army and the Inter-

Services Intelligence—are simply the most alarming manifestations of the seething hate that has in recent years pitted Sindhi against Punjabi, *Muhajir* against Punjabi, and *Muhajir* against Pathan. The drug money coupled with the easy access of Kalashnikovs have resulted in the brutalization and criminalization of Pakistani society and polity.

After Zia's death in 1988, the restoration of democracy in Pakistan took place. It was optimistically assumed that restoration of democracy under youthful leaders like Benazir Bhutto, and later on Nawaz Sharif, might be able to achieve a long overdue political consensus in which supremacy of political institutions over the bureaucratic-military oligarchy would produce a workable synthesis between the contrasting forces of reformism and ethnic pluralism. Equally, the new political dispensation was expected to be cooptive in seeking the restoration of peace in Karachi, a reprieve from the 'Kalashnikov culture', a friendly regime in Kabul, and a tangible resolution of the Kashmir dispute.

However, 11 years of democracy (1988–1999) were not without road blocks and pitfalls. Pakistan during this period stumbled from one crisis to another. The major issues that confronted Pakistan in the 1990s displayed not only the centrality of Pakistan's problems of governance but also exposed the aimless drift on the part of the leadership, causing widespread disillusionment and fuelling fissiparous tendencies. It is pertinent to note that the democratic regimes of both Benazir Bhutto and Nawaz Sharif had lived under the shadow of the military. The 'Troika system' of power sharing comprising the president, the prime minister and the army reserved the veto power for the army. The restoration of democracy in Pakistan was a semi-restoration of democracy or at best a military-backed regime. A state structure dominated by the non-representative institutions—namely the military and the bureaucracy was not inclined to a transformation that readily asserted the ascendancy of the elected institutions—the parliament, in particular. However, both Benazir and Sharif, respectively, failed to resolve the contradiction between the state structure and political processes in favour of a party-based system by removing a formidable wall of structural obstacles rooted in the very nature of the Pakistani state. Nawaz Sharif during his second term succeeded in amending Article 52-B of the Eighth Amendment. But Sharif became a democratic despot and finally he was deposed by General Pervez Musharraf in October 1999 and the military took over the reigns of power once again.

Even after five decades of its creation, Pakistan is struggling to establish a viable political system. Democracy and democratic institutions have yet to take roots. Its polity has been battered by long spells of military rule and even longer periods of religious, ethnic and economic turmoil. And since the 1990s, relentless Islamization has made things more difficult and has done enough damage to Pakistan itself. The dilemma of state and civil society is evident in the ethnic arena, which is still largely undefined despite its centrality in Pakistan's national experience. In Pakistan, ethnic pluralism is usually dismissed by the policy-makers and reduced to a mere law and order issue. The existing nature of state structure does not provide space for regional autonomy within the federal framework but instead tries to place a lid on the ethnic cauldron through coercion and a so-called Islamic ideology. This is likely to be counter productive by posing a challenge to the very integrity of the country.

Half a century of political failures, civil and military misrule, institutional decay and deepening crises have shaken public faith in the leaders. Today Pakistan is running out of options. It has tried military dictatorship, army-backed civilian dictatorship and democracy. There is a seeming litany of failures which has prompted some analysts and academics to term Pakistan a 'failed state' or a 'failing state'. Some observers describe it in much stronger terms like an 'anarchic state'. And the forecasts for Pakistan include its disintegration into more than one state. However, to call Pakistan a failed state is harsh. An unstable Pakistan is in no one's interest. The issues on Pakistan's national agenda which require urgent and utmost attention are revival of the economy, decentralization of power, provincial autonomy, religious tolerance, people's participation in polity, and curbing the menace of narco power and terrorism. Only restoration of democracy and devolution of real administrative and political power can save Pakistan.

This study consists of nine chapters. The opening chapter concentrates on the struggle for democracy in Pakistan from 1947 to 1958 and from 1971 to 1977. An analysis of the political processes and their underlying socio-economic dynamics along with the bearings of regional and international factors, from 1947 to 1958 suggests that while the state was being constructed, the institutional balance of power shifted in favour of the bureaucracy and the military. The post-military regime, the democratic experiment under Z. A. Bhutto (1971–1977), provides an insight into the patterns of conflict that led the military elite to the restoration of a military-hegemonic system.

Chapter II gives a portrait of Pakistan's premier institution, namely, the military. It analyzes the role of the military in governance in Pakistan. It seeks to explain how and why the military overtly intervened in politics. The chapter also examines the internal dynamics and the changing role and parameters of the military in Pakistan.

Chapter III aims to highlight the mismanagement of the country's economy and current economic crisis focusing on Pakistan's feudal structure, high defence expenditure and burgeoning debt burden. It also seeks to analyze the internal compulsions of Pakistan's political economy and the challenge of economic revival before the present regime.

Chapter IV considers the ineluctable dilemmas of Pakistan, how to weave a viable national identity out of diverse regional and linguistic loyalties and their political aspirations. It also puts into perspective the different movements, ranging from autonomy to political segregation along ethnic lines, that are accruing in Pakistan.

Chapter V highlights that religion has been misused rather than used in the state's construction of nation-building in Pakistan. At various points of time in its political history, religion has been exploited by the rulers of Pakistan to gain popularity, legitimacy and to fight political opponents. The culture of terrorism and *Jihad*, supposedly sanctioned by militant Islam, has bled Pakistani society in terms of accentuation of sectarian tensions and violences.

Chapter VI focuses on the menace of narco power, which has assumed the role of the fourth pillar in Pakistan, by exploring the triangular linkages and the nexus between politics and narcotics, the army and the ISI, and narcotics and terrorism. The relationship between narcotics and the civil society is taken into account to depict the menace of drug addiction and ethnic violence.

Chapter VII seeks to examine the dialectics of the restoration of the democratic process in Pakistan. From 1988 to 1999 a crisis of governability had emerged as a concomitant of the democratic process because the 'Troika system' of power sharing blended the authoritarian tradition with democracy. The military continued to be the strongest political force that could veto Pakistan's transition to democracy.

Chapter VIII describes and explains the phenomenon of the October 1999 coup of General Pervez Musharraf focusing on its background, nature and modality, its legitimatization tactics and so-called civilianization efforts. The future and prospects of democracy are also taken into account.

The final chapter (IX) presents the basic thrust of the work at a more abstract and general level, highlighting linkages between authoritarianism, democracy and development and the nature and direction of change in Pakistan.

Chapter I

Struggle for Democracy:
1947–1958 and 1971–1977

Even after half a century of its creation Pakistan is struggling to build a democratic polity. After 53 years of its existence, Pakistan fails to find leaders and has to fall back on her old masters, the armed forces, to save her from the 'evil' politicians that the military establishment had itself groomed. Unfortunately, democracy was never allowed to flourish in Pakistan. Since 1958, time and again, democracy has been strangled by the periodic imposition of martial law. The right to freedom and political activities has been denied and the constitution trampled under military boots.

However, Pakistan did have a long period (1947–1958) characterized by the trappings of a parliamentary government, but throughout this period the soul of democracy had long been smothered in the absence of general elections and a lack of interest aggregation and participation through political parties as the vehicle for mobilization. Effective power was, throughout, firmly in the hands of a bureaucratic-military oligarchy, notwithstanding successive changes in the form of government and the installation of political parties and political leaders in apparent charge of the state apparatus. After the long spells of military rule, Zulfikar Ali Bhutto's advent to power in 1971 seems to have ushered in an era of historic significance, for not only was it the first civilian government but also the longest to remain in power in Pakistan. However, in due course of time, Bhutto turned authoritarian. He was his own enemy, his arrogance and authoritarianism coupled with his failure to evolve grassroots civilian institutions led to his downfall. General Zia-ul-Haq's military coup in July 1977 displaced Bhutto and once again the chapter of democracy in the chequered political history of Pakistan was closed.

Pakistan is an early and rather curious product of the post-1945 decolonization process. Since its birth in 1947, Pakistan has undergone a turbulent process of nation-building seeking to create institutions and sufficient consensus necessary for stable internal politics. It provides a fascinating case study of the construction of state. The interplay of domestic, regional and international factors weakened the position of political parties and politicians within the evolving structure of the Pakistani state by tipping the institutional balance in favour of the civil and military bureaucracy. The failure of democracy and the ascendancy of military rule in Pakistan is commonly interpreted in terms of the weaknesses in its political party system and difficulties inherent in welding together a linguistically and culturally heterogeneous society. But such an explanation has neglected the complex dynamics underlying the political processes which have contributed to making military intervention the norm rather than an aberration in Pakistan.

This chapter focuses on two early phases of democratic experiment in Pakistan. The first section attempts to answer why, from 1947 to 1958, democracy failed and the bureaucracy and the military came to assume the predominant role in decision-making within the state structure. This will be done through a close and careful scrutiny of the different possible ways in which the interplay of regional and global factors influenced domestic politics and the economy, distorting relations between the centre and the provinces and the dialectics between state formation and political processes. The subsequent section provides an insight into the patterns of civil-military relations and conflicts that emerged in a post-military regime from 1971 to 1977. It also aims to explain why Bhutto failed to subordinate the military, which led to the resurgence of the military-hegemonic system.

State Formation and Political Processes: 1947–1958

The first 11 years of independence were crucial to moulding and shaping Pakistan's political and administrative profile. A new state structure was carved out of the chaos, bloodshed and dislocation caused by partition. Very few states in the world started with greater contradictions and handicaps than Pakistan on the morrow of independence. Pakistan faced serious administrative, political and economic problems along with the outbreak of communal riots and gigantic problems of refugee rehabilitation. However, Pakistan managed to survive despite several odds, defying the belief that it would collapse under the weight of its problems. However, state-building in the precarious circumstances in the early years of the young nation entrenched the centre and the bureaucratic-military elite at the cost of political institutions and political processes. Pakistan shaped up as a centralized and administrative polity which muzzled the growth of autonomous and viable political institutions and political processes. A centralized polity with an entrenched bureaucratic apparatus and a strong military saved Pakistan from collapsing in the early years of independence. However, this shifted attention from the task of institution building and processes that were urgently needed to inculcate in the diversified population a sense of participation, and give encouragement and vitality to the national sentiments that were manifested in the last stages of the freedom movement.[1]

Civilian Institution Building

Pakistan's self-abasing failure to institute even a formal democracy, coupled with periodic free and fair elections at the national and provincial levels, furnishes the obverse side of the British colonial legacy in the subcontinent. The contrasting inheritances of Pakistan and India in terms of state apparatus, coupled with the relative strengths and weaknesses of political parties, moulded the divergent

---

[1]Hasan-Askari Rizvi, *Military, State and Society in Pakistan* (London: Macmillan Press Ltd., 2000), pp. 57–58.

political developments in the first decade after partition in the two countries.

Colonial Inheritance

The absence of central-state apparatus in the territories constituting Pakistan gave a rather different turn to the unfolding dialectics between state formation and political processes. The imperatives of constructing an entirely new central authority from scratch, over territories which for long had been governed from New Delhi, together with the weakness or near non-existence of the Muslim League's organizational machinery, witnessed the administrative bureaucracy gaining an edge over the political arms of the state. The provinces continued to be the main arena of political activity in Pakistan. Those engaged in constructing and managing the new central government apparatus were politicians with the weakest or no social bases of support in the province and they were not able to stand their ground against civil servants trained in the true tradition of colonial bureaucratic authoritarianism. Already handicapped by a meagre share of spoils of partition, the centre was confronted with the challenges of severe socio-economic dislocations coupled with an adverse security environment. The outbreak of the Kashmir war provided an added impetus to the consolidation of central authority in Pakistan, but simultaneously 'sharpened the contradictions between state formation and political processes and, by extension, between the newly constructed centre and the provinces. In the early days of independence fears of reincorporation of areas within Pakistan into the Indian union served to blur the differences between external threats to security and central authority.'[2]

Moreover, Pakistan's threat perception entailed the diversion of scarce resources extracted from the provinces into defence efforts before political processes could become clearly defined. According to a perceptive scholar,

> strained relations with the provinces were hardly conducive for the smooth functioning of political processes given that the main national party had barely scratched the surface in the vast majority of the constituencies. This is where reliance on civil

---

[2]Ayesha Jalal, *Democracy and Authoritarianism in South Asia: A Comparative and Historical Perspective* (Cambridge: Cambridge University Press, 1995), p. 37.

bureaucrats seemed the only option for a central leadership sensing not its own but possibly the states' rapid demise. So it was not merely the absence of democratic ideals that spurred Pakistan's political leaders from Jinnah onwards into seeking comfort in bureaucratic authoritarianism.[3]

Weaknesses of Political Parties
When Pakistan came into existence it had no well-developed party organization which had a significant bearing on the process of state formation in Pakistan. An eminent Pakistani historian believes that Pakistan has not been able to steer its way to stable, consensus based political culture leading to national harmony, due to the absence of national political parties.[4] The Muslim League (ML), which took credit for the creation of Pakistan, has never been able to transform itself from a nationalist movement into a national party that could lead the nation on the path to democracy, constitutionalism and planned economic development. The ML was not comparable in organizational terms to the Congress Party of India, as it failed to perform the twin tasks of institution-building and political mobilization. The Congress Party in India was not only a mass party but also performed the tasks of interest articulation and aggregation and has played a predominant role in the politics of India for three decades. Moreover, the aggregate character of the Congress coupled with the Nehruvian model of consensus politics was a source of great strength.

Unlike the Congress Party, established in 1885, that gradually became a mass party, the ML, established in 1906 by a group of enlightened Muslims to protect their rights and interests, never became a mass party until 1939–1940. It did not promote the culture of internal discussion. Controlled by a small group of leaders, its claim as the spokesman of the Muslims was often challenged by a number of other Muslim organizations which were fighting for independence but did not support the idea of a separate state for the Muslims. It was only after 1937 that the ML made inroads into the Muslim-majority provinces of Punjab and Bengal. A large number of political leaders who occupied important positions in the political system of Pakistan joined the ML during the period 1937–1947, particularly

---

[3]Ibid., p. 50.
[4]M. Rafique Afzal, *Political Parties in Pakistan, 1947–1958*, Vol. I (Islamabad: National Commission on Historical and Cultural Research, 1976), p. 79.

from 1941 to 1947. They had no time to gain the experience of working together as a team and they lacked the norm of disciplined co-operation. Muslim politics in undivided India even in the heyday of the movement for Pakistan was characterized by intrigue, bickering and personal enmity between rival groups and individuals.[5]

An astute scholar, Khalid Bin Sayeed, believes that a parliamentary form of government only works well among homogeneous societies and that Pakistan, which is heterogeneous both physically and culturally, could not sustain the unity that had developed from the Indian Muslims' resistance to being absorbed into the wider Hindu culture.[6] After 1947, submerged differences and the ethnic diversity which was temporarily subsumed in the wholeness of a Pakistani Muslim identity, resurfaced and the League itself became the first casualty of politics where personal loyalties overrode party interests.[7]

The ML suffered from another problem. Most of its senior members who held cabinet posts at the federal level hailed from the Muslim minority provinces and lacked a popular base in Pakistani territory. They were more at ease with the bureaucratic elite, most of whom also came from the Muslim minority provinces, rather than with the leaders hailing from the Pakistani provinces whom they viewed as parochial and lacking sufficient commitment to the party.[8] As a result, the ML leadership was not inclined towards holding early elections. The situation was dangerous for them in East Pakistan (which constituted a majority of Pakistan's population) where their hold was very weak. The ML leadership feared a revolt by the province-based leaders and kept a firm hold over the party by

---

[5]K. J. Newman, 'Pakistan's Preventive Autocracy and Its Causes', *Pacific Affairs*, Vol. XXXII, No. 1 (March 1959), p. 20; 'The Constitutional Evolution of Pakistan', *International Affairs*, Vol. XXXVIII, No. 3 (July 1962), pp. 353–64; also see Reginald Coupland, *India: A Restatement* (London: Oxford University Press, 1945).

[6]Khalid Bin Sayeed, 'Collapse of Parliamentary Democracy in Pakistan', *The Middle East Journal*, Vol. XIII, No. 4 (Autumn 1959), p. 389.

[7]Iftikhar H. Malik, *State and Civil Society in Pakistan: Politics of Authority, Ideology and Ethnicity* (New York: St. Martin's Press, Inc., 1997), p. 30.

[8]Mohammad Waseem, *Politics and State in Pakistan* (Islamabad: National Institute of Historical and Cultural Research, 1994), pp. 89–90 and 108. Also see Omar Noman, *Pakistan: Political and Economic History Since 1947* (London: Kegan Paul International, 1990), pp. 9–10.

assigning key offices to the *Muhajirs* (Muslim migrants from India) or those provincial leaders who were coopted into the system.[9]

The ML could not develop mechanisms and skills to deal with internal dissensions and conflicts. The ML after Jinnah's death and the Pakistan People's Party (PPP) after Bhutto's execution faced difficulties in maintaining their organizational boundaries and discovering charisma to solve internal disputes. As particularistic cleavages began to reemerge, so too did the pattern of playing off powerful intra-provincial interests against each other, and in both cases this ultimately rebounded to the advantage of the rural notables and the bureaucracy. The political vacuum created by Liaquat's assassination and the lack of any accepted procedure for the solution of intra-party rivalries further encouraged factionalism, squabbling and personal jealousy, especially in the North-West Frontier Province (NWFP), Sindh, and the Punjab. The hollowness of the ML party organization was laid bare in the March 1954 elections, when the strength of the ML was crushed, reduced from an overwhelming majority in the provincial legislature to a group of 10 in a House of 309 members.

Problems of membership and of formulating a viable manifesto together with the absence of a realistic policy based on a synthesis of the polarizing forces of religion and reform catapulted the PML into chaos. The disintegration of the party led to a coercive attitude towards other dissenters. Unlike the Congress Party of India, it neither had the opportunity and tradition, nor the stature of leaders to ensure a process of collective leadership or political adjustment through give and take. The PML itself underwent many changes through splits and further splits.

The ML was essentially a party which lived not by programme, but by its leaders. After *Quaid-i-Azam* (the great leader) Muhammad Ali Jinnah's death, it languished as a coalition of Punjabi-Bengali groups, with the North-West Frontier and Sindhi groups sulking on the sidelines. According to a perceptive scholar, 'Instead of developing itself into a full-fledged grassroots party, the PML turned out to be a coalition interested only in gaining power. Its higher echelons engrossed themselves in intrigues and ignored the imperatives of nation-building. The League aligned itself with the non-representative ruling elites who have since used its name and cadres for their own interests. Ghulam Muhammad, Iskander Mirza,

---

[9]Rizvi, *Military, State and Society in Pakistan*, p. 69.

Ayub Khan, Yahya Khan, Zia-ul-Haq and Ghulam Ishaq Khan all used the League to acquire legitimacy.'[10]

The opposition, without whose constructive criticism and watchdog role no democracy can thrive, has always been discouraged from coming together. Any opposition to the ML was considered tantamount to opposition to Pakistan.[11] The foundation of the Awami League in 1949 and other ideological and regional coalitions only incurred the League's suspicion and wrath.

Other political parties in Pakistan have been similarly personality-centred or regional in character. During the 1970 elections in former United Pakistan, the Awami Party and the PPP had gained massive electoral victories but proved to be 'regional parties' at best.

Various governments employed the state apparatus to crush the growth of an opposition through several repressive measures such as arrests, restriction on their political activities and enactment of the Public Representative Offices (Disqualification) Act 1949 (PRODA). Thus, the opposition was deliberately rendered ineffective and dismissed to the periphery of the power structure of Pakistan. Consequently, no tradition of healthy opposition could take firm root, something that is an integral part of the democratic process. Besides, governments in their attempts to win support in the Assembly often bribed members and other important opponents with cabinet posts or granted them import licences or other similar privileges.

Leadership Crisis Pakistan faced a serious crisis of political leadership within a couple of years after its creation. The first year of independence was marked by heavy dependence on the charismatic personality of Jinnah; he was Governor General and President of the Constituent Assembly, and, above all, the founder of the state, recognized as the father of the nation. He overshadowed the administrative process at the federal and provincial levels. Jinnah had the stature, charismatic appeal and unrivalled prestige that commanded and compelled unquestioned acceptance of his leadership all over

---

[10]Malik, *State and Civil Society in Pakistan: Politics of Authority, Ideology and Ethnicity,* p. 31.

[11]Liaquat Ali Khan is reported to have said: 'The formation of new political parties in opposition to the Muslim League is against the interest of Pakistan. If the Muslim League is not made strong and powerful and the mushroom growth of parties is not checked immediately I assure you that Pakistan which was achieved after great sacrifices, will not survive.' *The Statesman* (Calcutta), 28 October 1950.

Pakistan. But he died in September 1948, only 13 months after independence. Liaquat Ali Khan, his lieutenant and first prime minister, partially filled the gap, but he was assassinated in October 1951.

Politics in Pakistan after the assassination of Liaquat Ali Khan was characterized by an absence of competent leadership which led to the politics of non-consensus. The bureaucrats turned politicians who came to power after Liaquat Ali in West Pakistan headed by Ghulam Muhammad, Chaudhri Muhammad Ali, and Iskander Mirza, had absolutely no faith in the people or in democratic institutions. In this respect, India had a very big advantage over Pakistan in terms of the extraordinary leadership of Nehru for 17 years in the nation's formative phase. His leadership gave the parliamentary political system tremendous support, provided it with a set of basic norms and values which he constantly reiterated in his role as the nation's school master, and enabled the system to bear the load of an expanding framework of political participation, economic and social mobilization, and open competition and criticism.

Jinnah, who has wrongly been publicized as a brilliant founder of a state,[12] failed as an institution builder. Obviously, Jinnah failed here. For the political and administrative framework of the new state, he preferred to follow the traditions and legacies handed down by the British[13] and arrogated more powers to himself by assuming the office of governor general. He imposed a highly centralized constitutional system like that adopted by the Government of India Act of 1935 on a country that was both culturally and physically heterogeneous. Control of the ML cabinet and the political machinery was handed over to the governors and bureaucrats. It was a Mudie or a Cunningham who sent detailed reports about the cabinet and party factions.[14] The main tenor of their reports was that the politicians were

---

[12]Ayesha Jalal in her well documented study claims that Jinnah had not envisaged the founding of a state when he set out on his quest for power, which only extended to seeking parity with the Congress Party. He bluffed all through about the concept of Pakistan which he left intentionally undefined; and when the concept materialized in 'a motheaten and truncated form', he was most unhappy but unable to back out. See by the same author, *The Sole Spokesman: Jinnah, The Muslim League and the Demand for Pakistan* (Cambridge: Cambridge University Press, 1983).

[13]Ayesha Jalal 'Inheriting the Raj: Jinnah and the Governor-Generalship Issue', *Modern Asian Studies*, Vol. XIX, No. 1 (1985), pp. 29–53.

[14]Under Jinnah, three of the four provincial governors in West Punjab, the Frontier and East Bengal were British.

not allowing the government machinery to function with its pre-independence bureaucratic efficiency. A dying man, Jinnah could only think of short-term remedies. He decided to place the politicians under bureaucratic tutelage.[15] His successor governments, outdid him in establishing bureaucratic control over politicians.[16]

Extraordinary powers had been vested in the Governor General, which greatly strengthened the hands of these officials, who easily bypassed the authority of the cabinet and, indeed, the parliament. The provincial governments were subordinated to the centre through the bureaucracy which rode roughshod over the politicians holding office. As Khalid Bin Sayeed observes: 'Under the dominating personality of the *Quaid-i-Azam* and his successor, Liaquat Ali Khan, the civil servants effectively controlled the entire administration in the provinces and politicians were kept in power subject to their willingness to obey central government *directives which itself was dominated and run by the bureaucrats.*'[17]

Liaquat's[18] mysterious assassination left the ambitious bureaucracy in total command. A strong nexus also grew between the civil-bureaucracy and the military. Both were drawn and continue to be drawn from the same, mostly land-owning social class and Punjabi-Pathan ethnic groups. It is not surprising, as an eminent scholar observes, that in Pakistan's first two decades, 'the locus of power centred on the civil services rather than either the political leadership, whom it dominated, or the army with which it closely collaborated.'[19]

As the political forces fragmented and the political institutions declined, the bureaucratic elite gained the upper hand and

---

[15]Khalid Bin Sayeed, *The Political System of Pakistan* (Boston: Houghton Mifflin Co., 1967), pp. 62–63. Also see his *Politics in Pakistan: The Nature and Direction of Change* (New York: Praeger Publishers, 1980), p. 26.

[16]Ibid.

[17]Khalid Bin Sayeed, 'Collapse of Parliamentary Democracy in Pakistan', p. 383, emphasis added.

[18]Liaquat Ali Khan had no regard and respect for the sovereign parliament of Pakistan. He openly stated: 'This House (Council of Muslim League) now carries more weight than the Parliament and every word uttered here should be in consonance with its dignity and responsibility. So far as I am concerned, I had decided in the very beginning, and I reaffirm it today that I have always considered myself as the Prime Minister of the League. I never regarded myself as the Prime Minister (chosen by the members of Constituent Assembly)', *Dawn* (Karachi), 9 October 1950.

[19]Hamza Alavi, 'Class and State', in Hassan Gardezi and Jamil Rashid (eds.), *Pakistan: The Roots of Dictatorship* (Delhi: Oxford University Press, 1983), p. 72.

dominated policy making. The appointment of Ghulam Muhammad, a former bureaucrat, as governor general in October 1951, who was succeeded by another bureaucrat with an army background, Iskander Mirza, in August 1955, set the stage for the ascendency of the bureaucracy, supported by the military in the background. They used their knowledge and experience of administration and their connections with their erstwhile colleagues in the senior echelons of the bureaucracy to strengthen their position and manipulate the divided and fragmented political forces. They had close connections with the Army Chief, General Ayub Khan, who was reluctant to come into the limelight, but extended support to them in their resolve to establish a centralized bureaucratic and administrative polity.[20] They engaged in alliance-building with the feudal, industrial, and commercial elite to entrench their position. The 'ruling alliance, drawn mainly from the top echelons of the bureaucracy and the army', adopted 'a concerted strategy' to exploit and manipulate rivalries among the political leaders, which accentuated political fragmentation and ministerial crises.[21] When, in 1954, the political leaders attempted to take on the bureaucratic-military axis by reducing the power of the Governor General, and had completed the draft of a constitution that reduced the head of state to a titular office in the British parliamentary tradition, the Governor General retaliated by dissolving the Constituent Assembly and removing the government. The confirmation of the dismissal by the Federal Court sealed the fate of democracy in Pakistan.[22] The bureaucratic-military elite pursued centralized and authoritarian governance, changed federal and provincial governments at will, and excluded those who questioned their political management.

---

[20]Rizvi, *Military, State and Society in Pakistan*, p.71.

[21]Ayesha Jalal, *The State of Martial Rule: The Origin of Pakistan's Political Economy of Defence* (Cambridge: Cambridge University Press, 1990), pp. 295–96; also see by the same author, *Democracy and Authoritarianism in South Asia*, p. 54.

[22] For details consult Allen McGrath, *The Destruction of Pakistan's Democracy* (Karachi: Oxford University Press, 1996), pp. 102–17.

Social and Ethnic Conflicts and the Emergence of Civil-Military Oligarchy

Social and ethnic conflicts had strong repercussions on Pakistan's polity and facilitated the emergence of a civil–military oligarchy. The new state had many ethnic groups—Punjabis, Baluchis, Sindhis, Bengalis and Pathans—each of which had a variety of subgroups based on ethno-linguistic, occupational, and caste divisions. During the pre-independence period ML leaders grossly underestimated the potency of regional and linguistic forces, pointing out that Islam recognized no regional or linguistic loyalties. However, after its creation Pakistan revealed an entirely different picture. Soon after independence the formidable challenge faced by the ML leaders was the growing ethnic and regional conflict between the Punjabis and Bengalis and the Punjabis and other ethnic groups like the Sindhis and the Pakhtuns.

Ethnic Conflicts The fact was that a geographically and ethnically split country was to be run by a political party like the ML, which had neither the organization nor the experience of its counterpart, the Indian National Congress. Pakistan's political leaders failed to realize 'that a political party like the ML would have to be restructured in such a way that it would develop, on the one hand, grass-roots support throughout the country and, on the other, the skills and the machinery to run the government. This meant that besides being a well-knit organization at the government level, the party would have to provide leadership both at the religious and ethnic levels. The ML leaders simply did not have either the imagination or the resources to develop such a party.'[23]

As a result of these internecine conflicts, the civil and military oligarchy emerged dominant, but they could not provide a clear sense of direction and national unity because the dominance of civil and military bureaucracies in effect meant the dominance of the Punjabi and West Pakistan groups.

In multi-ethnic Pakistan, the Bengalis who were geographically and culturally distinct from West Pakistan constituted the majority population of Pakistan. With 54 per cent Bengali population, it was clear that election on the basis of adult franchise would shift the

---

[23]Sayeed, *Politics in Pakistan: The Nature and Direction of Change*, p. 32.

power away from the Punjabi-*Muhajir* elite to the Bengalis. The reluctance of the central leadership, according to a perceptive scholar, 'to resort to parliamentary democracy was inextricably linked with ethnic divisions.'[24]

The representation of the two regional groups (East and West) in the major institutions—the Constituent Assembly, the civil services and the army, reveals Punjabi domination. In 1953 the Constituent Assembly had 79 members, 33 of whom were Bengalis. The Punjabis dominated the civil services and the army. In addition to this, there was a Dacca-Karachi-Peshawar axis. Bengalis were able to win the support of the Frontier and Sindhi groups because of the resentment that they often displayed towards Punjabi domination. The Punjabis dominated the civil services, and in the army, next to the Punjabis, the Pathans were influential. As far as the civil services are concerned, in 1948, only two East Pakistani bureaucrats held top positions in the civil services compared to 16 West Pakistani senior officials (both Punjabi and *Muhajireen*).[25] By mid-1950, according to one estimate, Bengalis were outnumbered by West Pakistanis in the ratio of five to one.[26] This development disturbed non-Punjabi and non-Urdu speaking communities. Under the quota system in civil service recruitment, East Bengalis could hope to occupy some of the key positions in the future, whereas in the army West Pakistani domination was so complete that East Bengalis could not hope to change the situation for a long time to come. Besides, the majority of ruling class and the state-apparatus were based in West Pakistan. In order to prevent the Bengali population from feeling its own strength and occupying a leading position in the politics of Pakistan, the new ruling class institutionalized a form of ethnic discrimination.

Already, the demographic balance favoured East Pakistan in any democratic framework. Efforts were immediately made, and continued throughout Pakistan's history to expand the Western wing— through the attempted annexation of Jammu and Kashmir, the attempts to persuade some of the Rajput rulers to accede to Pakistan,

---

[24]Omar Noman, *The Political Economy of Pakistan 1947–85* (London: Routledge and Kegan Paul, 1988), p. 9.

[25]Rounaq Jahan, *Pakistan: Failure in National Integration* (New York: Columbia University Press, 1972), pp. 26 and 107. Also see Asaf Hussain, *Elite Politics in an Ideological State* (Folkestone: Dawson, 1979), p. 65.

[26]K. B. Sayeed, *Pakistan: The Formative Phase 1857–1948* (Karachi: Pakistan Publishing House, 1968), p. 392.

the unhappiness about Gurdaspur district not having been included in Pakistan. Jasjit Singh aptly remarks that 'Ethnicity has played an important role in the process, especially in shaping the attitudes and actions of the dominant groups (Punjabi and Pathan) in the power structure of Pakistan. This would even indicate that ethnicity may have, in fact, played a much greater role in the partition of the sub-continent and its further break up than is usually assumed.'[27]

The major constitutional conflicts that took place in Pakistan arose largely over the question of representation to be accorded to the major regional groups in the central legislature of Pakistan. The contradiction was first highlighted by the language question. It was decided by Jinnah and approved by the League's high command that Urdu would be the national language of the country. The Bengalis argued that there should be two state languages, Urdu and Bengali.

Besides, Pakistan deliberately and systematically developed regional disparities between the two wings on political and racial grounds. The central government's attitude toward East Pakistan and its citizenry was a 'parody of English colonialism.'[28] Economic policy formulated under the influence of West Pakistani civil servants had been such that industrialization in West Pakistan had forged ahead leaving East Pakistan far behind. In addition, central government expenditure because of the location of Karachi and the concentration of the army in West Pakistan was much greater in West Pakistan than in East Pakistan. East Bengal contributed much more to foreign earnings of the country than the West and yet it was lagging far behind West Pakistan in economic development. Almost immediately after partition East Pakistan's economic exploitation began, its resources were utilized for the development of West Pakistan. The industrial enterprises set up in East Pakistan, were, in main, controlled by non-Bengali businessmen and financed by West Pakistani capital. It was, according to a perceptive scholar, 'a classical colonial situation, raw materials from the East brought in foreign exchange, which was used to develop Karachi and the Punjab. The goods produced in the West were off-loaded in the East.'[29]

---

[27]Jasjit Singh, 'The Army in the Power Structure of Pakistan', *Strategic Analysis*, Vol. XVIII, No. 7 (October 1995), p. 861.
[28]Tariq Ali, *Can Pakistan Survive: The Death of a State* (Harmondsworth: Penguin Books, 1983), p. 46.
[29]Ibid.

The Bengalis had often displayed their resentment towards Punjabi domination in the civil services and in the army. Some of the landlord politicians from Punjab, Sindh and the Frontier shared the same cultural and political outlook as the Urdu speaking Bengali Prime Minister Nazimuddin (1951–1953), and his associates or even the later Bengali Prime Minister, Mohammad Ali Bogra (1953–1955). But these similarities soon dissolved into differences, the Punjabi land-owning politicians being much closer both in outlook and interests to the Punjabi civil servants and military officers than the Bengalis could ever be. Punjabis, by playing a deliberately designed ethnicized role in the politics of Pakistan, had manipulated economic, political, and social policies to maximize their power. This sensitized Pathan, Baluchi, and Sindhi ethnic boundaries. The unprivileged, dissident ethnic elites started asserting their cultural and linguistic identities as nationalities, and they demanded vis-à-vis the predominant and privileged ethnic group of Pakistan, a fairer distribution of positions in the bureaucracy and the army. Military use of ethnic force (predominantly Punjabi) by political elites against other ethnic groups was reinforced in Bengal in 1971 and Baluchistan in 1974 and in Karachi in the 1980s onwards. The praetorian role of the army to hold ethnic and national identities together through coercion could be interpreted in terms of the military's predominantly Punjabi recruits who identified the state as well as its socialisation with a nationalistic ethic.[30]

Ayesha Jalal, focusing on institutional imbalances and the question of 'ethnicity' and provincialism, observes that

'in strategically situated countries like Pakistan, tensions between the centre and the provinces are not merely a reflection of the difficulties involved in integrating linguistically and culturally diverse constituent units. The problem is at the same time more complex—basic, because demands of provinces and linguistic groups within them are not often demands for a larger share of the state's financial resources, and more complex, because finances are generally limited, especially when the state's strategic perceptions have resulted in a political economy of defence characterised by the maintenance of defence budgets well beyond its resource

[30]Asaf Hussain, 'Ethnicity, National Identity and Praetorianism: The Case of Pakistan', *Asian Survey*, Vol. XVI, No. 10 (October 1976), pp. 929–30.

capacities. The response in either case tends to be the centralization of state authority and the pursuit of development policies aimed at maximising revenues rather than social welfare—a process in which Pakistan saw the non-elected institutions assuming dominance over the elected institutions of the state. These non-elected institutions carried a legacy of uneven recruitment patterns from the colonial area, thus exacerbating the problem of integrating diverse linguistic and social economic groups.[31]

In the wake of ethnic conflicts the orthodox and conservative Islamic parties, most of which lost their credibility in the last phase of the independence movement due to their refusal to endorse the ML demand for Pakistan, found the confusion in Pakistani politics suitable for staging a comeback by demanding the establishment of an Islamic state on conservative lines. The ML, unable to cope with the political situation, tried to win them by yielding to some of their demands. This emboldened them and they began to raise narrow sectarian issues and launched a political onslaught on the Ahmadiya community, demanding they be declared non-Muslims. These controversies further confounded Pakistani politics and accelerated fragmentation and decay of the political process.[32]

Bureaucracy Overrules Politics

In a young country like Pakistan, the bureaucracy has constantly overstepped, bypassed, dismissed and denigrated the mass verdict by simply opting for authoritarianism. The public servants have acted as masters and kingmakers, missing no opportunity to malign the politicians among the people. While politicians have been presented as mischievous, corrupt and inefficient, their favours have been nevertheless sought to legitimize authoritarian regimes from Malik Ghulam Muhammad through to Ghulam Ishaq Khan. A constant erosion of civil authority has been matched by an all-transcending state power.

In the post-Liaquat era Ghulam Muhammad's ascendancy marked the second phase in Pakistan of bureaucratic ascendancy, demonstrating the emerging power of bureaucrats who openly

---

[31]Jalal, *The State of Martial Rule: The Origin of Pakistan's Political Economy of Defence*, p. 3.
[32]Rizvi, *Military, State and Society in Pakistan*, p. 70.

played a political role and manipulated politicians to suit their purpose. The first blatant instance of the attitude of civil servants to politicians was Nazimuddin's removal by Ghulam Muhammad in 1953. Prime Minister Nazimuddin, an honest but weak Bengali Leaguer, who enjoyed a majority in the Constituent Assembly, was dismissed by the Governor General Ghulam Muhammad, who never held electoral office and came from the British India's Audit and Accounts Service. He was courted by a coterie of ambitious bureaucrats who deeply abhorred politicians and political processes. Ghulam Muhammad buried himself in palace intrigues fearing that the Prime Minister would sweep the polls by means of the Bengali ethnic majority. He was duly assisted by Iskander Mirza, a cunning civil servant with 28 years' experience, and the ambitious Commander-in-Chief (C-in-C) General Ayub Khan, who was keen to establish closer strategic relations with Western powers in order to build Pakistan's defence establishment.[33]

Nazimuddin was the first but not the last casualty of the bureaucracy and military's onslaught on the politicians. However, at one stroke, the Bengalis in particular and politicians in general had been thwarted and a message was sent to others 'to behave'. Ghulam Muhammad used the Government of India Act of 1935 to justify his action on the basis of the law and order situation both in East Pakistan and Punjab. In Bengal there had been language riots in 1952, in Punjab there had been anti-Ahmadi riots in 1953. A partial martial law had been imposed in Lahore to suppress the riots and anti-Ahmadi movement which was a command performance by the ambitious Punjabi Chief Minister, Mumtaz Daultana, an aristocrat, who in collusion with the *Muhajir*-Punjabi bureaucracy, tried to create problems for Khawaja with an eye to capture power. Nazimuddin was dismissed and Daultana gained nothing at all. However, the state had succeeded in creating a further polarization of the faction-prone politicians.

This exemplifies how the political process was working. In the case of martial law in Lahore the decision was prompted by pressure from the civil services (particularly from Iskander Mirza, who was then defence secretary) and carried out by the army. The dismissal of Khawaja Nazimuddin as prime minister was obvi-

---

[33]Malik, *State and Civil Society in Pakistan: Politics of Authority, Ideology and Ethnicity*, pp. 61–62.

ously a decision not taken by the central legislatures. This unconstitutional action of Ghulam Muhammad unambiguously demonstrated the political supremacy of the civil services and the army.

Another example of the bureaucratic manipulation of the state structure is the establishment of the One Unit scheme which was ingeniously conceived to counter-balance the Bengali majority in any elected assembly. It delighted many Punjabi politicians as it facilitated their domination of the four provinces in the Western wing and gave them parity with East Pakistanis. The fear of Bengali domination in these politicians and their benefactors in the state was justified when the United Front won a clear majority over the Muslim League in the provincial elections of March 1954 in East Pakistan. While the Front led by stalwarts like Fazlul-Haq, H. S. Suhrawardy and Maulana Bhashani won around 300 seats, the League had only 10. The overwhelming electoral victory of the United Front 'marked the first major defeat to be inflicted on the bureaucracy and its favoured coterie of politicians.'[34] The Front aimed at ruling the whole of Pakistan given the chance and their 21-point manifesto promised land reforms, the formulation of a constitution and social welfare-oriented measures that disturbed the bureaucracy-military and landed aristocracy axis. Consequently, after a series of vulgar provocations, Ghulam Muhammad dissolved the newly elected Assembly on 30 May 1954, only two months after the elections and proclaimed Governor's rule. The ex-Major General Iskandar Mirza was sent to replace the veteran politician, Khaliquzzaman, as the new provincial governor. Mirza's military-bureaucratic status was ideal for the job that he had been assigned. The United Front leaders were arrested as were thousand of their supporters. Mirza threatened the Bengali politicians with the imposition of martial law. The state structure had shown once again how far it would go to preserve its own petty interests.

In October 1954, the people of East Pakistan took an independent stance vis-à-vis the domination of the bureaucracy by introducing the proposals for constitutional amendment designed to curb the powers of the Governor General. In a sharp reaction to it, on 24 October 1954, the Governor General declared a 'state of emergency'

---

[34]Tariq Ali, *Can Pakistan Survive*, p. 47.

and dissolved the Constituent Assembly.[35] The Governor General had not only relied on his supporters in the Punjabi group, the civil services and the army, but also formed a new cabinet called a ministry of 'all talents', remarkable only for its utterly unrepresentative character. It included General Ayub Khan, the Commander-in-Chief as Defence Minister,[36] the Governor General himself, an ex-civil servant as the Minister of the Interior and Chaudhri Mohammed Ali, a former head of the civil service, as Finance Minister. The Prime Minister was still Muhammed Ali Bogra, who had lost all effective power. It could be said that real power was in the hands of administrators in the government who had the backing of the army.

The regime sought to control democracy because the West Pakistani Punjabi leaders were apprehensive even under the parity system of representation in the Assembly. The military-bureaucratic oligarchy was worried about West Pakistan. As it continued to suffer defeats in successive by-elections, it became clear that if free elections were permitted the ML would lose three provinces. The bureaucracy was petrified. Its recurring nightmare was a combination of Bengal and the non-Punjabi provinces in West Pakistan, which would represent a large majority in any national or federal legislative assembly. The scheme of 'One Unit' was conceived to prevent any such development. This entailed the abolition of provinces in the western part of the country, and the formation of a party which could unite the landed gentry of all regions. It was imagined that a 'united' West Pakistan would be better able to combat the demands of East Bengal.

The *de facto* central elite, being aware of the dangers that vernacular elites from Bengal armed with a mandate for maximum provincial autonomy could pose—in terms of repercussions on the economy and the military's strategic position—went on to devise

---

[35] *Dawn* colourfully commented that 'There have indeed been times—such as that October night in 1954—when, with a General to the right of him and a General to the left of him, a half mad Governor-General imposed upon a captured Prime Minister the dissolution of the Constituent Assembly and the virtual setting up of a semi-dictatorial executive.' Editorial, 'Revolution', *Dawn* (Karachi), 11 August 1957.

[36] The induction of Ayub Khan in the new cabinet as Defence Minister and also as C-in-C was not only unprecedented but also unprincipled and wholly opposed to the idea of a civilian supremacy over the military establishment. In his capacity as the Defence Minister the army chief became his own boss.

and impose the One Unit plan integrating West Pakistan.[37] It has been reported that General Ayub had already prepared a plan for the integration of West Pakistan. Ayub Khan argued that strategically and economically West Pakistan should be welded into one unit. To contain the resistance from the provinces of Sindh and the North-West Frontier, the ruling oligarchs used the technique of arbitrary dismissals in Sindh, NWFP and even in the Punjab.[38] Such unchecked methods of dismissal and installation of pliable regimes in the provinces demonstrated the new dictum that absolute power leads to absolute coercion.

Free and open use of coercion and terror to eliminate opposition and the imposition of integration further hardened the deep-seated opposition of Sindhi and Pathan leaders to what they regarded as Punjabi domination. On 14 October 1955, the new 'province' of West Pakistan came into existence. A 'short sighted bureaucracy, desperate to balance East and West, had thus injected the national question into the heart of West Pakistan politics.'[39] The furious opposition of the non-Punjabi provinces to the imposition of the One Unit system in West Pakistan 'was a warning against basing state authority on an administrative centralization while the political system was purportedly federal in structure. Yet it was the absence of any effective system of local self-government in the territories constituting Pakistan, in the West more than in the East, which offers the more striking comment on the bankruptcy of the methods adopted by the state to extend its sway over both economy and society.'[40] For the civil services and army 'to have allowed political parties to mobilize the rural areas prior to the consolidation of the administra-

---

[37]A series of one unit documents drafted by Daultana referred to the fact that West Pakistan, in its confrontation with East Bengal, should speak as one entity because the politicians of East Bengal had often resorted to the 'small brother's big brother' role of West disruption. The cunning course of action recommended was: The first necessity of the present context, therefore, is that we must clear the decks before we launch our political campaign. In other words, 'We must silence and render inoperative all opposition of which we are morally convinced that is motivated by evil.' For details see Sayeed, *The Political System of Pakistan*, p. 76.

[38]*Dawn*, 24 October 1954 and 12 December 1954.

[39]Tariq Ali, *Can Pakistan Survive*, p. 49.

[40]Jalal, *State of Martial Rule: The Origin of Pakistan's Political Economy of Defence*, p. 299.

tive machinery was tantamount to losing the old world with no absolute certainty of holding on to the new.'[41]

Ghulam Muhammad's resignation in 1955 saw him replaced by Mirza. Another bureaucrat turned Prime Minister Chaudhri Mohammad Ali gave the country its first constitution in 1956 which safeguarded a strong centre, preserved parity between the two wings and guaranteed One Unit in West Pakistan. The main function of the new constitution was 'to institutionalize political administration against the Bengalis by denying them the weight they should have had as a majority of the population. The president was given wide ranging powers, and the central government was to be so powerful that provincial autonomy was reduced to a farcical status.'[42] Hastily formulated clauses were inserted in the constitution to protect the bureaucracy from being dismissed without the authorization of the president. Thus, the civil services obtained a higher position than the assemblies and the national constitution without giving up its attempt to wield more powers. Naturally, this accentuated the ethnic divide in the country as the 'Bengalis', especially, resented the *Muhajir*-Punjabi domination of the country.[43]

Adverse Regional Strategic Environment and Consolidation of State Authority

Strategic and economic consequences of partition in general and Pakistan's adversial relations with India in particular influenced the shaping of polity of the new state. Pakistan's strategic defence has only contributed to enhance its internal socio-economic and political dilemmas. At the same time defence vis-à-vis India offered added impetus for the consolidation of state authority in Pakistan.

---

[41] Ibid., p. 300.

[42] Tariq Ali, *Can Pakistan Survive*, p. 49.

[43] Ataur Rahman Khan, then Chief Minister of East Pakistan summed up the feelings of most Bengali politicians when he observed in a parliamentary debate: 'As a matter of fact I may tell you, it may be a great weakness with me that I feel a peculiar sensation when I come from Dacca to Karachi. I feel physically, apart from mental feeling, that I am living here in a foreign country, I did not feel as much when I went to Zurich, to Geneva or Switzerland, or London as much as I feel here in my own country that I am in a foreign land.' Constituent Assembly of Pakistan, *Debates*, Vol. I, No. 4, 19 March 1956, p. 216.

Pakistan's Threat Perception
Pakistan's defence policy was, and is, inseparable from its foreign policy to a much greater degree than in most other countries. In 1947 there was a serious shortage of officers, especially those with staff experience. Pakistan had only one major general, two brigadiers and six colonels in the immediate aftermath of independence as against the requirement of 13 generals, 40 brigadiers and 53 colonels.[44] Besides, Pakistan had no defence industry and was totally dependent upon external supplies for even the most simple arms. Pakistan developed problems with India in the first couple of years which contributed to shaping the Pakistan military's perception of India as an adversary. Pakistan's security was also adversely affected by Afghanistan's irredentist claims on Pakistani territory. Pakistan's quarrels with India—over wide ranging issues, from the distribution of assets of the British Indian government and military to water disputes to territorial disputes in Kashmir—and its division into two wings separated by 1,000 miles of Indian territory made the matter worse and created immense problems for its military planners. As Wilcox aptly remarks, 'Military needs had to command foreign policy. And because foreign and defence policies are for the new states matters of survival, they seriously affect domestic policy. By this chain of logic, the leaders of the Pakistan army were propelled into the centre of decision-making, and became first its arbiter and then its monopolist.'[45] In addition, against the background of long standing confrontation with India and a fear that Pakistan might be vanquished and subjugated, the army stood out in the public eye as the only basis of the nation's survival. The military-bureaucratic oligarchy in Pakistan fostered tensions with India and cultivated fear to capitalize on it. Unlike India, where civilians dominate the defence policy process, the military in Pakistan was and is chiefly responsible for all strategic and structural decisions, and attempts to reduce their role in the decision-making process have never been successful.

---

[44]Major General Fazal Muqeem Khan, *The Story of the Pakistan Army* (Karachi: Oxford University Press, 1963), p. 222.

[45]Wayne A. Wilcox, 'Political Role of Army in Pakistan: Some Reflections' in S. P. Varma and V. Narain (eds.), *Pakistan Political System in Crisis: Emergence of Bangladesh* (Jaipur: University of Rajasthan, 1972), p. 35. Also see Cohen, 'Pakistan', in Edward A. Kolodziej and Robert E. Harkavy (eds.), *Security Policies of Developing Countries* (Lexington: Lexington Books, 1982), pp. 93–118.

However, in this context it is pertinent to note that given Pakistan's security handicap vis-à-vis India's military preponderance, Pakistan came into being as an 'insecure state' and this very insecurity led to the beginning of the Kashmir conflict and the obsession with attaining military parity with India. Pakistan, facing serious problems and challenges of consolidation, sought to blame India for the difficulties in solving its problems, and uncertain of its own identity, assumed a posture of hostility with India to justify its own existence and to define itself. 'The idea that a country has a foreign enemy is easy for the people to understand. It can also provide a powerful stimulus to national unity. For Pakistan, this role was filled by India.'[46] Failure to grab Jammu and Kashmir by force rankled, and this intensified the hostility towards India.

Priority to Defence Requirements Defence requirements enjoyed the highest priority in Pakistan. The civilians and military leaders were equally convinced that Pakistan's troubled relations with India—a stronger military power and Afghanistan's irredentist territorial claims presented a serious threat to national identity and territorial integrity which led them to allocate the largest share of the national budget to the military. From 1947 to 1958 Pakistan had seven prime ministers and eight cabinets belonging to different political parties, but they all shared the perspective that Pakistan must have a strong and powerful military for coping with the antagonistic regional environment. For example, in October 1948, the first Prime Minister Liaquat Ali Khan (August 1947–October 1951) said, 'the defence of the state is our foremost consideration. It dominates all other governmental activities'.[47] In a similar vein, Prime Minister Mohammad Ali Bogra (April 1953–August 1955) asserted that he would much rather starve the country than allow any weakening of its defence.[48] Governor General Iskander Mirza (March 1956–October 1958) declared that it was the 'foremost duty of every Pakistani to strengthen our armed forces so that the country could live in peace.'[49] The National Assembly supported the policy of strong

[46]Hasan Askari Rizvi, *The Military and Politics in Pakistan* (Lahore: Progressive Publishers, 1976), p. 39.
[47]*News Chronicle*, 9 October 1948.
[48]*Dawn* (Karachi), 17 August 1953.
[49]Ibid., 1 August 1957.

defence and the government never faced problems in obtaining the former's approval for the defence expenditure in the national budget.

It is well known that Pakistan spent on an average 60.69 per cent of its national budget on defence from 1947 to 1958, which was quite high given the country's actual social and economic problems. Even after the United States started giving military aid in 1954, defence expenditure in Pakistan has continued to increase instead of going down. According to one observer, Pakistan provides a typical example of a country where 'a poverty of resources for human needs contrasts with the affluence under which military programmes operate. The threats that touch people in their daily lives—joblessness, crime, illness, hunger—rank lower in the scale of government priorities than preparations for war.'[50]

The Strategic Doctrine Pakistan's strategic doctrine was shaped against the backdrop of an adverse regional security environment, in terms of India's military preponderance, Pakistan's security handicaps and the resources constraints, making it difficult to carry on a long-drawn war. According to an eminent scholar, 'A short war was possible only if Pakistan had the capability to raise the cost of the war quickly to unacceptable limits for the adversary.... A pre-requisite for this doctrine was the maintenance of a highly professional trained and well-equipped military with strong fire-power and mobilization.... Pakistan's preferred option was to build pressure on India in Kashmir by engaging in limited military operations there or by extending military support to Kashmiri activists. This strategy was less costly for Pakistan and tied large number of Indian troops in Kashmir.'[51]

Pakistan could not pursue its strategic doctrine without external cooperation as it lacked sufficient domestic resources to develop the required capability. It was therefore not surprising that the military attached such importance to security relations with the United States. International conventions were also important for building diplomatic clout for its disputes with India and Afghanistan.

---

[50]Ruth Leger Sivard, *World Military and Social Expenditure 1977* (Lessburg, Virginia: WMSE Publications, 1977), p. 5.
[51]Rizvi, *Military, State and Society in Pakistan*, p. 66.

Military-Strategic Alliance with the US and Weapons Procurement

Pakistan's policy-makers employed astute diplomacy and extra-regional ties as essential for dealing with an antagonistic regional environment in terms of getting diplomatic support vis-à-vis India, and weapons procurement. Power asymmetry between Pakistan and India to the advantage of the latter and the former's inability to cope with security pressures due to the paucity of domestic resources, deficient technological industrial base, and the urgent need of building strong defence, all led to Pakistan's policy-makers diligently cultivating external linkages and connections.[52]

Prime Minister Liaquat Ali Khan visited the USA to seek support in 1950 in return for a military alliance. But the response from the US was disappointing. After his assassination, power shifted to the bureaucratic-military axis. Ayub had been 'nagging and nudging the defence establishment in the US and Britain to buttress the Pakistan Army since early 1951.'[53] The United States was then seeking cold war partners as Secretary of State Dulles saw the need for enlarging the 'containment' doctrine in West Asia and on China's frontiers Pakistan stood ready to be recruited, or at least its Generals did.[54] In the wake of the declining influence and capabilities of the UK, the United States came to believe that the 'Persian/Iraq sector could not be defended without the help from Pakistan' and a State Department policy statement made it explicit that the 'kingpin of

---

[52]Ibid., p. 64. Also see his 'Pakistan's Threat Perception and Weapons Procurement', in Thomas Wander, Eric Arnett and Paul Bracken (eds.), *The Diffusion of Advanced Weaponry: Technologies, Regional Implications and Responses* (Washington, D.C.: American Association for Advancement of Science, 1994), pp. 193–210.

[53]Jalal, *The State of Martial Rule: The Origin of Pakistan's Political Economy of Defence*, p. 125.

[54]One of the factors that influenced the US decision-makers in extending military aid to a country like Pakistan was that the army with its monolithic unity was much more capable than traditional political parties in serving as a bastion against the quasi-military organization of communist parties. Indeed, a US President's Committee had approved military intervention in developing countries in times of political crises, and concluded that 'the military officer corps is a major rallying point of the defence against communist expansion and penetration.' *Supplement to the Composite Report of President's Committee to Study the United States Military Assistance Program*, vol. 2 (Washington, D.C.: US Government Printing Office, 1959), p. 79.

United States interests in Pakistan was its army.'[55] Pakistan was to serve the role of a strategic base for the US in defence of its oil interests in the Persian Gulf region. US military advisers were attached directly to the Pakistan forces at the General Headquarters and began to wield great influence with the military.[56] The repetition of the 1950s military assistance programme a generation later had given rise to the proverb in Pakistan in the mid-1980s, that the country was ruled by 'three-As' Allah, Army and America, with order shifting from time to time. In the negotiation of Mutual Defence Assistance with the United States in May 1954, it was clear that the prime mover and supreme architect of this special relationship with the US was General Ayub Khan who strenuously wooed and won the Americans. And it seemed equally clear that he did so quite independently, so far as his cabinet 'masters' were concerned.[57] The US arms assistance, historically, has been the root cause of a qualitative jump in Pakistan's military capabilities besides the quantitative effect in force levels. As a result of this alliance with the US the army's tools were not only expanded, but greatly enhanced in quality and sophistication.[58] Along with the equipment came training, and, most important in the long run, exposure to the most current and prestigious military tradition. Pakistan's participation in the South East Asia Treaty Organization (SEATO) and Central Treaty Organization (CENTO) also enabled the armed forces to cover up its deficiencies; it gave the Pakistani armed forces experience of warfare and increased their confidence, striking power and efficiency.

---

[55]Jalal, *The State of Martial Rule: The Origin of Pakistan's Political Economy of Defence*, p. 125.

[56]Tariq Ali, *Pakistan: Military Rule or People's Power* (London: Jonathan Cape, 1970), p. 44.

[57]Mohammad Ahmed, *My Chief* (Lahore: Longmans, Green and Company, 1960), pp. 75–76; and Muqeen Khan, *The Story of Pakistan Army*, p. 154.

[58]In terms of the badly needed military hardware the total assistance extended to Pakistan from 1954 to 1965 amounted to between $1.2 and $1.5 billion. Selig S. Harrison, *Washington Post* (Washington, D.C.), 12 August 1965; *New York Times* (New York), 29 August 1965; and *Times of India* (New Delhi), 29 November 1969. Until 1965, the bulk of military assistance to Pakistan came from the US under the provisions of the Mutual Defence Assistance Agreement Programme. From 1955 to 1965 Pakistan received $672 million in direct transfer of defence materials and services and almost $709 million in security supporting assistance and defence-related public law. See US House, *Mutual Development and Cooperation Act of 1973, Hearings*, 93rd Congress, 1st Session, pp. 127, 132.

The alliance with the US also drew forth economic assistance worth $3 billion for the country between 1947 through till 30 June 1965.[59]

Moreover, the American connection developed in the mid-1950s played a significant role in shaping the military's professional and political profile. Not only did this give confidence to the military to withstand India's military superiority, it also strengthened its position in the domestic context. The acquisition of modern technology and organizational skills which would be applied to the civil sectors, as well as better training and weapons, accentuated the already existing institutional imbalance between the professional task-oriented and confident military and the weak and incoherent political institutions. The growing strength of the military enabled the service headquarters to enjoy greater autonomy in professional and service matters and disbursement of the defence expenditure. They became 'too powerful' for the political leaders to tamper with and [it] virtually ran itself without outside interference.[60] The military autonomy strengthened overtime and the top brass resented any interference by the civilian government in what they considered to be their professional and internal service affairs. All army chiefs from January 1951 to December 1971 (Ayub Khan, Mohammad Musa and Yahya Khan, as against eight army chiefs in India during the same period) served for extended terms.

It is a well-established fact that since the early 1950s the army had treated the twin affairs of defence and foreign policy as 'reserved' subjects. Conduct of 'Operation Malta' and 'Gibraltar Force' in 1965, imposition of military solution of East Bengal problem (1971), Pakistan Afghan policy (1979), 'Operation Topac' (1988) and Kargil Aggression (1999) exemplify this point.

In this context, it is worth noting that the first military coup (Rawalpindi Conspiracy Case, 1951) failed to get off the ground; but it was motivated by the belief that a military solution to the Kashmir

---

[59]*Principles of Foreign Economic Assistance* (Washington, D.C.: US AID, 1963), p. 20. See Alavi, 'US Aid to Pakistan: An Evaluation', *The Economic Weekly*, Special Number, July 1963, pp. 1209–16; and Ataur Rahman, *Pakistan and America: Dependency Relations* (New Delhi: Young Asia Publications, 1982). Also see Shirin Tahir-Kheli, *The United States and Pakistan: The Evolution of an Influence Relationship* (New York: Praeger Special Studies, 1982).

[60]Stephen P. Cohen, 'State Building in Pakistan', in Ali Banuazizi and Myron Weiner (eds.), *The State, Religion and Ethnic Politics* (Lahore: Vanguard Books, 1987), p. 315.

issue was feasible, and disagreed with the civilian governments' policy on Kashmir, which was perceived as not pushing the military solution. This is not surprising, since the leader of the abortive coup attempt, Major General Akbar Khan, had taken a leading role in the invasion of Jammu and Kashmir in 1947. The underlying conflict may have had more to do with Ayub Khan trying to remove a potential threat from the hero of the Kashmir war, Akbar Khan. They represented two divergent points of view, not only with regard to Kashmir, but also in a broader geo-strategic perspective: Akbar was anti-imperialist, while Ayub was pro-West. But the episode certainly revealed that in spite of superficial similarities, the army was not all that cohesive, and internal rivalries within the army were certainly an important factor.[61]

Dismantling the Political System

The pattern of political process during the first decade of Pakistan's existence represented the kind of squabbles, petty intrigues and kaleidoscopic changes in alliances amongst members of National and Provincial Assemblies in their spineless abdication of power. The internecine feuding among the West Pakistani and East Pakistani politicians ranging 'between the grotesque and macabre,'[62] shows that no major political group either in West or East Pakistan was capable of uniting and running a government in pursuit of a clear and coherent political programme without the support of the civil and military bureaucracy.

The presence of ineffective party organization coupled with the absence of programmatic content to party politics—the political leadership ceased to have any real standing amongst the people. The isolation of the weak and unrepresentative politicians made them especially vulnerable before the bureaucracy which in sharp contrast was cohesive, tightly organized, disciplined and powerful. In such a situation, what the politicians were performing was conferring the mantle of political legitimacy to civil-military oligarchs through the charade of a democratic process, absorbing public

---

[61]Jalal, *The State of Martial Rule: The Origin of Pakistan's Political Economy of Defence*, pp. 120–24.
[62]*The Economist* (London), 11 October 1958, pp. 1–2.

discontent and channelling grievances. Besides, civil servants had mastered the methods of manipulating the feudal, ethnic and political factions, thus dividing and ruling the politicians. During the Mirza years, the office of governor general and later the president's office epitomized bureaucratic control and manipulation of the political leaders. The cabinet instability discredited the political leaders and parliamentary politics in general.

The first instance which showed the direct interest of a section of the military in politics was the Ralwalpindi conspiracy case, 1951. A mystery shrouded this case as the details were never made public and the trial was held in camera. By the time Pakistan's first prime minister became the target of an evidently hired assassin, the institutional balance had begun gravitating away from the political centre in Karachi to the military headquarters in Rawalpindi.

With the dismissal of the Constituent Assembly on 24 October 1954, the bureaucratic-military alliance and their cohorts in political and business circles in West Pakistan congratulated themselves for having successfully established a 'constitutional dictatorship'. It now became infinitely easier to keep the lid on domestic troubles and marshal support for their cause internationally. East Bengal was under Mirza's reliable jackboot; Punjab had been brought into line and the smaller provinces were unlikely to pose any serious threat without one or the other of the two main component units of the state. Ayub's evident role in preparing the blueprint of the integration of the provinces of West Pakistan was another instance of the army's increased influence in political decision-making.[63] In his autobiography Ayub Khan intended to bear a testimony to that fact and outlined the general's belief that a controlled form of democracy was the only appropriate system of government for Pakistan.

To make matters worse, the reign of Iskander Mirza signified bureaucratic manipulation at its peak. President Iskander Mirza, jockeying for power under centralist presidency, survived in a Bismarkian style by dividing his opponents and attempting to change the constitution in a shorter time scale (two years) than the eight years it had taken to create the Governor General system.

---

[63]The full text of memorandum is published in Mohammad Ayub Khan, *Friends Not Masters: A Political Autobiography* (London: Oxford University Press, 1967). Also see Muqeem Khan, *The Story of Pakistan Army*, pp. 186–91; and Mohammad Ahmed, *My Chief*, pp. 74–76.

General Ayub Khan who was watching the situation closely wrote, the President had 'thoroughly exploited the weaknesses in the constitution and had got everyone connected with the political life of the country utterly exposed and discredited.'[64] However, Mirza was pursuing his Machiavellian policies with the support of Ayub Khan who as a C-in-C had been the most powerful member of the central government during 1954–1955. A perceptive scholar on Pakistani politics observes, 'Mirza and Ayub were the two dominant leaders of the civil-military oligarchy that had decided that Pakistan could be governed best by tightening the grip of these two institutions on its government and people.'[65] It is also noteworthy that Pakistan had six prime ministers and one C-in-C in eight years, whereas in the same period India had one prime minister and six C-in-Cs.

Among the major political leaders of that period according to Sayeed, 'Suhrawardy was perhaps the only leader who was firmly committed to freeing the political process from the clutches of civil-military oligarchy.[66] Suhrawardy, who was Prime Minister from September 1956 to October 1957 tried to build a coalition between the Awami League party and the West Pakistan Republican Party. By supporting the One Unit plan, he had won considerable support among the Punjabi politicians, both Republicans and Muslim Leaguers, but Mirza fearing that a coalition between the Awami League Party and the Republican Party would weaken his own position, succeeded in pressurizing Suhrawardy to resign.

Even after his resignation, when Firoz Khan Noon of Punjab became the prime minister, Suhrawardy pursued his plan of forging an alliance between Bengal and Punjab, something that had not been attempted before. In class terms, Suhrawardy's plan involved an alliance between the lower middle-class groups of East Pakistan represented by the Awami League and the landowning groups of Punjab represented by the Republican Party. This alliance was likely to include big mercantile and industrial groups also. Besides, the fact that the Punjabi leaders were hopelessly divided, an almost insurmountable obstacle that Suhrawardy also faced was the opposition of President Mirza and probably General Ayub because his

---

[64]Ayub Khan, *Friends Not Masters*, p. 56.
[65]Sayeed, *Politics in Pakistan: The Nature and Direction of Change*, p. 45.
[66]Ibid.

plan ran counter to their interests. According to Sayeed, 'If his plan had succeeded and the general elections held, political parties supported by the class interests of the big bourgeoisie, the landed interests, and the lower middle class would have not only cut across ethnic divisions but might have outflanked the military and civil service oligarchs.'[67]

By 1956, confronted with the crisis of its very existence the League leaders began to mobilize the masses of West Pakistan. Nishtar made vigorous efforts to build the organizational base of the League to mobilize the masses by arranging public meetings.[68] The impact of the League efforts alarmed the military. In East Bengal, the economic discontent developed into a smuggling menace, and Bengali political leaders intensified their demand for provincial autonomy.

From 1954–1958, the negative repercussions of economic policies, geared to sustain needs of defence and requirements of international allies, had paved the way to a wide array of social discontent and protest which, on the eve of the first general election various political groups were seeking to exploit.

It is pertinent to ask how and why a military already dominant by 1951 decided to directly take over the reigns of power only in 1958.[69] The foregoing analysis of the 1950s has suggested how Pakistan's predominantly Punjabi civil services and army manipulated their international connections and the opportunities offered by endemic provincial factionalism to consolidate state authority at the expense of the political process. They were successful in thwarting the growth of organized parties with bases of support in all the provinces of Pakistan. But, so long as the 'facade of parliamentary government' was kept alive, there was nothing to stop the mushrooming of small and medium size oppositional groupings. In addition to it, these

---

[67]Ibid., pp. 45–46.

[68]Saeed Shafqat, *Civil–Military Relations in Pakistan: From Zulfikar Ali ·Bhutto to Benazir Bhutto* (Boulder: Westview Press, 1997), p. 33.

[69]In 1954, when Governor General Ghulam Muhammad offered power to the C-in-C, the latter refused for a variety to reasons. The G.H.Q. was greatly preoccupied with the reconstruction of the army which had suffered as a result of partition and the Kashmir war. Moreover, any overt involvement in the political process at that time without adequate consolidation of the General's power within the army might have whetted the appetite of the youngest officers. However, that was perhaps more a postponement than an outright refusal.

could after a national election conceivably unite 'to endanger, if not altogether undo, a state structure which was being designed to give primacy to the institutional interests of the bureaucratic-military oligarchy and its allies—in particular among Karachi based industrialists and some prominent Punjabi, landed and business families.'[70]

The very fact of a military's direct takeover in October 1958 suggests, in spite of the dominance of the army, the internal structures of the state were still vulnerable enough to be threatened by political forces. Though fragmented and regionalized these were, they could challenge the state's claim to legitimacy and exploit latent tension both within and between the central and provincial arms of the civil services.

There were strong domestic, regional and international compulsions for the bureaucratic-military axis to seek to depolitise Pakistani society before it stepped into the era of mass-mobilization. The country's first ever general election was scheduled to be held in March 1959. In the wake of a deepening fiscal crisis coupled with increasing social and political grievances, the bureaucratic-military axis and their allies outside the state became understandably apprehensive about the mass upsurge in political activity on the eve of promised national elections. They were worried because of the threat of the non-Punjabi electorate in West Pakistan voting for parties committed to dismantling the One Unit system. In East Pakistan parties calling for greater provincial autonomy were likely to emerge victorious.

As far as international compulsions are concerned, some Pakistani scholars maintain that a return to democratic politics would not have been conducive to US strategic interests, because some political parties and masses did not favour a military alliance with the West, and the military coup took place against the backdrop of the post-1951 developments in West Asia. According to one scholar, 'The primary reason for the coup was the overriding desire of the United States to protect its oil interest in the region, along with the maintenance of the Pakistan military's newly acquired privileges.'[71]

---

[70]Ayesha Jalal, *State of Martial Rule: The Origin of Pakistan's Political Economy of Defence*, p. 298.
[71]Bilal Hashmi, 'Dragon Seed: Military in the State', in Gardezi and Rashid (eds.), *Pakistan: Roots of Dictatorship*, p. 164.

The military takeover in 1958 resulted in the dismissal of the politicians who had provided a facade of parliamentary government, and the dismantling of the constitutional apparatus, through which new political forces were emerging and challenging the power of the bureaucratic-military axis, on the eve of the first general elections that were to be held in the country. Before the electoral process could acquire any legitimacy, the military elite decided to establish their hegemony by delegitimizing participatory politics, the remaining elements of democratic institutions and the political parties.

Thus, in the case of the military intervention of October 1958, with the already well-established dominant position of the army and the civil bureaucracy in the state apparatus, the 'power vacuum' theory does not hold true. The constraints on the state's autonomy of action—whether on account of domestic, regional or international factors—leads to the conclusion that the Pakistani army entered the political arena with the explicit intention to ward off challenges to its alliance with the civil services and certain dominant social and economic classes.

Post-Military Regime Democratic Experiment Under Bhutto: 1971–1977

In December 1971, the breakdown of the 'military-hegemonic political system' was accompanied by the collapse of the united Pakistani state. The partitioned Pakistani state was confronted with crisis of succession, authority and legitimacy. The military elites were clearly divided. Yahya and his associates made a last-ditch effort to retain power. However, 'rebel' group officers led by Lieutenant General Gul Hassan and Air Marshal Rahim Khan, Chief of the Pakistan Air Force, persuaded the senior generals to transfer power to the civilian leaders.[72] In this context one observer aptly remarks,

---

[72]This interpretation of events acquired credibility by the works of Shahid Javed Burki, *Pakistan Under Bhutto: 1971–77* (London: The Macmillan Press, 1980), pp. 69–70; Fazal Muqeem Khan, *Pakistan's Crisis of Leadership* (Islamabad: National Book Foundation, 1973), pp. 129–30. Also see Lieutenant General Gul Hassan

'...Bhutto was an obvious choice for a military high command which, once saner counsels prevailed, accepted that vacating the political arena willingly would leave the door open until the time was ripe to capture it again.'[73]

Lieutenant General Gul Hassan and Air Marshal Rahim Khan who had been instrumental in guiding the PPP to power; envisioned some form of guardian rule for the military in the political system.[74] However, neither an alliance nor a partnership grew between the civilian leadership and the military generals, instead an uneasy but necessary transition took shape. Although Bhutto had risen to power with the aid of the military, he was quick to emphasize that he was a duly elected leader.[75]

Bhutto assumed power under extremely adverse circumstances. At that time the country was facing the gravest crisis in its history. If we compare Pakistan in 1947 with Pakistan in 1971, the political problems appear to be almost identical: the search for national identity, the development of political rules of the game and consensus. Bhutto was confronted with the formidable twin task of rebuilding democratic institutions and the confidence (of a collapsed nation), which were not easy to accomplish in the post-military state. While making the transition from a military-hegemonic to a democratic set-up, the most difficult task was how to reorient the various elites, leaders, and social groups and classes, towards the patterns of democratic reform, when for so long they had been ruled by the military. Heeger has perceptively pointed out that a post-military state is very much like a new state to the extent that both are 'marginally institutionalized.'[76] A new system of civilian political institutions and roles remained to be organized and somehow integrated with the surviving governmental institutions. In the process,

Khan, *Memoirs of Lt Gen. Gul Hassan Khan* (Karachi: Oxford University Press, 1993), pp. xi–xii, 346–50.

[73]Jalal, *The State of Martial Rule: The Origin of Pakistan's Political Economy of Defence*, p. 313.

[74]Salman Taseer, *Bhutto: A Political Biography* (New Delhi: Vikas Publishing House, 1980), pp. 148–49; Burki, *Pakistan Under Bhutto: 1971–77*, p. 70.

[75]Z. A. Bhutto, *President of Pakistan, Speeches and Statements: 20 December 1971–31 March 1972* (Karachi: The Department of Films and Publications, Government of Pakistan, 1972), p. 3.

[76]For details refer to Gerald A. Heeger's post-military regime thesis, see by the same author 'Politics in the Post-Military State: Some Reflections on the Pakistani Experience', *World Politics*, Vol. XXIX, No. 4 (January 1977), pp. 242–62.

the boundaries of the various institutions—governmental, party, military, police—would have to be delineated.

Reorganization and Restructuring Under Bhutto

Bhutto was successful in bringing various interest groups under the PPP's wing through his populistic style of politics. Now he had to find a way of keeping the conflicting ideological strands they represented from clashing in louder discord. And he 'had to do so without weakening his own position vis-à-vis the civil-bureaucracy and the army—the bent but unbroken crutches for the effective exercise of state power, especially at the centre where most of it was concentrated.'[77]

Notwithstanding the PPP's majority, Bhutto's survival depended on the deals he could strike with the civil-bureaucracy and the army. The cooperation of one was a precondition for the implementation of his ambitious reform programmes, while the tacit support of the other was vital for the very survival of his regime. Pakistan might have entered the era of mass participation but the structure of the state had not as yet been brought into conformity with an emergent social reality. According to Ayesha Jalal, 'Extending his control over the mandarins and praetorian guard, jealously watching his impregnable hold over the underprivileged social groups, and also placating the dominant interest groups—petrified by his populistic rhetoric—without toning down his party's promises required more cunning and tact than is possible in a single life-time.'[78]

Pattern of Civil-Military Relations To bring the military under civilian control, Bhutto adopted several measures, such as imposing constitutional constraints on the political role of the military, instituting changes in the military command structure and the creation of a para-military force—Federal Security Force (FSF) etc. To confine the role of the military to defence and security matters, the 1973 constitution clearly defined the function of the military. Bhutto abolished what he termed the 'anachronistic and obsolete' post of the C-in-C, all the services chiefs (the army, navy

---

[77]Jalal, *The State of Martial Rule: The Origin of Pakistan's Political Economy of Defence*, p. 314.
[78]Ibid.

and the air force) were given the same rank and seniority.[79] Another step was to fix the tenure of the Chief of Staff for a term of four years, later reduced to three. Bhutto also shifted the Naval Headquarters from Karachi to Islamabad, ostensibly to promote coordination among the services, but also to keep a close watch over the navy's top brass.

In the process of restructuring the higher command, the prime minister was given primacy in defence policy by making him chairman of the Defence Council, which was to consist of some ministers and secretaries dealing with departments related to defence problems, plus the chairman of the Joint Chiefs of Staff and the three service chiefs. The prime minister was also made responsible for coordinating defence with home and foreign policies Committee.[80]

On the one hand, Bhutto's strategy was to impose checks on the political role of the military, on the other hand, he failed to curtail defence expenditure, and instead sanctioned increase in the cost of maintaining the coercive arm of the state. During his rule defence spending stood around 6 per cent of GNP or 47 per cent of the annual budget. During the Bhutto regime, 'a *modus vivendi* was worked out between Bhutto and the military, whereby the military obtained the hardware they wanted and, in return stayed out of domestic issues. In view of the fact that the military's performance as well as its prestige had suffered as a consequence of its internal involvement, it was not difficult for the military to agree to this arrangement, which could succeed so long as the civilian government functioned effectively and no crisis precipitated....'[81] Bhutto mistook the temporary subservience of the military-bureaucratic oligarchy for permanent weakness. 'He genuinely believed that he had tamed the generals and bureaucrats, and that under his benign control the same old structures would suffice.'[82] He fatally underestimated the autonomous power of the army as a political institution in Pakistan politics.

---

[79]Bhutto, *President of Pakistan, Speeches and Statements: 20 December 1971–31 March 1972*, p. 110.

[80]Satish Kumar, *The New Pakistan* (New Delhi: Vikas Publishing House, 1978), p. 327.

[81]Shirin Tahir-Kheli, 'The Military in Contemporary Pakistan', *Armed Forces and Society*, Vol. VI, No. 4 (Summer: 1980), p. 647.

[82]Tariq Ali, *Can Pakistan Survive*, p. 101.

Bhutto's relying increasingly on the coercive instruments of the state, especially the FSF which was created with the explicit intention of limiting his reliance on the army, he made the too familiar error of seeking coercion as the best means of acquiring greater autonomous action. Bhutto's excessive zeal in disengaging the military from politics proved to be his most serious error. This can be exemplified from the fact that in March 1973, a group of army officers led by retired Brigadier F. B. Ali and Colonel Alim Afridi, attempted a coup against the Bhutto regime. Moreover, Bhutto became so occupied with imposing civilian control over the military that he failed to pay adequate attention to the civilian political institutions, particularly political parties.[83]

Bhutto tried to curb the power of the bureaucracy by introducing certain structural reforms in the civil services, yet its hold on the state remained essentially undiminished. However, the rapid expansion of the public sector following Bhutto's populist measures—land reforms, labour reforms, nationalization of industries, industrial units and banks—saw the regime become more dependent than ever on the bureaucracy. Bhutto sought to keep the upper hand by allowing the new recruits as well as professional civil servants to exploit the new job opportunities to gain entry into the higher ranks of the economic strata.[84]

Economic Reforms In the economic arena, Bhutto carried out a number of reforms such as nationalization of banks, insurance companies, iron, steel, petro-chemical, gas and tractors—creating for the first time a public sector in Pakistan. The series of land reforms introduced by the new regime in fact changed very little in terms of production relations in the countryside, and failed to destroy the grip of the landlords. In addition the land reforms strengthened the big landlords at the expense of the 'kulaks'. Burki has accurately pointed out that the decision to impose state ownership over the wheat-flour, rice-milling and cotton-milling industries, far from being a leftward move, was in reality designed to aid the rural gentry by removing the links between middlemen and the rural

---

[83]Shafqat, *Civil–Military Relations in Pakistan: From Zulfikar Ali Bhutto to Benazir Bhutto*, p. 167.
[84]Jalal, *The State of Martial Rule: The Origin of Pakistan's Political Economy of Defence*, p. 315.

middle class.[85] Once the PPP had decided to leave property relation in the countryside intact, most of their other economic reforms proved to be merely cosmetic.

However, Bhutto's economic reformism such as nationalization measures had adversely affected the powerful financial-industrial groups. They resisted these policies. Bhutto's major failure was his inability to co-opt the financial-industrial groups. He underestimated their strength and capacity for resistance. Excluded from the political and economic decision-making arenas, these groups not only remained hostile towards the Bhutto regime, but in the later years of his rule, encouraged and supported the opposition groups. The PPP increasingly became identified with feudal interests. With urban professionals weakened and the potential of small-medium business groups not politically realized, the PPP's reformism was perceived as pro-feudal and anti-big business.[86]

Centre-Province Relations It is important to note that although Bhutto adopted the parliamentary system, it was not exactly the Westminster model. It was rather a semi-parliamentary system which stood somewhat between the authoritarian models of the Muslim world and the undiluted democracy provided in the Indian constitution. For instance, the 1973 constitution provided certain provisions, which are normally not found in the parliamentary system of government.

As far as the centre-province relationships were concerned Bhutto employed strong-arm tactics towards the non-PPP regimes, stifled the democratic process and established an authoritarian regime. In 1973 in a move which was to give a strong provincial dimension to the widening opposition to the regime, Bhutto rid himself of the non-PPP governments in Baluchistan and the NWFP charging them with anti-state activities in collusion with Kabul and New Delhi. He began showing utter disregard for the much celebrated provincial autonomy provisions in the 1973 constitution. The 1973 constitution was constantly amended by a pliant parliament to give Bhutto extraordinary powers. This provided a legal cover for a variety of political misadventures. The decision to 'try

---

[85]Shahid Javed Burki, *Pakistan: Under Bhutto 1971–77* (London: Macmillan, 1980), pp. 159–62.
[86]For details consult Shafqat, *Civil–Military Relations in Pakistan*, pp. 115–59.

Wali Khan, the leader of the National Awami Party which had been one of the two coalition partners in Baluchistan and the NWFP, for conspiring against the state was an uncanny replay of the Ayub regime's Agartala case against Sheikh Mujibur Rahman and the Awami League.[87] Later in the year, Bhutto took the ominous step of calling in the army to crush a tribal uprising in Baluchistan. As the situation took on civil war proportions, Bhutto relied heavily on the army to put down the Baluchi armed revolt against the federal government. By December 1973, the Pakistan army was again in the political arena fighting a full-scale war to protect the integrity of the state as akin to the 1971 military crackdown in East Bengal.[88] Bhutto's downfall and the end of civilian rule can be attributed to the PPP's refusal to tolerate a meaningful regional autonomy or accept the principle of power-sharing within a federal framework. Bhutto's Baluch adventure had put a noose around his own neck and doomed democracy in the country. It laid the basis for the military coup of July 1977. In this context Tariq Ali succinctly remarks, 'when Bhutto and his defence minister General Tikka Khan ordered four army divisions to crush the Baluch, they sealed the fate of their own regime. The offensive against Baluchistan permitted a discredited, enfeebled high command to recoup what it had lost with the debacle in East Bengal and re-enter the political stage.'[89]

Ideological Conflict Despite the disintegration of Pakistan, ideological conflict had emerged with new intensity, and this remained a major obstacle to the building of national consensus regarding the nature and direction of Pakistan's political system. Like Jinnah, Bhutto saw Islam as a civilianization, a culture and a way of life and thought that an Islamic revival in the fundamental sense could not meet the challenges of the time. Bhutto's frequent references to the progressive ideal, his policies of socio-economic reform, and the pre-eminence of socialist faction in the PPP were some factors that alarmed the Jamaat-i-Islami fundamentalists who sensed that their power was being undermined.

---

[87]Ayesha Jalal, *Democracy and Authoritarianism in South Asia*, p. 83.
[88]Christina Lamb, *Waiting for Allah: Pakistan's Struggle for Democracy* (London: Viking, 1991), p. 276.
[89]Tariq Ali, *Can Pakistan Survive*, p. 123.

Moreover, Bhutto portrayed himself as the *Quaid-i-Awam* (the leader of the people) to ward off charges by religious parties. In the wake of the oil boom in 1973, the strength of the externally financed religious opposition grew. The fundamentalist Jamaat-i-Islami calling for an 'Islami revival' aroused the religious sensibilities of a people dispirited by military defeat and held out the temptation for the various social groups. Instead of addressing the causes of middle-class alienation, Bhutto tried to establish his regime's Islamic credentials by normlessly making concessions to the religious parties. By doing so, Bhutto further antagonized the left.

Institution Building in the Post-Military Regime

Bhutto needed to build up the PPP as an institutional counter weight to the non-elected arms of the state. However, the scope of party-building suffered due to prolonged bouts of direct military intervention in the political process. In a post-military regime, politics is characterized by dissent, conflict and violence. Under such conditions, regime building becomes a top priority and party-building remains a low priority. The PPP emerged as a response to the military regime, so it was loosely organized, faction–ridden and composed of contradictory group support bases. Besides, as a legacy of the military regime, various forms of conflicts emerged with new intensity.[90] Bhutto and the PPP thus became preoccupied with regime-building. Consequently this led to centralization, and the threats of regionalism evoked authoritarian responses from the civilian regime very much like those of the military regime. Thus, despite the transition from military to party rule, democratic process remained fragile, and opposition parties and associational group activity was suppressed as the party in power sought dominance. Bhutto merely sought the subordination of bureaucratic-military institutions under his personal control.

Given the fact that the PPP was loosely organized, faction-ridden, it had a contradictory social class base, and lacked ideological coherence. Bhutto chose to use the party as a vehicle for patronage.[91] The party became an instrument of attaining access to governmental

---

[90]For details consult Heeger, 'Politics in the Post-Military State: Some Reflections on the Pakistani Experience' pp. 254–57.
[91]Shafaqt, *Civil–Military Relations in Pakistan*, pp. 257–58.

resources to distribute rewards to its supporters or adherents. This strategy of keeping a mass based but loosely organized umbrella party to promote personal power failed Bhutto. Bhutto gave priority to regime building instead of party-building coupled with socio-economic reforms, which resulted in failure in providing an alternative to the military hegemonic system.[92]

Bhutto made pronounced use of patrimonialism to extend the PPP rule in Baluchistan and NWFP where the PPP's opponents, the National Awami Party (NAP) and the Jamiatul Ulama-i-Islam (JUI) had coalition governments. Moreover, he did not allow the opposition to function freely outside the legislative assemblies. He banned the NAP, and got the ban approved by the Supreme Court. Even in Punjab and Sindh provinces loyal to the PPP, Bhutto tended to utilize his patrimonial linkage rather than adopting institutional paths as principal channels between the province and the centre. Thus, the political culture which Bhutto symbolized was characterized by complete intolerance of democratic opposition, irrespective of the means which may have to be adopted for the purpose.[93] Similarly, complete intolerance of dissent within the PPP was also a part of Bhutto's political style.

Bhutto gave a populist turn to Pakistani politics. The overplaying of the populism card proved to be counterproductive in a society where the emerging new interest groups did not induce the displacement of those that were already well-entrenched. He gave a special twist to the Pakistani variety of populism: he sought to compensate for his lack of institutionalized political support by constructing extremely powerful patrimonial para-military apparatus—especially the Federal Security Force. There is no disputing the fact that despite the nominal impact of many of the PPP's reforms, Bhutto was extremely popular among the rural and urban underprivileged.

Caught in the web of new and emerging discrepancies in the structural context of his popular initiatives, Bhutto leaned more and more on the coercive instruments of state authority. The army was called out by the civil government on five occasions to maintain law and order between July 1972–June 1974. In due course the reliance on the armed forces continued to increase.

---

[92]Ibid.
[93]Satish Kumar, *The New Pakistan*, pp. 324–30.

By the time Bhutto called for national elections in 1977, financial industrial groups, the bureaucracy, the military, the trader-merchants classes, and religious groups had become alienated by Bhutto's policies. The opposition leaders led by the Pakistan National Alliance (PNA)—a conglomeration of nine parties—believed Bhutto's rule was authoritarian and coercive and feared if he continued to rule, Pakistan would become a single-party dictatorship.[94] Charging the regime with massive electoral rigging, the PNA took the matter to the streets. Bhutto was not able to counter it effectively on account of two reasons. First, Bhutto had neglected party-building, therefore failed to mobilize his party. Second, he considered the PNA movement as a law and order problem, not as a political one. The PNA strategy was to stage mass protests and create a disorderly situation and incite the military to overthrow Bhutto's government.[95] By April–end the agitation became characterized by widespread violence, engulfing nearly all the towns of Pakistan. Both sides, i.e., the PPP and the PNA, were too adamant in their attitudes to reach any solution. As the agitation against Bhutto continued to mount, he imposed limited martial law on 21 April 1977, and Karachi, Lahore, and Hyderabad were placed under military control. Once the military came in to support the civilian government, the PNA provoked[96] military officers through slogans and demanded the overthrow of Bhutto's government.[97] Thus, on 5 July 1977, the 'military intervened in complex circumstances of "invitation" from the opposition political leaders and ambitious generals to resurrect military hegemonic political system with new zeal and orientation.'[98] The ghost of military rule which Bhutto believed to have exorcised materialized once again. Bhutto attempted to construct a populist state and to conciliate conflicting social classes through his own personal power. Bhutto's mistake lay in his failure to create a institutionalized support base by building a strong grassroots political party to counter the bureaucratic-military axis and its allies' onslaught against his populist regime.

---

[94]Shafaqt, *Civil–Military Relations in Pakistan*, p. 260.

[95]Ibid.

[96]Mohammad Asghar Khan, *Generals in Politics 1958–1982* (New Delhi: Vikas Publishing House, 1983), pp. 116–18.

[97]Writing from his cell Bhutto alleged that the military and the PNA acted in concert to overthrow his government. For details refer Zulfikar Ali Bhutto, *If I am Assassinated* (New Delhi: Vikas Publishing House, 1979), p. 145.

[98]Shafaqt, *Civil–Military Relations in Pakistan*, p. 261.

Chapter II

Military and Governance

In the twentieth century, the armed forces have become a universal and integral part of a nation's political system and no longer remains completely aloof from politics in any nation. If politics is concerned, as in David Easton's celebrated words, with the authoritative allocation of values and power within a society[1], the military as a vital institution in the polity can hardly be wished out of participatory bounds, at least as an institutional interest group with a stake in political decision-making. The varying roles that the military plays in politics range from minimal legitimate influence through recognized channels by virtue of their position and responsibilities within the political system to the other extreme of total displacement of the civilian government in the form of illegitimate overt military intervention in politics.

A conventional view is that 'state ultimately rests on institutionalized violence and therefore the armed forces are the foundation of the state. A more modern concept is that the state derives its legitimacy and consequently raison d'etre from the democratic will of the citizens and the armed forces are only an instrumentality

---

[1]David Easton, *The Political System: An Inquiry into the State of Political Science* (New York: Alfred A. Knopf, 1953), pp. 129–31.

to secure the democratic functioning of the state from external and internal threats.'[2]

In India the armed forces are seen as the instrumentalities of a democratic government and the forces themselves accept this philosophy unquestioningly. In Pakistan the self-image of the armed forces is that of a guardian of Pakistan ideology—the two nation theory. The role of the armed forces as an ultimate arbiter has wide acceptance among the public in Pakistan. For slightly less than half of its existence Pakistan has been under military rule or military dominated governance. Even in the rest of the period the army had significant influence in politics.

Pakistan, a typical case of praetorianism, is one of the several Third World countries where the military always keeps the contingency plan for a takeover ready. Pakistan's history since 1958 has been dominated by the recurring cycles of military intervention, consolidation and collapse. Pakistan has been subjected to periodic military intervention in politics so frequently that it has become almost a regular part of Pakistan's political process.'[3] On four occasions so far, the military has intervened overtly and imposed martial law throughout the country—in October 1958, March 1969, July 1977 and October 1999—and justified its extreme action on the ground of chaotic conditions prevailing in the country. Pakistan has essentially been ruled directly by 'the men on horseback' for 25 years of the 53 years of its existence, and indirectly for another two decades.

With military rule becoming the prevalent mode in Pakistan, the Indo-Pakistani subcontinent provides an illustration of the contrasting as well as changing patterns of civil–military relations. In sharp contrast, India, which though consanguineous with Pakistan in a number of ways ranging from history to colonial experience and post-independence problems, displays a unique pattern of civilian control over the military coupled with a remarkable combination of political stability and orderliness unparalleled in the Third World.'[4]

---

[2]K. Subrahmanyam, 'Military and Governance', in V. A. Pai Panandiker (ed.), *Problems of Governance in South Asia* (New Delhi: Konark Publishers Pvt. Ltd., 2000), p. 201.

[3]See Veena Kukreja, *Military Intervention in Politics: A Case Study of Pakistan* (New Delhi: NBO, 1985).

[4]Veena Kukreja, *Civil–Military Relations in South Asia: Pakistan, Bangladesh and India* (New Delhi: Sage Publications, 1991), pp. 185–228.

To understand Pakistan, one must try to understand the Pakistan Army. The objective of this chapter is to focus on the role of the military in governance and how this situation has developed. In addition, it also seeks to describe and analyze the internal dynamics of the military and its changing role and parameters in Pakistan. Finally, it will discuss how the military in Pakistan (as the most formidable and autonomous political actor) is capable of influencing the nature and direction of political change.

The Army: Final Arbiter in Pakistan

In Pakistan, the army is the ultimate arbiter in the affairs of the state. Throughout Pakistan's history the military has retained the central locus of power. From 1947 to 1958, the military elite had played an indirect or a 'back seat driver's' role in policy-making processes and helped in the rehabilitation of refugees. It also provided aid to the civil authority during the time of natural calamities (such as flood, periodic epidemics or food shortage) and communal riots. The first instance which was of direct interest to the military in politics was the Rawalpindi Conspiracy Case in 1951, in which the Chief of General Staff, General Akbar Khan, charismatic and politically well connected, figured as the prime accused. General Akbar Khan had earlier masterminded the invasion of Kashmir in October 1947. He was allowed to bypass the normal channels and deal directly with Prime Minister Liaquat Ali Khan. In this context, an eminent defence analyst Subrahmanyam aptly remarks, 'Such involvement of army officers in unconventional operations in disregard to traditional command and control was bound to encourage tendencies for political thinking and activism in the armed forces. Pakistan has had a series of court martials from the case of General Akbar Khan to the recent one on General Abbasi which illustrates that once there is an attempt at political intervention by the army, that becomes a trend.'[5] Ayub's evident role in preparing the blueprint of the integration of the provinces of West Pakistan was another instance of the army's increased influence in political

---

[5]Subrahmanyam, 'Military and Governance', p. 213.

decision-making. The declaration of limited martial law in Lahore to quell domestic disorder in 1953 engaged the army in the internal security and paved the way for the military's role expansion. Powerful bureaucrats like Ghulam Muhammad, Iskander Mirza and Chaudhri Muhammad Ali helped draw the defence establishment into domestic politics, and developed military and strategic alliance with the United States, enthusiastically supported by an ambitious army Commander-in-Chief, Ayub Khan. With the erosion of political authority, both at the central and provincial levels, the bureaucrats assumed the role of the state with willing feudalists ready to play a subordinate role. Eventually, the army emerged as the power-broker and moved to take complete control, which was eventually consummated through a formal/direct take-over in 1958. It is now widely accepted that the military coup of Ayub Khan had the tacit support of the United States, the biggest aid donor both on economic and military fronts.

The military regime of Yayha Khan failed to handle the politicized ethnicity in favour of the Eastern Wing, which demanded its share in power after the electoral victory in 1970. The military ruler became partisan and did not permit the Awami League to take-over the reigns of power despite the clear electoral mandate as it would have negative repercussions on the position and prerogative of the military. With the emergence of Bangladesh in 1971, the army was politically incapable of continuing to rule. It temporarily assumed a low-key profile and allowed Z. A. Bhutto to takeover as president, who had the political mandate of the 1970 elections to his credit. He attempted to reorganize the power structures in Pakistan but was only partially successful. He had to soon rely on the army for maintenance of law and order. Between July 1972 and June 1974, the army was called out 5 times to enforce law and order, the most severe being one in Baluchistan where 10,000 people were estimated killed in 17 months' operations, employing ground and air forces.'[6] After the 1977 rigged elections, the situation became worse and martial law was imposed in Hyderabad, Karachi and Lahore, and the army was sent into Sindh, without even consulting Jatoi, the chief minister. In this context, a scholar comments, 'It was the military that was at the forefront of the forces that

[6]Christina Lamb, *Waiting for Allah: Pakistan's Struggle for Democracy* (New Delhi: Viking, 1991), p. 276.

engineered the downfall of the PPP government in 1977, and the regime of Gen. Zia has the distinction of being the first unmitigated military regime in Pakistan.[7] In sum, in 1977, Pakistani politicians both in the government and in the opposition, gave the army another chance to stage a come-back as the country embraced the longest martial law in its history.

Under Zia-ul-Haq, the army acquired the constitutional basis to function as a legitimate political power-broker in Pakistan. The Eighth Amendment was the constitutional provision to that end. Even after the restoration of democracy in 1988, the army continued to play a significant role in the politics of Pakistan. However, its style appears to have undergone a very distinct change. The army's role as a supra party mediator in political crisis still appears to be acceptable to the people of Pakistan. After the 1988 elections, to become prime minister, Benazir Bhutto had to strike a deal with the then Chief of the Army Staff, General Mirza Aslam Beg, and she promised that she would not meddle in the military's internal affairs such as transfers, promotions and retirements of senior army officers and nuclear and Afghan policies.[8] Thus, the army reserved its decisive role in the formulation of foreign and security policies. In sum, it retained effective power to ensure that the elected political leadership will have no power over the military itself. It continued to control the crucial levers of power and policy-making while staying in the background. For the army, it was a situation of having your cake and eating it too. They determined policy in areas most important to them without getting into the mess of day-to-day governance. They formulated the Kashmir policy, the Afghan policy and where they failed, the blame was put on the civilian government. Thus, army supremacy in Pakistan's politics continued but with a significant difference. Instead of ruling directly, the army's approach was to be able to control the levers of power, defence and foreign policy while actively staying out of politics.'[9]

[7]Hamza Alavi, 'Class and State', in Hassan Gardezi and Jamil Rashid (eds.) *Pakistan: The Roots of Dictatorship* (Delhi: Oxford University Press, 1983), p. 41.

[8]Veena Kukreja, 'Restoration of Democracy in Pakistan: One Year of Benazir's Rule', *Strategic Analysis*, Vol. XII, No. 9 (February 1990), pp. 1164–65.

[9]Veena Kukreja, 'Pakistan's 1993 Election: Back to Square One', *Strategic Analysis*, Vol. XVI, No. 10 (January 1994), p. 1364.

After the 1997 election, Nawaz Sharif emerged as the elected Prime Minister with a two-third majority in the parliament and had attained dominance over the presidency which had been the fountain-head of power for the military since the early 1980s. He repealed the notorious Eighth Amendment, tamed the judiciary and forced the Army Chief, General Karamat to resign in October 1998. Never before in the history of Pakistan did the elected political leaders enjoy such powers. But 'this', as Jasjit Singh aptly remarks 'itself signified the tension inherent within the power structure of Pakistan and it was inevitable that the country would be pushed toward brinkmanship by the traditional *chaudhris* of power brokerage.'[10]

Internal Dynamics of the Military

The organizational resources and internal dynamics of the military establishment, especially its traditions, cohesion, capabilities and disposition of the officer corps, shape the military's role in the polity. The predominant role of the military both in internal politics[11] and in the formation of regional and foreign policies as well as ever-escalating defence expenditure in terms of resource allocation in the national exchequer, has occasionally raised questions.

The British Apolitical Tradition

There is a common belief that since the Pakistan Army was an offshoot of the British Indian Army, its conduct, especially apolitical professionalism, should be similar. But in Pakistan the army has eroded this tradition of non-involvement by intervening decisively and frequently, whereas in India the principle of civilian control over the military remains intact. The question arises why is an

---

[10]Jasjit Singh, 'The Army in Pakistan', in Jasjit Singh (ed.), *Kargil 1999: Pakistan's Fourth War for Kashmir* (New Delhi: Knowledge World, 1999), p. 23.

[11]For a review of theoretical literature on civil–military relations, consult Veena Kukreja, 'Civil–Military Relations in Developing Countries', *India Quarterly*, Vol. XLV, Nos. 2–3 (April–September 1989), pp. 154–92.

army that grew out of the Indian Army so different? In this context, the emphasis on the 'non-political' tradition of the British Indian Army lingering in Pakistan is not only misleading but also a misrepresentation of facts. The concept of an apolitical military-bureaucracy may be valid to a larger extent in those countries where the democratic institutions have developed over a longer period of time. But it is fallacious to extend the same assertion to the post-colonial societies.[12] In fact, the British Indian Army, from its very inception was trained to be the custodian of law and order and to promote colonial interests at the cost of different indigenous and regional interests within the subcontinent. Besides, the emphasis on an overall civilian control over the military was subordinate to the civil authority in London. Its relation with the civil authority in India was marked by 'separate sphere' of military and civilian influence. It was more of an equal partner than subordinate to it.[13]

It is also a gross mistake to highlight the British experience of merely 29 years vis-à-vis the post-independence 53 years' experience. Indianization of the Indian Army[14] started only in 1918. The pace improved slightly after 1932 but by 1947 only a few Indians attained the substantive rank of lieutenant colonel. The senior-most officer was only a major general.

Inheritance of Military Tradition from Muslim Rulers

The creation of Pakistan on the basis of religion also led to its army having to 'adapt to Islamic principles and practices.'[15] This in itself started to alter the secular moorings inherited from the Indian Army. At the same time, according to Jasjit Singh, 'Pakistan and its Army

---

[12]See Bilal Hashmi, 'Dragon Seed: Military in the State', in Gardezi and Rashid (eds.), *Pakistan: The Roots of Dictatorship*, p. 149.

[13]Hasan Askari Rizvi, *The Military and Politics in Pakistan* (Lahore: Progressive Publishers, 1976), pp. 15–25.

[14]For details see Indian Statutory Commission, *Report of the Indian Statutory Commission*, Vol. 2 (survey CMD 3568), (London: His Majesty's Stationery Office, 1930); William Gutteridge, 'The Indianization of the Indian Army 1918–45: A Case Study' *Race*, Vol. IV, No. 2 (May 1963), pp. 39–48.

[15]Stephen P. Cohen, *The Pakistan Army* (New Delhi: Himalayan Books, 1984), p. 34.

have felt an overriding compulsion to detach and distance themselves from, if not actually deny, the historical linkage with their Indian past, except where Islam could be used to bolster the legitimacy of the new state formed in its name. History has often been invented for this purpose.'[16] The official history of the Pakistan Army focusing on the inheritance of military tradition from Muslim rulers claims that the officers and men of the army are descended from 'the men who fought Alexander the Great, who...established the first Muslim stronghold in India and who campaigned in the days of the great Mughal Emperors helping to *conquer and stabilize nearly the whole of the subcontinent'* (emphasis added).[17] Such selective distortions have had an important role in shaping the perception of Pakistanis in general and the military men in particular.[18] The implicit conclusion, of course, is that the military tradition of Pakistan is derived from their ancestors who helped establish and expand Muslim rule in the subcontinent. After independence, the Pakistani Army emphasized Islam as the unifying force, though the basic structures remained largely based on the British model. In 1950, General Akbar Khan suggested the establishment of a Vietnam-like people's army but Sandhurst remained the model at the decision-making levels.[19]

Ethnic Recruitment Pattern: Punjabi Domination of the Army

The army of Pakistan was formed virtually from scratch in 1947, when the state itself was created. The military forces were split in a proportion of 64:34 on the basis of the proportion of non-Muslims and Muslims. The actual proportion of Muslims in the British Indian Army was lower; and a significant proportion of them did not opt to serve with Pakistan.[20] More important, the British Indian Army was

---

[16]Jasjit Singh, 'The Army in the Power Structure of Pakistan', *Strategic Analysis*, Vol. XVIII, No. 7 (October 1995), p. 856.

[17]Major General Fazal Muqeem Khan, *The Story of the Pakistan Army* (Karachi: Oxford University Press, 1963), p. 3.

[18]Jasjit Singh, 'The Army in the Power Structure of Pakistan', p. 857.

[19]Cohen, *The Pakistan Army*, p. 46.

[20]Jasjit Singh, 'The Army in the Power Structure of Pakistan', p. 857.

organized on the basis of 'class regiments.' However, after the revolt of 1857, the British did not keep any all-Muslim Units in the army; and Muslims were the only group in the army not to have their own regiment.[21] Muslim officers and soldiers, who constituted over 25 per cent of the British Indian Army strength in 1947, were spread among different regiments. The new Pakistan Army was almost entirely Muslim. Pakistan did move on to organizing class regiments based on provincial ethnicity. But this was really cosmetic and the central role of Punjabi and Pathan officers and soldiers continued.

Ethnic Imbalances

Pakistan officially discarded the British concept of 'martial races' for recruitment to the army and somewhat expanded the recruit base. However, ethnic imbalances persist in the army. The Punjab continues to provide the preponderant bulk of officers and other ranks; official estimates put its share as 65 and 70 per cent respectively. The Punjab is expected to sustain its entrenched position because of its strategic importance and it constitutes 56 per cent of Pakistan's population. The Pathans or Pashtuns are the second largest group in the army, constituting about 22–25 per cent of its officers and other ranks. North-West Frontier Province (NWFP) and tribal areas are 16 per cent of Pakistan's population; if the Pathans living in Baluchistan are added, their ratio is expected to rise to about 19 per cent. The Baluch and Sindhi-speaking people (3 to 13 per cent of Pakistan's population respectively) are under-represented in the army, especially in the higher echelons.[22] The Urdu speaking population is fairly represented at the officer level but there are a very small number of *Muhajir* (Muslim migrants from India) at the soldier level. They are known to be over-represented in the air force and the navy.

Traditionally, the Salt Range and Potwar (Potohar) region of northern Punjab and the adjoining districts of NWFP are known as the army heartland, providing a large number of soldiers,

[21]Cohen, *The Pakistan Army*, p. 37.

[22]Hasan Askari Rizvi, *Military, State and Society in Pakistan* (London: Macmillan Press Ltd., 2000), p. 240.

commissioned and non-commissioned officers. In the present-day administrative set-up, the district/tehsils of Jhelum, Chakwal and Pinddaden Khan described as the Salt Range area coupled with Attock, Campbellpur, Rawalpindi and Gujarat in the Punjab and Kohat, Mardan and Peshawar in NWFP, have established their reputation as the major suppliers of manpower for the army. According to one study, the recruitment base is slowly expanding. Over the 'last three decades, other areas in the Punjab and north-western region have made manpower available for recruitment. The Punjab's districts of Sargodha, Khushab and Mianwali provide a reasonable number of recruits, especially for other ranks. Furthermore, officers and other ranks also come from urban districts like Lahore, Gujranwala, Faislabad and the Canal Colonies. In case of NWFP, the districts of Kohat, Mardan and Bannu are still the main recruiting areas, although other regions are gradually coming up.'[23]

Thus, the recruitment base within the Punjab and NWFP has slightly expanded. The Punjabis and the Pathans continue to dominate the army as they have a decisive edge over the Baluch, Sindhis and *Muhajirs* in the population.

In pre-1971 Pakistan, the under-representation of the Bengalis caused much criticism of the recruitment policy in East Pakistan. The British treated the Bengalis as a non-martial race and their recruitment was deliberately discouraged. At the time of independence, the Bengalis constituted 1 per cent of the total strength of Pakistan's armed forces, their numerical strength in the army was 155 which rose to 13,000 in 1965. First infantry East Bengal Regiment—Senior Tiger—was set up in February 1948, but in the initial stages, a number of West Pakistanis were assigned to it as officers and senior commissioned officers (SCOs). Later, Bengalis replaced them and by 1968, four such regiments were in place. However, the Bengali representation remained inadequate in the army, especially from the middle to the upper level. In 1955, according to one estimate, East Pakistan's representation was a mere 1.57 per cent. It was highest in the air force being 10 per cent.[24] By 1963, the proportion of Bengalis in the army had increased to 5 per cent for

---

[23]Ibid.
[24]*Dawn* (Karachi), 8 January 1955.

the officers.[25] At that time only 7.4 per cent of the troops were Bengalis which improved slightly in post-1965. Only one Bengali attained the rank of lieutenant general and another became major general at the beginning of 1971. Their representation was much better in the air force and the navy, although it was never more than one-third.[26] Considering that East Pakistan was one of the regions (along with Bihar and Uttar Pradesh) that originally fostered the idea of Pakistan, and constituted the majority population of the state, the segregation and discrimination of Bengalis was to have a serious repercussion. With the passage of time Bengali army officers and soldiers became the backbone of the armed resistance of the Pakistan army during the civil war in 1971.[27] Moreover, the military was always perceived by ordinary Bengalis as an outside and alien force.

In more recent years, Pakistan has maintained four major infantry regiments: the Punjab, Baluch, Frontier Force and Sindhi Regiments. But this does not suggest that other ethnic groups and communities find fairer representation in the army corresponding to their share in the national population. Some units even in the Baluch regiment has no Baluchis and very few Pathans and Sindhis. The reason may not entirely be due to the perpetuating ethnic dominance by the Punjabi-Pathan army. Political dissent and violent disturbances have really been centred in Baluchistan and Sindh as 'both provinces had never fully accepted the foundation of Pakistan, especially in its shape that retained a Punjabi domination.'[28]

Over the years, according to Stephen Cohen, the Punjabi-Pathan group has not retained its special position in the army but has strengthened it. As Cohen comments, 'In brief, the history of Pakistan Army was the history of the Punjabi Muslim and the Pathan; this seemed entirely natural as much as there was hardly any other Muslims in the army.'[29]

Another study, considering the 1979 recruitment to the Pakistani Military Academy as guide, reveals that the officer corps has 70 per cent from the Punjab, 14 per cent from the NWFP, 9 per

---

[25]Rounaq Jahan, *Pakistan: Failure in National Integration* (New York: Columbia University Press, 1972), p. 62.
[26]Rizvi, *The Military and Politics in Pakistan*, pp. 135–45.
[27]Jasjit Singh, 'The Army in the Power Structure of Pakistan', pp. 857–58.
[28]Ibid., p. 858.
[29]Cohen, *The Pakistan Army*, p. 43.

cent from Sindh, 3 per cent from Baluchistan and 1.9 per cent from 'Azad' Kashmir. This indicates that the proportion of Punjabis has increased notably since 1947. The recruitment within a state is also not evenly spread. For instance, by the late 1970s over 75 per cent of all ex-servicemen came from three districts of the Punjab, namely, Rawalpindi, Jhelum and Campbellpur and the two adjoining districts of the NWFP, Kohat and Mardan. The recruits mostly belong to the landowner and landless farmer classes.[30] The existence of the Northern Command in Rawalpindi since the British era has left a continuing legacy in favour of the Punjab and the neighbouring frontier. Cohen, however, believes that the theory of the Punjabi domination is the product of the actual numerical imbalance between the Punjab and the other provinces and the bluff, rough Punjabi style (which has an undercurrent of treachery, according to Mengal and others), complicated by a Punjabi–centred strategic orientation. Moreover, it is concerned with the 'strategic core area' that the province had obtained.'[31] However, the continuing ethnic imbalance for whatever reason is perplexing and demoralizing.

Ethnic imbalances generate controversy because the army has been 'instrumental in creating a centralized and authoritarian polity which ensured its dominance of the state power. Whenever the ethnic and regional elite asserted their ethnic identity and regional rights, the power elite perceived it as a threat to the state and mobilized the state apparatus, especially the Army, to suppress these efforts ostensibly to protect national integrity.'[32] These trends were reinforced by the establishment of military rule which curbed political participation for the ethnic and regional identities.[33] Those who suffered under these political arrangements questioned the role of the military.

---

[30]Jasjit Singh, 'The Army in Pakistan', p. 28.

[31]Cohen, *The Pakistan Army*, p. 115.

[32]Rizvi, *Military, State and Society in Pakistan*, p. 241. Also see Asaf Hussain, 'Ethnicity, National Identity and Praetorianism: The Case of Pakistan', *Asian Survey*, Vol. XVI, No. 10 (October 1976), pp. 135–45.

[33]Refer Samina Ahmed, 'Centralization, Authoritarianism, and the Management of Ethnic Relations in Pakistan', in Michael E. Brown and Sumit Ganguly (eds.), *Government Policies and Ethnic Relations in Asia and the Pacific* (Cambridge, Mass: The MIT Press, 1997), pp. 83–127.

In addition, regional and ethnic imbalances also attract attention for other reasons. For example, the prosperity and welfare of many areas and families in the Punjab and NWFP are closely linked with the military. For peasants, the army offers a 'safety net' against poverty. This works to the advantage of the ethnic groups and the regions well represented in the military, giving a cause of complaint to the under-represented ones. Moreover, in the wake of the military's pronounced role during the Afghanistan crisis in terms of Inter-Services Intelligence's (ISI's) involvement with the *Mujahideen* and its total support to the Taliban operation has led the Pakistani critics to portray the army—a Punjabi institution—as aggressive, power hungry and ruthless.

Exploring linkage between the Punjabi-Pathan domination of the army, and the psyche of the Pakistani Army, Jasjit Singh, maintains that it 'has its roots in the West Punjab-North-West Frontier culture.' This culture characterizes 'unwillingness to accept defeat, transferring the responsibility for it to someone else, a strong urge to dominate, a certain recklessness and a deep desire for revenge etc., some of the traits are represented by the Pakistan army.'[34]

Pakistani Army inherited professionalism from the fighting tradition of North-West India and the new shape that the British gave to the army in India. But because of the narrow base of recruitment of its manpower, a greater role is played by the clan and tribal factor which tends to deal with professional matters also in a narrow clannish perspective. Within the army, according to Jasjit Singh, 'clan culture increases the pressure to prove to each other that each one is more aggressive and courageous than the other with little forethought to the consequences of the action. Kargil is but one example.'[35]

Military's Social Background and Orientation

During the last five decades the socio-economic composition of the army officers has undergone a transformation. Stephen Cohen finds three distinct generational phases in the history of the Pakistan

---

[34]Jasjit Singh, 'Nothing Uniform About Them', *The Sunday Times of India* (New Delhi), 25 November 1999, p. 17.
[35]Ibid.

Army: the British generation (1947–1953); the American generation (1954–1971); and the Pakistani generation (1972 onwards).[36]

The British Generation (1947–1953) The British generation included the pre-independence officers trained at the Royal Military Academy, Sandhurst, i.e., the King's Commissioned Officers (KCOs), and the Indian Military Academy, Dehra Dun, called the Indian Commissioned Officers (ICOs), and those given emergency commission during the Second World War. The British were careful in inducting Indians into the officer cadre. Those sent to Sandhurst came from loyal, prestigious and upper strata families who joined the army as a matter of prestige rather than to earn a living. The social base of recruitment slightly expanded with the start of the Dehra Dun Academy in 1932, but it was predominantly upper and upper-middle and the families with military service tradition.[37]

The Anglicized KCOs and ICOs in addition to the British officers, filled the senior slots in the Pakistani Army at the time of partition and set its tone in line with British training and professional orientation. However, the post-partition communal riots and the war in Kashmir had strong bearings on their psyche and outlook and 'Pakistanized' them in their attitude towards their counterparts in India.[38]

The American Generation (1954–1971) The American generation refers to the period when Pakistan joined the alliance system and the military obtained American military aid, and its officers received American training. The US-military and strategic alliance with Pakistan that developed in the mid-1950s exposed them to American military equipment, training and cultural influences which eroded the British influence, especially in the case of those who joined the army in the early years of independence. However, the basic pattern of ideas and orientations of the Pakistan Army inherited from the British survived. They could not break out of the British mould in such a decisive manner that one could talk of a distinct American generation. The air force, which relied more

[36]Cohen, *The Pakistan Army*, pp. 55–75.
[37]Rizvi, *Military, State and Society in Pakistan*, p. 242.
[38]Ibid.

heavily on American aircraft and equipment, was more Americanized in social orientation. This was also partly true of the navy.[39]

The Pakistani Generation (1972 onwards) The post-1972 officers have been described as the Pakistani generation. The major shift began to take place as the army expanded in the 1960s, more so after the early 1970s. According to Hasan Askari Rizvi, 'Most of those who joined the officers corps in the 1970s and later came from modest rural backgrounds and urban lower-middle and lower class backgrounds as job opportunities declined in the civilian sector. They looked on the army more as a career opportunity than as a family tradition or love for the profession.'[40] The new officers were thus more politicized and ambitious than their predecessors, who came from a relatively better social background and were not directly exposed to political pressures in their pre-military days. The new officers who are likely to occupy top staff command positions by the end of the first decade of the twenty-first century have a different orientation towards the society. They are quite materialistic in their orientation and are eager to lead a luxurious lifestyle. Some of them tasted power during the Zia years.

The traditionally cautious approach towards politics and the civil-society is disappearing. The junior officers freely make partisan political statements and express low, often contemptuous, opinions about civilians. The erosion of professional conduct, craving for quick material gains and the moral fibre of young officers have caused concern within military circles.

External Dynamics of the Military: Pakistan's Security Environment

Pakistan's defence policy has hinged on the crucial pillar of national security since the country's creation. It has been compounded by

---

[39]Ibid, p. 243. For a discussion of continuity and change in the Army, see Ayaz Amir, 'The Khaki Clan', *Herald* (Karachi), February 1986, pp. 40–42; A. R. Siddiqi, *The Military in Pakistan: Image and Reality* (Lahore: Vanguard, 1996), pp. 64–65.
[40]Rizvi, *Military, State and Society in Pakistan*, p. 243.

hostility from its larger neighbour India. Pakistan's quarrels with India—over a wide range of issues ranging from religion to water to territorial disputes in Kashmir—has serious ramifications for Pakistan's national security.

A post-independence war over Kashmir in the wake of mass migration and little in way of defence infrastructure except for a few scattered cantonments but no ammunition factories, made Pakistan follow a rigorous policy to overcome its handicaps. The dominant elite with an obvious pro-Western orientation and a bi-polarised world provided incentives to enter into an alliance-based relationship.

Pakistan's preoccupation with the security threat and the attendant priority for defence partially led to the supremacy of the defence ministry and the General Head Quarter (GHQ) in the wake of weakened parliamentary processes in the post-Jinnah years.

Jinnah always recognized the apolitical role of the army and always emphasized the supremacy of the civilian government. To him, the armed forces 'were the servants of the people.'[41] However, the military's opinion was given weight in the formulation of security policy. For example, in October 1947, the Supreme Commander, Field Marshal Auchinleck, persuaded Jinnah to reverse his order to the Commander-in-Chief, Pakistan Army, for sending the army into Kashmir after India secured its accession and sent its troops there.[42] Later, Pakistan's decision to induct its troops in Kashmir was also made on the advice of the Army Chief.[43] Under Liaquat Ali Khan, while he himself held the position of defence minister, the GHQ being in Rawalpindi, the defence ministry and the army tended to be more autonomous at the behest of powerful bureaucrats. Ayub Khan, Iskander Mirza, Ghulam Muhammad and their cohorts made and pursued Pakistan's defence policy entirely according to their own biases and ambitions, mostly over and above

---

[41]For details consult, M. Asghar Khan, 'Quaid-i-Azam on Soldiers and Politics', *Defence Journal*, Vol. IV, No. 11 (1978), p. 10.

[42]Allen Campbell-Johnson, *Mission with Mountbatten* (London: Robert Hale, 1951), p. 22.

[43]On 20 April 1948, General Douglas Gracey suggested in his report that if the troops were not sent to Kashmir, Pakistan's security would be jeopardized. The government of Pakistan accepted the report and formally committed the regular troops to Kashmir in early May. See Chaudhri Muhammad Ali, *The Emergence of Pakistan* (New York: Columbia University Press, 1967), pp. 305–06.

the political authorities. Pakistan's defence needs as advocated by the defence establishment, helped by the Cold War pushed Pakistan into closer relations with the United States.[44]

Compulsion of Hostility Towards India

From its very inception Pakistan has been suffering from an acute sense of insecurity vis-à-vis India. 'It projected itself not only as small and disadvantaged but as on the defensive against a real and present threat, with its survival at stake.'[45] These insecurities coupled with an identity crisis led Pakistan to assume a posture of hostility towards India. This perception goes as an input into the decision-making apparatus, and policy formulations, on their basis is further strengthened the same 'national psyche'. This is a vicious circle. This also promoted an enemy image of each other which has created a mindset of hostility and antagonism at the elite level. Besides, the Pakistan army has a vested interest in propagating the territorial conflict with India. There is 'an atavistic compulsion in Pakistan's power structures mindset which believes that its survival and security could only be secured by the fragmentation of India.'[46]

The insecurity in the Pakistani psyche has led to its obsession to attain parity with India's capabilities. This paved the way for militarization of the economy, at the cost of economic development.

The insecurity coupled with an identity crisis that were embedded in the Pakistani nation at its commencement, are still prevalent, and have even worsened with the events in the last 50 years. Furthermore, after the separation of East Pakistan, Pakistanis

---

[44]According to P. I. Cheema, four factors seems to have compelled Pakistan to abandon the option of non-alignment: the fear of India, the domestic political and economic problems, the ruling elite and the dictates of the international climate. But by far the most important factor was the perception that even after partition India was not reconciled to the establishment of Pakistan and would do everything to destroy the new state at the first opportunity. See P. I. Cheema, *Pakistan's Defence Policy, 1947–58* (London: Macmillan, 1990), p. 164.

[45]Thomas Perry Thornton, 'Fifty Years of Insecurity', in Seling Harrison, Paul Kreisberg and Dennis Kux, *India and Pakistan: The First Fifty Years* (New York: Cambridge University Press, 1999), p. 171.

[46]J. N. Dixit, *Anatomy of a Flawed Inheritance: Indo-Pakistan Relations: 1970–94* (New Delhi: Konark Publishers Pvt. Ltd., 1995), p. 244.

have been looking for various ways such as bleeding India through thousand wounds, that is, proxy war, and nuclear first use, to take revenge. In this context a perceptive observer succinctly remarks: 'In many ways Pakistan needs to maintain hostility with India to justify its own existence and to define itself.'[47] Pakistan's hostility towards India has its roots in ideology—the two-nation theory, the basis of Pakistani nationhood—but has been fostered by the military-bureaucratic axis for more than five decades. The armed forces have a stake in projecting Kashmir as a vexed territorial issue to keep filling their coffers to the brim. Without the raison d'etre of territorial dispute with India, the budgetary demands of the Pakistani armed forces will be relegated to secondary importance.

Escalating Defence Expenditure

As far as the defence expenditure is concerned, Pakistan, like China, does not provide any details and announces only the overall figure of its defence expenditure. However, it is possible to arrive at some broad trend indicators. Pakistan since its emergence braced itself for a 'political economy of defence.' From 1947 to 58 its defence expenditure was between 55 and 60 per cent of the country's total revenue. However, it increased after the US started giving aid to Pakistan in 1954.

Table 2.1 reveals that the most dramatic shift in Pakistan's defence expenditure had taken place following the Indo-Pak war of 1965 when in terms of the proportion of its GDP, it jumped from 4.82 per cent to 9.86 per cent. Pakistan's defence expenditure predictably escalated again in 1971–1972, when the army was deployed in a repressive role in East Pakistan and because of the costs of the war later in the year. Although with the break-up of Pakistan and emergence of Bangladesh the defence needs reduced markedly, the defence expenditure continued to grow, increasing by 39.70 per cent in 1974–1975 over the previous year, followed by another jump of 33.07 per cent two years later. These 'repeated increases in its defence allocations were also influenced significantly by Pakistan's domestic equation between its civil-military-political leaders and

[47]Jasjit Singh, 'The Army in the Power Structure of Pakistan', pp. 860–61.

interests. High levels of defence spending during the 1970s also resulted in remarkable growth of force levels. The effect was a substantive increase in the military power, especially between January 1972 (after the war) and December 1979 (before the Soviet intervention in Afghanistan). When the size of the army nearly doubled, the navy grew three times, and the air force, combat aircraft grew one-and-a half times.'[48]

During the 1981–1990 decade, defence expenditure grew at a cumulative rate of 315.7 per cent. Pakistan's defence expenditure was maintained at a much higher level after 1980 when Pakistan resumed its proxy war against India. Moreover, from 1979 to 1992, $350 million were spent for its nuclear programme.

Military and Strategic Ties with the US

Army leadership asserted the primacy of arms in politics. One of the characteristics of the army has been its desire for an external linkage and support in strategic and military terms from the very beginning. Pakistan's rulers were definitely looking for a strong reliable friend to strengthen its defence and side with it in its conflict with India. Pakistan developed a strategic alliance with the US. It is a well known fact that General Ayub Khan played a significant role in the negotiation of Mutual Defence Assistance with the US. Moreover, the decision to participate in South East Asia Treaty Organization (SEATO) and Central Treaty Organization (CENTO) was taken on his initiative. The US military and economic aid and Pakistan's participation in SEATO and CENTO enhanced the Pakistan military's capabilities qualitatively as well as quantitatively. At the same time the US influence and involvement in Pakistan's army became pervasive. Pakistan also developed military and strategic ties with China after the Sino-Indian war of 1962 following Kautilaya's dictum that 'enemy's enemy is your friend.' At the same time the relationship with the US and China has invariably been an important factor as an incentive to military adventurism by Pakistan, whether in 1965 and 1971, later in the proxy war against India since 1984 or in the Kargil aggression in 1999.

---

[48]Jasjit Singh, 'The Army in Pakistan', p. 50.

Table 2.1

Pakistan's Defence Expenditure, 1961–1999

Year	Defex (bn Rs.)	GDP Current Prices	Population (mns)	Defence Forces (.000)	Federal Govt. Exp. (bn Rs.)	Defex/ GDP (%)	Defex/ Federal Govt.Exp.
1961–62	1.109	19.139	97.5	250	1.986	5.79	55.84
1962–63	0.954	20.489	101.1	250	1.795	4.66	53.15
1963–64	1.157	22.945	104.7	253	2.337	5.04	49.51
1964–65	1.262	26.202	108.5	253	2.734	4.82	46.16
1965–66	2.855	28.969	112.5	278	4.498	9.86	63.47
1966–67	2.794	32.622	116.7	278	3.765	8.56	74.21
1967–68	2.182	35.542	121.0	351	4.077	6.14	53.52
1968–69	2.427	37.985	124.0	357	4.371	6.39	55.53
1969–70	2.749	43.347	127.0	390	5.009	6.34	53.91
1970–71	3.202	46.006	131.0	390	5.751	6.96	55.68
1971–72	3.726	49.784	135.0	404	6.926	7.48	53.80
1972–73	4.440	61.414	63.34	350	8.406	7.23	52.82
1973–74	4.949	81.690	65.89	466	11.954	6.06	41.40
1974–75	6.914	103.557	69.89	500	14.384	6.68	48.07
1975–76	6.103	119.736	72.12	502	17.709	5.10	34.46
1976–77	.121	135.982	74.33	604	20.609	5.97	39.41
1977–78	9.675	159.840	76.60	588	25.454	6.05	38.01
1978–79	10.302	177.844	78.94	518	29.861	5.79	34.50
1979–80	12.655	210.253	81.36	544	37.948	6.02	33.35
1980–81	15.300	278.196	83.84	549	46.348	5.50	33.01
1981–82	18.631	324.159	86.44	560	51.116	5.75	36.45
1982–83	23.224	364.159	89.12	588	59.076	6.37	39.91
1983–84	26.798	419.802	91.88	588	75.902	6.38	35.31
1984–85	31.794	427.157	94.73	479	90.074	6.73	35.30
1985–86	34.763	514.532	97.67	483	100.043	6.76	34.75
1986–87	41.325	572.479	100.70	483	111.856	7.22	36.94
1987–88	47.015	675.389	103.82	481	136.151	6.96	34.53
1988–89	51.053	769.745	107.04	481	156.417	6.63	32.64
1989–90	57.926	855.943	110.36	520	173.273	6.77	33.43
1990–91	64.623	1,020.600	113.78	55	183.060	6.33	34.63
1991–92	75.751	1,211.385	117.31	565	199.000	6.25	38.67
1992–93	87.461	1,341.629	120.83	580	235.000	6.52	37.91
1993–94	91.776	1,573.097	124.48	580	258.000	5.83	34.31
1994–95	104.512	1,882.071	128.08	540	295.017	5.55	34.52
1995–96	119.658	2,165.598	131.63	577	334.737	5.26	34.43
1996–97	127.441	2,404.633	135.28	587	398.209	5.30	32.00
1997–98	134.020	2,759.525	139.02	587	461.907	4.86	29.02
1998–99	145.000	2,960.000 E		587	606.300	4.90	23.92
			+	513 R			

Note: Population till 1971 includes East Pakistan.

Sources:

1. Economic Survey 1997–1998, Government of Pakistan.
2. World Military Expenditures and Arms Transfers, Arms Control and Disarmament Agency (ACDA), US Government, Washington.
3. Pakistan Government budget (for defence expenditure) for various years.
4. Jasjit Singh (ed). *Kargil 1999: Pakistan's Fourth War for Kashmir*, (New Delhi: Knowledge World, 1999), p. 51.

Military Aid and Arms Acquisition

As far as the military aid arms acquisition is concerned, as a result of Soviet military intervention in Afghanistan the US had provided $3.2 billion military and security-related economic aid to Pakistan over a five-year period (1981–1986). It is generally believed that nearly 60 per cent of the weapons and equipment supplied to Afghan *Mujahideen* (freedom fighters) from 1981 to 1991 through Pakistan was siphoned off in Pakistan. Pakistan's diversification of sources of weapon supplies has particularly intensified since 1990 when the US administration was forced to cut the aid. Even with the US, most foreign military sales (FMS) agreements were rapidly converted into commercial arrangements. As a result, US commercial arms sales to Pakistan had gone down. Despite the Pressler Amendment, therefore, American supplies more or less continued to reach Pakistan and were worth $1.03 billion in 1994. Pakistan continued to acquire substantive quantities of arms during the 1990s.

The sources of Pakistan's weapon supplies has undergone fundamental changes since the 1950s although the US and China have continued to be its most reliable suppliers. The US arms embargo in 1965 was Pakistan's first major crisis that deepened the urgency to diversify the sources, especially to a more reliable supplier. It is against this backdrop that China started the supply of arms to Pakistan and emerged as the most reliable supplier of weapons for Pakistan, more even than the United States. However, according to a noted scholar, 'Pakistan has continued its quest for US weapons essentially for three reasons: (1) as a symbol of strategic and political support and engagement by the United States; (2) diversification of sources of weapons systems; and (3) for higher-end technology weapons.'[49] China, on the other hand, has been Pakistan's major and trusted supplier of weapons at low costs for more than three decades. The comparative proportion of US weapons in Pakistan's military inventory, contrary to conventional wisdom, has been coming down over the years.[50]

Pakistan's defence expenditure figures do not take into account the costs of acquisition of major weapon systems. Pakistan

---

[49]Ibid., p. 52.
[50]Ibid.

has received substantive loans and aid from the USA, Saudi Arabia and other countries specifically for acquisition of arms. The actual resources invested in, and supporting, the military power, therefore, were significantly higher than what the official defence expenditure figures reveal. Thus, high level defence expenditures naturally show an adverse impact on the economic growth and development.

Of late, the high defence expenditure came under criticism for two main reasons. First, Pakistan's sinking economy in the late 1990s and especially the pressure of bourgeoning debts made many in Pakistan look critically at the resources being made available to the military. The review proposals have ranged from suggestions for organizational changes in the military, reduction in defence expenditure to its rationalization and a sticker control on its disbursement. There are demands that the annual budget statement should provide some details of the defence expenditure rather than the current practice of a one-line statement. Second, there is a growing realization that more resources should be made available to the social sector (such as, health care, education and environment) which is not less important than the defence sector. So far Pakistan has tried to achieve external security at the cost of societal security and allocated more resources to the military and neglected socio-economic development.

Changing Role and Parameters of the Army

The army's role and position in the power structure of Pakistan has undergone shifts and changes over the years. In the 1950s and 1960s it assumed the role of an agent of modernization and socio-economic change. In the 1970s it moved to conquer its own people in the East Pakistan crisis and Baluchistan as a Punjabi dominated army of an otherwise ruthless state. In the 1980s it emphasized its role as the defender of ideology.

Military as an Agent of Modernization

Ayub Khan, in order to seek legitimacy propagated his image as a modernizer. His economic development and modernization strategy won high praise and his period (from October 1958 to March 1969) was labelled as the 'decade of development'. Pakistan became a shining example for the rest of the developing countries. Ayub's political innovation of Basic Democracies was acclaimed by many as a plausible alternative to Western democracy and the Communist system. He also earned the title of 'Muslim de Gaulle' or a 'Great legislator'. Yet Ayub's regime fell in March 1969, as a result of mass movements and urban agitations. Gross quantitative indicators of economic growth supported the Ayub regime's claims regarding impressive economic development. However, behind the gross growth rates lie the stark realities of the socio-economic exploitation of the large mass of people. The policies of the Ayub regime led to an incredible concentration of wealth in a few hands. It was the deepening of regional and class inequalities during the Ayub era which provided the East Pakistani political opposition with the impetus to take themselves out of the clutches of the West Pakistani military-bureaucratic-industrial establishment.

Military as a Partisan and Ruthless Institution

Under the leadership of Yahya Khan, the army had displayed an obstinate commitment to preserve a system of a strong central government and it sought to prevent the replacement of this system by a six-point autonomous order even at the risk of the break-up of the country. What made the army positively hostile to Sheikh Mujibur Rahman and his Awami League was that the latter threatened to reduce this vast and magnificent fighting machine to humbler proportions. Therefore, the military and the dominant power groups in the Western wing considered transfer of power to Awami League as an even greater threat than East Pakistan's outright secession.

Military as Defender of the Ideology

Under Zia-ul-Haq's regime, organized efforts were taken to induct an Islamic dimension at the officer level. The lower middle-class, middle-rank officers accepted the army's enhanced role not only as defenders of the country but also as soldiers of Islam. Islam replaced the symbols of the British Indian Army. Some observers have tried to conceptualize a dialectical relationship between Islam, Pakistan and the military.[51] One cannot deny the inter-relationship between Islam, Pakistan and the army, but to consider the latter as the guarantor for the others is an oversimplification, as Muslim society even under non-Muslim colonial rule produced dynamic leaders like Syed Ahmed Khan, Jinnah and Iqbal.[52]

The political ethos in Pakistan (since Pakistan's first military regime in 1958) reveals that the Pakistani Army has 'incrementally acquired an institutional identity and role which is supra-governmental and which transcends all other constitutional arrangements of governance in Pakistan'.[53] Pakistani Army had declared itself, maintains Subrahmanyam, 'the ideological guardian of the two-nation theory on which the Pakistani people believe the nation is founded. In other words, the Pakistani army considers itself above the constitution and as the last resort of redressal when things go wrong.'[54] It has become the final repository of the responsibility of protecting and consolidating its nationhood. Besides, in Pakistan, the sovereignty does not rest with the people as in a secular democracy, but in Almighty God, Allah, himself. The Pakistan Army, according to Dixit, 'claims to be the shadow of God responsible for exercising state sovereignty for the welfare of the Pakistani people of which they claim to be the

---

[51]Asaf Hussain maintains that without Islam, Pakistan would not have come into existence; without Pakistan the military would not be able to exist; and without military, Islam and Pakistan would be threatened. In perpetuating such a state the military was perpetuating Islam. See Asaf Hussain, *Elite Politics in an Ideological State* (Folkestone, Kent: Dawson, 1979), p. 133.

[52]Consult Iftikhar H. Malik, *State and Civil Society in Pakistan: Politics of Authority, Ideology and Ethnicity* (New York: St. Martin's Press, INC, 1997), p. 77.

[53]J. N. Dixit, 'A Difficult Neighbour', *The Hindustan Times* (New Delhi), 27 October 1999, p. 13.

[54]Subrahmanyam, 'Battle Fatigues: Predictable Replay in Pakistan', *The Times of India* (New Delhi), 18 October 1999, p. 14.

most competent judge.'[55] The Pakistani Army does not, therefore, have the basic democratic orientation by which it would consider itself an apolitical instrumentality of a democratic state.

A number of important developments since the 1980s have had a profound impact on the traditional balance of power inside Pakistan. In the wake of the Soviet invasion of Afghanistan, cultivation of poppy and cannabis was encouraged by Zia-ul-Haq's regime to finance terrorist activities in India. General Zia's support for poppy cultivation gave a new dimension to international drug trafficking and terrorism in India. His target was to destabilize India. The successor regimes were unable and unwilling to control the menace and power of drug barons. The second development was the growth in power and influence of the ISI directorate which conducted the proxy war in Afghanistan, and in India. The ISI, in addition to amassing weapons and waging wars in the neighbouring countries, has become a force to reckon with in domestic politics. The military also influences the political process through the intelligence agencies. The military relies on the Military Intelligence and the ISI to pursue its political agenda. Intelligence-gathering has become increasingly important for senior commanders pursuing behind-the-scene political intervention. This is also important for advancing the military's professional and corporate interests. The third aspect is the introduction of radical religious indoctrination of the country in general and the army in particular.

Army's Indirect and 'Non-Takeover' Role from the Sidelines

After the demise of General Zia in 1988, a new-pattern of 'soft' or 'non-takeover' intervention developed in which the emphasis shifted from assuming power directly, to playing a more subtle, but still ubiquitous role from the sidelines. The military had an important influence over foreign security and key domestic issues and it continued to moderate confrontations among feuding politicians or state institutions. The army remained pivotal in the power structure along

---

[55]Dixit, 'A Difficult Neighbour', p. 13.

with the president and the prime minister under the system which was described as the Triangle of Power or the 'Troika'.[56]

Islam and the Military

It is worth noting that Islam being integral to Pakistan military ideology was repeatedly invoked during the wars in 1965 and 1971 to galvanize the soldiers and civilians for the defence of the country. When Zia-ul-Haq assumed command of the army in March 1976, he gave the motto of 'Iman' (faith) 'Taqwa' (piety and abstinence), and 'Jihad-fi-Sibilillah' (holy war in the name of God), which reflected his strong religious inclinations. However, this was not a major departure because Islamic principles, teachings, history and Muslim war heroes and their battles have always been a part of military education training and ideology. Islam was emphasized 'as an identity and a motivational force coupled with professionalism and service discipline. Religious extremism and linkages with Islamic movements or groups were discouraged. The military represented the moderate and liberal face of Islam.'[57]

However, some developments during the Zia years had far-reaching repercussions for the role of Islam in the army. First, Zia-ul-Haq used Islam and conservatism and orthodoxy in the army. This fitted nicely with the transformation in the orientation of the new breed of officers who came from the middle to lower strata of the society, hailing mainly from small towns and urban areas with conservative religious values. The institution of 'regimental priest' was upgraded and strengthened the bias in favour of Islamic conservatism.[58] According to a perceptive scholar, 'The middle level officers, recruited from more traditional sectors of Pakistani society increased the salience of Islam and the struggle to turn Pakistan's military officers into good Muslims.... The earlier officer class who succeeded by a "second generation" of petit bourgeois origin and "fascist" outlook'.[59]

---

[56]Rizvi, *Military, State and Society in Pakistan*, pp. 1–2.

[57]Ibid., p. 245.

[58]Ibid.

[59]Eqbal Ahmad, 'Pakistan: Sign–Posts to a Police State', *Journal of Contemporary Asia*, Vol. IV, No. 4 (1974), p. 425.

Some of the Islamic groups were allowed to make inroads into the army, something of an anathema in the past. Zia-ul-Haq had a strong inclination towards the Tableghi Jamaat, a purely religious organization which does not involve itself in politics, and he was the first head of state to attend its annual congregation at Raiwind. Encouraged by this, a good number of officers and men began openly to associate with the Tableghi Jamaat. Other conservative Islamic sectarian groups were also able to develop connections with the personnel of the three services, especially the army.[60] The other group that gained access to the army and the bureaucracy was the Jamaat-i-Islami which had a favourable disposition toward the Zia regime and was associated with the government's Afghanistan policy. The Jamaat-i-Islami with its overt Islamic political agenda penetrated these institutions, and religion thus became an important part of the public profile of the in-service personnel.

The Afghanistan experience reinforced Islamic zeal among army personnel. The withdrawal of the Soviet forces from Afghanistan in 1988 created a sense of euphoria among them and the thinking process of many army personnel (including some senior officers) was frozen in the Afghanistan experience. They often argued for an Afghanistan-style armed resistance to bring an end to non-Muslim domination of the Muslims, especially in Kashmir.

The Soviet withdrawal also strengthened religious zealots inside and outside the military. A small group of religious zealots in the army were arrested in September 1995 for the planning and take-over of the Army Headquarters and the civilian government in order to establish a strict Islamic order.[61]

As a result of the introduction of orthodox Islamic orientation in the military, perhaps for the first time in Pakistan, military doctrine was sought to be interpreted in religious terms. General Zia in his foreword to Brigadier S. K. Malik's book *The Quranic Concept of War* states, 'the professional soldier in a Muslim army, pursuing the goals of a Muslim State cannot become "professional" if, in all his activities, he does not take on the "colour of Allah" '.[62]

---

[60]Rizvi, *Military, State and Society in Pakistan*, p. 246.
[61]Zafar Abbas, 'Day of Reckoning', *The Herald*, January 1996, pp. 89–95.
[62]Foreword to Brig. S. K. Malik, *The Quranic Concept of War* (Lahore: Wajidalis, 1979).

Strategic Doctrine of Terror

As Pakistan moved towards greater Islamization in the 1970s and 1980s it also sought increased inspiration from religion for its strategic doctrine. General Zia encouraged such efforts. The Pakistan military believes in the 'strategic doctrine of terror' and 'total war' and links it to nuclear deterrence. Since 1990, Pakistani leaders have been using the tactic of nuclear blackmail, which succeeded in deterring India from attacking Pakistan in retaliation as exemplified in the case of the Kargil aggression and ongoing proxy war in Jammu and Kashmir. Pakistan has considered nuclear weapons as a major means of imposing terror over a professed but stronger enemy, i.e., India. Pakistan has threatened to use nuclear weapons against India, time and again, since they remain weapons of mass terror.[63] In sum, under the nuclear umbrella, Pakistan feels more confident of waging its low cost proxy war against India. This has also provided strategic advantage to the army vis-à-vis India.

The present Chief of Army Staff, General Pervez Musharraf, like Zia, is also a Deobandi in many ways, which symbolizes the ethos and religious orientation of the present day army of Pakistan. During the Zia era, Musharraf had developed a close relationship with the ISI and Islamic fundamentalist groups like the Harkat-ul-Mujahideen.[64]

Linkages between Militant Islam, Terrorism and Export of *Jihad*

Growing influence of Jamaat-i-Islami on the army during the Bhutto period and Islamization of the army under Zia-ul-Haq led to its 'transition to militant Islamic orientation, therefore also acquired a nationalist character.'[65] But contrary to conventional wisdom this has not adversely affected its professionalism. On the other hand, this has provided a strong religious motivation in support of

---

[63] Jasjit Singh, 'The Army in Pakistan', p. 46.
[64] B. Raman, 'Gen. Pervez Musharraf: His Past and Present', *Corde*@vsnl.com. 1 July 1999.
[65] Singh, 'Nothing Uniform About Them', p. 17.

aggressive action.[66] The army has even interpreted the *Quran* since the late 1970s to justify the use of terrorism in pursuit of warfare. In 1979, it came out with an interpretation of the *Holy Quran*, which argued in favour of a total war where terror was to be a central element in the run up to the war, during hostilities and for war termination.[67] Successive generations of officers have been exhorted to think in terms of the use of terror as a weapon sanctioned by the *Holy Quran*. The linkages between militant Islam, terrorism, and export of *Jihad* are exemplified through the Taliban phenomenon.

Guerrilla warfare is also a part of the army's strategic thought. From its birth, the Pakistani army has been over-sensitive to the asymmetry that existed in relation to India, which has been propagated as its enemy number one. It has, therefore, sought to merge irregular guerrilla warfare with regular organized military operation.

While most professional armies study and train to fight irregular warfare, the Pakistan army, from the very beginning, studied it for waging such warfare. It has also practiced it from the start. The synthesis of regular and irregular warfare was finally achieved in the Taliban operation after almost two decades of experience in Afghanistan. Unlike the Turkish armed forces, which have been a bastion of secularism, the Pakistan military, though starting with British colonial traditions, has become politicized and now Islamaized, specially at the level of junior officers. This was evident by the bearded soldiers manning the government buildings in Pakistan after the latest military intervention. Besides, they have been nurturing militant and terrorist organizations to export *Jihad* to various parts of the world. Pakistan attempted to replicate the Afghan model in India. However, the same strategy has failed miserably in Kargil when it came face to face with the more dedicated and professional Indian military.

In this context, commenting on the role of Islam in the army, a prolific writer asserted that 'As long as Islam is coupled with professionalism and service discipline, it is a source of strength. However, whenever the imperatives of military profession are subordinated to extraneous considerations, no matter what is their source,

---

[66]Ibid.
[67]Malik, *The Quranic Concept of War*, pp. 58–59.

the military faces internal problems.'[68] Zia's policies led to the rise of religious conservatism in cross-sections of the military. One observer of military affairs comments that Islam could serve as a 'force multiplier' for a Muslim army when it was not being used as a 'substituting professional hard and software in the shape of weapons and training.'[69] According to Rizvi, 'the major challenge the military faces in the twenty-first century is the maintenance of a professional and cohesive disposition as the new breed of officers takes over its command. The delicate balance between Islam and service discipline is going to be another important concern, especially because a number of Islamic groups continue to work on the new breed of officers and other ranks.'[70]

Military's Penetration of Civilian Institutions: The Economy and Society

The long years of direct and indirect rule have enabled the military to spread out so widely into civilian institutions, the economy and society that its clout and influence no longer depend on controlling the levers of power. It is derived from its organizational strength and its significant presence in all sectors of government and society.[71]

Military's presence is firmly established in all walks of life. It has carved out a role and position in the public and private sectors, industry, business, agriculture, education, scientific development, health care, communication and transportation. Such an omnipresence ensures a significant role for the military in the state and society even if the generals do not directly rule. Several factors have contributed to this. First, the military regimes of Ayub Khan and Zia-ul-Haq, respectively, included their personnel in government and semi-government jobs and civilian professions. Ayub Khan during his rule appointed senior officers, mostly retired, to

---

[68]Rizvi, *Military, State and Society in Pakistan*, p. 247.
[69]A. R. Siddiqi, 'Army: Chickens are Coming Home to Roost', *The Nation* (Lahore), 23 October 1995. Also see Talat Masood, 'Lessons for the Military', *The News* (Lahore), 19 October 1995.
[70]*Rizvi, Military, State and Society in Pakistan*, p. 248.
[71]Ibid., p. 233.

senior jobs with high salaries and perks in government and semi-government corporations or autonomous bodies. General Zia in 1980 fixed a 10 per cent minimum quota for military personnel in civilian jobs which provided a basis for their induction into all government and semi-government services. Besides, the private sector was encouraged to accommodate them. The military also contributed to improving their socio-economic condition by distributing agricultural land and material awards.

Second, the military has been able to translate its dominance over the state structure to become deeply entrenched in the political economy. The military has expanded its role in the economy by active involvement in industry, commerce, and business, developing a stake in the government's economic policies and industrial and commercial strategies. Army's control of vast industrial and business empires has enabled it to amass sufficient clout in the economy and to develop a capacity for looking after the welfare of its personnel without relying on the civilian government.[72] The most impressive result of more than five decades of dominance over the state apparatus has been the military establishment's extensive tentacles throughout the economy. Each of the three defence services of Pakistan have trusts and foundations with large investments in the national economy.

Third, the military's ethnic homogeneity has helped in raising its political profile. The preponderant bulk of military officers are recruited from Punjab and NWFP and it also contributes to its clout. Thus, the linkages between ethnicity and recruitment pattern of the army are interesting and relevant to politics.

Finally, the civilian governments at the federal and provincial levels, overwhelmed by the problems of governance and maintenance of law and order, 'seek the military's support more often than was the case in the past for the performance of their basic function which in turn adds to the relevance and importance of the military for the orderly functioning of the polity.'[73]

As the foregoing discussion suggests, Pakistan army plays complex and equally baffling multiple roles. Cohen summed this up succinctly: 'There are armies that guard their nation's borders,

---

[72]Ibid., pp. 236–37.
[73]Ibid., p. 233.

there are those that are concerned with protecting their own position in society, and there are those who defend a cause or an idea. The Pakistan army does all three.'[74] For a weak, mutually divisive, economically and politically fragile Pakistan, unable to afford a huge defence establishment, it is imperative to disengage the army from its varying roles. In the context, the army officials reflecting 'new thinking', who feel that the army as an institution has suffered erosion in terms of professional capabilities due to its interventionist and vetoing role in domestic politics, can help politicians in evolving a common viable political culture based on plural and democratic traditions.[75]

---

[74]Cohen, *The Pakistan Army,* p. 105.
[75]Malik, *State and Civil Society in Pakistan: Politics of Authority, Ideology and Ethnicity,* pp. 79–80.

Chapter III

Political Economy:
Near the Brink of Collapse

Pakistan at the moment is in the midst of, perhaps, the worst economic crisis in her history. Economic growth over the last few years has remained stagnant, with its revenues not even sufficient to cover debt servicing requirements. Islamabad is heavily dependent on international donor agencies and bank borrowings just to keep itself afloat. The rising deficit in the balance of trade, exacerbated by declining exports and spiralling import bills, has created an untenable situation. Most observers agree that Pakistan may not even be able to pay for essential imports like oil, if the International Monetary Fund (IMF) suspends lending for the structural adjustment programme. The economy, experts say, has reached its lowest point since the breaking away of Bangladesh from Pakistan in 1971. The very integrity and survival of Pakistan is in question as the economy is on the brink of collapse. Since 1987 the bleak picture of the country's economy and its future has been reported and highlighted by both the Pakistani and international press. According to one observer, Pakistan's current economic problems stem from three factors, namely: (1) existing feudal order in the country, (2) high defence expenditure, and (3) bourgeoning debt burden.[1]

---

[1]Sreedhar, 'Pakistan's Economic Dilemma', *Strategic Analysis*, Vol. XXII, No. 3 (June 1998), p. 445.

At independence, the feudal landlords of Pakistan, the *zamindars*, *khans* and *sardars*, emerged as a dominant class in the country, later to be joined by an embryonic national bourgeoisie comprised mainly of immigrants from the industrially more developed provinces of India. One could hardly expect these feudal lords as agents of modernization. There were two half-hearted efforts to bring out land reforms in 1959 and 1972, including an act to abolish the *Sardari* system, but they failed to substantially weaken the grip of the feudal class on land ownership.

Since its creation, Pakistan has been according a very high priority to defence. It has been obviously spending a major portion of its total revenues to modernize the military apparatus. The Pakistani political leaders' conception of hostile India, its identity crisis, and its border tensions with India and Afghanistan have all helped to boost the military expenditure disproportionately at the cost of development projects.

The third reason for the problems in Pakistan relates to debt burden. Until the 1990s, Pakistan survived by borrowing from the international monetary system. But thereafter, due to the changes in the international system, Pakistan's economy started feeling the pinch. Pakistan is today entangled in one of the classical models of debt trap—how to repay the old loans and yet keep the economy going. In the international monetary system, Pakistan's credibility is quickly getting eroded and this by itself has created problems for fresh borrowing. This chapter aims to analyze the performance of Pakistan's economy since independence with a focus on these three areas. It also takes into account the internal compulsion of economy and the challenges before the Musharraf regime.

Pakistan's Political Economy: An Overview

The analysis of the nexus between state and political economy in Pakistan provides some interesting insights into the ways the state and economy influence social dynamics underlying political processes in Pakistan. An examination of the state–class relationship in the different phases of the post-independence history of Pakistan highlights the persisting problems of economic inequalities and social injustice. According to a perceptive scholar,

> The absence of any substantive restructuring of existing associations of dominance and privilege in civil society have since the late 1960s served to magnify competition and conflict in ever-expanding political arenas and sharply increased the trans-actional costs of governance, forcing greater reliance on the states' coercive apparatus, irrespective of its formally democratic or authoritarian facade.[2]

An outstanding difference between India and Pakistan in the initial two decades of independence was the relative cost of defence to the central exchequer. The share of defence as a proportion of total government expenditure has been extraordinarily high since Pakistan's creation. In the first decade after independence, defence along with the cost of civil administration, swallowed more than three-quarters of the central government's revenue budget. With the advent of military regimes in Pakistan, defence and civil administration continued to claim the lion's share of the central government resources leaving little for development purposes. India, on the other hand, prior to the Sino-Indian war in 1962, never spent more on defence than 12 to 14 per cent of the central government expenditure[3] and therefore continued to spend relatively more on social services.

During the last five decades, the central government's expenditure in Pakistan reveals neglect of the social sector at the expense of defence spending. The defence budget coupled with the costs of administration, expenditure on para-military forces as well as interest payments on military debt accumulated over the years has greatly limited Pakistan's policy options with disastrous effects on its political trajectory. Given the centralized nature of the state structure, it seems reasonable to portray Pakistan's political economy as more defence than development oriented.[4]

---

[2]Ayesha Jalal, *Democracy and Authoritarianism in South Asia* (Cambridge: Cambridge University Press, 1995), p. 123.
[3]Y. Lakshmi, *Trends in India's Defence Expenditure* (New Delhi: ABC, 1988), pp. 23–40.
[4]Ayesha Jalal, *Democracy and Authoritarianism in South Asia*, pp. 140–56.

The present sorry economic predicament is at least partly due to Pakistan's unrealistic drive to achieve parity with India in military terms to remove the power asymmetry between them. The predominance of the armed forces in Pakistani polity, the military's unidimensional approach to nation-building, resulted in skewed priorities, with defence expenditure becoming priority number one. And high defence expenditure has been rationalized on account of security threat from India. In this process, Pakistan's socio-economic structure was messed up. The National Assembly also supported the policy of strong defence. There was consensus among the politicians with regard to the maintenance of strong armed forces against India. It is noteworthy that Pakistan gives only a one line statement of the military expenditure without mentioning details of overall figures. It also does not take into account the costs of acquisition of major weapons system.

Table 3.1 reveals that Pakistan spent on an average, 60.69 per cent of its national budget on defence from 1947 to 58, which was quite high—given the fact that the country was facing acute social and economic problems. Even after 1954, when Pakistan began to obtain military equipment and weapons from the US, the defence expenditure continued to increase instead of going down.

Table 3.1
Pakistan's Defence Expenditure, 1947–1958 (in million Rupees)

Year	Defence Expenditure	Total Expenditure Met from Revenue	Defence Expenditure as Percentage of Total Expenditure
1947–48	153.8	236.0	63.16
1948–49	461.5	647.0	71.32
1949–50	625.4	856.0	73.06
1950–51	649.9	1266.2	51.32
1951–52	779.1	1442.3	54.01
1952–53	783.4	1320.1	59.34
1953–54	653.2	1108.7	58.69
1954–55	635.1	1172.6	54.16
1955–56	917.7	1433.4	64.02
1956–57	800.9	1330.7	60.18
1957–58	854.2	1521.8	56.13

Source: Adopted from Hasan Askari Rizvi, *Military, State and Society in Pakistan*, London: Macmillan Press Ltd., 2000, p. 63.

It is interesting to note that after the emergence of Bangladesh, though the size of Pakistan was almost halved in territory, there was no reduction in the strength of the armed forces nor any reduction in the budgetary allocations. Between 1971 and 1980, the defence expenditure grew at a cumulative rate of 377.8 per cent in current Pakistani rupees. During the 11 year rule of General Zia-ul-Haq, the defence budget more than doubled during the first decade every five years, and in the last year of his rule, it reached an all time high. Table 3.2 reveals it increased from Rs 10,302 million in 1978–79 to Rs 23,224 million in 1982–1983 and in 1987–1988 it touched Rs 47,105 million. In 1988–1989, it reached Rs 51,053 billion. In fact, during the 11 years rule of General Zia, the defence budget of Pakistan registered an annual increase of over 16 per cent. And as percentage of GDP, it hovered around 7 per cent during the second half, and 8 per cent in the last year of his rule.

Table 3.2
Pakistan's Defence Expenditure, 1978–1989 (Rs. mn)

Year	DE	% Increase of DE Over Previous Year	GDP (fc)	DE as % of GDP	DE as % of Fed Govt. Expenditure
1978–79	10,302	06.48	177,844	05.79	34.50
1979–80	12,655	22.84	210,253	06.02	33.35
1980–81	15,300	20.90	247,029	06.19	33.01
1981–82	18,631	21.77	289,788	06.43	36.45
1982–83	23,244	24.65	327,909	07.08	39.31
1983–84	26,798	15.39	375,792	07.13	35.31
1984–85	31,794	18.64	435,015	07.31	35.30
1985–86	34,763	09.34	489,376	07.10	34.75
1986–87	38,619	11.09	545,888	07.61	36.94
1987–88	47,105	21.97	618,036	07.61	34.53
1988–89	51,053	08.38	596,300	08.56	32.63

Source: Compiled from Pakistan Economic Survey, an annual publication of the Government of Pakistan.

Pakistan's defence expenditure was maintained at a much higher level after 1988 when Pakistan resumed its proxy war against India. Pakistan has also spent $250 million from 1979 to 1992 for its nuclear programme, seeking to provide a credible nuclear deterrent. After Zia's death in mid-1988, the subsequent elections brought back civilian rule in Pakistan in 1988. Benazir Bhutto, despite her promise to prune the defence budget, could not do so because of the predominance of the Pakistani military in the body polity. This got reflected in the third budget her government presented to the National Assembly in 1990–1991 which registered a mere 9.79 per cent increase over the preceding year.

As a result, the incidence of defence expenditure on Pakistani economy became one of the highest in this part of the world. During the decade 1988–1998, except for two years, 1990–1991 and 1991–1992, defence expenditure always exceeded developmental expenditure. This high level of defence expenditure naturally shows an adverse impact on economic growth and development. According to one study, covering a period of over four decades since 1960, 'An examination of budgetary trade-off in Pakistan found that economic services as a whole were adversely affected by military expenditures.'[5] For the last several years, many financial institutions have been pressing the Pakistani leadership to cut back defence expenditure. However, the Pakistan elite have resisted.

A political economy of defence, by its very nature, hinders the state's development activities, especially when economic resources are scarce and the appetites of the non-elected institutions insatiable. The investigation of the relations between political and economic power in Pakistan suggests a separation between state power and class power. So it is significant to consider the nature of the links between the non-elected institutions and the dominant social classes.

Unlike India's political economy of development in a liberal democratic setup, the political economy of defence in Pakistan has rested on a particular kind of relative autonomy of the state from the dominant social classes. The persistence of military rule and the prolonged suspension of political processes has enabled the Pakistani state to refine the art of social engineering to a much larger extent than the Indian state. The military-bureaucratic state of Pakistan has been able to determine whom to include and exclude from the development process.[6]

---

[5]Jasjit Singh, 'Pakistan's Nuclear Posturing: Hitching its Stars to India's Wagon', *The Times of India* (New Delhi), 13 November 1996, p. 11.
[6]Ayesha Jalal, *Democracy and Authoritarianism in South Asia*, p. 156.

The big landowning families of West Pakistan have remained junior partner of the civil bureaucracy and the military axis which has managed Pakistan's affairs since the early 1950s, but they have not failed to extract economic compensation for their subordinate role in the power structure. Despite an inability to turn economic power into direct political control, the dominant social classes in Pakistan have done quite as well as their Indian counterparts in negotiating terms with the state in support of their material and other interests. Tentative attempts by the Pakistani state to bring about land reforms were successfully hindered through stiff resistance from West Pakistan's big landlords irrespective of the democratic or authoritarian nature of the regime. In this context, the middling strata was also aligned with the bigger landlords against state encroachments on agricultural interests. This is an indication of the limitation on the state's relative autonomy of action from the dominant agrarian class.

In 1952–1953, Punjab's bigger landlords subverted an attempt by the more progressive wing of the Muslim League to introduce redistributive reform by refusing to bring their produce to the market and precipitating a 'man-made famine' in that province.[7]

Even after fifty-three years of independence, the feudal landlords continue to maintain their predominance on the nation state of Pakistan. According to Abul Fazal, '...the landlord's relationship with peasants continued to be pro-capitalist. It was characterized by super exploitation, actual insecurity of tenure and lawlessness. This double aspect of the landlord class in Pakistan—a commodity relationship with the world market and a coercive relationship with the peasant—appears to have imparted a stability to the formation, especially in Sindh and Southern Punjab. The reason was a lack of industry which could mechanize agriculture and absorb the surplus labour power enabling the peasants to escape the situation of dependence.'[8]

This landed class never permitted any land reforms which could alter the social equilibrium to any significant extent during the last five decades. The two attempts to implement land reforms in

---

[7]Ibid., p. 145.
[8]M. Abul Fazal, 'Feudalism', *The Nation* (Lahore), 10 and 11 June 1997.

1959 and 1972 by Ayub Khan and Zulfikar Ali Bhutto respectively were symbolic rather than substantive in their impact.[9] The result of this extraordinary situation was that a majority of the rural population became dependent on the landlords for their survival. This resulted in a complete economic hold of the landlord class over the masses, enabling them to get people of their choice elected to the National Assembly and Provincial Assemblies. Finally, because of their timely participation in the Pakistani movement and the leadership role thrust on them by the absence of adequate Muslim presence in other fields of economic endeavour, it was the landed aristocracy that grabbed the sinews of state power at an early stage. And they have succeeded since then to block any measure designed to extend social justice and equitable socio-economic order.

The reluctance of Pakistan's mainly Punjabi-dominated military and bureaucratic state to implement effective land reforms or impose an agriculture income tax, strongly demanded by nascent industrial groups and also by Bengali middle class professionals, has been presented by some theorist as evidence of its 'organic alliance' with the landed elite of Pakistan. However, Ayesha Jalal considers it a 'politics of compromise'. In other words, it is simply a matter of expediency in response to effective social and political engineering by the military-bureaucratic state.[10]

Pakistan's appallingly low rates of saving, coupled with a technically weak industrial structure, has necessitated far greater dependence on imports and consequently, been much more of a drag on development processes. It can be cited as 'a classic example of a case where artificial prosperity was maintained by heavy doses of foreign aid and overseas remittances of Pakistan.'[11]

Unlike India after independence, the Pakistani ruling elite did not opt for long-term planning and time bound targets. They did not think of building a self-reliant economy. The development of large scale basic indigenous industries was discouraged due to the easy and cheap availability of goods and service through foreign aid. At another level, Pakistan failed to implement even basic economic development. Some of the macro level economic indicators point towards this. The domestic saving ratio to the GDP/GNP

[9]Ibid.
[10]Ayesha Jalal, *Democracy and Authoritarianism in South Asia*, pp. 146–47.
[11]Sreedhar, 'Pakistan's Economic Dilemma', p. 446.

remained one of the lowest among developing countries. Low savings resulting in low capital formation have, in turn, resulted in the absence of any meaningful industrialization such as steel, iron, transport and communication, and power.

An overview of Pakistan's economic performance suggests that it has been mismanaged since 1947. The little so-called development that took place in the late 1950s and 1960s was accidental and not due to governmental policies. The absence of institutional frameworks for the governance of the state to channelize the aspirations of people has resulted in a chaotic situation.

During the 1950s and 1960s, Pakistan received liberal doses of economic aid from the West as an alliance partner of Cold War politics, which enabled the ruling elite to present a picture of economic prosperity to the rest of the world. The emergence of detente or relaxation in Cold War denied aid from the West, but the oil boom of the Persian Gulf compensated Pakistan in terms of resource availability. The overseas remittances sustained the economy in the 1970s. When the oil boom was coming to an end by the end of the 1970s, the Soviet military intervention in Afghanistan in December 1979 gave birth to the Second Cold War and Pakistan reaped maximum benefits in terms of economic and military aid. However, the Soviet withdrawal from Afghanistan in 1989 created a grave economic situation as the bubble of borrowed dollars burst.

So far as the problem of bourgeoning debt is concerned, as has been mentioned earlier, the money that flowed into the Pakistani economy was largely borrowed from both external and internal sources. The money so borrowed was not used for any productive purposes. This automatically resulted in the creation of economic assets which could repay loans. The borrowed money created artificial prosperity in the beginning, but as the years passed, Pakistan got caught in the classical 'debt trap' scenario feared by most developmental economists. Moreover, Pakistan's domestic and external debt and its servicing had shown a rising trend in recent years.

In addition, the strategy of relying on foreign aid for economic development unfolded serious distortions such as expansion of the consumer goods industry in preference to heavy industry programmes, stagnation of agriculture and lag in agricultural production. The net result was that there was no real increase in per capita income.

Capitalist Development Model: 1947–1958

The *Quaid-i-Azam*, M. A. Jinnah, even before the establishment of Pakistan, had influenced the development of certain economic and commercial institutions and had clearly indicated that the central philosophy behind economic policy would be based on principles of capitalism and private enterprise. Against this kind of economic development with the entrepreneurial class drawn from certain commercial communities that had come from India and with their investment decisions guided almost solely by the profit motive, it was bound to result in both class and regional conflicts. In the formulation of economic policies, the interests of certain dominant classes or groups like the bureaucrats, the lawyers, the upper-middle class intelligentsia, and the landlords had been upper-most in the minds of the policy makers. The ruling elite argued that the policies that had been pursued were probably the only practical measures essential for the speedy development of the country. Moreover, in reality, the interests of the great majority of people who lived in the rural areas of West Punjab, Sindh, the Frontier and East Bengal, namely, the small peasants, the tenants and the landless labourers, did not fit into such policies. Most of these refugees were poor peasants and could have been rehabilitated if the large estates in West Punjab had been broken up through land reforms. Jinnah, as the founder of the state and the Governor General of Pakistan, could have used his political influence and constitutional power to introduce land reforms as an emergency measure. Unfortunately, this was not done even though Mian Iftikharuddin, minister for rehabilitation of refugees in the West Punjab government, pressed for such reforms and resigned when his plea was rejected.[12]

Pakistan's economic history shows that the rulers of Pakistan after 1947 followed a course of action that had no relation to the historical aspirations of a people who had suffered the oppression of exploitative class relations under centuries of colonial mode of production. The economic policy adopted after 1947 was based on capitalist development principles as the Pakistan state geared to the interests of the merchant industrial groups. Their

---

[12]K. B. Sayeed, *Politics in Pakistan: The Nature and Direction of Change* (Praeger: Praeger Publishers, 1980), p. 27.

influence and importance grew in the 1950s. Most of the big industrialists were drawn from certain trading communities like Memon, Bohra, Khoja and Chinioti.

On the eve of independence, the leadership of the Muslim League party was dominated by a feudalistic aristocracy and a group of independently rich professionals and merchants. Having assumed the rule of the new nation with the help of a British trained bureaucracy, 'the leadership embarked upon safeguarding its narrow personal and class interests. Although lip service was paid to "genius" and "Islamic tradition" of the people, no attempt was made to free them from the age-old forms of oppression.'[13]

The four trading communities (Memon, Bohra, Khoja and Chinioti) controlled 35 per cent of investment in all firms, that is, both private and corporate. All these communities, except the Chiniotis, who belonged to a small town in Punjab, came from India. Owing to declining profits in international trade, and with profits ranging between 50 to 100 per cent of invested capital in a single year in manufacturing, these trading communities became industrialists. They were encouraged by the industrial policies of the government. In this context, an eminent scholar observes,

> The expansion of the private sector and the growing concentration of wealth in the hands of certain families or groups of merchant capitalists belonging to certain ethnic communities came about because of the deliberate policies that the government followed. The policy not only to tolerate but to create inequalities of income and wealth in the commercial and industrial sectors was followed because the government's considered view was that these were absolutely essential for the economic development of the country.[14]

With this increasing industrial wealth concentrated in a few groups, there was an increase in political influence but not the power of the big business groups.

For a non-governmental group to become powerful, it must have certain bases of support in the country ... a number of merchants communities who became industrialists came from India and thus

---

[13]Jamil Rashid and Hassan Gardezi, 'Independent Pakistan: Its Political Economy', in Hassan Gardezi and Jamil Rashid (eds.), *Pakistan: The Roots of Dictatorship* (Delhi: Oxford University Press, 1983), p. 5.
[14]Sayeed, *Politics in Pakistan: The Nature and Direction of Change*, p. 48.

had no social base in Pakistan. Similarly in terms of population they represented 0.26 per cent of population but controlled 41.5 per cent of Muslim private firms and 29 per cent of all firms.[15]

At the time of independence, given Pakistan's grimmer strategic and economic realities, it could not expect to meet the crushing expenditure for its strategic defence without expanding the states' administrative machinery and taking the politically dangerous path of digging deeply and widely into provincial resources. Alternatively, Pakistan had to solicit foreign aid, and in this way, increased its dependence on the centres of the international capitalist system. Pakistan developed a special military relationship with the United States and became a member of the Central Treaty Organization and the South East Asia Treaty Organization.

The dividends that accrued to Pakistan from this special relationship not only helped Pakistan to develop its military capabilities but also launch its economic development plan. Economic assistance in the form of US Public Law 480 and other agricultural commodity programmes, grant for economic development, technical assistance development grants and loans of various kinds extended to Pakistan from 1947 to 1965 amounted to $3 billion.[16] Economic assistance and the way it was channeled also produced certain desired political consequences from the US point of view.

In the early 1950s, experts from the Harvard University came to Pakistan to formulate the country's Five Year Plans. These experts conceived and executed a design for development based on the economic doctrines that guided the rise of capitalism in the West. The Planning Commission, which had attached to it an advisory team from Harvard University, played a crucial role in using commodity aid as a leverage to persuade to dismantle the detailed import controls. Thus, decontrol through liberalization of imports and the availability of raw materials through commodity aid, led to the growth of the private sector.

The political consequences of economic assistance were that Pakistan's economic development should be along capitalist lines leading to the strengthening of the private sector. Pakistani capitalists themselves did not play an important role in the formulation and

---

[15]Ibid., p. 49.
[16]Ibid., p. 50.

implementation of these policies. They functioned mostly as the beneficiaries of such policies. It was the military elite that 'propped' them up and 'pampered' them with the help of foreign aid that they acquired from the United States.[17] It has been maintained by Hamza Alavi that the bureaucratic-military oligarchy mediated between the competing demands of the three propertied classes—the indigenous bourgeoisie, the neo-colonial metropolitan bourgeoisie, and the land-owning class—and in playing this role the bureaucratic-military oligarchy represented the relative autonomy of the post-colonial state of Pakistan.[18]

Ayub Era (1958–1969):
Deepening Regional and Class Disparities

With the advent of Ayub Khan in 1958, the country entered a new phase of economic planning under the philosophy of laissez-faire. 'The military pacts had', according to Jamil Rashid and Hassan N. Gardezi 'greatly bolstered the confidence of the ruling coalition of the army, bureaucracy, landed aristocracy and prospering comprador bourgeoisie, and with renewed vigour they pursued their objective of economic growth regardless of any consideration of social justice.'[19]

The Ayub regime was a period of exemplary economic growth, averaging around 5.5 per cent annually. Per capita incomes grew at the rate of 3.5 per cent annually, large-scale manufacturing grew at almost 17 per cent annually, and by 1968, 90 per cent of all exports had been freed from administrative control and the government relied only on tariffs to restrict demands.[20]

During the Ayub era, Pakistan became one of the few developing countries that openly and officially advocated the

---

[17]Ibid., p. 51.

[18]Hamza Alavi, 'The State in Post-Colonial Societies: Pakistan and Bangladesh', in Kathleen Gough and Hari P. Sharma, (eds.), *Imperialism and Revolution in South Asia* (New Delhi: Monthly Review Press, 1973), pp. 159–61.

[19]Jamil Rashid and Hassan N. Gardezi, 'Independent Pakistan: Its Political Economy', p. 9.

[20]Omar Noman, *Pakistan: A Political and Economic History Since 1947* (London: Kegal Paul International Ltd., 1988), p. 26.

capitalist doctrine of 'functional inequality' under which the private entrepreneurs were to receive maximum incentive based on the assumption that government should tolerate 'some initial growth in income inequalities to reach high levels of saving and investment.'[21] The Ayub regime openly flaunted the ideology that 'the underdeveloped countries must consciously accept a philosophy of growth and shelve for the distant future ideas about equitable distribution and welfare state.'[22] Therefore, the so-called entrepreneurial classes were being pampered, protected, and mollycoddled through various policies such as tax benefits, cheap credits, import permits, and availability of foreign exchange because they had the initiative, industry, capacity to save, and willingness to plan those savings into investments. Similarly, surpluses were offered[23] to those industrialists only who could convert these surpluses to socially productive and useful economic and industrial growth.

Thus, the entrepreneurial elite, who were emerging as powerful interest groups even before 1958 also made significant gains under the Ayub regime. The regime's policy of economic development through private enterprise helped in consolidating the power of the 'new', 'able', 'ruthless' group of industrial entrepreneurs.[24] Papanek's book, *Pakistan's Development: Social Goals and Private Incentives* introduced the famous phrase 'robber barons' to describe Pakistani industrialists and businessmen. The book demonstrated, without inhibition or reservation, how the Pakistani peasants were squeezed in order to create industrial tycoons.[25] The economic policies had reduced the peasant and urban workers to a state of dire poverty in spite of record rates of increases in the gross domestic

---

[21]Government of Pakistan, Planning Commission, *Second Five Year Plan 1960–65* (Karachi, 1968), p. 49.

[22]Mahbubul Haq, *The Strategy of Economic Planning: The Case of Pakistan* (Lahore: Oxford University Press, 1963), p. 30.

[23]Surpluses were extracted, particularly from the Bengali peasants, through the foreign exchange earning of jute, and to a lesser extent from the West Pakistan peasants through wheat procurement at less than world market prices.

[24]See Rashid Amjad, *Private Industrial Investment in Pakistan: 1960–1970* (Cambridge: Cambridge University Press, 1982). Also refer Talukdar Maniruzzaman, 'Group Interest in Pakistan Politics, 1947–58', *Pacific Affairs*, Vol. XXXIX, No. 49 (1966), pp. 88–91.

[25]Gustav F. Papanek, *Pakistan's Development: Social Goals and Private Incentives* (Cambridge: Harvard University Press, 1968), see chapter VII, 'Squeezing-The Peasants', pp. 184–225.

product in the 1960s. In addition, the country had accumulated an enormous foreign debt.

Ayub Khan in an effort to project his image as that of a great reformer and a Pakistani Nasser, introduced land reforms. The ceilings recommended by the Land Reform Commission were 500 acres of irrigated and 1,000 acres of non-irrigated land for holdings. The owners were allowed to maintain an extra 150 acres for orchards for livestock. Furthermore, there were enough loopholes to permit landholding above the fixed ceiling. For example, there was an option for making gifts or voluntary surrender. Many landlords redistributed land among relatives and friends, and thus avoided exceeding the ceiling while effectively retaining control of the land.[26] At that time, 6,000 landowners representing 0.10 per cent of the total agricultural population in the country possessed 7.5 million acres of land estimates over 500 acres, making together 15 per cent of the private land in the country. This was an alarming figure.[27] On the other hand, more than 2.2 million persons owned less than 5 acres and another 2.5 million landless farmers were either *haris* (landless peasants), share-croppers or simply tenants. The farmers with small holdings also equally suffered from land fragmentation for which the *ishtmaal-i-arazi* (land consolidation scheme) was adopted in the reforms of 1959.

As Table 3.3 reveals, 6,000 *zamindars* (landowners) and *waderas* (Sindhi landlords) owned 1,236 acres on an average, compared to the national average of 9.5 acres. Acquisition of the extra land was almost impossible due to bureaucratic bottlenecks, loopholes in land reforms. Only 5 per cent of the land was surrendered to the government.[28] The land reforms were cosmetic rather than substantive in their impact, having affected no more than 1.6 per cent of the cultivable land. Many observers maintain that Punjabi domination of the military and the landed interests of

---

[26]Gunnar Myrdal, *Asian Drama: An Inquiry into the Poverty of Nations*, Vol. 1 (New York: Pantheon, 1968), p. 329.

[27]Asaf Hussain, *Elite politics in an Ideological State: The Case of Pakistan* (Folkestone: Dawson, 1979), pp. 55 and 91.

[28]Khalid Bin Sayeed, 'Pakistan's Constitutional Autocracy', *Pacific Affairs*, Vol. XXVI, No. 4 (Winter, 1963–64), p. 365.

the officers prevented the martial law from undertaking any revolutionary land reforms.[29]

Table 3.3
Landownership in West Pakistan, 1959

Average Landholding (in acres)	Percentage of Landlords	Percentage of Landowned
5 or less	64.5	15.0
5 to 25	28.5	31.7
25 to 100	5.7	22.4
100 to 500	0.1	15.9
500 and more	0.1	15.9

Source: Government of Pakistan, *Report of the Land Reform Commission* (1959), Appendix I.

In fact, the Pakistani landlords had never had it so good as under the Ayub regime which supposedly was anti-feudal. For example, the most powerful representative of the landowning class, the Nawab of Kalabagh, was installed as Governor of West Pakistan, a key position from which he could put into effect policies designed to promote the interests of the landowning class which he did vigorously. Agriculture and related subjects were provincial subjects under the federal constitution and were in his domain.[30]

In fact, the impact of the so-called 'Green Revolution' on the different strata of the rural population has been quite uneven. Because it was mainly those who cultivated large landholdings who have benefited more from the new developments and those who cultivate small holdings have benefited less. One consequence of the Green Revolution has been to widen disparities in income and wealth among the different strata of the rural population. It has also had the effect of widening the disparities among the regions. A further consequence of the Green Revolution, which follows from the secondary effects of changes in patterns of rural incomes and expenditures, is that in the case of those farmers whose physical

---

[29]Hamza Alavi, 'Class and State', in Gardezi and Rashid (eds.), *Pakistan: The Roots of Dictatorship*, pp. 60–61.
[30]Herbert Feldman, *Revolution in Pakistan* (London: Oxford University Press, 1967), p. 59.

farm output has not gone up, their real incomes have deteriorated absolutely, as a result of the inflationary pressures and the greatly increased demands for manufactured consumer goods.[31]

In sum, the benefits of the Green Revolution were confined to the big and medium sized farmers of Punjab. The small farmers felt that the initial programmes of the Green Revolution disfavoured them and that large-scale agri-business farming endangered their survival.

Efforts in support of agricultural development under the Third Five Year Plan (1965–1970) emphasized the development of middle and upper middle class 'farmers' while carefully reassuring the status of the already powerful owners. This gradual 'moderniza-tion from above' of agriculture illustrates the conservative character of Ayub's land programme. Social change in terms of land tenure revision and redistribution was virtually non-existent under Ayub.[32]

Gross quantitative indicators of economic growth supported Ayub's claims regarding the 'miraculous' and 'dramatic' economic development. And the US cited the Ayub regime as a role model for developing countries. Gross growth rates, however, do not explain the whole picture adequately. Behind this number game lies the stark realities of the socio-economic exploitation of the larger masses of people.

The rapid economic growth created regional and class inequalities and was accompanied with a fall in living standards for substantial sections of the population. In addition, the nation's economic wealth got concentrated into a few hands. Mahbubbul Haq revealed that by 1968, 22 families controlled 66 per cent of industrial assets, 70 per cent of insurance funds, and 80 per cent of bank assets.[33] This elite consisted of a mere two score families who followed narrow and nepotistic political and economic practices.[34]

---

[31]Hamza Alavi, 'Elite Farmer Strategy and Regional Disparities in Agricultural Development', in Gardezi and Rashid (eds.), *Pakistan: The Roots of Dictatorship*, pp. 307–10.

[32]Government of Pakistan, Planning Commission, *The Mid Plan Review of the Third Five Year Plan 1965–70* (Karachi, 1968), p. 1.

[33]*Business Recorder* (Karachi), 25 April 1968, p. 1.

[34]For an excellent account of the levels of economic concentration in Pakistan see Lawrence J. White, *Industrial Concentration and Economic Power in Pakistan* (Princeton: Princeton University Press, 1974), p. 35; and Stanley A. Kochanek, *Interest Groups and Development: Business and Politics in Pakistan* (New Delhi:

Many sons of these families became high ranking military officers and moved from there into prosperous businesses, maintaining family connections. Top bureaucrats were recruited with the same family and 'old boy' school ties. This business-military-bureaucratic coterie or trial was based almost and entirely in West Pakistan. Moreover, its self-serving practices restricted institutional growth by precluding access to economic and political power. It also restricted the development of management talent at a time when Pakistan required the very best effort in all areas of endeavour. From the political point of view, the restriction on access to power proved most serious as the counter elite vented their frustration by violence against the regime.[35]

The Ayub regime produced meaningless growth rates by means of the establishment of import substitution consumer industries under the patronage of, and in partnership with foreign monopoly capital. According to one scholar, 'this type of lopsided industrialization fed on cheap labour provided by the impoverished masses, while social inequalities were maintained and deepened.'[36] Once industries were developed and surplus generated, the question arose as to how to dispose of the commodities produced, as per capita income was still low in the areas of production. East Bengal, 'a captive colony, presented good marketing opportunities for the robber baron of Pakistan's industry.'[37] The export earnings from peasant produced jute and cotton were appropriated by the manufacturers so that they could import machinery and technology. Defence expenditure was already concentrated in the western part of the country. During the so-called decade of development the per capita gross domestic product of East Pakistan grew by only 17 per cent at 1959–1960 constant prices compared to 42 per cent in West Pakistan. Inter-regional resources transfers imperilled already fragile living standards in the predominantly agrarian Eastern wing. When Ayub seized power East

Oxford University Press, 1983), pp. 87–104, and Rashid Amjad, 'Industrial Concentration and Economic Power', in Gardezi and Rashid (eds.), *Pakistan: The Roots of Dictatorship*, pp. 228–69.

[35]Louis Dupree, 'The Military is Dead! Long Live the Military', *American Universities Field Staff Report* (South Asian Series), Vol. XII, No. 3 (1969). Also see David Loshak, *Pakistan Crises* (London: Heinemann, 1977), pp. 27–28.

[36]Gardezi and Rashid, 'Independent Pakistan: Its Political Economy', in Gardezi and Rashid (eds.), *Pakistan: The Roots of Dictatorship*, p. 10.

[37]Ibid.

Pakistan's per capita income was 30 per cent less than that of West Pakistan. By the time he was thrown out of office in 1969 the difference was as much as 61 per cent.[38]

Thus, the laissez-faire economics resulted in such distortions in the relations of production that the masses of both parts of the Federal Union suffered heavily and eventually rose in revolt against the Ayub regime. The workers resented the decline in real wages at a time when industrial expansion was proceeding at a rapid pace. The small farmers felt that the Green Revolution had worked against them, and that large-scale agri-business farming jeopardized their survival. It was the deepening of regional and class inequalities during the Ayub era which led to his downfall.[39]

Bhutto's Socialist Democracy: 1971–1977

In the 1970 elections, the Pakistan People's Party (PPP) charter recognized that the only way to eliminate the problem of social inequality caused by the rapid growth of capitalism was through socialism, but it also recognized that Pakistan would have its own form of socialism that incorporated Islamic values.[40] In the economic arena, the Bhutto government announced the take-over of 31 large firms and 10 basic industries. Life insurances companies owned by Pakistani nationals were also nationalized. The government, apart from nationalizing more firms, abolished the Managing Agency system and suspended the stock trading of about eighteen firms. In every instance, the government made clear that the former owners would be compensated. The government was committed to a mixed economy rather than total socialism.

The PPP, in its election manifesto in 1970, declared land reforms to be a 'national necessity' and raised the well-known slogan of *roti, kapra aur makan* (bread, clothes and shelter). Much radical rhetoric adorned Zulfikar Ali Bhutto's land reforms of 1972. Yet, as in

---

[38]Omar Noman, *The Political Economy of Pakistan, 1947–1985*, p. 41.

[39]Gardezi and Rashid, 'Independent Pakistan: Its Political Economy', in Gardezi and Rashid (eds.), *Pakistan: The Roots of Dictatorship*, pp. 10–11.

[40]Anwar H. Syed, *The Discourses and Politics of Zulfikar Ali Bhutto* (New Delhi: St. Martin's Press, 1992), p. 62.

1959, the authors of the legislation were more concerned about winning popular legitimacy than delivering substantial benefits to the poor. As in 1959, the ceilings were on individual rather than on family ownership. According to Bhutto's land reforms of 1972, the maximum ceiling envisaged the reduction of landholdings per individual from 500 to 150 irrigated acres and from 1,000 to 300 unirrigated acres. Land above the ceilings was acquired without any compensation and it would be distributed among the landless peasants. Farmers having debt liabilities on account of the 1959 Land Reforms were exempted from paying them. All previous records and land transfers were to be scrutinized so as to plug the loopholes in the early reforms. A system of cooperative farming through self-sufficient agrarian villages was planned for the long term. As usual, the bureaucracy gave out exaggerated figures on land transfers to the peasants and raised expectations.[41]

On the eve of the 1977 general elections, the government announced a new package of land reforms. The peasants were promised the distribution of all cultivable state waste land in an eight point National Charter for Peasants. Bhutto also abolished the old land revenue systems and replaced it by an agricultural income tax system. Another set of land reforms reduced the individual ownership of landholdings to 100 acres of irrigated land or 200 acres of unirrigated land. Given the usual corruption and the ascendancy of feudals in the system, according to one estimate, only 1 per cent of cultivable land was distributed among 1,30,000 tenants.[42] However, many landlords had preempted the reforms by transferring land to their immediate relations without risk of loss.

It is noteworthy that some significant economic steps, such as labour reforms and education and health reforms, taken by the Bhutto government, from 1972 to 1974 were designed by the PPP left, a faction of the PPP. But these steps proved dangerous and had a damaging effect because the political weight of the groups that benefited was not as great as that of the groups which did not benefit or, in some cases, even suffered. For example, the combined strength of the industrial labour in the large manufacturing sector (the

[41]For details see Ghazala Meenai, 'Pakistan People's Party', in Pandav Nayak (ed.), *Pakistan: Society and Politics* (New Delhi: South Asian Publishers, 1984), pp. 155–56.
[42]M. G. Weinbaum, 'The March 1977 Elections in Pakistan: Where Everyone Lost', *Asian Survey*, Vol. XXII, No. 7 (July 1977), p. 604.

recipients of credit from the financial institutions under the government control), and the college teachers was considerably less than that of the small sized industrial entrepreneurs who had to bear the cost of labour reforms, and the urban classes who were denied opportunities for obtaining quality education and improvement of the health system. The groups that had not been satisfied had also been supporters of the PPP. Bhutto's nationalization measures, which later adversely affected small-scale entrepreneurs and several private industrial firms, led to an alliance between religious elites (the Ulama) and the entrepreneurs that proved to be a major force in removing him from office in 1977.[43]

Although Bhutto had come to power on a socialist platform, he began to lean towards the right and move away from his socialist ideology. From 1974 to 1977, after the departure of the left faction—when Bhutto took full command of the policy making—economic measures were not aimed at helping any of the more important parts of Bhutto's large middle class constituency. At the same time, Bhutto's several economic moves led to deterioration in income distribution, in term of a decline in the share in total wealth of the middle class.[44]

However, according to Hamza Alavi, nearly all the land reform legislations helped to strengthen the growing economic power of the landlords who had been increasingly relying on government funds for modernizing agriculture.[45] The government's policies gave the landed gentry a boost. Initially, the PPP did harbour a few Sindhi landlords but later many more from all over the country came under its wings. It has been reported that feudal elements in the PPP owned 75 per cent of resumable land in Punjab, 60 per cent in NWFP and 40 per cent in Sindh.[46] By reducing the landholding limits, Bhutto tried to force big landlords

[43]Kemal A. Faruki, 'Pakistan: Islamic Government and Society', in John L. Espositio (ed.), *Islam in Asia: Religion, Politics and Society* (Oxford: Oxford University Press, 1987), p. 584.

[44]Shahid Javed Burki, *Pakistan Under Bhutto: 1971–77* (London: Macmillan Press Ltd., 1980), p. 135.

[45]Hamza Alavi, 'Elite Farmer Strategy and Regional Disparities', in Gardezi and Rashid (eds.), *Pakistan: The Roots of Dictatorship*, pp. 293–95 and Shanaz J. Rouse, 'Systematic Injustice and Inequalities in Maliki and Raiya in Punjab Village', in Ibid., pp. 311–27.

[46]Ghazala Meenai, 'Pakistan People's Party', p. 162.

into adopting modern methods of farming for which the government gave enormous funds. Prices shot up as a result. The landowners got large amounts as subsidies for fertilizers and tubewell sinkings. As a consequence, a class of rich peasants emerged in the countryside. Besides rich peasants, a new class of bureaucrat-capitalists who were managing the state sector industries came up.[47]

Apart from this, the government's decision to take-over management of 4,000 agro-industries helped the landlords to overcome the challenge from the middle peasantry. The nationalization of wheat flour, rice milling industries, etc. was done to appease the big landlords.[48]

The aggregate growth of the economy under the PPP, as measured by annual rise in GNP, was 4.6 per cent per year. The share of the public sector in total investment grew from 5 per cent in 1971 to 74 per cent in 1977, leading to a subsequent decrease in private investment as people transferred their wealth to foreign countries. Large scale manufacturing declined substantially, growing at a rate of less than 2 per cent annually compared at the rate of 1.91 per cent with growth rate that exceeded 10 per cent in the 1960s. There was a decline in per capita agricultural production. Industry and educational institutions were nationalized, the efficiency of industry declined,[49] and people became disenchanted with Bhutto's economic policies.

In the 1977 elections, unlike in 1970, he relied on elite groups to win, having lost confidence in the masses.[50] Out of the top 50 leaders in his party, there were 27 landlords, 6 tribal chiefs, 5 businessmen, and 7 middle class professionals but only 1 trade union leader. This was a significant change; his previous government had included four radical socialist cabinet ministers.[51]

Apart from these economic setbacks during the Bhutto era, the middle class also suffered political and social deprivation with the re-entry of old established groups as large landlords and such

---

[47]'Inside Pakistan', *Frontier*, Vol. IX, No. 46 (18 June 1977), p. 2.

[48]Ghazala Meenai, 'Pakistan Peoples Party', p. 162.

[49]Shahid Javed Burki and Craig Baxter, *Pakistan Under the Military: Eleven Years of Zia-ul-Haq* (Boulder, Colo: Westview Press, 1991), p. 94.

[50]General Faiz Ali Chisti, *Betrayals of Another Kind: Islam, Democracy and the Army in Pakistan* (Delhi: Tri-Colour Books, 1989), pp. 34–35.

[51]Omar Noman, *Pakistan: A Political and Economic History Since 1947*, pp. 103–04.

new groups as industrial workers and peasants. And consequently, the middle class, the main base of the regime, got disenchanted with Bhutto.[52]

Bhutto's economic policies did not change the class system, instead, it helped to perpetuate the exploitative status quo. It did not challenge the basic power of landed aristocracy. Rather it provided a cover to the rural gentry for continued enjoyment of their class privileges. In lieu of making a token surrender of land in excess of official limits, they enjoyed generous tax concessions, loans and monetary compensations.

In sum, Bhutto's so-called socialist policy 'did not bring any radical change in Pakistan's capitalist-oriented development, except for introducing a bias against large industrialists and reasserting the power of big landlords who now benefited from the investment funds diverted through nationalized financial institutions.'[53] There were some modifications in labour laws, minimum wages, anti-monopoly legislations, all of which only marginally helped the under-privileged and poor masses of Pakistan. According to one scholar, 'At best, the Bhutto era was a weak social democratic attempt to rearrange the economic structure to the satisfaction of new class alliance which has emerged at the end of the second martial law regime of Yahya Khan.'[54]

With a Bonapartist strategy Bhutto proceeded to build a new class alliance in favour of his social-democratic platform among all these segments—landlords, professionals, white-collar workers, middle peasants and radicals. At the same time he did not want to reduce the role of large industrialists and businessmen beyond a certain limit. Bhutto knew 'that by superimposing a framework of mixed economy on a partially feudal, partially dependent capitalist society, the economic power of the dominant classes, would be pre-served. He thus, set himself the contradictory task of balancing the political power of the dominant classes, while at the same time posing as the representative of the peasants and workers.'[55]

---

[52]Ibid., pp. 191–93.
[53]Rashid and Gardezi, 'Independent Pakistan: Its Political Economy', in Gardezi and Rashid (eds.), *Pakistan: The Roots of Dictatorship*, p. 12.
[54]Ibid.
[55]Ibid., p. 13. Also see Ajjaz Ahmad, 'Democracy and Dictatorship', in Ibid., p. 104.

It is true that Bhutto failed in breaking the power of the ruling alliance of the big bourgeoisie, the landlords and the military-bureaucratic elite. But his populistic programmes did bring a mass awakening among the peasants and workers for their rights. For the first time the poor peasants of Pakistan realized that they counted in the arithmetic of politics.

Zia's Era of Artificial Prosperity (1977–1988)

After replacing Z. A. Bhutto, the military regime, in the economic field, in order to get support from the economic elite, had chosen to move along a rightist course of action. The first step of the government to reassure the support of the main propertied classes, i.e., the industrialists, the petty bourgeoisie, and the landowning groups was the abandonment of all the economic, so-called socialistic policies pursued by Zulfikar Ali Bhutto. For example, denationalization of the flour mills and rice-husking mills was announced soon after the imposition of martial law. As regards the cotton ginning or spinning factories, of the 579 such factories that had been taken over in 1976 by the Bhutto government, 279 were returned to their owners.[56]

Landlords also seem to be the beneficiaries under the martial law regime as the landowning influentials had brought about the eviction of tenants from their lands with the help of the police and the Frontier constabulary. In its search for support base, the regime spared the landed aristocracy from reforms or agricultural tax. Even the *Sharia* (Islamic Law) Court, in a verdict on an appeal against land reforms, decreed the irrevocability of the Islamic guarantee of private property and questioned the legality of the land reforms.

In the absence of an elected representative cabinet, the martial law regime became more dependent on businessmen, industrialists and the advice of bureaucrats. The budgets reflected the biases pertaining to these two groups. While the first one asked

---

[56]Sayeed, *Politics in Pakistan: The Nature and Direction of Change*, p. 179.

for liberal import and industrial policies, meaning a bigger free list for imported goods, lower duties, decreased income tax, reduction in interest rate, generous banking terms for letters of credit, liberalization of the export finance scheme, abolition of tax on the issue of bonus shares and harsh labour laws, the second group with increased expenditures on administration and other non-developmental accounts, devised budgets of high indirect taxes and cut in social services for the lower income group.[57]

Under both conditions, the burden of expenditure increased without sufficient increased revenue from the industrialists. If anything, taxes like excise duties were passed on to the consumers, putting pressure on the retail price level and keeping higher wholesale profits. The military regime filled the budgetary gap by relying on foreign aid loans.

This kind of budgetary policy led to the vicious circle of unending foreign dependency—whether foreign governmental aid loans or private remittances from overseas Pakistanis. It was a situation where the budget showed that while non-developmental expenditure was increasing at a faster rate, in a poor country like Pakistan, the productive investment declined. This led to a reliance on external resources which increased the debt liabilities.

During Zia's period the economy in statistical terms represented a rosy picture. In comparison to the Z. A. Bhutto period, in Zia's era growth rates were much higher. The aggregate growth of the economy under the PPP, as measured by the annual rise of GNP, was 4.6 per cent per year. During the Zia period the average annual GDP growth was 6.3 per cent from 1978 to 1983. The manufacturing growth rate was 9 per cent. Substantially above the 3.8 per cent average and from 1972 to 1978 all sectors except services and construction showed improved growth performances, and from 1983 to 1988 the economy grew at an even better pace. The GDP grew at an annual rate of 6.6 per cent and large scale manufacturing at an average annual rate of 16.6 per cent.

One significant cause for impressive growth rates was significant rise in remittances due to migration of people to West Asia to find jobs. Approximately ten million people, 11 per cent of the total population, benefited directly from this exodus. According to Shahid Javed Burki, 'From 1975 to 1985, Pakistan received a total

---

[57]Ibid.

of $25 billion in remittances from the workers in Middle East and good portion of which went to the poorer segments of the society.[58] The impact of this money helped in neutralizing the agitational zeal of the poor and the middle class against the military ruler.

The other cause of buoyancy in the economy during the Zia era was the large amount of US assistance coming to Pakistan in the wake of Soviet invasion of Afghanistan in December 1979. Zia's military junta drew its main strength from its manoeuvering in the international sphere, in terms of its return to the Western camp and its integration in the renewed Cold War designs of the Regan Administration. Soviet military intervention in Afghanistan had opened up a bonanza of military and economic aid denied by the United States to the previous government for being less than cooperative camp followers. The movement of Soviet forces into Afghanistan endangered the strategic interests of the United States in the region. In order to wage a proxy war via Pakistan, the United States propagated Pakistan as a 'frontline-state', agreed to provide the Zia regime with a $3.2 billion aid package and a lifting of the embargo on arms supplies. Zia-ul-Haq reaped maximum benefits from United States' strategic compulsions. Assistance from the United States after 1982 totalled around $5 billion, making Pakistan the third largest recipient of US aid in the 1980s.[59]

Perhaps the most vulnerable feature of the economy was its excessive dependence on international aid, decreasing overseas remittances, burgeoning foreign debt and continuing privatization of the economy. Furthermore, the long-term implications of excessive dependence on foreign assistance (as more than half of the funds for the country's development budget were covered by external resources) were alarming. Moreover, debt servicing, in part offset by aid, was likely to be a large hurdle in the future.[60] Despite the improvement in the external finance position during 1985–1986, the balance of payments position remained structurally weak, as reflected in the rise in debt service payments to United States. Pakistan has accumulated a large debt. On 30 June 1985, it stood

---

[58]Shahid Javed Burki, 'Pakistan Under Zia, 1977–1988', *Asian Survey*, Vol. XXVIII, No. 10 (October 1988), pp. 1082–1100, especially p. 1093.

[59]Hafeez Malik, 'The Afghan Crisis and Its Impact on Pakistan', *Journal of South Asian and Middle Eastern Studies*, Vol. V, No. 3 (Spring 1982), pp. 40–52.

[60]*Pakistan Economic Survey*, 1985–86 (Islamabad, 1986), p. 46.

at $12.6 billion constituting 30.9 per cent of the GNP. Debt servicing rose to $1.2 billion in the 1987–1988 fiscal year, nearly two and a half times more than the $494 million the country had to pay from 1978 to 1989. Debt servicing constituted 2.8 per cent of the GNP, compared to 2.1 per cent in 1978–1979.

However, the real alarming trend in the budgets presented by the Zia regime was the sharp increase in the defence expenditure. Since 1977, defence expenditure had increased by 44.5 per cent. For two years, 1975–1977, it was fairly stable, but the take-over of administration by army officers had led to increased expenses on defence. In fact in the 11 years rule of General Zia, the defence budget of Pakistan registered an annual increase of over 16 per cent.

Additionally, Zia's Afghan policy had long-term negative implications. The support lent by Zia to the Afghan resistance movement, produced a parallel arms and drug economy with serious implications for the fragile weave of Pakistan's social fabric.

In order to perpetuate its power and seek legitimacy, Zia-ul-Haq sought to Islamize the economy.[61] However, in actual practice, in the ingeniously devised so-called 'Islamization' of the economy, the regime was appealing to the historical categories of feudalist Islam and justifying social and economic relationships based on a decadent status quo of feudalism and comprador capitalism by imposing the medieval forms of *mudaraba* (profit sharing), *muzaraa* (share-cropping), *zakat* (charity at the ratio of 2.5 per cent), *ushr* (tax at the ratio of one-tenth), *riba* (usury), etc., which originated 1400 years ago and developed in different social contexts.[62] Terms such as 'Islamic Economy', 'Islamic Banking', were coined as Zia-ul-Haq succinctly remarks, 'in a purely tendentious way to serve the interests of international capitalism by interpreting Islam in feudalist and bourgeois terms.... Real Quaranic Islam has been discarded by the military elite of Pakistan for the reason that its application would do away with the institutions of feudalism and capitalism. The feudal/medieval form of *fiqhi* Islam suits the interests of the ruling elite, because feudal Islam is in the main reactionary, medievalistic

---

[61]See Khalid M. Ishaque, 'The Islamic Approach to Economic Activity and Development', *Pakistan Economist*, Vol. XVII, No. 20 (July 1977), pp. 13–23.
[62]See Veena Kukreja, 'The Zia Regime: Legitimation Through Islamization', *Strategic Analysis*, Vol. XV, No. 3 (June 1992), pp. 185–89.

and dogmatic. It promotes the interests of feudal landlords and compraders."[63]

Economic Downturn: 1988–1999

Benazir Bhutto came to power after the death of General Zia in 1988. Her government inherited a bankrupt economy. The shortsighted policies pursued by the Zia regime succeeded in creating for the time being, an artificial world of pseudo billions providing chewing gum. But this economic oasis, in the due course of time, began to dry up with the burgeoning foreign debt and decreasing overseas remittances. The size of the government's fiscal deficit increased considerably and the price situation deteriorated. The growth rate of both savings and investments declined substantially. The deficit in the balance of payments widened. Thus, a total view of the economic scene suggested that the economy lacked a sound industrial base and was totally dependent on external aid, credits and remittances.[64] Any change in these variables could lead to an economic collapse and its attendant political fall out.

During her first stint in power (1988–1990), on the economic front, unlike her father's policies of nationalization and public sector expansion, Benazir attempted to bring the private sector to the forefront of economic activity in Pakistan but the economy remained stagnant. However, on the economic front Benazir Bhutto did not formulate a coherent policy. In principle, the PPP abandoned its socialist goals and resolved to pursue

---

[63]Zia-ul-Haq, 'Islamization of Society in Pakistan', in Mohammad Asghar Khan (ed.), *Islam, Politics and the State: The Pakistan Experience* (London: Zed Press, 1985), p. 122. Also see his, 'Pakistan and Islamic Ideology', in Gardezi and Rashid (eds.), *Pakistan: The Roots of Dictatorship*, pp. 369–81; and Hassan N. Gardezi, 'The Resurgence of Islam: Islamic Ideology and Encounters with Imperialism', in Gardezi and Rashid (eds.), *Pakistan: The Roots of Dictatorship*, pp. 353–65; Omar Asghar Khan, 'Political and Economic Aspects of Islamization', in Asghar Khan (ed.), *Islam, Politics and the State: The Pakistan Experience*, pp. 149–61.

[64]For major economic indicators consult, *Pakistan Economic Survey 1987–88 and 1988–89* (Islamabad), and *International Monetary Fund Financial Statistics* (Washington, D.C., 1989). Also see *Pak and Gulf Economist*, 22–28 July 1989, pp. 16–20.

privatization, but reluctantly and without clarity of purpose.[65] A high powered committee was constituted under the chairmanship of Farooq Leghari that assigned to the Pakistan Industrial Development Corporation (PIDC) the task of reinvigorating industrialization, facilitating decentralization, and encouraging privatization.

But the PPP government was slow to formulate a systematic privatization policy. Inflation, unemployment, and stagnation in the industrial enterprises, specially in the public sector, demanded immediate attention and policy action, which the Bhutto government did not seem able to provide. Instead of devising an economic policy, the government indulged in the politics of patronage, providing jobs to PPP supporters in the public sector, which irritated the bureaucracy and increased inefficiency. In sum, the PPP regime had neither the will to streamline the public sector nor was serious in encouraging privatization. Thus, the confidence of the industrialists, who were skeptical of Bhutto anyway, was weakened. While the government did not formulate a coherent privatization policy, it was able to attract foreign investment. In 1989 a number of multinational corporations began to open projects in oil exploration, textile, and fruit preservation industries.[66] Her stress on sizeable increases in allocations for health and education in the 1989–1990 budget was clear evidence of her orientation. She gave her approval to a fait accompli, a deal negotiated by Zia's regime in accordance with the IMF economy-reconstructing guidelines under which Pakistan received $1.168 billion from the IMF and the World Bank. The government lacked popular support and used the elite class, especially the landowning elite to mobilize the masses through various kinds of influence, peddling.[67]

In sum, the return of democracy in 1988 had not altered the situation in any significant way. In fact, the armed forces continued to remain in the helm of affairs and protected the interests of the feudal class.

---

[65]Arif Nizami, 'A Balance Sheet in the Deficit', *The Nation* (Lahore), 2 December 1989.

[66]Saeed Shafqat, 'Pakistan Under Benazir', *Asian Survey*, Vol. XXXVI, No. 2 (July 1996), pp. 665–66.

[67]Hassan Gardezi, *A Reexamination of the Social Political History of Pakistan: Reproduction of Class Relations and Ideology* (New York: The Edwin Mellen Press, 1991), p. 137.

After Benazir's removal, Nawaz Sharif came to power. His primary interest was in the economy, which did fairly well under his leadership notwithstanding its continued vulnerability to mounting debt and a population growth rate of 3.1 per cent. The average per capita GDP growth rate during his tenure was more than 13 per cent. Privatization and increased exports seemed to be the primary focus of the government, and numerous measures were enacted to expedite the pace of growth through privatization. Sharif privatized some government institutions by providing incentives to foreign investment, his reforms opened several industries to private enterprise, and his government offered liberal tax and tariff incentives to new industries. It also liberalized foreign exchange, opened export trade to foreign firms, returned almost all industrial units and financial institutions to the private sector, and opened new banks.[68]

The budget deficit no doubt was brought down but it was still far away from the IMF set target of 5.8 per cent. Moreover, to reduce the deficit, all the cuts were applied in social sector allocations and in the Annual Development Plan. Allocations for education were cut by 58 per cent, health by 70 per cent and public works programmes by more than 50 per cent. The defence budget, on the other hand, was raised by 11.6 per cent. The budget deficit was financed by foreign (38.1 per cent) and domestic (61.9 per cent) borrowings and debt servicing constituted the largest item of expenditure.

Benazir's second term came at a time when Pakistan faced serious political and economic problems. In 1993, it was reported that the country was heading fast towards a state of bankruptcy. There were massive debt repayments due, remittances had slowed down and the IMF refused to renew loans and demanded that the government must first initiate a credible, comprehensive and decisive policy package to clean up the country's economic and fiscal mess.[69]

Pakistan was living beyond its means for so many years, the country had accumulated such a huge amount of public debt

---

[68]Government of Pakistan, Economic Advisory Wing, *Economic Survey: 1993–94* (Islamabad: Finance Division, June 1994), pp. 3, 201–202.

[69]B. M. Bhatia, 'Near the Brink', *The Hindustan Times* (New Delhi), 25 October 1996, p. 11.

that annual interest charges had come to account for 45 per cent of the expenditure of the federal government. Interest payments and defence expenditure put together exceeded the aggregate annual revenue receipts of the government. Obviously the present level of fiscal imbalance and the current accounts deficit that the country was facing were simply unsustainable. In a highly unusual move, the army—which was consuming 26 per cent of the budget—presented its own report to President Legari, characterizing the economic situation as grave. Drastic measures were required to remedy the situation.

But Benazir avoided certain quick fix approaches that were politically dicey. She could not afford to impose taxes on agriculture and the feudal landlords who supported her government.[70] By the end of the 1980s, a stage had been reached in the Pakistan budget where any developmental work needed to be done with borrowed funds. This situation had become worse by the turn of the decade with the aid inflow becoming necessary to repay the instalments of old debts. In other words, the net aid available for development started getting lesser and lesser. With other macro-economic parameters already in disarray, the economy started experiencing hyper inflation.

The borrowed money kept an artificial prosperity in the beginning, but as the years passed, Pakistan got caught in the classical 'debt trap' scenario feared by most development economists. The country's total public debt burden was reported to be around Rs (Pakistani) 1.02 trillion by the end of June 1997. In addition, there was a short term debt of $10 billion borrowed with interest liability of 7.5 per cent. As a per cent of Gross Domestic Product, Pakistan's total public debt was 90 per cent.[71]

Debt servicing was the single largest item of expenditure in the federal budget. In 1997–1998 budget, it was estimated at Rs. 247.86 billion, which amounted to around 54 per cent of expenditure and 78 per cent of the total tax revenue.[72] Thus, it became crystal

---

[70] Ahmed Rashid, 'Bhutto's Burden: Pakistan in Deep Economic Crises', *The Times of India*, 23 September 1996, p. 13.

[71] Aftab Ahmed Khan, 'Massive Growth in Public Debt', *The News* (Lahore), 28 July 1997. Also consult Shahid Kandar, 'Can We Repay Our Debt?', *The Nation*, 21 December 1997.

[72] Ibid.

clear that an unsustainable deficit was bound to have a destabilising impact on the economy.

Pakistan's debt trap has been very impressively explained by one observer who maintains that Pakistan today is trapped in a vicious debt trap whereby it needs to borrow more than Rs 60 crore every single day of the calendar year to survive. That translates into an additional debt of Rs 5 crore every working hour of the day, Rs 8 lakhs every minute or close to Rs 15,000 every second.[73]

In addition, Pakistan's fragile economy turned into shambles under the weight of international sanctions imposed after its tit for tat response to India's nuclear tests of May 1998. Thus, while economic downturn has been a consistent feature of Pakistan's economy for over a decade, the situation became particularly precarious since the nuclear tests in 1998 and the Kargil misadventure the following year. Besides, there was an allegation that Sharif's family was amassing wealth while preaching austerity to the nation.

Musharraf Regime: Challenge of Economic Revival

The ongoing economic crisis presents a serious dilemma for the Musharraf regime. The central dilemma faced by budget makers is the debt overhang. Debt servicing costs have increased from a mere Rs 90.5 billion in 1990–1991 to a shocking Rs 287 billion in 1998–1999, growing at an annual average of roughly 20 per cent. Since gross domestic product and revenue growth cannot keep pace with the increasing debt servicing burden, the problem is exacerbated with every passing year. This leads to a balance of payments problem, central to the IMF demand that the budget deficit be reduced.

General Musharraf had given the economy's 'state of collapse' as one of the key reasons behind the military intervention last October. The military regime followed a two pronged economic policy, hinging on 'economic revival' and 'poverty alleviation.' While the military rulers continue with their mantra of reviving investor

---

[73]Farooq Saleem, 'Pakistan Under a Mountain Debt', *The News*, 16 March 1997.

confidence, it appears that the biggest impediments to this revival are the interests of the military establishment itself.

Investment needed for economic revival comes from three different avenues: the public sector, the private sector and foreign investors. Usually a mix of all three is needed, with one feeding on the other. At a time when private and foreign investors are fighting shy, the role of public investment becomes paramount.

A revival strategy led by public investment is thus fore-stalled by the existing fiscal status quo. As such, given high debt servicing, liability and the imperative of containing the fiscal deficit, fiscal space can only be created by reducing defence expenditure. However, in the budget 2000–2001, defence allocation witnessed an increase by 11 per cent from the previous year. This exemplifies that the military regime does not seem ready to revive public investment at its own cost.[74]

The other element of economic revival is the improvement in capacity utilization of the existing productive capacity, judged essentially by the overall improvement of GDP growth and its various components. Overall growth in GDP was at 4.4 per cent in 1999–2000, up from the revised figures of 3.15 per cent for the previous year. This growth is singularly attributed to better per-formance of the agriculture sector. A record wheat crop of 19 million tons helped in lowering the import bill and contributed to growth.

On the manufacturing front, the dismal performance of the previous years continued. Manufacturing growth in 1999–2000 fell to an abysmal 1.5 per cent from roughly 4 per cent the previous year. The absence of an industrial policy, low investment are all responsible for industrial stagnation. While these are all long-term structural problems, the same worn-out policies were adopted to-wards the manufacturing sector in the course of the last year.

Like several governments before him, the present military ruler has included speedy privatization, broadening of tax base,[75] increasing revenues, reduction of subsidiaries, reforms in civil ser-vice, banking, agriculture and industry, curbs on smuggling and

---

[74]Asad Sayeed, 'Behind the Facade of Economic Revival', *The Herald* (Karachi), November 2000. Reproduced in *Strategic Digest*, Vol. XXXI, No. 1 (January 2001), p. 22.
[75]Samina Ibrahim, 'A Nation of Tax Evaders', *Newsline* (Karachi), May 2000. Reproduced in *Strategic Digest*, Vol. XXX, No. 7 (July 2000), pp. 887–990.

weeding out corruption in the long list of promises to the IMF. Curtailing state expenses, tight monetary and fiscal control, decentralization and devolution of power are also part of the programme. At present the underground black economy is at an all-time high of Rs 1,500 billion, the quantum figures of the smuggled goods markets have hit Rs 360 billion, income tax evasion is depriving the exchequer of Rs 100 billion and loss in General Sales Tax (GST) revenue is estimated at Rs 60 billion. And the most glaring example of the government's lack of will and conviction to implement urgent economic reforms is in their lacklustre performance over the smuggling and general sales tax issues. Without a major change in the restructuring of the economy and without major reform efforts, particularly directed at developing the country's institutional base, the economy's present downward trend will continue.[76]

The only area where there was an attempt to confront structural problems was on the revenue generation side. Initially the government made a great show about concentrating on agricultural income tax, taxing the traders and taking on the smugglers. But their intentions simmered down with time. As in the past, the government's drive for agricultural tax ran up against the country's martial political economy. On the one hand, the military does not want to open another front vis-à-vis the agriculturalists, on the other, its own officer corps own huge landholdings which remain tax exempt. The two combine to ensure that this institution—supposedly apolitical and working in the national interest—is adverse to taking on free riders in the agricultural sector.

Unless backed by tough economic and structural reforms, the IMF loan package on the anvil is no magic wand that will resuscitate Pakistan's battered economy. Unless the government has the resolve to take difficult decisions, and economic reforms are implemented on a war footing, recent IMF package will be just another in a long line of IMF packages that have failed to revive the economy.[77]

---

[76]Shahid Javed Burki 'Managing Pakistan's Present Economy: International Obligations vs. Internal Compulsions', *Pakistan Horizon* (April–July 2000), reproduced in *Strategic Digest*, Vol. XXXI, No. 1 (January 2001), pp. 10–16.

[77]Taimur Siddiqui, 'Operation Rescue?', *Newsline* (Karachi), May 2000. Reproduced in *Strategic Digest*, Vol. XXX, No. 7 (July 2000), p. 898.

The other slogan which the regime has flagged over the last one year is poverty alleviation. But if one separates rhetoric from reality, a different picture emerges. The earmarked funds constitute roughly 0.6 per cent of the GDP and merely 3 per cent of the total federal government expenditure earmarked for the current fiscal year. At the same time, defence allocation constitutes 5.02 per cent of GDP and 22.8 per cent of total federal government expenditure. It is obvious where the actual priorities of this government lie.

Moreover, contrary to government claims, resources for this meagre amount of poverty alleviation funds have not come from a reduction in the defence budget. It is actually the social sector expenditures for the ongoing fiscal year that have been slashed to provide for this fund (expenditure for the Social Action Programme has been cut by Rs 5.8 billion) as well as the diversion of funds from previous heads such as Physical Planning and Housing.

The economic and non-economic interests of the military establishment as well as their reading of the ground reality leaves little room for reallocating resources and altering policies which are pro-poor and pro-welfare.[78]

Moreover, under the pressure of the IMF, prices of utilities have increased precipitously in the last year, fuelling inflationary pressure across the board. The currency has been devalued 11 per cent in the last three months, leading to further imported inflation and currency speculation.

In this context, Asad Sayeed aptly remarks, 'Developments in economic policy and performance over the last one year demonstrate vividly that unless and until the corporate interests of the military are reigned in, sustainable economic development in Pakistan will remain a mirage.'[79]

In the wake of post-11 September scenario, the resumption of Pakistan's military-strategic partnership with the US is being viewed by some Pakistani economists as a great opportunity for economic revival. The Bush administration has rewarded Pakistani President-cum-General Musharraf with massive economic and military aid, for providing critical support to the US-led war against

---

[78]Sayeed, 'Behind the Facade of Economic Revival', p. 25.
[79]Ibid.

terrorism. It appears that Pakistan as a 'frontline state' has squeezed financial advantage out of its support to the US campaign against the Taliban and Osama bin Laden. The US and Japan have lifted the 1998 economic sanctions imposed on both India and Pakistan, but Pakistan has got a string of other goodies too. The IMF has sanctioned additional instalments of an ongoing loan despite Pakistan's failure to meet key conditions like revenue targets. The IMF is now working on a new poverty reduction loan to Pakistan and the World Bank has announced a new loan too. The European Union has abolished tariffs on Pakistani garments, a key export of that country. The US has announced that an aid of $100 million more may be on its way. The rescheduling of loan payments with the Paris club donors and the IMF seems to give the country some much-needed economic breathing space.

The bonanza of economic aid for Pakistan may look like a financial coup, but the gains are largely illusory. First, Pakistan's economy is bound to suffer enormous damage by joining the US war against terrorism in Afghanistan. Second, the history of debt relief reveals that recipients are typically as badly or worse off after a doze of debt relief than before.[80]

Besides, industrial production and manufacturing are reeling from the impact of the US-led war on Afghanistan which resulted in a substantial loss of export orders.

Looking at the refugee factor, one finds that there are apparently 2.5 to 3 million Afghan refugees already in Pakistan (as a result of the Soviet invasion of Afghanistan in 1979). The new wave of refugees have entered Pakistan and that too will have an impact on Pakistan's economy. It will cause political problems too. So Pakistan is going to pay a heavy prize for Afghanistan II, and it seems doubtful if all the aid and debt relief it gets will compensate. Moreover, debt relief rarely helps an indebted country. For example, Pakistan got massive aid from Western donors after the Soviet military intervention in Afghanistan in 1979. But even concessional loans have to be repaid, so more aid meant more debt. Because this was poorly used, the debt became unsustainable.

---

[80]Swaminathan S. Anklesaria Aiyar, 'Illusory Bonanza for Pakistan', *The Sunday Times of India* (New Delhi), 28 October 2001, p. 11.

The bonanza of economic and military aid to Pakistan after 1979 did not make it prosperous. In this context an eminent economist succinctly remarks,

> Gross mismanagement by venal, incompetent rulers meant wasteful spending, eroding institutions and political loot. The billions Pakistan got during Afghanistan I left it bust. The billions it will now get for Afghanistan II will have the same result unless Pakistan puts its house in order and greatly improves governance and prudence. This is something Pakistanis will have to do themselves—it cannot be provided by foreign donors.[81]

---

[81]Ibid.

Chapter IV

Ethnic Divide: Aspirations and Political Power

The most serious threat to Pakistan's polity since its emergence has been from conflictive ethnic militancy. During the last two decades this threat in particular has come from Sindh, where various plural communities in pursuit of self-definition continually antagonize each other and add further strains on the federation. Unfortunately, the powerful Pakistani ruling elite has remained reluctant to accept the plural composition of society and have reduced it to law and order problems, rather than part of governability.[1] The religious elites have also frowned upon ethnic diversity. However, today Pakistan is facing internal turmoil. All the ethnic groups, Baluchis, Pathans, Sindhis, are highly discontented. *Muhajirs* (Muslim refugee migrants from India) feel left out and let down by the Punjabi ruling classes.

The situation in Karachi over the past few years has raised a number of issues, including the relationship between the state and ethnic communities, Pakistani nationalism and ethnic nationalism, the army, the bureaucracy and the political leadership. Thus, violent ethnic spates in Sindh present the most serious threat to Pakistani state and civil society. This also poses the ineluctable dilemma to the

---

[1] Iftikhar H. Malik, *State and Civil Society in Pakistan: Politics of Authority, Ideology and Ethnicity* (New York: St. Martin's Press Inc., 1997), p. 168.

ruling elites of how to weave and weld together different and distinct ethnic groups into a nation.

The foundation of Pakistan was based on Islam. Religion was a great unifying factor for the Muslims in the pre-independence era and resulted in the two-nation theory and the birth of Pakistan. The ethnic factor gained importance after the creation of Pakistan. Though Islam was the foundation, ethnicity became the driving force in politics.

Very soon after the birth of Pakistan, the identity of 'the Muslim Nation' dissolved, giving way to ethnic, sectarian, and other groups, which started pressurising and demanding for a fairer distribution of the expected rewards of independence from the British. According to an eminent scholar,

> To counter such demands, the privileged groups—Punjabis and *Muhajirs* decided to deploy Islamic ideology in Pakistan for the first time, in a manner in which it had never featured in the Pakistan movement itself. They now put forward the conception of Pakistan as an Islamic State and society and the concept of citizen as a Muslim. This view, therefore, repudiated the legitimacy of regional ethnic identities and the demands that were articulated in that idiom.[2]

Aijaz Ahmed believes that the 'concept of an "Islamic nation" is the main ideological weapon in the hands of the regionally-based dominant classes in their struggle to deny the rights, even the separate existence, of the oppressed nationalities....'[3]

The partition of the Indian subcontinent was based on the theory that religion is the basis of nationhood. The claim that all the Muslims of India constituted a nation and, therefore, they should have a separate homeland carved out of British India, was a denial of other factors, such as language, culture, history, etc., as the basis for constituting an ethnic community. The underlying assumption of the two-nation theory is that a community can be homogeneous on the basis of religion alone. However, the fact is that no human grouping

---

[2]Hamza Alavi, 'Class and State', in Hassan Gardezi and Jamil Rashid (eds.), *Pakistan: The Roots of Dictatorship* (Delhi: Oxford University Press, 1983), p. 58.

[3]Aijaz Ahmed, 'Democracy and Dictatorship', Hassan Gardezi and Jamil Rashid (eds.), *Pakistan: The Roots of Dictatorship* (Delhi: Oxford University Press, 1983), p. 16.

can be homogeneous on the basis of religion. In this context, Asghar Ali Engineer aptly remarks that 'Religion at best, is one important factor for unity but not the only factor, the Pakistanis are discovering this today. The Bengalis discovered it yesterday.'[4]

The Pakistani establishment viewed ethnic heterogeneity and cultural pluralism as a threat to the whole country and laid emphasis on religious commonality. By ignoring and 'dismissing ethnic heterogeneity and demands for provincial, autonomy, devolution of power, decentralization and equitable policies governing relations with the Centre, the ruling elites have sought refuge in ad hoc measures and no comprehensive plan has been undertaken to coopt such plural forces through bargaining and appropriate political and economic measures.'[5] The breaking away of the former eastern wing of the country exemplifies the bankruptcy of this policy.

The disintegration of Pakistan and the emergence of Bangladesh in 1971 dealt the first blow to the two-nation theory. The emergence of Bangladesh proved a milestone, as it reinforced the aspirations of many ethnic movements in West Pakistan. The successful secession of Bangladesh was considered a resurgence of regional and ethnic identities. It was followed by the Pakhtun and Baluchi nationalistic assertion in the 1970s, Sindhi nationalism in the 1980s and *Muhajir* movements in the 1990s. However, successive regimes instead of accommodating these forces with polity and granting political concessions, have exacerbated them through neglect and 'back wash' effects of development. It is worth stating that ethnic politics took a nasty turn in mid-1980s when Pakistan simmered under the longest period of martial law in its history. The new generation of ethnic leaders (especially in urban Sindh), opted for militancy. With easy availability of arms, the ethnic strife became increasingly explosive in the absence of political platforms and bargaining processes. Urban guerrillas, backed by the rank and file of their respective ethnic communities, financed by their business or landed-cohorts and sometimes from drug syndicates, reduced life

---

[4]Asghar Ali Engineer, 'Pakistan's Polity and its Viability', *The Hindu* (Delhi), 14 October 2000, p. 10.
[5]Iftikhar H. Malik, *State and Civil Society in Pakistan: Politics of Authority, Ideology and Ethnicity*, p. 168.

in Karachi and Hyderabad to a routine arson, looting, street battled sniper and fire and prolonged curfews.[6]

Ethnic Politics in Pakistan

Ethnic politics in Pakistan is a story of ambiguous, often turbulent relations between the Centre and the Provinces, and also the net result of political economic and cultural alienation. At another level, it is a saga of majority–minority discord, aggravated by rapid demographic changes pushing new economic forces and contestations over census statistics, quotas and jobs.[7] The state has continuously fiddled with ethnicity, and the military regimes in the 1960s and 1980s in particular played a significant role in ethnic marginalization.

This chapter aims to highlight the similarities and the distinctiveness in the genesis of ethnic movements in Pakistan as well as in the diverse and complex forms of demand articulation and aggregation. A comparative perspective of ethnic movements seeks to highlight the similarities, simultaneities and differences in forms, content and style of such movements. It also underlines with equal intensity, the implications and criticality of transnational linkages therein.

A classical divide between the 'centrists', who are of Punjabi origin and the 'autonomy seekers', who belong to the remaining four provinces, has existed since the time the Pakistan movement began looking a reality. They have taken diametrically opposite stands over the issue of the political structure of Pakistan. The centrists, who have held power uninterruptedly since partition, view their opponents' demands as 'autarchic' and anti-Pakistani. They have repeatedly stressed on a doctrinaire uniformity, whose basis is the conformity to the principle of 'one nation (Pakistan),

---

[6]Ibid., p. 169. Also see Salamat Ali, 'Sindh Erupts on Wave of Ethnic Killings', *Far Eastern Economic Review*, 7 June 1990; and *Newsweek* (New York), 11 June 1990.

[7]Iftikhar H. Malik, *State and Civil Society in Pakistan: Politics of Authority, Ideology and Ethnicity*, p. 171.

one language (Urdu) and one people (Muslims).[8] Thus, in the psyche of Pakistan's ruling elite, nation-building and state-building had become virtually synonymous even after the bifurcation of the state structure in Pakistan in 1971, the unitarian character of the state prevailed in spirit. Notwithstanding its federal form, provincialism continued to be a dirty word in the political vocabulary of the central leadership. For instance, in 1974, Bhutto maintained that regionalism or provincialism connoting the pre-eminence of nation, parochial loyalties, vis-à-vis the state of Pakistan, would lead to a catastrophe.[9] The official aversion to democracy and constitutionalism has not allowed various regional and ethnic forces to enter mainstream politico-economic institutions. Instead of opting for logical and egalitarian politics based on consensus, the regimes have sought to carve out an overarching Pakistani identity at the expense of ethnic pluralism. On the other hand, the autonomy seekers have placed their faith in a confederal political structure for Pakistan as they insist that Pakistan should be recognized as a multi-national state where the federal government acts upon the express wish of the confederating provinces and not the other way round as has happened in the past 50 years.[10] By the early 1950s, these battle lines took sharper contours, and provincial leaders looked upon the enforcement of an artificially fostered ideology as nothing but a veneer to cover the lust for power of the politicians.

By the use of ideological jargon and schemes such as parity, One Unit, martial law or civilian rule, the powerful ruling elite has denied heterogeneous communities any participation in national affairs, or has simply manipulated plurality in order to perpetuate its own power. The elitist and ethnically discretionary character of the state itself betrayed official efforts at national integration and an added momentum was provided by migration, urbanization, archaic means of communications, and weakening of the civil sector. Regional/territorial identification, provincialisation, historical and cultural postulates, lingual communalities and

---

[8]Aabha Dixit, *Ethno-Nationalism in Pakistan*, Delhi Papers 3 (Delhi: Institute for Defence Studies and Analyses, January 1996), p. 6.
[9]Lawrence Ziring, 'Pakistan's Nationalities Dilemma: Domestic and International Implications', in Lawrence Ziring (ed.), *The Sub-Continent in World Politics* (New York: 1975), p. 96.
[10]Aabha Dixit, *Ethno-Nationalism in Pakistan*, p. 6.

economic denominators have with variation, continued to play a vital role in the formation and transformation of ethno-nationalism in the country.

Punjabis: The Dominant Ethnic Group

Demographically, the Punjabis comprise the largest single ethnic group of Pakistan's current population and have since 1947, maintained political dominance of the federal government. The Punjabis number 62 million representing about 48 per cent of Pakistan's total population. Punjabis are, in effect, the successors to British rule, and as a predominant group wield a great deal of power and influence within Pakistan. Language plays a major role in the self-definition of the ethnic groups in Pakistan. As is the case with the Bengalis, the Baluchis, Pashtuns, Sindhis and *Muhajirs*, the Punjabis have their own distinct language.

Of the major ethnicities, the Punjabis exhibit the most cultural influence and control over the national governmental apparatus of Pakistan, though *Muhajirs* at one point also represented a growing power block. The degree of power and influence that Punjabis yield in the government of Pakistan is due in a large part to their inheritance of power from British rule. During the British administration of the region now called Pakistan, which was then part of India, certain groups were viewed as more desirable than others in terms of their capabilities and attitudes. The British viewed Punjabis as the ethnicity that showed the most promise in the region, believing that Punjabis would adapt quickly to British modes of military operations and practices and therefore best serve British interests.[11] As a result, the British most often chose Punjabis for recruitment in the British colonial armies—shortly after partition, Punjabis constituted 66 per cent of Pakistan's officer corps. Today, Punjabis represent 70 per cent of Pakistan's army. Pakhtuns hold the balance of military positions, while almost no Baluchis or Sindhis appear within the military's higher ranks. As a result, Punjabis

---

[11]C. D. Hurst, 'Pakistan's Ethnic Divide', *Studies in Conflict and Terrorism*, Vol. XIX (1996), p. 181.

exert significantly more control over Pakistan's military institutions than any other ethnicity.

The Punjabi predominance of the military, in turn, led to the formation of a Punjabi elite class, whose greater access to education and influential positions in the government paved the way for later Punjabi control of the bureaucracies and government departments. When the military directly took-over reigns of power by military coups led by General Ayub Khan in 1958, and later by Army Chief of Staff Zia-ul-Haq in 1977, the Punjabi-dominated military instituted campaigns of 'Punjabaization'[12] in Pakistan's government. In removing the other ethnicities from positions in the bureaucracy in favour of people of Punjabi origin, Punjabi leaders consolidated their presence in the affairs of Pakistan for decades. An example of the clout that the Punjabis have wielded in Pakistani politics is evident in the decision to move Pakistan's capital from Karachi in Sindh to Islamabad in the Punjab during Ayub Khan's regime, a choice that was highly unpopular with the other ethnicities in Pakistan but was carried out nonetheless.

Pakistan's military establishment—indeed its economic, political and bureaucratic establishments as well—is Punjabi dominated, to all purposes its unstated guiding dictum is that all Muslims are equal but Punjabi Muslims are more equal than others. It is this attitude and the colonial exploitation of what was once East Pakistan that led to the emergence of Bangladesh as a sovereign state in 1971. Unfortunately for Pakistan, its military establishment has learnt nothing from history, instead of redressing the genuine grievances of ethnic categories like the *Muhajirs*, Sindhis, Pathans and Baluchs, it persists with the policy of making Islamic fundamentalism the nation's cementing ideology.

As the most powerful and highly compensated ethnicity in Pakistan's government, the Punjabis are often the targets of the other ethnicities of Pakistan. Many of the disenfranchised view the Punjabis as having received a greater share of Pakistan's wealth than is their due. In an effort to fend off the opposition of the Baluchs, Sindhis, and sometimes the Pashtuns, the Punjabi-dominated governments of Islamabad have frequently entered into

---

[12]This term is further elaborated upon in the work by Feroz Ahmed, 'The Rise of Muhajir in Pakistan', *Pakistan Progressive*, Vol. X, Nos. 2–3 (Summer–Fall, 1989), p. 35.

alliances with elements of the Pashtun leadership, who make up the next largest ethnic segment of Pakistan's military. Further, the Punjabi ruling elite had at one time joined forces with *Muhajir* merchant, and middle classes, cooperating for mutual political support. In recent years, however, the *Muhajirs* have lost their clout in the power structure in Islamabad, leading to its conflict with Punjabis and ethnic Sindhi groups. Today, with the watchful eye and strong hand of a Punjabi-dominated military, the Punjabis carefully maintain a balance of power in their favour.

In the past few years, there has been considerable growth in ethnic feelings among culturally and linguistically different people of the Punjab. Broadly, there are three distinct regions in the Punjab, which are characterized by their own dialects of the Punjabi language and an embryonic feeling of cultural exclusivity. The Potohar region that covers the north-western parts of the province consists of the districts of Dera Ghazi Khan, Dera Ismail Khan and Rawalpindi, where the dialect Hindko is spoken, while the lower Punjab encompasses the districts of Multan, Bahawalpur and Sialkot, where the Siraiki dialect is spoken, and the rest of the districts make up the most prosperous and powerful heartland of the entire country. The 1981 census, for the first time ever, listed Siraiki as a separate language rather than as a dialect of Punjabi. As a result, Siraiki was reported to be the language of 9.8 per cent of Pakistan's and 14.9 per cent of Punjab's households. This makes the Siraikis the fourth largest community after Punjabis, Pushtuns and Sindhis. However, the question still persists about the stability, territorial compactness, economic cohesion, and consciousness aspect of Siraiki-speaking people.[13] The Hindko-speaking (2.4 per cent) are beginning to demand a province for themselves, while districts like Dera Ghazi Khan want to bifurcate from the Punjab or join up with the NWFP, where the movement for a Greater Pashtunistan is making headway following the winding down of the Afghan crisis and the creation of a Baluch–Pathan hiatus. A recent trend, noticeable in the Potohar and Siraiki regions, is the growth of animosities directed against the heartland of the Punjab. Even within the

---

[13]See Government of Pakistan, *Main Findings of the 1981 Population Census, Statistical Division, Population Census Organisation* (Islamabad: Government of Pakistan, 1983).

Punjab, it is now being increasingly felt that there are the rulers
and the ruled.[14]

Ethnic Movement in East Pakistan

Pakistan was barely a year old when its central government was
first challenged by the Bengali ethnic group. This first major ethnic
movement took shape in East Pakistan, where Bengali nationalism
was being channelled into an anti-West Pakistan movement.

Genesis and Grievances

It became the first formidable problem of nation-building and the
enigma was further compounded by the fact that it was the largest
socio-cultural subgroup which constituted a majority (54 per cent)
of Pakistan's population. The shortsighted and discriminatory policies pursued by the power elite of Pakistan mainly composed of
West Pakistani politicians. Civil and military officers, sowed the
seeds of regionalism which stood as an impediment in the process
of political integration and ultimately resulted in the break-up of
Pakistan in 1971. The core leadership of the Muslim League and
the civil-bureaucracy came from the predominantly Punjabis and
Muhajirs who had stake in central power. With a majority Bengali
population, it was clear that elections on the basis of adult franchise
would shift the power away from the Punjabi-*Muhajir* elite to the
Bengalis. The reluctance of the central leadership to introduce the
parliamentary democracy was directly linked with ethnic division of
the country.[15]

In due course of time, the denial of due participation to the
Bengalis in running the state, cultural subjugation and economic
disparity and deprivation gave rise to regional sentiments which
posed obstacles in the process of political integration. In this context,

---

[14]Aabha Dixit, *Ethno-Nationalism in Pakistan*, pp. 31–32.
[15]Omar Noman, *The Political Economy of Pakistan 1947–85* (London: Routledge
and Kegan Paul, 1988), p. 9.

a Bangladeshi scholar aptly remarks: 'The history of United Pakistan from 1947 to 1971 is one of constant conflict between the Pakistani nationalism which could barely acquire a definite identity, and the emerging regionalism or sub-nationalism.'[16] Rounaq Jahan, an eminent Bangladeshi scholar in her seminal study remarks: 'The power structure inherited had effected little Bengali participation, and the policy pursued by the "national elite" in the early years, a policy of one state, one government, one economy, one language, one culture tended to perpetuate this imbalance, and was a factor in the growth of Bengali alienation in the first decade of Pakistan's existence.'[17]

One of the distinct features which distinguished Pakistan from other countries of the Third World was the geographical incongruity—as its two major constituent parts, East and West Pakistan—were separated by 1,000 miles of Indian territory. Geographical separation made communication difficult between the two wings and in the process, did not allow a common pattern of social mobilization to emerge. Only a small elite from the East interacted with the West.

The linguistic traditions of East and West Pakistan were varied and the Bengali language had become the vehicle for the expression of a renaissance in Bengali culture and society. It had secular connotations, which propelled the West Pakistan elite to try and ignore the language and instead foist Urdu, a minority language but with a close association to the Indian Muslim heritage and Pakistan movement. The Bengali educated proto-elites opposed Urdu openly and forcefully. The Muslim League leadership in West Pakistan also considered Urdu as a symbol of national integration. The Bengali language movement was suppressed and on 21 February 1952, some activists were killed by the police in Dhaka. This date became a symbol of resistance against the Punjabi-dominated West Pakistani ruling elite.[18]

---

[16]G. W. Chowdhury, *The Last Days of United Nation* (London: C. Hurst and Company, 1974), p. 1.

[17]Rounaq Jahan, *Pakistan: Failure in National Integration* (New York: Columbia University Press, 1972), p. 28.

[18]Tariq Rahman, 'Language and Ethnicity in Pakistan', *Asian Survey*, Vol. XXXVII, No. 9 (September 1997), p. 836. Also see Rounaq Jahan, *Pakistan: Failure in National Integration*, p. 13.

It seems, the attempts to impose certain unitarian cultural-religious concepts and a centralized constitution brought Pakistan to the verge of disintegration. The economic policy of the power elite also had a destabilizing and disequilibrating impact for the political system of Pakistan. According to Kamruddin Ahmad,

> the sociological paradox relating to the deterioration of Bengalis after independence can be explained only in the background of history and psychology. After the independence the people of West Pakistan started feeling that they got a country of their own, the resources of which belong wholly to them. They belong to a nation; the army, the bureaucrats, the police belong wholly to them and are in the control of their leaders.... On the contrary, the people of East Pakistan could not feel the joys of freedom. Governors, Chief Secretaries, till 1956 were all outsiders.... The heads of autonomous bodies were non-Bengalis.[19]

The under representation of the Bengalis in the political and bureaucratic structure further aggravated the East-West divide. In the new state of Pakistan, the Bengalis had very little representation in the civil-military bureaucracy. According to Rounaq Jahan, Bengalis constituted 5 per cent of the military elite and 10 per cent of entrepreneurial class.[20] So far as the under-representation of East Pakistan in the military is concerned, Sayeed in his authoritative study on the role of military in Pakistan, put the figure even lower—at 2 per cent.[21]

Given the heterogeneous base of a country like Pakistan, the exclusiveness of the power elite and the kind of policies it pursued had a dysfunctional impact on Pakistan's political system. These West Pakistani elites, in pursuing policies of development favouring the growth of West Pakistan, could invoke certain respectable economic doctrines supported by advisory groups of Western economists. In this context, an eminent scholar aptly remarks that 'the "coalition

---

[19]Kamruddin Ahmad, *The Social History of East Pakistan* (Dacca: Crescent Book Store, 1967), pp. 178–79.
[20]Rounaq Jahan, *Pakistan: Failure in National Integration*, pp. 24–25.
[21]Khalid Bin Sayeed, 'The Role of the Military in Pakistan', in Jacques Van Doorn (ed.), *Armed Forces and Society* (Mouton: The Hague, 1968), p. 71.

of brains and guns" in Pakistan was not only against the members of East Pakistan but also against the brains of East Pakistan.'[22]

In due course of time, as regional economic disparity, imbalance and exploitation increased particularly in East Pakistan, it provoked bitter opposition and resentment towards the central government more than anything else, and contributed to the break-up of Pakistan.[23] Just seven months after the creation of Pakistan, a member of the Constituent Assembly of Pakistan pinpointed that a strong feeling was growing among the East Pakistanis that they are being neglected and treated merely as a colony of West Pakistan.[24]

It is noteworthy that at the time of partition neither East Pakistan nor West Pakistan had any significant industry. Both were producers of agricultural products like rice, jute, wheat and cotton. Economic difference between the two wings was not remarkable in the beginning. But due to the economic policies and development strategy formulated by the West Pakistani elite, industrial growth and development took place in the Western wing at the cost of East Pakistan. Economic disparity has been systematically perpetuated by the policy makers of Pakistan in the successive Five Year Plans, i.e. 1955–1960, 1960–1965 and 1965–1970. East Pakistan was denied its due share in various sectors of the economy, such as public sector development expenditure, revenue expenditure, foreign trade, allocation of foreign aid and foreign exchange. It is worth stating that while in 1947 East Pakistan had more cotton textile mills than West Pakistan, by the 1970s it ended as the biggest market for export of finished textile goods from West Pakistan.[25] During the third plan (1960–1965) the per capita development and revenue expenditure in West Pakistan were Rs 521.05 and Rs 390.35, respectively, whereas the expenditures for

---

[22]Khalid Bin Sayeed, *Politics in Pakistan: Nature and Direction of Change* (Praeger: Praeger Publishers, 1980), p. 81. Also see Kamaluddin Ahmed, 'Economic Disparity and the Breaker up of Erstwhile Pakistan', in Pandav Nayak (ed.), *Pakistan: Society and Politics* (New Delhi: South Asian Publishers, 1984), pp. 70–78.
[23]Ibid., pp. 65–82.
[24]Rehman Sobhan, 'The Problem of Regional Imbalance in the Economic Development of Pakistan', *Asian Survey*, Vol. II, No. 5 (July 1962), p. 31.
[25]Nural Islam, *Development Strategy of Bangladesh* (London: Oxford University Press, 1978), p. 3.

East Pakistan were as low as Rs 240 and Rs 70.29 respectively.[26] In this context, Richard Nations has observed that 'A double edifice of exploitation has build on the unique structure of two separate economies politically united within a single pseudo-national state. Both the traditional forms of social and imperial exploitation were compressed in Bengal.'[27] This resentment with regard to economic disparity and deprivation began to flare up as the power elite of West Pakistan was unresponsive and indifferent to the demands of East Pakistan.

The East Pakistani nationalist leadership took up the issue of economic disparity in their charter of demands. The Awami League, which brought out a pamphlet entitled 'Why Autonomy', mainly stressed the issue of economic imbalance. In fact, the economic demands put forward in the six points were the cornerstone of the programme to which Ayub, Bhutto and other West Pakistani leaders reacted very sharply.[28] An analysis of six points reveals that point three, four and five were related to the direct control and management of the economy by the regional governments to stop disparity permanently. The people of East Pakistan felt that they could choose and manage their own socio-economic strategy for development and therefore they considered the demand for autonomy as non-negotiable. On the contrary, the power elites of West Pakistan perceived in that demand 'a threat not only to their economic interests but also to the very stability of the social structure on which their power and privileges rested.'[29]

The serious threat to 'Pakistani Nationalism' came from the issue of economic disparity and deprivation. Although the basis of Pakistan was religion, it proved an ineffective basis for nationhood.[30] For the Bengali nationalist leaders, the economic disparity was the

---

[26]Government of Pakistan, Planning Commission, *Report of Advisory panels for Fourth Five Year Plan 1970–75,* Vol. I (Islamabad, July 1970), pp. 27–28.

[27]Richard Nations, 'The Economic Structure of Pakistan and Bangladesh', in Robin Blackburn (ed.), *Explosion in a Sub-continent* (Harmondsworth: Penguin, 1973), p. 272.

[28]For details see Kamaluddin Ahmad, 'Six-Point Movement and the Emergence of Bangladesh', *South Asian Studies,* Vol. XIII (July–December 1978), pp. 80–90.

[29]M. Anisur Rahman, 'East Pakistan: The Roots of Estrangement', *South Asian Review,* Vol. III, No. 3 (April 1970), pp. 238–39.

[30]William J. Barnds, 'Pakistan's Disintegration', *World Today,* Vol. XXVII (August 1971), p. 320.

most powerful instrument to radicalize the Bengali masses and muster their support. Indeed, growing economic aspirations on the one hand and economic disparity on the other hand intensified dissension and conflicts. The greatest fault of the power elites of Pakistan was their indifference and unresponsiveness to the demand for removing economic disparity.

In sum, economic disparity and deprivation ultimately led to the collapse of the State of Pakistan as these produced the most serious crisis for the political system. Unfortunately, the military rulers of Pakistan in the midst of crises wanted to suppress and silence the Bengalis forever. In a crisis-prone political system wherein majority of the people are aroused over a genuine grievance, any repressive and coercive measure is bound to be counter-productive and fatal. This has been true in the case of erstwhile Pakistan which broke up in 1971 with the help of the Indian army in the civil war, after about 25 years of its existence.

Pakhtun Regionalism

In the broader framework of over-centralism, the Pakhtun problem[31] of NWFP provides not only a classic case of political alienation but also shows how ethnic aspirations have been portrayed as separatism to undermine the legitimacy of their demand. Historically though, some groups of Pakhtuns had demanded an independent Pakhtunistan but after its merger with Pakistan, the issue was used as a leverage to bargain with the central government. However, the support rendered by Afghanistan to the movement for Pakhtunistan had posed a serious problem to the newly born state of Pakistan. What the Pakhtuns refer to as Pakhtunistan extends from inside Pakistan's north-western corner into Afghanistan and south into Iran. Their population of around 17 million constitutes about 13 per cent of Pakistan's overall population. As compared to Baluchi consciousness, the Pakhtuns of the

---

[31]Pakhtuns, Paktun, Pathan, Paktoon and Pashtuns have the same connotation. All these terms have been used here interchangeably.

NWFP could claim that their ethnicity was backed by greater historic depth as well a greater sense of cohesion.[32]

Historical Genesis

The area which comes under the present NWFP was under the suzerainty of various kingdoms at different points of history. The reign of the Pakhtuns under the auspices of the Afghan empire was founded in 1747. However, the existence of the Pakhtun state was brought to an end when the British established their own empire in the region. During the nineteenth century, the British had tried to convert Afghanistan into a buffer state separating their British Indian territory from the rising Czarist empire across the Central Asian river of Amu Darya. In 1893 the Durand line was drawn marking the boundary between India and Afghanistan. In the process, the Pakhtuns on this side of the Line were separated from those of Afghanistan. This division imposed on the Afghans was resented by them and that gave rise to Pakhtun nationalism.[33] This anti-British sentiment led to the formation of the Red Shirts by Khan Abdul Ghaffar Khan. The Pakhtunis were forced to join Pakistan against their will, after a referendum in 1947 which Abdul Ghaffar Khan and the Khudai Khidmatgars boycotted.

The Pakhtun leaders and the Red Shirts were throughout treated as traitors in Pakistan, because of their pre-partition support to the Congress and the demand for Pakhtunistan on the eve of partition, although the concept of Pakhtunistan was never clearly defined by Khan Abdul Gaffar Khan. However, after partition, its leadership recognized the emergence of Pakistan as a settled fact and espoused the reorganization of provincial boundaries under which all Pashtu speaking areas would be united as a single province and to be named Pakhtunistan and operating under the federal set-up of Pakistan. Abdul Wali Khan, who formed the Awami National Party, confined himself to demanding for regional autonomy.[34]

---

[32]K. B. Sayeed, *Politics in Pakistan: The Nature and Direction of Change*, p. 121.
[33]Kalim Bahadur, 'Ethnic Problems in Pakistan', *World Focus*, Vol. XV, Nos. 4–5 (April–May 1994), p. 27.
[34]Sukha Ranjan Chakravarty, 'The Paktoon National Movement', *Foreign Affairs Reports*, Vol. XXV, No. 1 (1976), p. 9.

The Pakhtunistan movement gained ground on two emotive issues—transborder linkage with the Pakhtuns in Afghanistan[35] and the fear of cultural, social and economic submergence at the hands of the dominant Punjabi-*Muhajir* elite in the state structure. According to Tahir Amin, the fear of being dominated by the Punjabis under the guise of Muslim Nationalism became the war cry of the Pathan ethno-national movement.[36]

As compared to Baluchi consciousness, the Pakhtuns of NWFP could claim that their ethnicity is backed by greater historic depth as well as a greater sense of cohesion. However, Pashtun nationalism has not expressed itself as violently as its Baluch variation. The reasons for this might have to do with the fact that although they have been discriminated against to some degree by Islamabad, in general, the Pashtuns have met with better treatment from Pakistan's regimes than have the Baluchs, Sindhis, or *Muhajirs*. Whereas the Baluchis and others were often excluded from the majority of Pakistan's leadership, the Pashtuns have a significant presence in the professional organizations and leadership of Pakistan, especially in its military. This presence extends back to British involvement in the region, when members of the Pashtun aristocracy were incorporated into the Punjabi-dominated government and military. Pashtun involvement has been maintained to this day.

The Pakhtuns held key positions in the civil and military bureaucracies of Pakistan and in terms of influence and number were ahead of the two smaller provinces, Sindh and Baluchistan, and were next to the Punjab in these institutions. Their share in the armed forces was between 15 to 20 per cent. Emphasizing the strategic significance of the province, the government had established the key military establishments in the Frontier.[37] A number of Pakhtuns from time to time had occupied the highest position in the

---

[35]S. M. M. Qureshi, 'Pakhtunistan: The Frontier Dispute Between Afghanistan and Pakistan', *Pacific Affairs*, Vol. XXXIX, Nos. 1–2 (Spring–Summer, 1966).

[36]Tahir Amin, *Ethno-National Movements of Pakistan* (Islamabad: Institute of Policy Studies, 1988), p. 86.

[37]Peshawar was the headquarters of the Pakistan Air Force and there were air force bases at Peshawar, Kohat, Risalpur and Chitral. In addition, there was the Pakistani Military Academy at Kakul and the Air Force College at Risalpur.

army and the bureaucracy.[38] However, such a presence of Pathans in the national power structure needs to be qualified. To begin with, most of the military recruitment has traditionally been from two settled districts, Kohat and Mardan. Consequently, the collective benefits of the military recruitment of the Pathans have accrued to only a small part of the NWFP as a whole.

Pakhtun Grievances

The Pakhtun sense of ethnic pride and achievement is often accompanied by the grievance that the NWFP had been kept in a state of underdevelopment largely because of the dominance of the central government by non-Pakhtuns and particularly by the Punjabis. Ever since the creation of Pakistan, the underdevelopment of the Frontier was the central theme of campaigns launched by Khan Abdul Ghaffar Khan and his son, Wali Khan. The NWFP lagged behind every other province, in both gross and per capita regional product. It also lagged behind Sindh and Punjab in the number of large-scale industrial units. Moreover, Punjab was the main beneficiary of the Green Revolution with 91.2 per cent of the tubewells located in that province, whereas in the Peshawar division, with its fertile agricultural areas, there were only 2.7 per cent of private tubewells in 1968.[39] Even after the establishment of the National Awami Party (NAP)-Jamiatul Ulama-i-Islam (JUI) coalition government in the Frontier in 1972, Pakhtun complaint relating to the preempting of the lucrative forces of revenue by the central government and their alleged unwillingness to make amends for this through generous allocation of central revenues to the province continued. These regional disparities were further heightened by the way the central government had allowed the industries to exploit the resources of the Frontier for the benefit of Punjab and Sindh. It can be exemplified by the fact that the NWFP, which is the biggest producer of raw tobacco, has no cigarette producing plants or factories.

---

[38]For details consult Sayeed, *Politics in Pakistan: Nature and Direction of Change*, p. 122.
[39]Ibid., p. 123.

The influx of around three million Afghan refugees fleeing from the Soviet invasion and Afghanistan's subsequent civil war had provided a greater push for the reestablishment of Pashtunistan, as the stress of the refugee problem strained the nerve of the NWFP. However, as with the other ethnic nationalists, the Pashtun movement is itself divided between the different options for the future. These differing views include the strengthening of the NWFP and its membership in a new Pakistan redesigned along confederation lines, the creation of a greater Afghanistan, which would incorporate the existing Pashtun regions of Pakistan, the outright secession of the province to truly return to a fully autonomous Pashtunistan.[40] A tribal uprising in the NWFP during November 1994 resulted in at least 200 deaths. The possibility of further violence has been threatened by elements of the Pakhtun leadership who demand from the Punjabi-dominated federal government, greater autonomy over their own affairs, and a larger share of Pakistan's economic future.[41]

In the Frontier, one of the major components of Pakistan consciousness or sub-nationalism was the intense devotion to the Pashto language and literature. The efforts of Khan Abdul Ghaffar Khan, the anti-British Pakhtun nationalist leader, transformed the Pashto language into such a symbol in Baluchistan as well as in the NWFP. However, because of the Afghan claim to Pakhtunistan and its support of Pashto, Pakistan's ruling elite was mistrustful of Pashto despite the National Awami Party's choice of Urdu as the official language of the NWFP during its brief rule in 1972. Pashto remains an identity marker and part of Pakhtun nationalism as expressed by the NAP's successor Awami National Party (ANP), which continues to challenge the domination of Pakistan's central government.

In October 1958, General Mohammad Ayub Khan, himself a Pashtun from Hazara district captured power but his ascendancy to power did not help the cause of Pashtunistan. After Bhutto assumed power there was a significant change in the policies towards the NWFP as emphasis was laid more on economic integration. However,

---

[40]Hurst, 'Pakistan's Ethnic Divide', p. 187. Also see Selig S. Harrison, 'Ethnicity and the Political Stalemate in Pakistan', in Ali Banuazizi and Myron Weiner (eds.), *The State, Religion and Ethnic Politics* (New York: Syracuse University Press, 1986), p. 290.

[41]Ahmed Rashid, 'Riches and Rubble: Karachi Collapse Rocks Bhutto Government', *Far Eastern Economic Review*, Vol. CLVIII, No. 2 (12 January 1998), p. 23.

Z. A. Bhutto's handling of political affairs in the province by appointing a non-representative person as the Governor without consulting the democratically elected party, brought him in confrontation with the ANP. He imposed central rule in 1973 in the NWFP on the pretext of a threat to the national security and in 1975 installed a puppet government and banned the ANP. This further multiplied the grievances of the Pashtuns as they felt they would never get a fair deal from the government. Initially when Zia came to power in Pakistan, to strengthen his support base, he sympathized with the Pashtun leaders who were anti-Bhutto elements. But after the execution of Z. A. Bhutto, there was apparently no threat to his rule. Thus, he hardened his stand towards the Pakhtun issue. The restoration of democracy in 1988 has not brought any significant change in the outlook of the leaders towards provincial autonomy. In 1997, the issue of renaming the NWFP as Pakhtunkhwa, associated with the ethnic aspiration and identity of the Pashtuns came to the forefront. The Nawaz Sharif government refused to consider this demand for fear of inflaming ethnic tensions in the province, and the ANP terminated its alliance with the Pakistan Muslim League (PML). According to one observer, the

> issue of Pakhtunkhwa is an emotional one and it should be evaluated in terms of the symbolic connotation of the demand. The federal government has demoralized the genuine Pashtun aspiration by picturising it as a separatist movement. This parochialism undermines creditability and the spirit of regionalism.[42]

Baluchi National Movement

Representing the smallest percentage of population at 4.2 per cent but claiming the largest percentage of Pakistan as their homeland, are the Baluchs. The Baluchs are a tribal community, consisting of 17

---

[42]Smruti S. Pattanaik, 'Pakistan's North-West Frontier: Under a New Name', *Strategic Analysis* Vol. XXII, No. 5 (August 1998), p. 779.

rough tribal groupings[43] with a total population of approximately 3 million people.

Baluchistan is an area of vital strategic importance to Pakistan. It occupies nearly 40 per cent of the country's land area. Baluchistan is at the strategic crossroads between Afghanistan and the Gulf of Oman to the South.

Baluch historians claim to be ethnically linked to the Kurdish tribes who migrated north from what is now Syria. Separating from the Kurds, the Baluchs slowly settled into what has become Iranian and Pakistani Baluchistan over the period between the sixth and fourteenth centuries.

Genesis and Grievances

The Baluch national movement had its origins in the pre-independence period, when the assertion of Baluch identity arose as a reaction to increasing integration of Baluch society within the liberal and modernistic trends exhibited by imperial Britain. Since the withdrawal of the British, the Baluchs tended to be in frequent conflict with the central authority against the latter's 'calculated disregard of their ethnic and cultural identities.'[44]

Like the Pakhtuns, the Baluchs were also never enthusiastic supporters of Pakistan. Ahmed Yar Khan, the last ruler of Kalat, had made it clear in the mid-1930s, that he wanted Baluchistan to be independent and claimed that Nepal and Kalat had the same status.

In 1947, Ahmed Yar Khan declared Kalat as independent. Pakistan rejected Khan's declaration and forcibly annexed Kalat. The Pakistani army occupied Kalat and forced the Khan of Kalat to sign accession documents. The forcible occupation of Baluchistan by Pakistan led to a short-lived revolt by the brother of the Khan of Kalat. The revolt did not last long, but it gave a fillip to the Baluch national movement which resurfaced in 1973.

---

[43]The main Baluch tribes are Mengals, Marris, Bugtis, Mohammad Hasnis, Zehris, Bizenjos, and Raisanis. Brahui, which is a different language from Baluchi, is spoken by the Brahui tribes in Kalat division.

[44]Kalim Bahadur, 'Ethnic Problems in Pakistan', pp. 27–28.

At every moment in Pakistan's history, the Baluchs were opposed to the machinations and intrigues of the military-bureaucratic complex that ruled the country. The One Unit Scheme, adopted in 1955, threatened to merge the distinct identity of the Baluchs with the rest of Pakistan. The Baluchi protested but their cries were ignored. Three years later, discontent in Baluchistan was utilized to justify the coup d'etat of General Ayub Khan. In 1959, there was a campaign of repression against the Baluchs; several hundred armed men led by the 80-year old Nauroz Khan, took to the arid hills of the province and fought back.[45]

As far as the Baluch grievances are concerned, ethnicity intertwined with a sense of political isolation and relative economic deprivation continued to be a potent force in evoking Baluch mobilization. Such a feeling was more intense amongst the Baluchs rather than the Pathans. Very few Baluchs have held key positions in the central government of Pakistan. According to one study, 'during 1947–1977 only four of the 179 persons who were named in Central Cabinets were ethnic Baluchs. Only one of them (Akbar Bugti) was named prior to the 1970s. As against this, a much larger number of Pathans were represented in the Central Cabinets.'[46] Baluch representation in civilian bureaucratic elites was 25 per cent with the Punjabi taking 48.89 per cent and the *Muhajir* 30.29 per cent.[47]

In the military too, though labelled by the British among the martial races, the number of Baluchs has been rather small. One study reveals that from the areas that later became Pakistan, British recruitment was 77 per cent from Punjab, 19.5 per cent from NWFP, 22 per cent from Sindh, and 0.6 per cent from Baluchistan.[48] In another study, the ethnic group strength of the Pakistan military officer corps in the 1970s was approximately estimated as 70 per cent Punjabi, 15 per cent Pathan, 10 per cent *Muhajir* and 5 per

---

[45]Tariq Ali, *Can Pakistan Survive*, p. 116.

[46]Shaheen Mozaffar, 'The Politics of Cabinet Formation in Pakistan: A Study of Recruitment to the Central Cabinets—1947–77' (Ph.D. Dissertation, Miami University, Ohio, 1980), cited in Robert G. Wirsing, *The Baluchis and Pathans* (London, 1981), Minority Rights Group Report, No. 48, p. 9.

[47]Stephen P. Cohen, 'Security Decision-Making in Pakistan', Report Prepared for the Office of the External Research, Department of State, September 1980, p. 40.

[48]*4th Triennial Census Central Government Employees* (Islamabad: Government of Pakistan, 1973).

cent Baluch and Sindhi. As regards higher military positions, it was maintained that till June 1959, out of 24 generals in the Pakistan army, 11 were Punjabis and 11 Pathans.[49] Even later, there was hardly any Baluch in the armed forces ranks. There are only a few hundred Baluchs in the entire Pakistani Army. The famous Baluch Regiment has no Baluch in it. The Kalat Scouts was a para-military force raised during the Ayub dictatorship. There were only two people from Kalat recruited to its ranks. The same is the case with the Sibi Scouts, created to police the Marri areas.

In the provincial framework, the Baluch sense of grievance hinged on the nativist/regional planks. According to one estimate, of 830 higher civil service posts in Baluchistan, only 181 were held by the Baluch in 1979. There was only one Baluch each holding the rank of secretary, director and deputy commissioner. As regards the police, all the high officials were non-Baluch also. And so was three-fourths of the police force.[50] The situation in the judicial services was equally dismal.

So far as the channeling of funds was concerned, it had been mainly in the hands of non-Baluch, predominantly Punjabi bureaucracy. It was alleged that the Baluch plea for control over decisions pertaining to development activities had been ignored. In addition to this has been the issue of internal colonization. The Baluch resented that Punjabi settlers had been grabbing prime farm land and the Punjabi real estate speculators had been buying up property in Quetta.[51]

The other grievances included the Baluch perception of the exploitative attitude of the centre in harnessing national resources of the province. They felt that the Punjabis were reaping the benefits of the vast untapped natural resources. In this view, the foreign imperialist interests backed by the Pakistani bureaucracy have been getting the lion's share in profits from the state resources which are being

---

[49]Asaf Hussain, *Elite Politics in an Ideological State: The Case of Pakistan* (Folkestone, Kent: Dawson, 1979), p. 129.

[50]Seling S. Harrison, *In Afghanistan Shadow: Baluch Nationalism and Soviet Temptations* (Washington, D.C.: Carnegie Endowment for International Peace, 1981), p. 164.

[51]Urmila Phadnis, 'Ethnic Movements in Pakistan', in Pandav Nayak (ed.), *Pakistan: Society and Politics* (New Delhi: South Asian Publishers, 1984), p. 195. Also see her *Ethnicity and Nation-Building in South Asia* (New Delhi: Sage Publications, 1990).

rapidly depleted without any lasting benefit to Baluchistan itself. Thus, apart from a dismally low rate of royalty paid by the centre to the state, gas has been piped not within Baluchistan but outside. Even its capital, Quetta, received gas long after it had been tapped.[52] Even education-wise Baluchistan remains the most backward province and outside Quetta, there is virtually no educational infrastructure.[53] Since 1951, a Baluchi language movement has sought to preserve Baluch cultural identity. Baluch identity is expressed by coining words of Baluch origin and by writing this language despite little official patronage.[54]

The formation of the NAP in 1957 reflected a Baluch–Sindhi–Pathan combine pledged to the principle of provincial autonomy. However, in the garrison state ethos of the Pakistani polity during the Ayub era, the issue of regional autonomy remained stifled if not muted.

During the 1970–1971 elections, the Baluch leadership attempted to mobilize political support from the landowning classes and peasantry as well as the petty bourgeoisie by stressing the un-derdevelopment of the province at the hands of a Punjabi dominated centre.

With the formation of the NAP–JUI coalition governments in Baluchistan in 1972, socio-economic cleavages amongst the Baluchs seemed to be subdued for a while. Instead contradictions between the central and regional elites assumed preeminence.

An immediate cause of clash between the centre and the provinces was the desire on the part of the latter to assure Pathans and Baluchs key positions in the provincial administration by pressurizing the personnel from other provinces to vacate their positions. This was viewed with hostility by the centre. Equally significant was the demand of the provincial government to have a greater share in the natural resources of the province. In the allocation of industries also, the provincial governments charged the centre of having a ham-handed policy towards them. The Baluch and Pathan leadership was also obviously desirous of widening and consolidating its political base by acquiring more political power. This was regarded with disdain and suspicion by

[52]Ibid.
[53]Siddiq Baluch, 'Baluch Perception of Things', *Dawn* (Karachi), 19 May 1987.
[54]Carina Jahani, *Standardization and Orthography in Balochi Language* (Upsalla, Sweden: Almquist and Wikeseth International, 1989), p. 233.

the PPP dominated centre which had virtually no base in these areas.[55]

The widening chasm between the central and provincial leadership had also brought to the surface an attempt on the part of the Pakistan People's Party (PPP) to penetrate these provinces by means, fair or foul, and the attempts of the latter to circumvent it.[56] Consequently, the Centre's intransigence led to the dissolution of provincial governments. It used a number of strategies—cooptive, divisive, collaborative and coercive—to achieve its objective. The NAP leadership was incarcerated on one pretext or another and the party outlawed for its 'antinational activities.'[57]

The Baluch insurgency had been sparked off by the dismissal of Ataullah Mengal's provincial government by the PPP government and reached its height during the period 1973–1977. It led to a brutal confrontation between 55,000 Baluchs and almost 70,000 Pakistani troops. Coercion was used to crush the Baluch insurgents on a large scale, the Bhutto regime used heavy and overwhelming Pakistani and Iranian fire power against them. In this process, inordinately large number of civilians were killed, especially in attacks targeted against Baluch villages suspected of harbouring insurgents.

The Pakistan Army's offensive was culled from the classics of counter-insurgency manuals. It concentrated on destroying the base of popular support on which the guerrillas depended. In August–September 1974, Punjabi soldiers under Jahanzeb's command encircled the Marri Tribal areas and massive artillery bombardment coupled with strafing from the air by French-supplied Mirages to take place.[58] The whole operation was a devastating blow against the Baluch resistance.

For five years, Baluchistan was torn apart by civil war. It also changed the character of Baluch nationalism for ever. It emerged in a new organization: the Baluchistan People's Liberation Front (BPLF).

---

[55]Phadnis, 'Ethnic Movements in Pakistan', p. 198.

[56]Z. A. Bhutto abolished the Sardari System in order to mobilize political support and establish the political presence of the federal government in Baluchistan.

[57]For details consult Satish Kumar, *The New Pakistan* (New Delhi: Vikas Publishing House, 1978), pp. 157–215. For the official viewpoint see *White Paper on Baluchistan* (Islamabad, Government of Pakistan, 1974).

[58]Tariq Ali, *Can Pakistan Survive*, p. 119.

The BPLF developed a network of armed militants that cut across tribal bonds and rivalries. The BPLF combines the principles of nomadism with Marxism–Leninism. Though christened in 1976, the BPLF is the direct outgrowth of guerrilla movement. It spearheaded the 1973–77 insurgency and believes in the inevitability of confrontation with the centre. The BPLF defined the Pakistani state 'as a reactionary construct governed by a militant bureaucratic dictatorship, which defended the interests of the propertied class in town and countryside and was, in its turn, backed by the United States and its leading relays in the region: Saudi Arabia and Iran.'[59]

Initially, the BPLF had the national liberation of all nationalities in Pakistan as its prime objective soon after it declared the formation of an independent Baluchistan as its goal. By 1978, its leadership had broadened this to a 'greater Baluchistan' which included the Baluch inhabited areas of Iran and Pakistan. However, by 1980 the controversy regarding independence or cooperation with other anti-government groups in a Pakistan-wide struggle had divided its rank and file.

However, in contrast to it the militant outlook of the Bizenjo led National Awami Party espoused greater provincial autonomy within an overall Pakistani framework. Urging for maximum political autonomy for the provincial units, it maintained that only four subjects (defence, foreign affairs, currency and communication) would be divested in the central government.'[60]

The Baluch ethnic movement has thus been shorn of its collective strength in the absence of an overarching united leadership. The ethnic movement has no doubt been fragmented and the multi-tribal Baluch community have yet to evolve a collectively agreed symbol to ignite and sustain an enduring national movement. The problem facing Baluchistan now is complex. Its population is heterogenous; while Baluchs constitute about half the population, the other half is made up of several other ethnic groups viz., the Pakhtuns, Brahuis, Sindhis and Punjabis. The Pathans are in a majority in Quetta District comprising 40 per cent of the population. The Soviet intervention has increased the problems of ethnic and tribal diversity. It had led to political parties in

---

[59]Ibid., p. 122.
[60]Seling S. Harrison, *In Afghanistan's Shadow: Baluch Nationalism and Soviet Temptations*, pp. 89–90.

Baluchistan becoming very factionalized and politicized. To add to the simmering tension, the arrival of Afghans influenced the moulding Baluch-Pathan tension.[61]

To be able to get the Baluchis into the national mainstream, Pakistani rulers will have to bring an authentic socio-economic change which may bring them at par with constituents units of Pakistan, namely, Punjab, NWFP and Sindh. Unless the government is able to come terms with the tribal sensitivity, the Baluch problem will continue and may progressively get out of hand.

Sindhi Nationalism

In post-1971 Pakistan, out of the country's four provinces Sindh has always been in the limelight and is popularly referred to as a province of permanent sectarian violence. Today the ethnic Sindhis form 13 per cent of the total population of Pakistan. Over the last several decades, Sindh has become a cauldron of various ethnic communities which have migrated into the area, due to social and political factors. The tragedy of Sindh has been that out of a total population of 19 million in the province, the Sindhis constitute less than half. About six million are *Muhajirs* (refugees) and Punjabis, four million are Baluchs and 0.5 million Pakhtuns.[62]

The ethnic politics of Sindh revolve around different points of conflict, such as, Sindh vs Centre, Sindhi vs *Muhajirs*, *Muhajirs* vs Punjabis, *Muhajirs* vs *Muhajirs*, Shia vs Sunni etc.[63]

Genesis and Grievances

The liberal or leftist approach to the ethnic problem in Sindh considers the 'economic contradictions within the Pakistan, especially Sindhi, socio-economic structure, responsible for creating class conflicts along

---

[61]Salamat Ali, 'Baluchistan: An Upheaval in Forecast', *Far Eastern Economic Review*, 19 October 1979, p. 42.
[62]Kalim Bahadur, 'Ethnic Problems in Pakistan', p. 28.
[63]For details consult, Mohd. Arif, 'Sindh in the Midst of Crisis', *Strategic Analysis*, Vol. XXIII, No. 11 (February 2000), pp. 1895–1908.

the lines of rural versus urban, feudal versus middle class and ruling elites versus have-nots. It also looks at the question of nationalities in a deterministic way, tracing its origin in the Pakistani capitalist economic order which it considers to be a derivative of the neo-colonial world order, carried on by the privileged classes in Pakistan. Such a system was destined to have cracks, which have appeared in the form of strong ethno-national or ethnoregional movements, for example, the SNA or the MQM.'[64]

The Sindhi nationalist movement had begun during the campaign to separate Sindh from the Bombay Presidency in the deep of British rule. Sindhi support to the Pakistan movement arose out of a desire of the Sindhi Muslim business classes to drive out their Hindu competitors. Although Sindhis had expressed civil support initially for partition, several events changed their enthusiasm for the creation of Pakistan. The first factor was an unforeseen side effect of partition. After partition the majority of refugees who left India by force or by choice from areas other than Punjab came to Sindh and settled principally in the cities, such as Karachi, Hyderabad and Sukkur. The *Muhajirs* became such a large percentage of urban Sindhi population that they gained a great measure of control over the region's cities. The *Muhajirs*, who were economically and educationally better off than Sindhis, pushed the Sindhis out of the competition. They captured government jobs and business. Further, although the Indian Punjabis had been able to assimilate quickly into the population of Pakistan's Punjab, the *Muhajirs* failed to do so to any significant degree in Sindh, creating sharp divisions in the Sindhi society. Moreover, as time progressed, the Punjabi-dominated government in Islamabad came to join in an alliance with the *Muhajir* middle classes for mutual political support. This led to 'preferential treatment' of the urban centred *Muhajirs* by Islamabad at the expense of more rural Sindhis.[65] When Jinnah decided to remove the Sindhi capital of Karachi from Sindhi control and place it under the auspices of the new federal bureaucracy, the Sindhis viewed the move as further evidence of a Punjabi-*Muhajir* conspiracy against the Sindhis. Although the decision was later abolished in favour of the One Unit scheme, this was also viewed as

---

[64]Iftikhar H. Malik, *State and Civil Society in Pakistan: Politics of Authority, Ideology and Ethnicity*, p. 217.
[65]Hurst, 'Pakistan's Ethnic Divide', p. 189.

a slap on the face by Sindhis who considered it as yet another attempt by the Punjabis to extend their control over other ethnic groups.[66]

Liaquat Ali Khan, the first Prime Minister of Pakistan, a *Muhajir*, was the principal leader of the *Muhajirs*. In the beginning, many of Pakistan's top bureaucrats were Urdu-speaking and exercised a high degree of influence over the country in the early formative years. This 'immigrants bureaucracy' relied on the support of the military elite, which hailed mainly from Punjab. This civil-military nexus brought Punjabis and Urdu speakers close to each other. Pakistan's successive political upheavals led to a Punjabi-*Muhajir* military elite imposing control over Sindh. More Punjabi entrepreneurs settled in Sindh to control business and commerce.

In Sindh the ethnic contradictions appeared rather forcefully, for it has been a multi-ethnic province since the Baluchs and Gujaratis emigrated there in the early years and were accepted as Sindhis. After independence, the Urdu-speaking refugees replaced the urban Hindus in Sindh, and the Sindhis, to their discomfort, realized that they are not only to deal with Punjabi domination of the state but also to compete with the relatively advanced *Muhajirs*.

In due course of time, the lateral influx of Punjabis, Pashtuns and others further changed the demographic situation to the detriment of the Sindhi salariat (see Table 4.1). Quoting from the census of 1981,[67] Hamza Alavi finds that 52 per cent of the population of Sindh consisted of Sindhi-speaking inhabitants, whereas Urdu speakers made up 22 per cent of the total population and 50 per cent of the population of Karachi, Hyderabad and Sukkur. In Karachi, 54.03 per cent of the population were Urdu speakers, 13.06 per cent were Punjabis, 8.7 per cent were Pashtuns from the NWFP and the rest were Afghans, Iranians, Sri Lankans, Burmese, Africans and others. The Biharis, Afghans, Iranians and Bangladeshis arrived in Karachi after the statistics for 1981 were published. Alavi is shocked that in the capital of Sindh only 6.3 per cent were Sindhi speakers which was a cause

---

[66]Ibid.

[67]It is interesting to note that ethnicity in the census of 1981 was based on 'language most often used in household.' The census for 1991 was postponed due to various pressures.

Table 4.1
Ethnic Percentage of Sindh, 1981

	Total	Urban	Rural
Muhajireen	24.1	54.4	2.2
Sindhis	55.7	20.0	81.5
Punjabis	10.6	14.0	8.2
Pashtuns	3.6	7.9	0.5
Baluchis	6.0	3.7	7.6

Source: Adopted from Iftikhar H. Malik, *State and Civil Society in Pakistan: Politics of Authority, Ideology and Ethnicity* (New York: St. Martin's Press, Inc., 1997), p. 202.

of grievance to Sindhi nationalists. He takes into account the class formation of the Karachi population where 40 per cent of the inhabitants live in slums—*Katchi Abadi* (rural and tribal areas)—and the affluent salariat inhabit prosperous areas, causing a severe sense of mutual antagonism.[68]

Economic statistics, like demographic figures, has played a significant role in generating a deep sense of alienation, ethnic redefinition and polarisation. Sindh, especially the urban areas, accounts for more than half of Pakistan's industrial concerns. It contributes 30 per cent of the GDP and 21.3 per cent of the agricultural GDP with the highest per capita income in the country. It also accounts for 43 per cent of the construction industry. Urban Sindh is the financial capital, housing the headquarters of most of the country's national banks, major branches of international banks, insurance companies and shipping concerns. Karachi remains the major port and the headquarters for the navy. Such activities have certainly created a sense of deprivation in the hinterland. The high proportion of Urdu speakers and Punjabis in educational institutions, civil and military departments, factories, banks, offices, hotels, airlines, police, hospitals and in the mills has increased a sense of alienation among a growing Sindhi middle-class as well as the landowning class who have their own apprehensions about being marginalized by the powerful class of businessmen.[69]

---

[68]Hamza Alavi, 'Nationhood and the Nationalities in Pakistan', *Economic and Political Weekly*. Vol. XXIX (8 July 1989), pp. 1530–31.
[69]Iftikhar H. Malik, *State and Civil Society in Pakistan: Politics of Authority, Ideology and Ethnicity*, p. 202–3.

Combined with the demographic and economic statistics, linguistic controversy has played a crucial role in ethnic mobilization.[70] The imposition of Urdu as the national language by the ruling class on other linguistic groups alienated the Sindhis. The Sindhi language and culture was overshadowed by the Urdu language and Hindustani culture of the Urdu-speaking people, which politicized the Sindhis.[71] The state, first by promoting Urdu at the expense of traditional languages and then by reversing its policy in 1971, agitated both Sindhis and *Muhajireen*. In 1972, soon after the creation of Bangladesh, there were riots over the Urdu-Sindhi controversy in Sindh (especially in Karachi). The first PPP government in Sindh under Mumtaz Ali Bhutto tried to coopt and pacify Sindhi nationalists, but antagonised the *Muhajirs* in the process, for they considered Urdu not merely as the national language but as a symbol of their own identity.[72] Eventually the regime relented and reverted to the pre-1947 policy of dual languages, maintaining Urdu and Sindhi side by side.[73]

Feroz Ahmed, a leading Sindhi intellectual, traces a number of causes, similar to those given by Alavi, for the resurgence of nationality sentiments in Sindh. Along with immigration, he pinpoints the ideological orientation of the power elites as the main reason for Sindhi alienation. 'Islam, integrity of Pakistan and the Urdu language became the code words for national domination. In the name of Pakistan's unity and integrity, the very foundation of unity was eroded.'[74] In addition, he blames the exploitation of Sindhi resources by the Punjabis and feels that Sindh has always suffered because of conspiracies against it. The refugees replaced the Hindu exploitative class and even Karachi was initially taken

---

[70]Ibid., p. 203.

[71]For an excellent account of language question in Sindh refer Feroz Ahmed, 'The Language Question in Sind', in Akbar S. Zaidi (ed.), *Regional Imbalances and Regional Questions in Pakistan* (Lahore: Vanguard Books, 1992). Also see Legislative Assembly Debates of Pakistan, 28 August 1972, pp. 504–08.

[72]Charles H. Kennedy, 'The Politics of Ethnicity in Sindh', *Asian Survey*, Vol. XXXI, No. 10 (October 1991).

[73]Iftikhar H. Malik, *State and Civil Society in Pakistan: Politics of Authority, Ideology and Ethnicity*, p. 203.

[74]Feroz Ahmed, 'Pakistan's Problem of National Integration', in Mohammad Asghar Khan (ed.), *Islam, Politics and the State: The Pakistan Experience* (London: Zed Press, 1985), p. 234.

away from Sindh. In this power politics, some Sindhi surrogates helped the Punjabi-*Muhajir* oligarchy so that the 'Sindhis would be reduced to the status of the American Indians.'[75] The execution of Z. A. Bhutto and use of extensive military power in 1983 during the Movement for the Restoration of Democracy (MRD) struggle in Sindh, brought the alienation of the Sindhis to a climax.

Bhutto's execution by General Zia-ul-Haq was seen as an assault by the Punjabi rulers on a Sindhi prime minister. This, combined with Zia's *Muhajir* ethnic background and open support for the *Muhajir* movement, sent the Sindhi cause into a higher degree of militancy. In the mid-1980s, Sindhi disenchantment with the Pakistani government erupted into open warfare. During Zia's regime, guerrilla units raised in the Sindh confronted the Punjabi federal troops from Islamabad. However, poorly organized and ill-prepared insurgency was eventually crushed by the use of coercive power of the state.[76] The severe repression of Sindhi nationalism was akin to Baluch nationalism. After the end of open hostilities, the Sindhi movement was strengthened by rising public opinion against Islamabad.[77]

After the twenty months of restoration of democracy, the dismissal of Benazir Bhutto, a Sindhi politician—whom the establishment had accepted reluctantly and then expelled unceremoniously—left a bitter taste in the province.

Sindhi ethno-nationalism, based on a separate Sindhi identity, had made inroads among young intellectuals largely due to the efforts of G. M. Syed, the veteran Sindhi politician who had been a one-time supporter of the demand for Pakistan. He was a charismatic leader with articulate ideas and sufficient economic resourcefulness to support his espousal of what was later known as Sindhi nationalism. He began his own political movement known as the Jeeye Sindh Movement.[78] In the late 1980s he became the unchallenged leader of Sindh National Alliance (SNA), which brought

---

[75]Ibid., p. 243.

[76]Seling S. Harrison, *In Afghanistan Shadow: Baluch Nationalism and Soviet Temptations*, p. 283.

[77]Hurst, 'Ethnic divide in Pakistan', p. 189.

[78]For his views, see G. M. Syed, *Struggle for a New Sind: A Brief Narrative of Working of Provincial Autonomy in Sind During the Decade (1937–1947)*, (Karachi: 1949); *Sindhi Culture* (Karachi: 1972).

together various ideological groups. However, the SNA failed to win any seat in the 1988, 1990 and 1993 elections, and Syed's dream of establishing a separate Sindhudesh by ousting the non-Sindhis was dashed to the ground.

Muhajir's Movement

The sudden and dramatic rise of the Muhajir Quami Movement (MQM) in Pakistan's Sindh province in the mid-1980s represents an important case study in cultural pluralism and is an example of very successful ethnic mobilization. The MQM's claim that Urdu-speaking *Muhajirs*, Muslims who left India after partition in 1947, constitute a fifth nationality (along with Punjabi, Pathan, Baluch and Sindhi) in Pakistan, was also a redefinition of political identity i.e., *Muhajir* for a community that had previously shunned particularistic identity in favour of a broader Muslim Pakistani identity.[79]

In 1984 General Zia-ul-Haq encouraged the Urdu-speaking minority in forming the MQM under the leadership of Altaf Hussain and Karachi became its operational base.[80] With repeated victories in the 1985 non-party election, national elections in 1988 and 1990, the MQM had established a virtual monopoly over representation of the Urdu-speaking community in Urban Sindh.

The MQM is exceptional in the recent history of Pakistan by virtue of its own specific characteristics—its predominantly urban, class-specific youthful membership, mobilized in the name of an 'imagined' ethnicity and motivated by radical ideas. It has been portrayed by its numerous opponents as a terrorist organization working for the Indian RAW or the former KGB to destabilize Pakistan.

Being an urban, youthful and organizationally well-knit party, the MQM has been able to mobilize some of the largest demonstrations in Karachi and Hyderabad at short notice even if it was

---

[79]Consult, Farhat Haq, 'Rise of the MQM in Pakistan: Politics of Ethnic Mobilization', *Asian Survey*, Vol. XXXV, No. 11 (November 1995), pp. 990–1004.
[80]Zia's interest in encouraging the MQM and providing it with training and fire arms was two-fold. First, it was seen to be a counterpoise to the PPP in the big cities of Sindh. Second, it aimed to divide Sindh on ethnic lines.

not in government. Its ward committees, *mohalla* (urban locality) units, regional sectors and overall provincial structures with international networks in the UK, the USA, and the Arabian Gulf have added to its political muscle. The MQM has received steady support from its financers and patrons and retained its own bands engaged in sniping, looting or kidnapping—as was witnessed in Hyderabad and Karachi, 1988 onwards.

Muhajir's Grievances

By the 1951 census, close to 55 per cent of the population of Karachi was *Muhajir*. During the first decade after partition, the Urdu-speaking *Muhajir* along with the Punjabis, had come to occupy a dominant position in Pakistan's political and bureaucratic arena.[81] According to one observer, 'For these centrist political elites Urdu as a national language and an emphasis on Islamic identity became the foundation for engineering a common national outlook within this multi-national state.'[82]

However, by the end of the 1950s the rising power of the military, an institution dominated by Punjabis and Pathans, pushed the Urdu-speaking elites to the status of junior partners in the power structure, the MQM alleged that Ayub Khan was guilty of systematic discrimination against the *Muhajirs* in urban Sindh and perceived Ayub's decision to move the capital from Karachi to Islamabad as a deliberate attempt to marginalize the *Muhajirs*.[83] But the shift in the power under Ayub Khan also brought technocratic elites into significant policy-making position, many of whom were Urdu-speaking *Muhajirs*. In Sindh, the *Muhajirs* continued to

---

[81]An account of important political offices from 1947 to 1958 shows both Punjabi-speaking refugees and Urdu-speaking refugees holding 18 out of total 27 offices of governor general/president, prime minister, provincial governors and chief ministers. See, Theodore P. Wright, Jr., 'Indian Muslim Refugees in the Politics of Pakistan', *Journal of Commonwealth and Comparative Politics* (July 1974), p. 191.

[82]Farhat Haq, 'Rise of the MQM in Pakistan', p. 991.

[83]During the December 1964 Presidential election, the *Muhajir* population of Karachi experienced the wrath of a Pathan (Pakhtun) backlash when Gohar Ayub Khan, son of President Ayub Khan launched a series of attacks on *Muhajir* communities because of their support for Fatima Jinnah, the sister of M.A. Jinnah, against Ayub Khan.

dominate the bureaucracy but Punjabis, and later Sindhis, claimed a greater share of such positions in the 1970s.[84]

During the 1960–1980 period, the *Muhajirs* witnessed a slow relative decline in their political and economic status. The young MQM supporters blame the quota system for what they believe to have been a dramatic decline in *Muhajir* socio-economic status. Many *Muhajirs* were aggrieved by Z. A. Bhutto's policies in the 1970s which were perceived as anti-*Muhajir* and pro-Sindhi.[85] The language controversy in 1972 further alienated the *Muhajirs* from Bhutto's government when the Sindh Assembly dominated by the Sindhi-speaking members of the PPP, passed a language bill declaring Sindhi to be a provincial language along with Urdu. This led to language riots in Karachi and the other *Muhajir*-dominated cities of Sindh.[86] Besides, the government decision to introduce an urban–rural quota in Sindh aroused the *Muhajirs'* fear of losing jobs and socio-economic status. Though, there has not been an absolute decline in the *Muhajir* share of jobs and admission, their share has dropped relative to that of the Punjabis, Pathans, and Sindhis. The alienation from Bhutto's government landed most *Muhajirs* on the anti-Bhutto platform of the Pakistan National alliance for the 1977 elections.

Initially, most *Muhajirs* supported Zia-ul-Haq's military regime. However, Zia's decade-long rule solidified Punjabi dominance and the share of the *Muhajirs* in the civil bureaucracy was further reduced under Zia. The *Muhajirs* have steadily seen their power and clout eroded in comparison with the other ethnicities. Under Zia's military regime, *Muhajirs* witnessed the loss of many of their positions to the politics of 'Punjabization'. Even after the restoration of democracy, Pakistan's governments have slowly pushed out the *Muhajirs'* representatives leaving *Muhajirs* worried about their future.

---

[84]See Feroz Ahmed, 'Ethnicity and Politics: The Rise of Muhajir Separatism', *South Asia Bulletin*, Vol. VIII (1988), pp. 55–57.

[85]For details consult, Moonis Ahmar, 'Ethnicity and State Power in Pakistan: The Karachi Crisis', *Asian Survey*, Vol. XXXVI, No. 10 (October 1996), pp. 1032–33.

[86]For Sindhi-Urdu language controversy, consult Tariq Rahman, 'Language and Politics in a Pakistan Province: The Sindhi Language Movement', *Asian Survey*, Vol. XXV, No. 11 (November 1995), pp. 1005–16.

Critics of the MQM argue that *Muhajirs* do not have any basis for claiming discrimination or oppression since they continue to be over-represented in key sectors of Pakistani society—the bureaucracy, management positions in the private sector, print and electronic media, the medical and legal professions, and educational institutions. Besides, some critics consider *Muhajir* nationalism a myth on account of two reasons. First, the term *Muhajir* is a temporary mark of identification for people who migrated from India to Pakistan at the time of partition. Second, *Muhajirs* do not belong to a single ethnic community but comprise various ethnic and racial groups having roots in the Indian provinces of Andhra Pradesh, Bihar, Gujarat, Madhya Pradesh, Uttar Pradesh, West Bengal and others.[87] Moreover, their demand for a new administrative set-up and better socio-economic status is totally contradictory to their previous 40 years of consistent opposition to the erosion of state power.

Supporters of *Muhajir* nationalism and the MQM point out that the search for identity among *Muhajirs* is logical and that many common factors can legitimize the feeling of a '*Muhajir* nation', common language, similar culture, common history of migration from India, and hostile and discriminatory attitude of ruling elites, collective sufferings at the hands of various regimes. *Muhajirs* accept the ideology of *Muhajir* nationalism based on equal rights and social justice. Their feelings of relative deprivation and loss of hope in the prevailing political order galvanized their sense of identity vis-à-vis Sindhi and other ethnic communities, setting the stage for confrontation with the state establishment. The MQM addressed this sense of 'relative deprivations' effectively, and thus became an extremely successful example of collective mobilization of ethnic loyalties.

During the 1980s and 1990s, the relative decline in the socio-economic status of the *Muhajirs* and the demographic factors provided fertile ground for ethnic mobilization of the Urdu-speaking community in urban Sindh. Large scale inter-province migration mainly from Punjab and NWFP to Sindh and continued existence of more than a million Afghan refugees, and the presence of millions of illegal immigrants have brought about a significant shift in the

---

[87]Moonis Ahmar, 'Ethnicity and State Power in Pakistan: The Karachi Crisis', pp. 1036–37.

ethnic composition of Sindh. According to one estimate, around 25,000 people, mostly from Punjab and NWFP, move to Karachi annually. The majority of these new migrants are in their twenties and are competing in the labour market.[88] The Punjabi and Pathan migration has added to the *Muhajir* perception of becoming marginalized and out of 26 demands put forward by the MQM in its 1988 Charter of Resolution, more than half concerned the population issue. Moreover, in Sindh, the urbanization spurred by internal and international migration exacerbated the already existing urban–rural divide between Sindhis and non-Sindhis.[89]

The arrival of Afghan refugees in the 1980s added to the volatile demographic situation in Karachi whose citizens associated the 'drug and arms mafia' with these new refugees, most of whom were Pathans. It was widely believed that a large portion of all the weapons supplied to Afghan *Mujahideen* fighters through Central Intelligence Agency (CIA) reached the private markets all over Pakistan. Undoubtedly, the easy availability of arms made the ethnic clashes more deadly and violent.[90]

But perhaps the single most important factor in the emergence of the MQM and *Muhajir* ethnicity was the rising nationalist sentiments of the Punjabis, Baluchs, Pathans and Sindhis. Until the mid-1980s, the dominant *Muhajir* response to nationalist assertions by other groups was to oppose ethnic particularism, support centrist forces, and commitment to the two-nation theory. The secession of East Pakistan and the emergence of Bangladesh was a defining moment for the *Muhajirs* in two specific ways. Bangladesh demonstrated the hollowness of the two-nation theory—the idea that Hindus and Muslims constituted two nations in the sub-continent the cornerstone of *Muhajir* Pakistani identity. The second important outcome for *Muhajir* identity was the Bihari refugee question.

In the 1980s, the *Muhajirs* reacted in response to their declining measure of power, to growing opposition from the Sindhi populance, and to their perception of an intransigent Punjabi control of Pakistan's bureaucracy and military. Altaf Husain's enigmatic

---

[88]Methab S. Karim, 'Karachi's Demographic Dilemma', *Dawn* (Karachi), *Friday Magazine* (Karachi), 27 February 1987, p. 1.
[89]Feroz Ahmed, 'Ethnicity, Class and State in Pakistan', *Economic and Political Weekly*, 23 November 1996, p. 3053.
[90]See Arif, 'Sindh in the Midst of Crisis', pp. 1898–99.

personality[91] coupled with oratorical skills and his ability to make his life experience a metaphor for the 'trials and tribulations' of the Urdu-speaking community in Pakistan enabled him to exercise complete control of the MQM until he went into voluntary exile in London in 1992. From 1987–1992 he gained control of the MQM. The MQM has used propaganda such as mass rallies, strikes, posters, graffiti, printed literature, audio and video cassettes to maintain its closed 'network'. Its titular leader, Altaf Hussain after his self exile in London—addressed as the *Quaid-i-Tehreek*—frequently used transcontinental satellite technology to address rallies in different countries.

Although unique in certain aspects, the MQM has suffered from a personality cult, with Altaf Hussain assuming the uncontested leadership by means of rhetoric, demagogy, ambiguity and coercion. For a long time, Hussain has remained the focal point through a combination of charisma, propaganda, machinations and the fascist structure of the movement. To many observers, Karachi had already become Pakistan's Beirut, largely due to the criminalization of ethnic dissent attributed to Altaf Hussain.

Altaf's wish for total control precluded any possibility of a democratic structure emerging within the organization. Critics of Altaf Hussain considered him unpardonable and the whole organization was run on the style of Nazi and fascist parties of Germany and Italy. They also accuse the MQM of adopting fascist methods in dealing with opponents and internal dissidents. They trace MQM's fascist record to when it was operating torture cells, using terrorist methods against the journalist community, and suppressing dissent within its own rank and file.

The Sindhi perception about *Muhajir* assertion of a separate identity is based on fears of loosing power if the present demographic status of the province is changed to the advantage of non-Sindhis, who now constitute more than 40 per cent of its population. Majority of the Sindhi elite is very suspicious of MQM demands and vowed not to allow any change in the province's administrative map. In a statement issued in July 1975, noted Sindhi intellectuals condemned the MQM's desire to divide Sindh and called

---

[91]For details see I. Bakhtiar, 'The Altaf Factor', *The Herald* (Karachi), January 1993, pp. 59–62. Also see Raymond Whitaker, 'Pakistan's Top Orator Divides Karachi Voters', *The Independent* (New York), 22 October 1990.

it an assault on the rights of Sindhis. These fears have provided the ruling PPP (1988–1990 and 1993–1996) an opportunity to strengthen its position in Sindh's rural areas as a viable counter to the MQM. By condemning the MQM agitation and its demand for *Muhajir* autonomy, the PPP has tried to portray the MQM as an anti-state and pro-Indian group, thus sending the message to the Punjabis that only the PPP is capable of ∴hwarting the organization's designs against the integrity of Pakistan.

Muhajir vs the State

The MQM had become a state within the state.[92] Karachi and the surrounding Sindhi region are the most troubled areas of Pakistan. The Sindh's major urban centre is regularly plagued with clashes between not only *Muhajirs* and Sindhis, but Sunni and Shia, vying political movements, and competing drug lords. The violence in Karachi remains unabated with new forces emerging. There were four separate conflicts involving rival criminal gangs, Sunni and Shia Muslims, native Sindhis and Urdu-speaking *Muhajirs*, and rival factions of the *Muhajir* community. In this inter and intra-ethnic fights the use of small arms is amazing. Extortion and illicit drug trafficking are part of normal business and have flourished under the cover of police-criminal nexus. This in turn has added to the violence making it more bloody.

The use of army, paramilitary and police to deal with a guerrilla war situation in Karachi and Hyderabad resulted in the further alienation of urban Sindh from Islamabad. The hostility between the MQM and the establishment deepened as a result of alleged extra-judicial killings of the MQM[93] members by the security forces. The stand-off between the government and the MQM with the implication for sustained violence has led to Karachi being called a 'bleeding wound of Pakistan.'[94]

---

[92]For details consult Moonis Ahmar, 'Ethnicity and State Power in Pakistan: The Karachi Crisis', pp. 1034–35.

[93]Mohammad Mirza, 'The Question of Custodial Killings', *Friday Times* (Lahore), 19–25 October 1995, p. 8.

[94]Moonis Ahmar, 'Ethnicity and State Power in Pakistan: The Karachi Crisis', p. 1035. Also see *India Today*, 15 July 1995.

The implications of the Karachi crisis are certainly different from the disturbances in Baluchistan in the mid-1970s and rural Sindh in the early and mid-1980s. Continuous turmoil in Karachi—the commercial centre of Pakistan—have caused massive damage to the economy[95] and society. The Karachi crisis is a major test case for Pakistani rulers, and its management is vital for the country's political and economic stability.

Politics of Coalition

After the restoration of democracy in Pakistan, the *Muhajirs* formed an alliance, first with the PPP government (1988–1990) and then with the Islamic Democratic Alliance (IDA) (1990–1993) and shared in cabinet positions both at provincial and federal levels. During the Benazir regime, the MQM ended the relationship in October 1989 and the army was called to restore order in the province.[96] However, a perpetual state of war with the PPP could not wipe out the cross-sectional support for the party, rather it weakened the MQM but strengthened its militant section.

History seemed to have come full circle in Pakistan in May 1992, when Nawaz Sharif reluctantly agreed to military action code-named 'Operation Clean-Up', to curb the dacoities and kidnapping in Sindh. Operation Clean-Up drove many MQM leaders and workers underground and allowed a splinter group, the MQM (Haqiqi), to claim to be the real MQM. The army tried to get rid of Altaf Hussain by patronizing the Haqiqi faction and enabled MQM (H) to start a turf battle against MQM (Altaf), forcing most top leaders and activists into hiding. Altaf Hussain turned his medical trip to London into self-exile. By the end of 1994, the Haqiqi faction had become discredited as a puppet of the army. Moreover, the three years repression of

---

[95]A research paper commissioned by the Karachi Chamber of Commerce and Industry revealed that 'a working day lost by strike in Karachi costs 1.3 billion rupees ($38 million and in 1995 a total 34 working days were lost as a result of strikes called by the MQM' cited from Moonis Ahmar, 'Ethnicity and State Power in Pakistan: The Karachi Crisis', p. 1035.

[96]See Zaffar Abbas, 'Sindh: Falling Apart?', *The Herald* (Karachi), May 1989, pp. 27–31. Also see Anwar Iqbal, 'Is the Tide Turning Against the MQM?', *The Muslim* (Islamabad), 17 May 1989.

MQM has not produced any result. The MQM's *Muhajir* base and the influence of its leader, Altaf Hussain, remains as strong as ever.

Massive use of state coercion under operation Clean-Up and criminal charges brought by the government against Altaf Hussain and MQM workers resulted in more and more radicalization of the party by frustrated ambitious workers. After brief cooperation in 1993, the MQM and the PPP reinitiated their polarization which pushed Karachi into the most violent phase in its history. The on-going militancy operation failed to stamp out violence and, despite massive cost and publicity, could not restore order in the city. Following cyclic phases in violence during 1995 had turned Karachi into an urban battlefield. Seeing the regime as vulnerable and lacking any policy initiative on strife-ridden Karachi, the MQM intensified its militancy in Karachi 'Bhutto's waterloo'. By early 1995 Karachi had become ungovernable largely due to ethnic violence. Gradually the conflict turned into civil war between the security forces and the MQM. Benazir and the MQM Altaf Hussain supported by hawkish elements in their respective organizations confronted each other in the worst showdown in Karachi's history which led to the killing of more than 1,200 citizens killed by mid-1995. Such polarization presented the most serious threat to the Pakistani state and civil society.[97] Today, *Muhajir* separatist sentiments are on the rise, the more radical elements of MQM agitate for a separate state of Karachi. While the governments in Islamabad and Sindh have become more and more brutal in their opposition to the MQM for fear of general anarchy and the loss of yet another province.

The MQM is now pursuing two contradictory strategies in response to the variety and intensity of challenges it faces. Recently it has occasionally used the name Muttahida Quami Movement (United National Movement), so far only as a tactical ploy since the MQM in all its incarnation remains confined to urban Sindh. Moreover, the MQM's rhetoric and actions have become more militant since the beginning of 1994; Altaf Hussain has accused the military of *Muhajir* genocide and compared the situation in urban Sindh to those in Bosnia and Indian Kashmir.[98]

---

[97]For details consult Iftikhar H. Malik, 'The State and Civil Society in Pakistan: From Crisis to Crisis', *Asian Survey*, Vol. XXVI, No. 7 (July 1996), pp. 673–90.
[98]Farhat Haq, 'Rise of the MQM in Pakistan', p. 1001. Also see Altaf Hussain in interview in *The Herald*, May 1994, p. 34.

The use of coercion to quell the MQM has not worked, nor will the MQM's drive to seek an autonomous status at the expense of Sindhi and other ethnic minorities. There is no military solution to the problem of Karachi. Karachi needs a constitutional package to deal with the economic, social and political deprivations. Moreover, the question of provincial autonomy is also imbibed with the problem of Sindh. *Muhajirs* cannot achieve economic and political autonomy without the support of other ethnicities.

The idea of a separate *Muhajir* state, as was mooted in the late 1980s among certain *Muhajir* sections, is quite impractical given the fact that *Muhajireen* are spread all over Pakistan. It has put forward the idea of the division of Sindh into two separate provinces, rural and urban respectively. Such an administrative division may not guarantee a resolution of the volatile pluralism in Karachi, rather it may exacerbate ethnic cleansing with the MQM expelling non-Urdu speakers from urban Sindh.[99]

The MQM may feel confident that no one can rule Pakistan peacefully while it is on the offensive; but it must not ignore the demographic realities of the 1990s, where Karachi has become the largest Pashtun city in the country. Equally, it needs to be remembered that there are more Baluchis in Karachi alone than in the entire province of Baluchistan and that Karachi has already become the sixth largest Punjabi town. Thus, the new imperatives demand more interdependence among these diversified communities.[100]

In sum, ethnicity is a factor to be reckoned with in Pakistan. At present, the nature of the state structure does not provide a favourable milieu for regional autonomy in the federal framework. The ethnic movements, howsoever inchoate and divided, continue to simmer. The coercive apparatus of the state may provide a tight lid on the ethnic cauldron without a safety valve which can only be in the form of an effective creditworthy mechanism for devolution of power to the federating units.

Today Pakistan is confronted with the problems of satisfying the needs of divergent ethnic interests within its borders while at the same time maintaining the integrity of its political boundaries. Islam has not been able to overcome national animosities nor was religion

---

[99]Iftikhar H. Malik, *State and Civil Society in Pakistan: Politics of Authority, Ideology and Ethnicity*, p. 254.
[100]Ibid., p. 255.

enough of a reason to prevent Bangladesh from breaking away. Politicized Islam is against the recognition of ethnic identities. Pakistan as an ideological state has always suppressed pluralism. In fact, pluralism is always thought to be a threat in ideological states. Fundamentalists demand that the exponents of five nationalities theory should be declared traitors. However, religious commonality alone cannot ensure political or even social and cultural homogeneity. The existence of ethnicity is an objective fact of life. It is imperative for Pakistan to restructure its system to accommodate this reality. Efforts towards achieving democracy, egalitarianism and devolution of real administrative and political power will save the day for Pakistan. Without this a sense of alienation could gain strength and lead to more frequent spates of ethnic militancy.

Chapter V

.

The Rising Tide of Islamic Fundamentalism in Pakistan

Contemporary Pakistan is under dark clouds of religious fundamentalism. It is in the name of Islam that the country has created an image of being the most potent source of religious terrorism, which poses a threat to peace and stability in large parts of the globe, let alone Pakistan itself. The biggest irony of Pakistan's history is that Islam, which was supposedly the raison d'etre of Pakistan, has not only been misused rather than used in its state construct of nation-building, but also became the biggest source of most of its internal conflicts in the last decade. During the last two decades, conflicts between different sects have sharpened, i.e., between Sunnis and Shias on one hand, and on the other between Sunnis themselves. These political conflicts are an expression of a deeper philosophical confusion as to what constitutes an Islamic state. History reveals no uniform pattern on which a religion-based state is structured.[1] Since religion had played an important role in the creation of Pakistan, the role of religion in the context of post-independence developments assumed significance. The *Ulama* (learned authorities on Islam) were in favour of Islam playing a dominant role in Pakistan. However, they were never clear and unanimous about

---

[1]Satish Kumar, 'Militant Islam: The Nemesis of Pakistan', *Aakrosh*, Vol. III, No. 6 (January 2000), reproduced in *Strategic Digest*, Vol. XXX, No. 8 (August 2000), p. 1075.

what the role should be. In contrast to this view, the modernist, Western-educated political leaders and intellectuals sought the Pakistani state to be based on the Western parliamentary model, with Islam playing a role only in the personal lives of the people.

Pakistan moved towards vigorous Islamization from the mid-1970s onwards, but all such attempts only further accentuated the sectarian conflicts and contradictions in Pakistan. In this context an eminent scholar succinctly remarks, 'Islamization in Pakistan has travelled a rocky road.... Greeted with skepticism by some and with enthusiasm by many, the process thus far has led to frustration, disillusionment and opposition.... Pakistanis have found it easier to rally under the umbrella of Islam in opposition movements, e.g., against the British and Hindu rule or, more recently, against the Bhutto regime, than to agree upon what Islam and an Islamic state are....'[2]

The increasing clout of militant organizations in the internal and external affairs of Pakistan could be explained in terms of Pakistani elites' failure to discover alternative sources of inspiration to sustain and strengthen the country. Ever since the emergence of Pakistan, the ruling elite, which comprises the army, the bureaucracy, and the political class, and the people of Pakistan, have permitted themselves to be held

hostage to the belief that since Islam was the only justification for the creation of Pakistan, it is in the name of Islam alone that Pakistan can be held together. And this despite the warning given by *Quaid-i-Azam* Muhammad Ali Jinnah ... that the political role of Islam was over after Pakistan had been achieved.[3]

At various points of time in Pakistan's history, religion has been exploited by the ruling elite to gain popularity and legitimacy and fight political opponents. Thus, in the case of Pakistan, religion has been used negatively rather than positively in terms of national integration. The unwillingness of Pakistan's leadership 'to rise up to popular expectations, and more importantly their cynical manipulation of religious emotions and concern of the masses, giving rise to

---

[2]John L. Esposito, 'Islam: Ideology and Politics in Pakistan', in Ali Banuazizi and Myron Weiner (eds.), *The State, Religion and Ethnic Politics: Pakistan, Iran and Afghanistan* (Lahore: Anguard Publishers, 1987), pp. 360–61.

[3]Satish Kumar, 'Militant Islam: The Nemesis of Pakistan', p. 1085.

unending social and political confusions and uncertainties have been the source of a human tragedy of an epic proportion.[4] The story of Pakistan's politics since its inception is one of the blatant pursuit of political self-interests by Pakistan's ruling elites disguised in religious discourse.

It is worth noting that in Pakistan, military rulers as well as civilian rulers with autocratic tendencies used Islam as an instrument. In the words of an eminent observer, 'The result was that Islamist elements over the years acquired extra- constitutional power and influence disproportionate to their support among the electorate. This extra-constitutional power has become a major source of instability and disruption in Pakistan, and a threat to peace in the region.'[5]

This chapter aims to analyze the factors involved in the Islamic upsurge and its consequences in Pakistan's society. It also discusses the use of Islamic idioms by the political leadership in Pakistan to promote its own political goals. It would also take into account the profound impact of the rise of sectarian Islamic fundamentalism and violence on the polity and society. Besides an attempt is made to read the portents of these developments as they are likely to contour the contemporary and future polity in Pakistan.

Consolidation of the Muslim Identity in Pre-Independent India

In fact the raison d'etre of the emergence of Pakistan was the Muslim desire to preserve and foster Islamic values. However, the consolidation of a distinct Muslim identity in India had started even before the idea of Pakistan was mooted in the minds of Muslim intellectuals. The quest for such an identity can be identified with the efforts of Syed Ahmed Khan and Amir Ali, for calling upon Muslims to strengthen the bonds of community, after the revolt of 1857. These efforts were akin to that of Shah Waliullah who urged the glorification of Islam in the wake of the disintegration of the

---

[4]Asim Roy, *Islam in South Asia: A Regional Perspective* (New Delhi: South Asian Publishers, 1996), pp. 149–50.
[5]Satish Kumar, 'Militant Islam: The Nemesis of Pakistan', p. 1076.

empire under Aurangzeb. In order to rehabilitate Islam or to secure the interests of the Indian Muslims, Shah Waliullah had gone as far as to invite Ahmed Shah Abdali to rid India of the scourge of the Marhattas. Fundamentalist revival sought to strip modern, innovative and foreign influence from the Islamic faith. The Indian Muslims under the impact of the Wahabi movement preached the slogan 'Back to the Koran' and sought to restore *Jihad* (holy war) for an Islamic ideal state. There had been the movements of the *Mujahideen* (one who participates in *Jihad*) led by Syed Ahmed Brelavi, dedicated to the establishment of an ideal Muslim state in the North-West Frontier, then part of the Sikh empire. In Bengal the Faraizi Movement led by Haji Shariatullah had similar aims. In both cases deterioration in the economic position of the Muslim peasantry had meant renewed interest in 'building' Islam in some insulated enclave.

Islam, however, became politically useful after the revolt of 1857. Its emotional appeal was noticed by the intellectuals. Freedom from religious encroachment became the new ideology and the Muslims of the subcontinent were convinced that their religion would continue to be in danger in the British regime. In this context, Abbas Rashid aptly remarks that the elite 'managed to foster a degree of general Muslim identification with issues like lack of education, discrimination in employment, inadequate political representation etc. Thus, while their use of Islam may have been subjectively opportunistic, it was nevertheless effective given the context.'[6] Later on, of course, the British policy of divide and rule widened the cleavages of Hindu-Muslim differences, encouraged the Muslim Leaguers and used them to counter the Congress to strengthen their rule. The widening gulf between the two communities was politically institutionalized when the Indian Council Act of 1909 gave constitutional recognition to separate electorates (for Muslims and non-Muslims). Besides, increasing influence of Hindu hardliners and later on Hindu militants in the Congress consolidated the differences between the two communities and the Muslims felt alienated. The Muslim League came into being more or less out

---

[6]Abbas Rashid, 'Pakistan: The Ideological Dimension, in Mohammad Asghar Khan (ed.), *Islam, Politics and The State: The Pakistan Experience* (London: Zed Press, 1985), p. 75.

of insecurity among the Muslims with the rise of radical Hindu religious groups.

Within the Muslim community, in contrast to the Western-ized elite, the orthodox religious leaders or traditionalists who strug-gled to attain a position of leadership, regarded the credentials of the former to lead the Muslim *Ulama* with contempt. They considered the Muslim League a bunch of loyalist toadies and accused them of cooperating with the Satans of Europe against the Islamist Caliphate and Pan-Islamism. They felt equally strongly about being Indian nationalists as being Pan-Islamicists. The orthodox religious leaders at the end of the First World War were instrumental in launching the Khilafat movement against the British and they were actively supported by the Congress. This for the first time mobilized the large number of Indian Muslims against the British on the basis of religion.[7] Though this movement was an exhibition of Hindu-Muslim unity, for the first time, it awakened the Muslims, rekindled their consciousness and made them aware of their potential to fight the British and politicized them. These changes, keenly observed by the educated Muslim elites, convinced them they could create a separate constituency for effective mass mobilization on the basis of religion to achieve their goal. After the 1937 elections, when the Congress captured power in 7 out of 11 constituencies, the Muslim insecurity about a possible Hindu domination became more entrenched in their psyche.[8]

For the first time during the British rule, creation of a separate entity for the Muslims within or without the British Empire was given a territorial shape by Mohammad Iqbal in his presidential address to the annual session of the Muslim League in 1930. However, Iqbal prescribed cultural uniqueness to be coterminous with territoriality. He definitely urged for autonomy rather than inde-pendence, nonetheless he was the first to impinge on the idea of territoriality to mobilise the Muslims. The Lahore resolution adopted by the Muslim League clearly defined the territoriality of the pro-posed Muslim state by including the north-western and eastern zones of India to be grouped together to constitute independent states where the unit would be autonomous. It is interesting to note

[7]Ibid.
[8]Smruti S. Pattanaik, 'Islam and the Ideology of Pakistan', *Strategic Analysis*, Vol. XXII, No. 9 (December 1998), p. 1275.

here that the resolution did not mention anything about the state being based on Islamic ideology. About the ideological basis of the two-nation theory, Iqbal is also known for his secular credentials.[9]

Islam and Politics: The Formative Phase

In 1947 Pakistan emerged as a nation, embodying Muslim aspirations, on the basis of the ideology of Islam. Mohammad Ali Jinnah, the founder of Pakistan who was westernized in his orientation, had no desire to make Pakistan a theocratic state ruled by religious priests. His idea of Pakistan as an embodiment of the fundamental principles of Islam was based on liberal ideology. The political elite thought that in due course of time, the introduction of liberal democracy would marginalize the fundamentalist orthodoxy, represented by the Jamaat-i-Islami and other right wing Islamic parties. The liberal elite led the Pakistan movement to create a modern democratic state in which the will of the people would be supreme. They saw no conflict between Islam and democracy. In fact, they often described the concept of democracy and equality as Islam's gifts for all of humankind. On the other hand were orthodox clerics who stood for a theocracy presided over by a priestly class. The two-nation theory and the use of religious idiom for the furtherance of purely political goals made a confrontation between the two forces unavoidable.[10] There has been an ongoing battle between them throughout the five decades of Pakistan's history. What made this contest unequal was the tendency on the part of the advocates of the democratic model to compete with their opponents on the latter's ground and to persist in the exploitation of religion for limited political gain.[11] Pakistan's constitutional history, therefore, has been one of struggle to make Pakistan a liberal democratic state on one hand and to make it conform as much as possible to Islamic orthodoxy on the other.

---

[9]Ibid., also see A. M. Zaidi (ed). *Evolution of Muslim Political Thought in India*, Vol. I (New Delhi: Michiko and Panjathan, n.d.), p. 66.

[10]I. A. Rehman, 'The Divine Right of Nawaz Sharif,' *Newsline* (Karachi), September 1998, p. 19.

[11]Ibid.

Jinnah's Secularism vs Religious Orthodoxy

After the creation of Pakistan, the leaders of the Pakistan movement, the ruling Muslim elites, emphasized the virtues of democratic and liberal governance. But orthodox elements would not let them build up such a system. The tug of war between the orthodox and liberal elements would characterize the debates on constitution-making in the formative years of Pakistan.

The orthodox section was ironically led by Maulana Maududi of Jamaat-i-Islami, who once considered Jinnah's idea of a Muslim nation 'fallacious formulation'[12] and was opposed to the formation of Pakistan. But once Pakistan was a reality, Maududi was a major centre of influence. He would ridicule the democratic liberal approach to constitution making and say: 'If a secular and Godless instead of Islamic constitution was to be introduced, what was the sense in all this struggle for a separate Muslim homeland?'[13]

The opponents of the Islamic state claim that Jinnah's ideal was a modern national secular state. Jinnah said that the new state would be a modern democratic state with sovereignty resting in the people, and the members of the 'new nation would have equal rights of citizenship regardless of their religion, caste and creed.'[14]

Jinnah, from the point of view of Islamic dogma, was not religious. Even in the movement for Pakistan he provided the tactics and not the thought behind it. He asked the people to be Pakistani first.[15] He never meant Pakistan to be a theocratic state. In his speech to the inaugural session of the Pakistan Constituent Assembly on 11 August 1947, he presented a clear picture of a secular state.

---

[12]Maududi is best known as the founder of the Jamaat-i-Islami and for his prolific writings on the nature of the Islamic State, which have inspired Islamic resurgence movements throughout the world. For a concise statement of his thought concerning the nature of an Islamic State, see *Islamic Law and Constitution* (Lahore: Islamic Publications, 1983).

[13]Quoted in Akbar S. Ahmed, *Pakistan Society: Islam, Ethnicity and Leadership in South Asia* (Delhi: Oxford University Press, 1988), p. 17.

[14]The Report of the Court of Inquiry, Punjab Disturbances of 1953 (Lahore, 1954), pp. 206–7. Also see Akbar S. Ahmed, *Pakistan Society: Islam, Ethnicity, and Leadership in South Asia*, p. 17, and Aziz Ahmed, *Islamic Modernism in India and Pakistan 1957–1964* (London: Oxford University Press, 1967), p. 214.

[15]See *Speeches of Quaid-i-Azam Mohammad Ali Jinnah as Governor General of Pakistan* (Islamabad: Ministry of Information and Broadcasting, n.d.). pp. 5–12.

He said: 'I think we should keep in front of us as our ideal and you will find that in course of time Hindus would cease to be Hindus and Muslims would cease to be Muslims, not in the religious sense, because that is the personal faith of each individual, but in the political sense as citizens of one nation.'[16]

Jinnah could possibly have added that they will continue to be Hindus and Muslims in a cultural sense. For this was an aspect of the new state that the westernized elite tended to ignore. As Abbas Rashid remarks aptly in this context, they felt

> that a less 'Islamic' Pakistan would automatically transform itself into a more liberal one. They mistook their position of relative strength in Pakistani society as evidence of a popular deep-rooted partiality towards western liberalism. This was a major error. Where they needed to articulate Islam in ways that would render it adequate to confront the real problems that the Muslim nation faced in the middle of the twentieth century—of disparity, hunger, disease, illiteracy, etc.—they were sidelining it into an exclusively personal realm. Instead of elaborating Islam's secular and liberal content, they were substituting for it a western, Eurocentric liberalism.[17]

On the other hand, the *Ulama*, after the creation of Pakistan, lacking credibility due to their known opposition to the formation of Pakistan, to prove their credentials and commitment to Islam, tried to press for Shariat to be the basis of the constitution. The demand became more convincing because 'the very ideology of Muslim nationalism, however ambiguously formulated and wrapped in populist terminology, contained immanently a religious character.'[18]

However, the orthodox or traditionalists also had no idea about 'how Islam could be presented in a positive ideological formulation, i.e., how to extrapolate from the religion of Islam the structure of economic and political systems that could be implemented in Pakistan....'[19] Maudidi, recognizing the nature of

---

[16]Ibid., p. 10. For details see Muhammad Munir, *From Jinnah to Zia: A Study of Ideological Convulsion* (Lahore: Vanguard Books, 1980), pp. 29–30.

[17]Abbas Rashid, 'Pakistan: The Ideological Dimension,' p. 83.

[18]Ishtiaq Ahmed, *The Concept of an Islamic State in Pakistan* (Lahore: Vanguard, 1991), p. 79.

[19]Abbas Rashid, 'Pakistan: The Ideological Dimension', p. 84.

opportunity, proceeded to occupy a significant position in the efforts to provide the specifics of an Islamic state—'a goal that the Objective Resolution adopted by the Constituent Assembly in March 1949 appeared to accept.'[20] It was (Islam) a powerful instrument in the hands of politicians in the time of 'uncertainty and confusion over the raison d'etre of Pakistani society and the goal it had meant to pursue.'[21]

In the formative phase of Pakistan, realizing the ethnic challenges to national integration, the political elites tried to reorient Islam in order to neutralize sub-national identities. Thus, the Islamic identity was displayed overzealously and people were urged to be sensitive to the Islamic ethos and culture as their only identity which is coterminous with their Pakistani identity (a state based on religion).

Objective Resolution: *Ulama's* Victory The Objective Resolution strove to embody an Islamic concept of a state that would serve as the foundation of Pakistan. The terms of Objective Resolution differ in all basic matters from the position Jinnah had taken in his speech of 11 August 1947. Whereas the founder of Pakistan had said sovereignty would rest with the people of Pakistan, the Resolution stated that it rests with the God Almighty. The sovereignty of the legislature being confined 'within the limits prescribed of Him' were counter to the democratic principles that there were no limits on the legislative power of a representative assembly. 'The first assault', as I. A. Rehman aptly observes, 'on the democratic model *Quaid-i-Azam* had for Pakistan was mounted by his successor in authority, Liaquat Ali Khan, when he produced the Objective Resolution. The Resolution was conceived as a measure to suppress the debate generated by a clash of interest between those who were solely concerned with state-building regardless of the means employed, and those who could not give up the aspirations of regional autonomy and national self-realization that the Lahore Resolution had aroused.'[22]

---

[20]Ibid.
[21]Ibid.
[22]I. R. Rehman, 'The Divine Right of Nawaz Sharif', p. 9.

The Ahmadis/Qudiani's Controversy

The orthodox religious views, for the first time in Pakistan's history, found political expression when their demand to expel the Ahmadias (viewed as heretical by most Muslims due to their rejection of the finality of Mohammad's prophethood) surfaced in 1953 in Punjab. The vulnerability of the westernized elites was exposed when they imposed martial law for the first time in Pakistani history to restore law and order. As Rashid Abbas has maintained, 'from being concerned exclusively with the defence of Pakistan's geographical frontiers, the army had taken its first step towards becoming an arbiter in the realm of ideology.'[23] However, for the first time, this also demonstrated the effectiveness of Islam as a political weapon in the hands of the opposition which consequently disarmed the politicians ideologically. Though many of the ruling elites were convinced about the misuse of Islam and its future implications, they lacked the strength to say so openly in an Islamic country without being criticised by fundamentalists who had strengthened their hold on certain sections of the masses.

The 1956 Constitution

The views of the *Ulama* were accommodated to a large extent in the 1956 constitution by endorsing certain Islamic principles and declaring Pakistan an Islamic Republic. No doubt, the constitution had an Islamic facade but the hard core was missing. By failing to address clearly the issue of Islam's role in the state, the 1956 Constitution added to the ideological confusion that existed regarding the nature and ideology of the Pakistani state.

One of the important factors in Pakistan's politics is the different interpretations of Islam which have made it difficult to evolve a common bond of allegiance. Thus, the government could not find a single binding link to evolve an Islamic ideology. There were internal incongruencies and contradictions in the ideas of orthodox religious bodies who are presumed to be authorities on religion and ideology. This was reported in Chief Justice Mohammad Munir's report which maintained '...keeping in view the several definitions given by the *Ulama*, need we make any comment except

---

[23]Abbas Rashid, 'Pakistan: The Ideological Dimension', p. 85.

that no two learned divines are agreed on this fundamental. If we attempt our own definition as each learned divine has done and that definition differs from that given by all others, we unanimously go out of the fold of Islam and if we adopt the definition given by one of the *Ulama*, we remain Muslims according to the view of the *alim* (scholar) but *kafirs* (infidels) according to the definition of everyone else.'[24] However, Islam was not declared the state religion by the 1956 constitution.

Role of Islam During Ayub's Rule

Major General Iskander Mirza abrogated the 1956 Constitution after his military coup in 1958. When General Ayub Khan himself seized power from Iskander Mirza a few weeks later, he wanted to introduce modern reformist Islam and tried to minimize the role of the religious elite. The Presidential Ordinance of 1962 actually dropped the word 'Islamic' from the country's title.[25] However, he reinstated the word Islamic Republic of Pakistan by introducing the First Constitution Amendment Bill, 1963, under pressure from religious parties. His secular credentials were confirmed with the implementation of the Family Law Ordinance of 1961. Ayub's ordinance on the 'Muslim Family Laws, 1962' invited sharp reaction from the right wing fundamentalists because they believed that the ordinance violated many injunctions of the *Quran* and *Sunnah* (Traditions of the Prophet) and the centuries old established practices of the Muslim society.[26]

However, as political trouble mounted for Ayub, the Advisory Council for Islamic Ideology that was provided for in the 1962 Constitution was set up under the chairmanship of Justice Abu Saalch Mohammad Akram and it gave 24 recommendations to the government relating to the controversial Muslim Family Laws Ordinance of 1962, interest (*usury*), the use of alcohol in official

---

[24]'Report of Court of Inquiry Constituted Under Punjab Act II of 1954 to Enquire into Punjab Disturbances of 1953, The Munir Report, Lahore: Superintendent, Government Printing, 1954, p. 259; cited in Muhammad Munir, *From Jinnah to Zia: A Study of Ideological Convulsion*, p. 146.

[25]Article 1(i) of the 1962 Constitution.

[26]Anwar Hussain Syed, *Pakistan—Islam, Politics and National Solidarity* (New York: Praeger, 1982), p. 110.

ceremonies, the sanctity of *Ramadan*, the revision of educational policies, the making of Islamic studies a compulsory subject in schools and colleges, the voluntary collection of *Zakat* (charity) etc. Ayub accepted most of the recommendations in a bid to win support for his badly floundering civilianizing process under the Basic Democracies scheme.

It is noteworthy that Ayub's contempt for the *Ulama* and his tight grip over the country's affairs kept sectarian controversies at bay. Unlike the early days of Pakistan when Muslim League leaders deferred to the *Ulama* and lost in the bargain, Ayub made only the most minimal concessions to them and Pakistan remained a forward looking modern nation, though he also kept the country bereft of democratic rights.

However, Ayub Khan did not hesitate to use the Islamic card as a political survival tactic. During the 1965 elections, he sought the help of orthodox religious groups to issue a *fatwa* (a ruling by a jurist on the legality or otherwise of an action) to delegitimize the contesting of Fatima Jinnah (Jinnah's sister), for presidentship of Pakistan on the religious ground that a woman cannot become head of an Islamic state. It is also well known that for the purpose of political legitimacy he cultivated *Pirs* (teachers) and *Mashaiks* (religious leaders).

In the late 1960s the *Ulama* also joined the widespread agitation against Ayub's authoritarian rule, probably because they believed that only in a democratic environment could they once again press their case for Islamization. As the general elections of 1970 approached, a polarization of the political right and left had already emerged.

During Yahya Khan's rule in 1971 the *Ulama* also supported the government for the army crackdown in East Pakistan because they considered Mujibur Rahman to be secular in orientation. Thus, it was not only the political leadership who gained from the partnership with these groups but the orthodox groups also consolidated themselves politically and became well entrenched in the system. Till Ayub Khan's advent, the policies pursued were in conformity with liberal Islam and religion was considered largely a private matter. However, during Ayub's period, under pressure, the liberals quickly yielded to the Islamist lobby for reasons of expediency and convenience. More often than not, such efforts lacked credibility, stemming from an opportunistic and often cynical use of religion by these who were seen as liberal and secular in conflict.[27]

The Bhutto Period: Resurgence of Political Islam

Z. A. Bhutto, who fell out with his patron Ayub over the issue of 'Tashkent Declaration', emerged as the symbol of democratic aspirations of the masses. But sensing a challenge from the fundamentalist Jamaat-i-Islami, he cleverly coined the phrase 'Islamic Socialism' to attract as large a number of people as possible. Bhutto after coming to power became the major architect of Islamic solidarity in national and international politics. The 1973 Constitution, betraying the impact of Islamic fundamentalism, contained many Islamic provisions stronger than the ones stipulated in all previous constitutions. For the first time Islam was declared the state religion. According to Article 31, one of the fundamental principles of state policy was to enable the Muslims of Pakistan to order their lives in accordance with the principles of Islam. The teaching of Islamiyat and Holy *Quran* was made compulsory for Muslims. The Council for Islamic Ideology (CII)[28] was formed to give advice to the state and provincial governments so that the existing laws could be passed and implemented according to the tenets of the *Quran* and *Sunnah*.[29] In 1974 the Jamiatul Ulama-i-Islam (JUI), Jamaat-i-Islami (JI), and Jamiatul Ulama-i-Pakistan (JUP) raised the question of declaring the Ahmadis or Qadianis as non-Muslims. Gradually the movement picked up momentum and finally Bhutto yielded to their demand by proclaiming the Ahmadis/Qadianis as non-Muslims through a constitutional amendment. The Islamization process initiated by Bhutto used emotive religious phrases like *Musawat-e-Muhammadi* (the equality of the followers of Mohammad) and *Islamic Musawat* (Islamic equality) as part of the political rhetoric to gain the

---

[27]Abbas Rashid, 'Pakistan: The Politics of Fundamentalism', in Kumar Rupesinghe and Khawar Mumtaz (eds.), *Internal Conflicts in South Asia* (London: Sage Publications, 1996), pp. 63–64.

[28]*The Constitution of Islamic Republic of Pakistan 1973*, pp. 122–24. Also see, Mohammed Munir, *From Jinnah to Zia: A Study of Ideological Convulsion*, p. 93.

[29]Consult Som Anand, 'Islamism and Pakistan's Social Realities', *Man and Development*, Vol. II, No. 1 (March 1980), pp. 97–100.

support for his policies.[30] Religious instructions were made compulsory for Muslim and non-Muslim students. In foreign affairs too Pakistan successfully used the changed environment to strengthen its political position and gain closer alignments in economic, social, cultural political and military affairs.

Before the elections in 1977, nine opposition parties came together under the banner of the Pakistan National Alliance (PNA). Apart from its economic demands it revived the demand for an Islamic state. Having lost the elections (in 1977 the elections were rigged), the PNA raised the slogan of *'Nizam-e-Mustafa'*, i.e., the pattern of government the holy prophet had given under his auspices to the state of Medina. Bhutto once again yielded in his effort to defuse the PNA onslaught and asked the CII to prepare within six months a plan for the enforcement of *Shariat* (Islamic law) in Pakistan. With the spread of anti-Bhutto campaigns in January–February 1977, he laid more emphasis on religious issues. The word socialism was replaced by the word *Musawat-e-Muhammadi*. More emphasis in the People's Party's programme for the future was on Islam.[31] The government tried to defuse the situation by announcing 'Islamic' reforms. Bhutto banned liquor shops, gambling, horse racing, night clubs, etc. and changed the weekly holiday from Sunday to Friday. However, Bhutto's choice to compete with orthodox clerics in political exploitation of religion proved suicidal.

The PNA was also backed up by armed forces for tactical reasons. Zia taking advantage of the turmoil in Pakistan was successful in preventing the opposition from concluding a deal with Bhutto. Consequently, Bhutto increasingly began depending on the army. Zia used the opportunity to intervene and remove Bhutto through a bloodless coup on 5 July 1977.

In this context, the composition and characteristics of the PNA and their subsequent collaboration with the military in an effort to rule Pakistan in the name of Islam are adequate testimony to the existence of a conspiracy on the part of Bhutto's civilian opponents—a large number of whom were affiliated with religious parties—and

---

[30]Riaz Hassan, 'Islamization: An Analysis of Religious, Political and Social Change in Pakistan', *Middle Eastern Studies*, Vol. XXI, No. 3 (July 1983), p. 263.
[31]*Dawn*, 4 March 1976.

the army high command to bring Bhutto down and replace the 'un-Islamic' regime with an 'Islamic' one.[32]

The definite appeal of Islamic slogans to General Head-quarters could plausibly be interpreted in terms of the changing ethos of Pakistan's military leadership.[33] A throw back to Islamic slogans appeared very attractive to the homespun officers—trained at Quetta and Karachi—who had suffered the humiliation of 1971 when the Sandhurst-trained generals were in command. The former now found solace in religion, which also provided them the main basis of legitimacy for the reimposition of military rule.[34]

Zia-ul-Haq: Legitimatization Through Islam

Zia-ul-Haq used Islam as a legitimization strategy for the consolidation of his autocratic military rule in an unprecedented manner and therefore cultivated and strengthened Islamist elements most vigorously. In marked contrast to the earlier two regimes of Ayub and Yahya, over 11 years Zia perpetuated his rule 'through a combination of repression, the shameless utilization of Islam and an elaborate series of carefully orchestrated political initiatives designed to lull the masses.'[35] Zia's obsession with 'puritanical and aggressive championing of the cause of Islam'[36] was apparently born out of his

---

[32]Mohammad Ayoob, 'Two Faces of Political Islam: Iran and Pakistan Compared', *Asian Survey*, Vol. XIX, No. 6 (January 1979), p. 538.

[33]Mohammad Ayoob, 'Pakistan Comes Full Circle', *India Quarterly*, Vol. XXIV, No. 1 (January–March 1978), pp. 17–18.

[34]Ibid., pp. 18–19.

[35]Tariq Ali, *Can Pakistan Survive: The Death of a State* (Harmondsworth: Penguin, 1983), p. 138. Also, see Marvin G. Weibaum and Stephen P. Cohen, 'Pakistan in 1982: Holding on', *Asian Survey*, Vol. XXIII, No. 2 (February 1983), pp. 123–31; and William L. Richter, 'Pakistan in 1984: Digging In', *Asian Survey*, Vol. XXV, No. 2 (February 1985), pp. 149–50. Also consult H. Alavi, 'Pakistan and Islam—Its Ethnicity and Ideology', *Mainstream*, 21 February 1987, pp. 151–52; and 28 February 1987, pp. 15–25.

[36]William L. Richter, 'The Political Dynamics of Islamic Resurgence in Pakistan', *Asian Survey*, Vol. XIX, No. 6 (June 1979), p. 555 and his 'Persistent Praetorianism: Pakistan's Third Military Regime', *Pacific Affairs*, Vol. LI, No. 3 (Fall 1978), pp. 277–93. For an excellent account of Islamic state in Pakistan within a

political motives or compulsions for survival in the wake of the changing social and political composition, and the ethos of the officer corps in the 1970s.[37] Being conscious of the need to broaden his political base on the one hand and the masses' attachment to Islam on the other hand, Zia shrewdly exploited religion to 'evoke an emotional response' in support of his regime.[38] By the proclamation of the 'Islamic System' in Pakistan, Zia legitimized his continuation which 'rescued' Pakistani ideology. He had, therefore, a 'divine mission' and the army acted as the defender of the state ideology.[39]

So far as the compatibility of democracy with Islam is concerned, Zia had used Islam as the very strategy for survival and stated on several occasions that Islam had no such things as political parties, western-type democracy, the division of power among the executive authority and autonomous legislative and independent judiciary.[40] He considered democracy as out of step with the Muslim

---

theoretical framework see Lawrence Ziring, 'From Islamic Republic to Islamic State in Pakistan', *Asian Survey*, Vol. XXIV, No. 9 (September 1984), pp. 931–46.

[37]For details consult Mohammad Ayoob, 'Pakistan Comes Full Circle', pp. 18–91 and his 'Two Faces of Political Islam: Iran and Pakistan Compared', pp. 538–39; and Tariq Ali, *Can Pakistan Survive*, pp. 139–42.

[38]Omar Asghar Khan, 'Political and Economic Aspects of Islamization', in Asghar Mohammad Khan (ed.), *Islam, Politics and The State: The Pakistan Experience*, p. 127, and J. Henry Korson, 'Islamization and Social Policy in Pakistan', *Journal of South Asian and Middle Eastern Studies*, Vol. VI, No. 2 (Winter, 1982), p. 72; also see *Morning News* (Dacca), 9 October 1979.

[39]See Zia's interview to the British Broadcasting Commission as reported in *Dawn* (Karachi), 18 October 1982. Also see Press Conference at Lahore, *Daily Jang* (Rawalpindi), 22 March 1982; *The Muslim* (Islamabad), 22 March 1982; *Far Eastern Economic Review*, 2 April 1982; and *Daily Jang* (Rawalpindi), 2 August 1982. See Munir D. Ahmed, 'The Current International Constellation in Pakistan', *Journal of South Asian and Middle Eastern Studies*, Vol. VI, No. 4 (Summer, 1983), pp. 80–81.

[40]It is important to note that Zia commissioned the Council for Islamic Ideology (CII) to work out guidelines on the future political structure pursuing Islamic lines. The CII in its report to the President in April 1982 recommended that the elections as well as the party system are consistent with Islam and proposed direct elections for 60 per cent of seats of the Council of Advisers. Zia flatly rejected these recommendations and sent them back to the CII for further deliberation. With a view to diminishing the importance of the CII and qualifying its recommendation, Zia let it be known that two or three other institutions, (without giving their names) had been working on this question on behalf of the regime and they would be submitting their proposals. See *Nawa-i-Waqt* (Lahore), 4 August 1982. Also see, Duran Khalid, 'The Final Replacement of the Parliamentary

psyche. Obviously Zia's intention was to deride democracy through a self-justifying interpretation of Islam.[41] He consistently circumvented the democratic process and condemned political parties and the opposition, popular participation and favoured the institution of 'Amir' or one man rule for the country. 'Muslims,' according to him, 'believe in one God, one prophet, and one book, and their tendency is that they should be ruled by one man.'[42]

Similarly, under the regime's grand Islamic framework the legal powers of the judiciary in Pakistan were constantly subject to coercion, harassment, bribery, blackmail and every uncivilized effort to convert it into a tool of the military regime and a mockery of the institution of judiciary. The possibility of the judiciary exercising even a semblance of independence was finally put to an end on 24 March 1981, by the eighteen-article Provisional Constitution Order (PCO).

Post-Zia perceptive analysts such as M. Ilyas Khan and Ziagham Khan have held Zia's attitude towards politics responsible for changing the nature and course of Pakistan's politics along dictatorial and fundamentalist-militant lines. According to them he rendered politics unworkable in Pakistan by blurring the distinction between politics and terrorism.[43] By raising the bogey of Al-Zulfikar and initiating a massive propaganda campaign against terrorism, he hanged, flogged and imprisoned pro-democracy political activists. In this context, Ilyas Khan and Zaigham Khan observe, 'In the new order (created by Zia), anything that was democratic was branded as un-Islamic which in effect meant that all political parties agitating for democracy found themselves battling a holy warrior instead of a military dictator.'[44]

Democracy By the "Islamic System" in Pakistan', in Wolfgang Peter Zingel and Stephanie Zingel and Lallament (eds.), *Pakistan in the 80s: Ideology, Regionalism, Economy, Foreign Policy* (Lahore: Vanguard Books, 1985), pp. 263–309.

[41]For an interesting discussion on Islam and modern democratic institutions, see Mohammad Munir, *From Jinnah to Zia: A Study of Ideological Convulsion*, pp. 114–22.

[42]Nisar Osmani, 'Presidential System More Suitable', *Dawn*, 28 March 1978; A. R. Changez, 'Political Parties Have No Place in an Islamic State', *The Pakistan Times* (Lahore), 16 September 1977; also see his interview with Smith Hempostone, in *Dawn*, 20 March 1979, and *The New York Times* (New York), 17 August 1979.

[43]M. Ilyas Khan and Ziagham Khan, 'Zia and Politics: Attitude and Impact', *The Herald* (Karachi), August 1999, p. 54.

[44]Ibid.

In addition, General Zia altered the entire system of governance, from a parliamentary democracy headed by an elected prime minister to an arrangement that later came to be known 'the troika system'. In this 'troika system', the prime minister was only one of the three key decision-makers (along with the President and the Army Chief) and often not the most powerful one. 'The message was clear: any politician, even if he was elected to office, was not to be trusted and that there must exist a mechanism to keep him in check.'[45]

Thus, Zia's laws and policies resulted in making vast sections of the population extremely vulnerable to the Islamic militancy by replacing a tolerant and liberal civil society with an intolerant and retrogressive one. An eminent Pakistani commentator has observed, 'The question here is not one of the interpretation of Islam, but of the motives and the context in which it was enforced: Zia did not employ Islam with the intention of inculcating positive values, such as peace, and honesty, imbibed by Islam. His uses of religion was limited to aggregating power with an authoritarian state, through the police, army, and bureaucracy; exercising arbitrary control; and the denial of human rights to the Pakistani citizenry. Islam was enforced to deny women the right of being equal witnesses and to stifle freedom of expression, association, and even religion. A survey of laws and policies instituted by Zia reveals that Islam was invariably employed where rights were to be curtailed, and not for the expansion thereof.'[46] Zia-ul-Haq used Islam to perpetuate his autocratic rule but left behind a legacy of division, disruption, contradiction and conflicts.

Zia, in order to consolidate his power, sought to transform the economy and society according to the basic tenets of Islam.[47] However, in actual practice, through the ingeniously devised so-called 'Islamization' of the economy the Zia regime was appealing to the historical categories of feudalist Islam and justifying social and economic relationships based on a decadent status quo of feudalism and comprador capitalism by imposing the prequranic medieval

---

[45]Ibid.

[46]Hina Jilani, 'Zia and the End of Civil Society', *The Herald* (Karachi), August 1999, p. 3.

[47]See Khalid M. Ishaque, 'The Islamic Approach to Economic Activity and Development', *Pakistan Economist*, Vol. XVII, No. 20 (July 1977), pp. 13–23.

forms of *mudaraba* (profit sharing), *muzaraa* (share-cropping), *zakat* (charity), *ushr* (tithe), and *riba* (usury), which originated and developed in different social contexts. For example, *mudaraba* was reinterpreted and projected as a sacred religious principle to justify the maximization of profits under capitalism, both industrial and comprador. Islamic or interest-free banking is being developed on the basis of the medieval concept of *mudaraba*.[48]

All that was left to the regime to do, in the name of Islamization, was to undertake cosmetic measures, although the word 'cosmetic' is an outrageous word to describe barbaric punishments that were prescribed under *Hudood* (punishment under Islamic Law) Ordinances.

Zia's introduction of Islamic measures like *zakat, ushr,* and *hudood* punishments accentuated sectarian tension between the Sunnis and Shias. The Shias, who constitute nearly 25 per cent of population, claim that their school of traditional-legal thought, namely, Jafari *fiqh*, is different in its prescription from the Hanafi-based Sunni *fiqh*. Shia demonstrations in 1980 against *zakat* had led to violence and bloodshed. Islamic resurgence under Zia brought to the surface the differences among various Sunni sects too, e.g., Deobandi, Barelvi, Wahabi, Ahle Hadith, and so forth.[49]

Finally, in a crude attempt to use Islam as a cloak to thwart the aspirations of the masses and political dissenters, Zia introduced a repressive code, partially modelled on medieval Islamic punishment,[50] such as, public flogging, amputation of the hands of burglars and criminals, stoning to death of adulterers, execution of political

---

[48]For details see Veena Kukreja, 'The Zia Regime: Legitimization Through Islamization', *Strategic Analysis,* Vol. XV, No. 3 (June 1992), pp. 5–8. For detailed account of interest from banking see Khurshid Ahmed (ed.), *Studies in Islamic Economics* (Leicesur: The Islamic Foundation, 1981); Muazzan Ali (ed.), *Islamic Banks and Strategy of Economic Cooperation* (London: New Century Publishers, 1982); and Zia ul Din Ahmed, et. al., *Money and Banking in Islam* (Islamabad: Institute of Policy Studies, 1983).

[49]Satish Kumar, 'Militant Islam: The Nemesis of Pakistan', p. 1076.

[50]For details account of the Constitutional (Amendment), Order 1979 and *Hudood* Ordinance see Javid Iqbal, 'Islamization in Pakistan', *Journal of South Asian and Middle Eastern Studies,* Vol. VIII, No. 5 (Spring, 1985), pp. 38–52; and Kalim Bahadur', 'Problem of Secularism in Pakistan,' Pandev Nayak (ed.), *Pakistan: Dilemmas of a Developing State* (Jaipur: Aalekh Publishers, 1985), pp. 29–42.

activists, torture of political prisoners including women,[51] aimed at 'brutalizing Pakistan political culture.'[52] In sum, the path of exploiting religious ideology, on which the regime had embarked, was one leading to political bankruptcy rather than ideological consolidation.

Jihad as a Foreign Policy Instrument

Moreover, Zia used Islamic fundamentalism cleverly in order to strengthen Pakistan's relations with the Muslim countries in order to strengthen his position domestically. According to Eqbal Ahmed during the 1980s, there was trend towards the growth of 'fundamentalists neo-totalitarian Muslim movements' which is contrary to the political culture and historical traditions of the Muslim majority.[53] The fundamentalists such as Muslim Brotherhood in the Arab world, the Jamaat-i-Islami in Pakistan, the Sharekat Islam in Indonesia, and the Islamic government of post-revolution Iran seek to restore the past in its idealized form. But none of these move-

---

[51]Anita M. Weiss, 'Women's Position in Pakistan: Socio-Cultural Effects of Islamization', *Asian Survey,* Vol. XXIII, No. 2 (February 1983).

[52]Tariq Ali, *Can Pakistan Survive,* pp. 138–39 and for very perceptive observations, see Nubar Housepain, 'Pakistan in Crisis: An Interview with Eqbal Ahmad', *Race and Class,* Vol. XXII, No. 2 (Autumn, 1980), pp. 129–30. See also *Pakistan: Human Rights Violations and the Decline of the Rule of Law* (London: Amnesty International Publication, 1982); and *Amnesty International Report* 1985 (London: Amnesty International, 1985), pp. 233–37. Similar evidence was presented to US Congressional sub-committee hearing by Amnesty and other monitoring agencies in September 1981, see, 'The Current Human Rights Situation in Pakistan' statement submitted for the record by Amnesty International USA in hearings before the sub-committee on International Security and Scientific Affairs, Asian and Pacific Affairs, and International Economic Policy and Trade of the House Foreign Affairs Committee, September 1981; 'Atrocities of Military Rule in Pakistan', prepared by *Pakistan Committee for Democracy and Justice* (New York, September 1981). For additional details, 'Repression in Pakistan', *Man and Development,* Vol. V, No. 2 (June 1983), pp. 126–40; Pakistan Democratic Forum, 'Six Years of Arbitrary Rule: Massive Repression in Pakistan to Perpetuate Military Dictatorship,' *New Perspectives,* Vol. XIII, No. 6 (1983), pp. 23–26; and Anwar Tamachi, 'Anatomy of Zia Regime: A Tragic Story of Repression', *Secular Democracy,* Vol. XV, No. 4 (April 1982), pp. 27–37.

[53]Quoted from Surendra Chopra, 'Islamic Fundamentalism and Pakistan's Foreign Policy', *India Quarterly,* Vol. XLIX, Nos.1–2 (January–June 1993), pp.1–36.

ments succeeded in attracting the majority of workers, peasants and intelligentsia.[54]

Zia's significant objective of Islamization was concurrent with the Soviet military intervention in Afghanistan in 1979 as the Soviet invasion was depicted as 'Islam is danger'. Thus, the interest of the US and Pakistan converged as the US wanted to wage proxy war with Soviet Union via Pakistan. The US arms started flowing into the hands of the *Mujahideens*. However, the arms were diverted to create terror in Kashmir also. Afghan conflict has militarized Pakistan society.

Though religious extremism grew during General Zia-ul-Haq's 11 years rule, it was during Z. A. Bhutto's period that clergy realized its clout when he bowed to its demand to declare Ahmadias as *kafirs*. General Zia used the clergy against Bhutto and brought it close to the corridors of power, agreeing to its demand to set up *zakat* and *salat* (prayer) committees and sponsoring *Ulama* and *Mashaikh* (spiritual leaders) conventions and financing them. As a result *madrassas* (religious schools) and mosques grew in number and influence. These mosques have now been increasingly moving towards a system of sectarian apartheid.[55]

Highlighting the impact of Pak–Afghanistan nexus in the field of militancy and terrorism, an eminent Pakistani journalist points out in his report that the number of registered religious institutions in the NWFP, according to official statistics, was above 1,000 in 1999. There was no official estimates of other *madrassas* run by individuals in various parts of Frontier and Tribal Areas, and the Northern Areas. According to conservative estimates, some 20,000 Afghan students were enrolled in various religious institutions in the NWFP and the overall strength of students at these seminaries is likely to be above 100,000. Officials in the country's security agencies believe that 15 to 20 of these religious institutions pose a potentially grave threat to law and order.[56]

In sum, Zia's cynical exploitation of Islam may have produced revulsion among the educated, but the Islamists appetite

---

[54]Eqbal Ahmed, 'Islam and Politics', in Mohammad Asghar Khan (ed.), *Islam, Politics and the State: The Pakistan Experience*, p. 25.

[55]M. K. Dhar, 'Iran Voices Concern Over Pak Violence', *The Hindustan Times* (New Delhi), 28 February 1995, p. 12.

[56]Behroz Khan, 'Sectarian Spill Over', *Newsline* (Karachi), October 1999, p. 76.

grew. It is apparent that Pakistan is paying the price for the fundamentalist policies it has been pursuing, which has led to the mushrooming of religious schools, mosques, and mullah inspired criminal
gangs which enjoy official protection and are often used to settle
political scores.[57] These schools sponsored by politico-religious parties
of the purist Deobandi–Wahabi sects continued to spread in an un-
regulated manner and became breeding grounds for sectarian intolerance and hatred.

Emerging reality of sectarian violence in terms of Shia–Sunni
conflict is sweeping Pakistan today. Besides, all the major religious
groups have their private militias. The issue of sectarian violence is
related to human right violation of Shias, as of other religious minorities.

Restoration of Democracy: Orthodoxy's Power Remains Unchanged

In 1988, a Shariat Ordinance was passed, in tune with Zia's
obsession with Islamization. After the death of Zia-ul-Haq, with the
restoration of democracy in Pakistan, Benazir Bhutto came to power
but she could not completely do away with Zia's Islamization legacy
in the face of assertion of the orthodox section. President Ishaq
Khan, Zia's close adviser in her 'Troika' government and the Senate
were against the reversal of Zia's Islamic policies. Thus in 1989, a
modified version of the 1985 Shariat Bill was passed but it was lapsed
when the Assemblies were dissolved in 1990. Due to her political
vulnerability Benazir could not repeal the anti-women *Hudood* laws.

Nawaz Sharif sought to start from where Zia had left. In
1990, Nawaz Sharif, Zia's protege passed Shariat Bill to gain political
legitimacy since the fairness of 1990 elections was questioned.
Certain provisions of this Bill were in consonance with the democratic principles. By enforcing the Shariat Act in 1991, the ruling
elites of Pakistan put the principle of democratic election outside the
jurisdiction of clerics and also saved the interest related laws which
had become extremely controversial.

---

[57]'Pakistan: Sectarian Violence Becomes an Ominous Menace', *The Nation*
(Islamabad), 1 September 1994.

Islamizing an Islamic State

By the declaration of Shariat or the social system of Islam, the supreme law, through the 15th Constitutional Amendment (1998), Nawaz Sharif like his predecessors had used the Islamic card for his political survival in the face of imminent economic collapse and growing sectarianism in the country. For the constitution already proclaims that Pakistan is an Islamic State and has vested the country's sovereignty with Allah. Sharif's opponents believed he was pushing Pakistan into a dangerous form of religious dictatorship and was likely to declare himself *Amir-ul-Momineen* (leader of Muslims).

What appears to have pushed Sharif along this dangerous path was that his country was confronted with grave economic crisis in terms of freezing of foreign currency accounts and crash in stock market. After the nuclear test the economic sanctions had placed the government in a tight corner. The US missile attacks on the terrorist bases in Afghanistan and Sudan gave rise to anti-US sentiments. The pressure on the government increased after the right-wing fundamentalist parties organized street demonstrations against the US-missile strikes. What questioned Sharif's legitimacy further was that he was reported to have prior information of United States' missile strikes. At this juncture, Islamization became a strategy of political survival for Sharif.

The amendment to the constitution aimed to change the complexion of state from democracy to theocratic and of the leader from elected representative to absolute monarch. Constitutional experts maintain that Sharif's game was to render constitution and the Parliament totally irrelevant and turn the country into a facist state, threatening the very existence of the present federal set-up.[58]

Musharraf's Regime and Religious Extremism

On the domestic front, the liberal forces that expected General Musharraf to reverse the rising wave of religious extremism have

---

[58] *Newsline*, September 1998, p. 17.

ended up feeling marginalized, having seen the regime buckle under pressure from the Islamist political lobby. Meanwhile, Islamist hard-liners, who were on the defensive in the initial days, have started to make a comeback with their characteristic assertiveness. After the regime's retreat on the issue of rationalizing the blasphemy law, the Islamist political forces have even found the courage to challenge the military establishment—something unheard of in the past.

Under the pressure from the US and a resurgent alliance between India and Russia on the Taliban issue, General Musharraf is speaking the tongue of Zia-ul-Haq. He is telling the world that *Jihad* in its true understanding delineates war culture and shuns terrorism and, therefore, the two should not be confused. In the process he is implying that his military regime has no control over the *Mujahideen* (whom he calls freedom fighters) and that their actions are purely voluntary. What this means is a projection that Pakistan is following *Jihad*, not terrorism.[59]

The military regime's rhetoric and policy on religious militancy appears to be divergent. While the government has been making overt noises about clamping down on the military forces, military government has given more room to the militants, and the crackdown on sectarian terrorists initiated by Shahbaz Sharif's government in Punjab, was stopped by Musharraf's government.

To win US approval, the self-elevating Musharraf knew that he had to silence the *Jihadis*. General Pervez Musharraf first made a show of acting against the fundamentalist militias and tried to regulate the functioning of the *madrassas* in August last year. He announced the banning of Lashkar-e-Jhangvi, a violent Sunni Muslim group, and Sipah-e-Mohammad, a violent Shia group, both of which have been implicated in attacks on mosques, funerals and drive-by shootings. Besides, he also announced the enactment of a tough anti-terrorist law and warned two other terrorist groups, the Sunni Sipaha-e-Sahaba and the Shia Tehrik-e-Jafria. On 20 August, the Sindh provincial government banned *Jihadi* groups from displaying sign-boards at their offices and collecting funds by placing

---

[59]In February 2000, General Musharraf in a television interview stated that '*Jihad* is required ... where Muslims are faced with revengeful actions ... *Jihad* organizations are not terrorist organization. Individual groups are responsible for terrorism and give a bad name to *Jihadi* organization.' See Zaigham Khan, 'Militants Versus the Military', *The Herald* (Karachi), May 2000, pp. 50–52.

donation boxes in public places. On 21 August, the police in Karachi raided the office of the above-mentioned organizations and the houses of their leaders, arresting over 200 of their activists and confiscating weapons.

The crackdown ended with a whimper as the affected organizations reacted in anger. All the 200 activists who were arrested were released shortly before midnight on 21 August. On 24 August, the Corps Commander of the Sindh province, Lieutenant General Tareeq Wasin Ghazi, told a hurriedly convened press conference in Karachi that no offcial campaign was going on against the *Jihadi* organizations to stop them from collecting funds.

No more successful was the effort to regulate the functioning *madrassas*, which are geared to mass production of fanatics who swell the ranks of fundamentalist Islamic militias. The ordinance promulgated in this connection on 19 August 2001, remained a piece of paper and *madrassas* remained factories for the mass production of zealots ready to die for *Jihad* all over the world.

The cosmetic nature of crackdown on the *Jihadi* organizations could be interpreted in terms of Musharraf's equations with the *Jihadis* which has a series of grey areas. Musharraf was keen to win over the US and West without taking punitive action against the *Jihadi* organizations nor touching their sources of funding.

Musharraf used the carrot-and-stick policy as the *Jihadis* on the way out from economic crisis. As part of the alleged 'deal', the military government, notwithstanding its public statements, turned a blind eye to the *Jihadi* activities. In return, petro-dollars from Saudi Sheikhs—with whom the *Jihadis* presumably have a certain leverage—helped bail out the cash-strapped Pakistani government.

Like Zia, Musharraf is internally promoting *madrassas* as a way to appease the religious support for his rule. Musharraf looks eastwards to bring Kashmir under Pakistan's control through an Islamic crusade. And the *madrassa*–educated volunteers are a low-cost way of keeping India perpetually off-balance.

Madrassas, therefore, are the labour suppliers, producing the raw material on which *Jihad* is driven. The wheels of which are well oiled by the wealthy Pakistani diaspora who pour in money along with Wahabis of Saudi Arabia. It is no surprise that the Lashkar-e-Toiba is linked with Ahle Hadith (Wahabi group), and its parent organization *Markaz-ad-Da'wa Wal Irshad* (Centre Islamic Invitation and Guidance) has so much money, according to reports that it can open a bank. The coming of the Jihad International Inc. or the Green International, as some analysts refer it, is the product of rapid Talibanization of Afghanistan and the religious extremism in Pakistan.

Kashmir, therefore, becomes a target of its eastern thrust. Keeping alive the Kashmir issue is to the advantage of the network. Kashmir means more funds, more *madrassas*, and more recruit to fight. For Islamabad regime it becomes a tool to divert the attention of people from the harsh realities governing the country.

Export of *Jihad*, Terrorism and Civil Society

It is a well-known fact that in the last two decades,

Pakistan fell prey to the temptation of nurturing militancy in the name of Islam and thought this to be an easy option as a means of promoting its strategic goals in the region, particularly in Afghanistan and India. Pakistan called it 'Jihad' ... obviously the intention was to mobilize and motivate the Pakistani army and irregular armed forces of all kinds in the name of Islam.[60]

Pakistan first employed this so called 'Islamic strategy' against the Soviet forces in Afghanistan from 1979 onwards. By labelling it as Islamic cause, Pakistan managed to receive financial support from Saudi Arabia and various other Muslim countries. The 'Islamic strategy' got support from the United States and China merely because it was directed against the Soviet Union, and they are now reaping its bitter consequences as now they are finding difficult to contain this Frankenstein monster. The involvement of Pakistan's ISI and participation of Jamaat-i-Islami workers, and activists of its students wing, the Islami-Jamaat-e-Taliba, in the Afghan *Jihad* is no secret. For Pakistan, Afghan *Jihad* served well and after the withdrawal of Soviet forces from Afghanistan in 1989, it started applying export of *Jihad* strategy against India. Pakistan believes that a Taliban controlled Afghanistan will be an ally and give its

---

[60]Satish Kumar, *Militant Islam: The Nemesis of Pakistan*, p. 1080.

army strategic depth vis-à-vis India.[61] The Taliban began as reformers, following a tradition in Muslim history based on the notion of *Jihad*—holy war against infidels. *Jihad* however, does not sanction the killing of fellow Muslims on the basis of ethnicity or sect. Yet the Taliban has used it for just that.[62] According to Ahmed Rashid some, 80,000 Pakistani militants have trained and fought with the Taliban since their emergence in 1994, which provides for a 'huge militant fundamentalist base for a Taliban-style Islamic revolution in Pakistan. The Taliban have thus established close ties not only with the military but with many sectors of Pakistani society, which now pose a threat to Pakistani stability.'[63]

Over the years, Afghanistan has been serving as breeding ground for *Jihadi* groups. The western regions of Pakistan and the southern regions have became vast network of training camps for highly motivated militant youth. After the withdrawal of the Soviet troops, a huge force of highly motivated, militarily trained militant Islamists looked for new pastures. These *Jihadi* groups are being exported with full backing of resource rich Muslim countries to conflict zones, like Bosnia, Kosovo, Chechnya, Dagestan, Philippines and Tajikistan[64] to undertake specific terrorist missions.

Pakistan's involvement in the post-Soviet Afghanistan civil war became more explicit as Taliban, a force which grew out of Afghan refugee students who got their religious and military training in Pakistani *madrassas*, started making its impact on the battlefield from 1994 onwards.

Pakistan created and nurtured Taliban-Al-Qaida for transnational terrorism to achieve predominance in the Islamic world. The Pakistan establishment apparently felt that by facilitating the various partners in the Taliban-Al-Qaida it can obtain their help in pursuing its own foreign policy objectives. The most commonly given rationale for this belief by people like General Hamid Gul, General Durani and General Aslam Beg was that this collective effort succeeded in defeating the Soviet Union when the latter occupied Afghanistan from

---

[61]Ahmed Rashid, 'The Taliban Exporting Extremism', *Foreign Affairs*, Vol. LXXVIII, No. 6, (November–December 1999), p. 118.
[62]Ibid., p. 126.
[63]Ahmed Rashid, 'Pakistan's Coup: Planting the Seeds of Democracy', *Current History* (December 1999), p. 413.
[64]'Afghanistan: Heart of Darkness', *Far Eastern Economic Review*, 5 August 1999, pp. 11–12.

1979 to 1989. When a superpower is defeated by this strategy, it will work in other places also. The Pakistani establishment refused to accept that it became possible only due to unrestrained help from the US and its allies all over the globe.

This misperception continued throughout 1990s when Pakistan slowly started escalating its operations in India. The end result of it was the Kargil aggression of Summer 1999. The coming of General Musharraf in power in October 1999 has not helped matters to any significant extent. General Musharraf did nothing to remove this misperception, fearing that any change in his country's Kashmir policy may cost him the very authority he is exercising due to vocal supports some of these groups have in Pakistan.

There is no lack of evidence to suggest that Pakistan considers Taliban as virtually an extension of its own military appa- ratus to jointly achieve the objectives of first capturing the whole of Afghanistan, then Kashmir, and then carry forward the exports of *Jihad*[65] into the rest of India, and later beyond South Asia into Central Asia. The success of the Taliban operation in Afghanistan has negative repercussion for India in terms of its spill-over effect in Kashmir.

It has far more serious implications for the security situation in the post-nuclear South Asia. Pakistan's fanatic groups like the Markazdawa-ul-Irshad, the Harkat-ul-Ansar, Hizbul-Mujahideen, Ja- maat-i-Islami, Lashkar-e-Toiba, and Jaish-e-Mohammad are involved in supporting a *Jihad* against India. Expansion of their appeal in the post-nuclear test period will only compound the concerns. The idea of nuclear weapons in the hands of these fanatics is absolutely spine chilling. In Pakistan, powerful voices are urging the exercise of nuclear option. A frenetic climate is being created where a minor mishap can turn Humphrey Hawksley's frightening fiction 'Dragonstrike', into a chilling reality.[66]

The massive increase of sectarian violence in Pakistan in the last two decades can be seen as the result of Islamization policies of successive regimes and the backlash of Pakistan-Afghan collusion in providing training to the militants. In 1997 alone, more than 3,000

---

[65]See Rahimullah Yusufzai, 'Exporting Jihad', *Newsline* (Karachi), September 1998, pp. 36–39.
[66]Also see, Ajoy Bagchi, 'The Gordian Knot', *The Pioneer* (New Delhi), 23 September 2000, p. 7.

people were killed in outbreaks of sectarian violence. The beginning of 1998 saw the Mominpura massacre in which 24 Shia worshippers were gunned down while offering prayers. The Lashkar-e-Jhangvi, a Sunni sectarian group, attempted to assassinate the then Prime Minister Nawaz Sharif in 1999.

Besides, Pakistan's government has encouraged the establishment of such a large number of Islamic militant organizations and groups (such as Taliban, Harkat-ul-Mujahideen, Lashkar-e-Toiba, Hizb-ul-Mujahideen, Hizb-e-Wahadat, Sipah-e-Sabaha Pakistan, Lashkar-e-Jhangvi, Sipah-e-Mohammed Pakistan,[67] and Jaish-e-Mohammad) in the last 10 to 15 years. The growth of such organizations continued unchecked even during the post-Zia democratic governments. The most typical of these organizations, and the one with the largest manpower and resources is the Lashkar-e-Toiba (army of the righteous). It is the militant outfit of the Markaz Dawa-Wal-Irshad and Ahle-Hadith, even though it is the latest to join the rank of *Jihadi* organizations. The Lashkar was formed after the Afghan *Jihad* against Soviet occupation was nearly over and it is primarily meant to train recruits to fight battle in Kashmir. There are many Pakistani *Jihadi* organizations operating on the Indian side in Kashmir, but the Lashkar is the largest of them. The members of the *Jihadi* organizations are mainly local men, assisted by fighters from other countries such as Pakistan and Afghanistan. But the case with Lashkar is exactly the opposite. Eight per cent of the Lashkar's soldiers belong to Pakistan.[68] It gained popularity for its role in the Kargil conflict and also for sending its *fidayeen* or suicide missions to blow up military cantonments in Kashmir.

Pakistan has to take the blame for the backlash of its Afghan policy in terms of increased militancy and terrorism at home. The decades long involvement and investment by Pakistan's secret agencies in Afghanistan had backfired, and the experience gained by militants in the use of explosive and light and heavy weapons are now being applied against its own people. Besides, thousands of volunteers affiliated with the militant religious organizations trained in guerrilla warfare in Afghanistan continue to report at the military-camps in the Taliban controlled areas of the country every month.

---

[67]For the antecedents and objectives of these organizations, see Ziagham Khan, 'Allah's Armies', *The Herald* (Karachi), January 1998, p. 28.
[68]Zaigham Khan, 'Allah's Army', *The Herald* (January 1998), p. 125.

What is worth noting about this activity is that no minimum age is set for recruitment, and boys in their early teens are often reported to be seen heading for the frontline.[69]

The symbiotic relationship between Islamic political parties and various militant Islamic outfits that came into existence during the anti-Soviet Afghan *Jihad* led to disastrous consequences for Pakistan itself in the post-Soviet period. According to a keen observer,

> Pakistan is paying a heavy price for its fundamentalist brigade's adventurism both in terms of loss of precious human lives, in the threats it constantly faces from the world's powerful states of tough economic and military sanction for its close ties with the Taliban government, and what are perceived as its links with terrorist network.[70]

Moreover, propping up of militant organizations had led to the militarization of society in Pakistan and widened the gulf between various groups since they competed with each other for material benefits. As a result, sectarian conflict in Pakistan acquired a far more violent hue than it had ever before in the country's history. The extremist sectarian politics after the emergence of militant organizations like Sipah-e-Sahaba and Tehrik-e-Jafaria have rendered sectarian conflict violent and bloody. However, the Islamic revival movements launched by obscurant religious groups like the Tablighi-Jamaat are the beginning of further radicalization of Pakistani society. In this context, the sectarian divide is cutting deeper and deeper into the social fabric, threatening religious harmony. The Tablighi-Jamaat movement is 'based on Deobandi or Wahabi movement, a Sunni orthodox belief system, implicitly excludes Shi'ites and Sufis, as well as other groups like Ahmadis.'[71] Violent sectarianism coupled with a heroin-Kalashnikov culture raises questions about Pakistan's survival as a state.

The unholy nexus in terms of close ideological and military ties between Pakistani religious extremists and the Taliban pose a grave threat to civil society in Pakistan. The Taliban's military success in Afghanistan and their missionary zeal has infected Pakistani brethren, influencing them with renewed fervour to bring a truly

---

[69]Behroz Khan, 'Sectarian Spill Over', p. 76.
[70]Ibid.
[71]Assia Haroon, 'Prophetic Times', *Newstime* (Karachi), No. 10 (April 1998), p. 35

Islamic state[72] in Pakistan. However, the prospects of a Taliban controlled Afghanistan is viewed as a threat to peace and security in Pakistan by liberal, secular and opinion-making circles in Pakistan.

In this atmosphere of heightened intolerance, the close ideological and military ties between Pakistani religious extremists and their Taliban allies could fuel further political instability and sectarian violence, making Pakistan itself a potential target of terrorism.

In this context an astute scholar aptly remarks,

> Together, the Islamic parties and the militant outfits have given rise to what may be called a 'jihadi' culture with Jihadi movements and Jihadi strategies which are deployed inside and outside the country by vested interests. The consequence, in terms of instability, disruption, disaffection, conflict, and contradiction, within Pakistan and outside, is there for anyone to see.[73]

The Pakistani leadership irrespective of its personal values, attitudes and lifestyles has chosen to ride the Islamic tiger and is now finding it difficult to dismount it. In the wake of their successes, the militant Islamic parties have started pressurizing the governments of Pakistan on matters of domestic and foreign policy.

As far as the Indian government's unilateral cease-fire initiative to Pakistan is concerned, *Jihadi* organizations like the Lashkar-e-Toiba and the Jaish-e-Mohammad rejected the offer of cease-fire. However, Pakistan agreed to de-escalation and the observance of 'maximum restraint' along the Line of Control. While the third extension of the cease-fire continued, the incidents of terrorism in India have increased as can be viewed by the attack on the Red Fort and the attempt to attack Srinagar Airport, in January 2001.

In the meantime, Pakistan is facing a Catch 22 situation. It is paying a heavy social and political price for patronizing the militants in terms of social and political costs since some of the above-mentioned militant groups are involved in religious and sectarian violence within Pakistan and the situation is likely to deteriorate. Any move to curb radical groups is likely to be met with resistance by hardliners in the military. Conservative political parties

---

[72]Jessica Stern, 'Pakistan's *Jihad* Culture', *Foreign Affairs*, Vol. LXXIX, No. 6 (November–December 2000), p. 118.
[73]Satish Kumar, 'Militant Islam: The Nemesis of Pakistan,' p. 1086.

have been warning the military regime of serious consequences if they give in to American pressure. As is evident by various statements from the Lashkar, a negotiated settlement to the Kashmir problem is not at all acceptable to its members, who reject the system of constitutional democracy and are in favour of an Islamic revolution. It is most likely that if organizations like the Lashkar are permitted to operate without a check they manage to establish a state within a state. In future, 'Lashkar and other similar organizations may decide to topple the system they despise. At that time Pakistan would become the victim of a *Jihad*, which it is waging against India in the name of Islam.'[74]

Today, the growing menace of religious fundamentalism is posing threats to religious tolerance, freedom of expression, civil society and civil liberties. The present regime confronts an acid test and its survival is at stake. The most frightening aspect of fundamentalism in Pakistan is that society itself is becoming fundamentalist and parties based on religion have formed their own armies. It is easier to face a fundamentalist government, not a fanatical society. Instead of the enlightened version of Islam it is the fundamentalist extremist Taliban kind of version which is being promoted and imposed in Pakistan.

Pakistan's peculiar brand of Islam is based on distortion, fundamentalism, misrule and terrorism. It has done to Pakistan irreparable damage in terms of dismantling of the civil structure of the country and pushing it in the path of self-destruction.

The issues on the Pakistan's national agenda which require immediate attention include management of the economic crisis, decentralization of power, religious tolerance, people's participation in policy-making and people's pressing need for relief from unemployment, insecurity and inflation. No theocracy which is by definition a highly centralized authoritarian entity, can solve these problems. In the present age no nation can avoid becoming a pariah without standing firmly by democracy, peace and the basic rights of all human being. There lies Pakistan's salvation.

---

[74]Sumita Kumar, 'Pakistan's Jihadi Apparatus: Goals and Methods', *Strategic Analysis*, Vol. XXIX, No. 12 (March 2001), p. 2196.

Can Pakistan Become a Moderate Islamic State?

Things changed dramatically after terrorist attacks on the World Trade Centre and the Pentagon on 11 September 2001. Faced with an American ultimatum that if he did not extend unconditional support to the war against terrorism, his country would be made bankrupt and its nuclear arsenal taken out, General Musharraf quickly fell in line. Pakistan was once again given the status of a 'frontline state' in promoting western strategic, objectives. Pakistan has had to take an ironic U-turn to become a US ally against the very terrorism it fuelled. Musharraf's willingness to cooperate with the US war on terrorism in Afghanistan overtly appeared to have changed his country's Afghan policy.

As the war on terrorism progressed, General Musharraf successfully delinked his country and the Taliban from the terrorist network and made the US focus exclusively on Al-Qaida and its leader Osama bin Laden.

In this background, the Pakistani establishment continued its terrorist attacks in India after a brief lull in September 2001. They refused to take cognizance of Indian protests. After gradually escalating tension, the Indian parliament was attacked on 13 December 2001. This has deeply scarred the collective psyche of the Indian nation.

After the fall of the Taliban in Afghanistan, Pakistan seems to have become the next battleground in the US war against terrorism. As the war in Afghanistan progressed, it became increasingly clear that Pakistan's involvement in the Taliban and Al-Qaida is complete and total. Already the seized documents by the US from places like Kabul and Kunduz reveal that the leadership in Islamabad is not averse to share even its nuclear secrets with the Taliban and Al-Qaida. As a result, General Musharraf has been compelled by the US to act against his rabid religious leaders and crackdown on his *Jihadi* militia who have been carrying out a common programme against the civilian populations of Kashmir and Afghanistan. According to a well-known analyst, 'The only reason the global alliance has spared Pakistan and General Musharraf from direct action is his total submission to the US and his promise to transform Pakistan into a "moderate Islamic State's status".[75]

In this context, it is noteworthy that General Musharraf in his speech of 12 January 2002, has committed himself to pushing Pakistan towards Islamic moderation and agreed to stop cross-border terrorism. The speech was a direct result of the ultimatum delivered by the British Prime Minister Tony Blair, on behalf of the US and the Western alliance, that General Musharraf should initiate far-reaching reforms to purge Pakistan of extremism and terrorism. The whole exercise was part of the war against terrorism, and it was only marginally to do with the Indo-Pakistan border confrontation.[76] By far the greater part of the general's speech dwelt on the urgent need for internal reform within Pakistan. The speech has been described by American interlocutors as 'historic', 'ground breaking', 'absolutely fundamental', and 'wholly honourable and positive.'

General Musharraf's so-called 'bold and visionary' speech was in fact clearly addressed to three distinct audiences—people in the West, particularly the United States, in his own country and India. He had two messages for the first two. The first was that Pakistan was breaking with Islamic fundamentalism and charting a new path towards becoming a modern, dynamic, Islamic welfare state. The functioning of mosques and *madrassas* was to be regulated so that they did not become centres of fundamentalist indoctrination and terrorist activity. The second message was that his country had enough of terrorism which had played havoc with its life, killing thousands of people in sectarian violence, filling it with hatred and intolerance, destroying the sanctity of its holy places, and projecting it as a retrogressive, non-performing state. Terrorism, whether domestic or meant for export would be dealt firmly. All this was aimed to please the western countries, particularly the United States, which are now deeply concerned over the rise of Islamic fundamentalism in Pakistan and its emergence as a world-wide exporter of terrorism. The conclusion that the speech was delivered with the

---

[75]K. Subrahmanyam, 'Put Kashmir on Ice: Pakistan Must Focus on Moderation', *The Times of India* (New Delhi), 3 December 2001, p. 10. Also see his 'America's Game Plan: Final Goal is a Moderate Pakistan', *The Times of India*, 11 November 2001, p. 12.

[76]K. Subrahmanyam, 'Washington's Waiting: Islamabad's Tokenism will not Work', *The Times of India*, 11 February 2002, p. 14.

expectation of a reward, is reinforced by his request to the US, towards the end, to mediate in the Kashmir issue.

General Musharraf was at his best when he spoke on 12 January to assure the world that Pakistan has burnt its bridges with the *Jihadis*, *Tabligis* (preachers) and other fundamentalists to become a moderate Islamic state. This was music to the ears of the West because no Islamic state, not even Turkey, had gone so far.[77]

However, the message to India was understandably different. There is hardly anything for India in the speech. He has not changed a comma in the policy Pakistan has been following towards India for the last fifty years. He is the same old, rigid and threatening General. One cannot find a word or gesture which can be stretched to show that General Musharraf is giving up the posture of hostility and moving towards measures to normalize the relationship. General Musharraf employs the same phrase—'We shall continue to give Kashmiris moral and diplomatic help'—which one of his illustrious military predecessor, Zia-ul-Haq used, to camouflage cross-border terrorism.[78]

The question uppermost that is in everyone's mind today is whether General Musharraf has the intention and the political will to bring about the transformation outlined by him. The structure as well as Pakistani's polity, was deliberately insulated with the virus of Islamic fundamentalism by General Zia-ul-Haq. For more than a decade that Zia ruled Pakistan,

> General Musharraf was also flourishing within the ranks of this structure and did not remain insulated from its growing religious radicalisation. The fact that he reached the diseased structure's pinnacle shows that he had assiduously used it to his best advantage.[79]

Since taking over the helm of the country, General Musharraf has actively used the country's religious establishment to promote Pakistan's agenda vis-à-vis India, particularly furthering the

---

[77]Kuldip Nayar, 'Not Enough in it for India', *The Hindu* (New Delhi), 16 February 2002, p. 11.
[78]Ibid.
[79]Ajoy Bagchi, 'The General Just Cannot Deliver', *The Pioneer* (New Delhi), 26 January 2002, p. 8.

concept of strategic depth in Afghanistan and giving impetus to terrorism in Jammu and Kashmir.

He cannot deliver on his promise. He is under intense US pressure to come clean. Pakistan gives the appearance of cracking down on terrorism, but in reality has not done so. The General has conveniently clubbed every scoundrel under the Pakistan sky as a *Jihadi* making it easier for him to camouflage the fraud being perpetrated in the guise of war against terrorism. Since 12 January, more than 1,900 persons have been rounded up in the crackdown and it is being trumpeted as a mark of the General's intentions. However, in fact, a majority of them are merely small-time activists of religious organizations like Sipah-e-Sahaba, Tehrik-e-Jafria of Pakistan and Tehrik-Nifaz Shariat-i-Mohammad. Besides the crackdown was superficial. In fact, most of them had fled even before Musharraf told the world about the crackdown. The leaders had locked up their offices, closed their bank accounts and moved out to safer pastures, all under the supervision of the ISI and other agencies. Moreover, the banned JeM, LeT etc. continue to operate under different names. Apart from this, except for the initial changes in Pakistan's ISI and army leadership, there have been no changes in the four months. No attempt is being made to mobilize public support for Musharraf's commitment to make the country a moderate Islamic state.

There is no evidence of Pakistan giving up using terrorism as a tool of its foreign policy. The kidnapping of Daniel Pearl, the *Wall Street Journal* columnist, by the notorious Omar Sheikh, who has been operating in India and Pakistan for several years, and who is on the list of 20 wanted terrorists whose deportation has been demanded by New Delhi, highlights that Islamabad's action against terrorist groups was only cosmetic. The same Sheikh was involved in the transmission of funds to Mohammad Atta. Alongwith his *Jihadi* colleagues he was also responsible for the 13 December attack on the Indian parliament, the 1 October car bombing at Jammu and Kashmir assembly and the 22 January attack at the American Centre in Kolkata.

Besides, reports suggest that Pakistan is restructuring the *Jihad* machine. Some parts of it are being relabelled to placate the fussy Americans, others are being re-assembled in Pakistan occupied Kashmir.[80] The aim is to enhance the 'plausibility of denial', needed for the next terrorist attack.[81]

The ground realities suggest that Musharraf has taken the trouble of appearing to distance himself from the extremist elements for his own political survival. However, conditions in Pakistan do not lend themselves to the transformation of Pakistan into a liberal, plural, and moderate Islamic welfare state. Civil society in Pakistan remains feudal and highly militarized. Tackling religious extremism nurtured on state patronage for more than three decades is not easy. Pakistan's army is a highly politicized force. The middle and lower echelons of the army's officers corps are themselves now full of fervent fundamentalist officers, many of them having graduated from a *madrassa*-style education rather than the public schools of the ruling elite. In sum, its officers' cadre manifestly betray Islamic fundamentalist traits. Ironically, Pakistan has followed the policy of export of *Jihad* as an instrument of state policy for too long. Nearly three decades of incremental Islamization of Pakistan civil society and Pakistan's power structure has resulted in an emotionally charged religious mind-set bordering on fanaticism. Without a popular urge for social change within Pakistan, no amount of American financial infusion and aid can possibly reverse this process.

In sum, Musharraf continues to walk the tightrope. He has bought himself and Pakistan time by seemingly taking superficial action against *Jihadi* groups. Pervez Musharraf's recent visit to Washington was a check-up call to see how sincere he is about his pledge to fight terrorism, not only internationally but domestically. This is a period of grave uncertainty and peril for Musharraf.

---

[80]The outfit Shoora-e-Furqan (Assembly of Believers) comprises thousands of Pakistani nationals and Taliban and Al-Qaida fighters airlifted by Islamabad in the wake of the siege of the northern Afghan town by the US-led forces.

[81]Manoj Joshi, 'December 13 and After: Angry India Disengages', *The Times of India* (New Delhi), 4 January 2002, p.10.

Chapter VI

The Menace of Narco Power: Parallel Government

The 1980s, in the aftermath of the Afghan crisis, witnessed Pakistan turning into a narco state. Drug trafficking/narco trade, one of the many scourges gifted to Pakistan by the Afghan war, acquired a high profile and assumed the dimensions of a full-fledged industry in Pakistan. In the process it has created a new strata in society—that of narco barons or drug lords. They are the new billionaires, rising from different social and class backgrounds, they now form a brotherhood. Each runs his own empire, its network reaching to almost every institution of the state. The drug money has corrupted the law enforcement agencies in the country and turned them into puppets in the hands of powerful drug barons. They also buy political power. The narco barons have reached the highest echelons of political power. They finance political parties and a change of face at the top does not affect their position. They run a parallel economy and are capable of destabilising any government if their business is threatened. The long arm of the law does not reach the barons of the drug world. They are influential politicians, tribal chiefs with *Lashkars* (armies) behind them and resourceful press barons. The network of the drug empire has gripped Pakistan's society, economy and polity.

The narco barons are among the pillars of the power structure—members of the National Assembly, the Senate, Ministers in the Federal and Provincial Cabinet with access to the highest offices in the land. The political clout of the drug barons is manifested by the fact that narco barons are believed to have become the fourth centre of political power in Pakistan along with the military, the bureaucracy (in the shape of the president under the 'Troika System'), and the elected political leadership. It is believed that narcotics money fuels the political system.[1] The United States' Central Intelligence Agency's report titled 'Heroin in Pakistan: Sowing the Wind' also claims that Pakistan is run by drugs and that heroin is becoming the lifeblood of Pakistan's economy and political system. Those who control the production and international transport of heroin are using their resources to purchase protection, to gain access to the highest political circles in the country, and to acquire a substantial share in the banks and industries being sold to private investors.[2]

Pakistan emerged on the international narcotics scene in the late 1970s and in the span of 10 years became one of the major sources and routes of heroin supply to the western world. The illicit traffic in drugs is Pakistan's most lucrative business today, fetching for its dealers a revenue of over 8 to 10 billion dollars, though some put the figure at 36 billion dollars. But even if the former figure is considered correct, it is higher than the country's annual budget.[3] Most of this money is earned through the smuggling of heroin to the United States and Western Europe. Drug money has changed the economic and social scene in the country. Although a small and powerful group of narco barons has reaped the major profits, members of the law-enforcing agencies, bureaucrats and hangers have also benefited from the trickle. With their penetration of state institutions, economy and society, the narco barons today are the most formidable force threatening the government's authority, political stability, and the economic and social equilibrium of the society.

---

[1] Jasjit Singh, 'India's Strategic Environment in Southern Asia', *Journal of Strategic Studies*, Vol. VII (1988), p. 11.

[2] US Central Intelligence Agency Report on 'Heroin in Pakistan: Sowing the Wind', reproduced in *Strategic Digest*, Vol. XXIII, No. 10 (October 1993), pp. 1593–1628.

[3] *Newsline* (Karachi), December 1993, reproduced in *Strategic Digest*, Vol. XX, No. 6 (June 1990), p. 2491.

Genesis of Drug Trafficking

Pakistan is enmeshed in a narco problem which is complex, multi-faceted and growing. So far as the genesis of narco trade is concerned, Pakistan falls under one of the two main areas of opium poppy cultivation in the world—the 'Golden Crescent' of South West Asia consisting of Afghanistan, Iran and Pakistan and the 'Golden Triangle' of Thailand, Myanmar and Laos. The 'Golden Crescent' region provides for 60 per cent of heroin reaching America and 80 per cent for Europe.[4] In Pakistan, opium is cultivated mainly in the remote mountain areas of the North-Western Frontier Province and the Afghanistan/Pakistan border. Opium cultivation and use has been continuing in this region for the last few centuries. Under the British rule opium production was licensed. In the eighteenth and nineteenth centuries, the British used to import opium from India to China for reducing the balance of payments' deficits caused by large tea purchases. The system of control on production was inherited by Pakistan when it became independent in 1947. Until the late 1970s, the opium usage and production levels were relatively static. The boom came after 1979.

Pakistan, a key participant in Golden Crescent's heroin trade, got a fillip in the late 1970s and early 1980s. The industry was used to fill the vacuum created by the crackdown in South-East Asia, which reduced supplies from the region. Drug trafficking became a thriving business in Pakistan since the beginning of the 1980s when, at the behest of the US, Islamabad came to be embroiled in the Afghan imbroglio.

Afghanistan and Pakistan alone shared nearly 6,000 metric tons of the total illicit production in 1999. The United Nation's Drug Agency sources estimated in 1993 that more than $30 billion worth of heroin manufactured in Pakistan and neighbouring Afghanistan found its way to Europe and America every year. According to US officials, more than 20 per cent of the heroin smuggled into the US originated in Pakistan.[5]

---

[4]Alison Jamieson, 'Global Drug Trafficking', *Conflict Studies*, No. CCXXXIV (September 1990), p. 3.
[5]Jasjit Singh, 'India's Strategic Environment in Southern Asia', p. 11, also see *POT* (Pakistan), 11 June 1993, p. 2123.

According to the Pakistan Narcotic Control Board (PNCB), thousands of acres of land in the Frontier's tribal belt came under poppy cultivation in the early 1980s. Total area of opium poppy cultivation in Afghanistan and Pakistan stood at 27,360 hectares at the end of 1993.[6] The conflict following the 1979 Soviet intervention in Afghanistan facilitated increased opium production. It also provided a source of funding for the anti-Soviet war efforts, and allowed traffickers to exploit the support to the *Mujahideen* (one who participates in *Jihad*) by Iran and Pakistan, by using those countries as transit routes.[7] As a part of the Cold War politics, the so-called refugees from Afghanistan to Pakistan were converted into *Mujahideen* and were provided money and weapons to fight the Red Army. They were also provided the needed ideological framework by declaring that their fight against the Red Army was a *Jihad* (holy war). In the name of mobilizing the money for *Jihad*, the drug barons of the Golden Crescent were activated by the major players supporting the *Mujahideen*. This increased the poppy cultivation, and poppy refining factories came up all along the Pak-Afghan border. Some drug barons used the confusion prevailing in Pakistan and Afghanistan to their advantage to get rich quickly. The drug problem became even more serious with the civil war and political anarchy reigning in Afghanistan in the aftermath of the fall of the communist-backed government in Kabul. With different warlords controlling different regions, there has been a tremendous increase in poppy cultivation in Afghanistan.

The North-West Frontier: Cradle of Heroin Criss

A study by the US Congress specialist Richard P. Cronier and Barbara Leitch Le Peer points out that Pakistan's opium is produced mainly in the mountainous under-developed tribal areas of North-West Frontier Province, where Islamabad's writ hardly runs. Today about 200 heroin refining laboratories are located in this rugged region dominated by the fiercely semi-autonomous Pathan tribals. Three major areas of

---

[6]United States, State Department Publication, *International Narcotics Control Strategy Report*, April 1994, p. 16.
[7]Ivelaw L. Griffith, 'From Cold War Geopolitics to Post-Cold War Geonarcotics', *International Journal*, Vol. XLIX, No. 1 (Winter, 1993–94), p. 21.

Pakistan where most of the processing of opium into heroin takes place are: Khyber Agency, a region of NWFP that is under the control of local tribes and has about 100 labs, while Malakand Agency and Bajpur Agency has about 50 each. There are about 100 labs centred near Peshawar. Other facilities that are located in southern and south-western Pakistan, also produce heroin for export.[8] In the markets of Peshawar and Landi Kotal, drug is being openly bartered for ultra-modern weapons. With poor irrigation and absence of commerce, this frontier province has found in drugs an alluring source of income. It was only in the early 1980s that with the 'technology' acquired by those who belonged to poppy growing areas that poppy was converted into the deadly heroin. This transfer of technology on the one hand, deprived the western narco-traders of a source of huge earnings and, on the other hand, opened a world of new 'opportunities' for the local traffickers.

With the help of ISI agents and army personnel, several refineries were set up to produce heroin, which is in great demand in the Western market. Ever since the ISI and the army came into the picture, opium refining techniques have become more sophisticated in this region. Chinese chemists were hired for refining laboratories at Landi Kotal and Derra to improve quality and production.[9] As heroin laboratories sprang up in Pakistan's tribal belt a local network was created for drug trafficking. Over the years the trade has become more organized and centralized. The syndicates have developed what in drug parlance is called 'vertical integration whereby the production, refining, trafficking and distribution up to the street level are controlled by a single gang, unlike the past where each area of activity was controlled by different cartels.'[10]

Baluchistan: A Major Conduit

According to US sources, Baluchistan became a major conduit for heroin in the early 1980s, after Iranian narcotics dealers and Iranian Baluch Sardars fleeing from the Khomeini regime settled in

---

[8]Mary H. Cooper, *The Business of Drugs* (Bombay: Popular Prakashan Ltd., 1993), p. 67.

[9]For details consult Brian Freemantle, *The Fix* (London: Michael Joseph, 1985).

[10]'War on Narcotics', (editorial), *The Hindustan Times* (New Delhi), 28 June 1989.

Quetta and Karachi. Iranian money underwrote the development of the Helmand Valley in Afghanistan as a major poppy growing region under Afghan *Mujahideen* Commanders. Baluch agents transported much of the Helmand crop to refining centres in Robat and Shorawak in Afghanistan and Nushi and Chagai in Pakistan. The role of Baluchistan in the international heroin trade had increased yearly. Also, now that Kandahar in Afghanistan is developing as a poppy growing and reportedly a heroin refining centre, the importance of Baluchistan has been growing.[11]

Major Regional Events: Pushing Pakistan into the International Narcotics Trade

The narcotics situation in Pakistan has acquired a notorious character in the Golden Crescent region for several reasons. Three regionally transforming events in 1979 propelled Pakistan from a largely uninvolved state on the margins of the international narcotics trade into one that not only produced and refined opium, but which provided key transportation routes, to the international market—all operated by indigenous mafias with long experience in international smuggling. With this movement of large quantities of heroin through Pakistan, it was only a matter of time before the country began to face its own epidemic of heroin addiction.

The first event was the Iranian Revolution in February 1979. The Khomeini Regime banned all forms of narcotics production and usage and executed several well-known drug lords after short trials in revolutionary Islamic courts. As the regime took hold, farmers stopped or severely limited poppy cultivation. This led to the flight of narcotics dealers from Iran. Most of them shifted their business to Pakistan and Afghanistan. With its long coastal belt and porous borders with Iran and Afghanistan, Pakistan's geographical position is ideal for drug trafficking to Europe and USA. The Iranian dealers poured their money for producing poppy in the Helmand

---

[11]See US Central Intelligence Agency Report on 'Heroin in Pakistan: Sowing the Wind', pp. 1610–13.

Valley in Afghanistan and made use of the old smuggling routes between the Makran coast, Karachi and the Gulf countries.[12]

The second event was the passage by the Zia regime in Pakistan of the Prohibition (Enforcement of Hudood) order of 1979. This order was part of General Zia's Islamisation policy. It made the production and distribution of intoxicants, including liquor and opium, illegal. This pushed the opium business underground and into the hands of the old smuggling networks of the NWFP and Punjab. The vast potential for expansion of opium farming in the poor and autonomous region of the NWFP led to refining of opium into heroin by these gangs who transferred it in clandestine channels for international export. Thus, General Zia's policies, in fact, increased the production of opium in the NWFP rather than decreased it. Iranian contacts in Karachi and links with narcotics traffickers in Thailand certainly smoothed the way, but these expert smugglers would eventually have succeeded on their own. Cultivation of poppy and cannabis were encouraged during the Zia regime to finance terrorist activities in India.

Finally, the Soviet military intervention in Afghanistan in December 1979 and the subsequent conflict disrupted the old smuggling route between Afghanistan and Europe via Iran, Turkey and across the Iran-Soviet border. This led to deflection of much of the trade in Pakistan, particularly through Baluchistan. The outbreak of the Afghan war and influx of eight lakh Afghan refugees into Baluchistan turned this province into a great drugs and arms bazaar. Aagha Baloch, a one time guerrilla commander during the Baluch insurgency against Bhutto's government in the 1970s, claims that the 'CIA and ISI patronised the tribes living in the Pushto speaking Baluchistan belt bordering Afghanistan to keep the *Mujahideen's* supply lines secure.'[13] During the Afghan war, the Inter-services Intelligence propped up most of these tribes against the pro-Communist regime tribes in the region and gave them a free hand to indulge in various activities ranging from gun-running to drug trafficking.

---

[12]These Iranian dealers provided Pakistan smugglers with access to international narcotics networks and reportedly brought in experts to train locals in the relatively simple chemical process of refining opium into morphine base and heroin.

[13]*Newsline*, May 1993.

The predominantly Muslim nations of Central Asia that became independent with the break-up of the Soviet Union are also slowly being sucked into the vortex of Pakistan-based narco trafficking. The Central Asian States bordering Afghanistan and Iran have opened up new lucrative land routes for the smuggling of heroin into Europe.[14] The routes travel from Afghanistan to the Central Asian Republic of Tajikstan or Uzbekistan and from there to Ukraine, Russia. Central Asia has boomed in the drugs trade over the last decade so much so that the five states comprising Central Asia are increasingly being referred to as 'a new Columbia.'[15]

Of late, Saudi Arabia is also being used as a transit point for small to medium sized heroin consignments for Europe and America from Pakistan. Drug trafficking has become a major irritant in Pakistan's relations with Saudi Arabia. In addition to these, regional factors in Pakistan's domestic politics and its policy of bleeding India through thousand cuts, led some of the politicians to patron this dangerous trade. Moreover, the post-Cold War mess made the region highly volatile leading to further worsening of the situation.

Major Drug Syndicates and Gangs

The multimillion drug trade in Pakistan is controlled by three major syndicates[16] which operate in close collaboration with Afghan drug barons and have close ties with ministers, members of the national assembly (MNAs) and tribal chiefs. The most powerful of the syndicates is the Ayub Afridi syndicate led by Haji Ayub Afridi, Iqbal Beg, Anwar Khattak, Alman Shah and Iqbal Shah. Based largely in Khyber Agency, the syndicate has major drug control in the region. The leading figure in the syndicate is Haji Ayub Afridi, whose election to the National Assembly from Federally Adminis-

---

[14]*News* (Lahore), 13 March 1993.

[15]Graham H. Turbiville Jr., 'Narcotics Trafficking in Central Asia: A New Columbia', *Military Review* (December 1992), p. 55. Also see Mark Galeotti, 'The Drugs War in Central Asia', *Jane's Intelligence Review* (October 1994), p. 462.

[16]Many professional smugglers, gangsters and criminals deal only in narcotic drugs and run a parallel government to manage their global network. These groups are well organized and are popularly known as 'drug syndicates'.

trated Tribal Areas (FATA) in 1990 provoked intense international criticism.[17]

The second syndicate comprises mainly Afridi from Khyber Agency. Led by Momin Khan Afridi, a former member of the National Assembly from FATA, the syndicate also includes well-known press barons with strong political and intelligence links.[18]

The third powerful drug syndicate operates in Baluchistan, which has now become the main route for drug trafficking. The syndicate, led by Ali Mohammad Notezai and Asim Kud, both members of the provincial assembly, are well entrenched in the provincial power structure. Both of them are important members of Akbar Bugti Jamhoori Watan Party (JWP).

The Lahore underworld is run by six gangs,[19] all of which answer in one degree or another to the crime boss of the old city, currently Sohail Zia Bhutt, an extremely well connected Kashmiri who is informally known as the 'King of Hira Madni.'[20] Each gang runs at least one heroin den in its area and has a supply network reaching out into other parts of Lahore.

Apart from these big syndicates, several other powerful Pakistan drug barons are also operating at the international level. Lal Kamal, a former minister in the Nawaz Sharif government, is said to be among the top drug barons. It is also reported that Nawaz Sharif's cousin-in-law Suhail Zia Bhutt, was involved in drug trafficking. Sohail Zia used his influence and the near untouchability that his associations gave him to advance the interests of his patron in the heroin business.

These narcotics syndicates, once entrenched, infiltrate the upper reaches of the power structure, establish a territorial base, alter the dynamics of national and regional power relationships and revamp the employment of foreign trade patterns, as they have done in South America. Those state apparatuses which have the potential to pose a threat to their business are sought to be assimilated into their empire. With multimillions in cash at their disposal these drug

---

[17]Zahid Hussain, 'Three Major Drug Syndicates in Pakistan', *Newsline* (May 1993), reproduced in *Strategic Digest*, Vol. XXIII, No. 10 (October 1993), p. 1642.
[18]Ibid.
[19]The six heroin gangs are as follows: Taksali Gate-Hira Mandi, Yakki Gate-Badami Bagh, Lohari Gate-Anarkali, Shah Alam Chowk, Delhi Gate and Misri Shah.
[20]CIA Report on Heroin in Pakistan, pp. 1616–17.

mafiosi can hire thiefs, smugglers, bankers, etc. to work for them, lease boats, aircrafts and even judges to protect their nefarious crimes. They coopt the police and bureaucrats, etc. into their system. The non-yielding ones are simply exterminated.

Major Drug Barons[21]

In the NWFP where poppy has been grown for centuries and where it has been the only cash crop in the region, two drug cartels— Afridi mafia and Yusufzai and Kakhattak elites—rule the roost. The Afridis are the foremost drug traffickers throughout Pakistan. They are located around Peshawar and also control the Khyber Pass, the great northern gateway to the Indian subcontinent, and are involved in some illegal trade or the other. One of the major drug barons in the NWFP in the 1980s was Malik Wali Khan Kuki Khel, leader of the Afridis, and a former member of the National Assembly (1960–1965). In 1984, with heroin now well embedded in the Afridi product line, the government began to pressurise the tribe to close the heroin labs on its territory. Malik Wali Kuki Khel denounced the government's attempt to control the 'natural wealth' of the Afridis, raised a tribal army of about 20,000, and tried to force a boycott of the 1985 elections.[22]

Malik Momin Khan Afridi is an old narcotics trafficker, who began operations through Thailand under cover of a Peshawar-based export/import business. He got elected to the National Assembly in 1958 from NA–34, a constituency incorporating non-contiguous tribal areas adjoining the district of Peshawar, Kohat, Bannu, and Dera Ismail Khan. Momin Khan essentially purchased his seat by buying off enough electors—the tribal seats all have a restricted franchise and none has more than 7,000 voters.

Muhammad Ayub Afridi (also known as Haji Ayub Zakha Khel), cited as the 'biggest drug baron in Pakistan' by the CIA report, supported General Zia and cooperated with the ISI in its large scale efforts to arm and assist the Afghan *Mujahideen*. During the 1980

---

[21]For Drug Baron's Who's Who, the first list of Narcotics Smugglers prepared by the ISI on 16 January 1993, consult *Pulse* (Islamabad), May 28–June 3 1993.
[22]CIA Report on 'Heroin in Pakistan: Sowing the Wind', p. 1606.

elections, Haji Ayub supported the Islami Jamhoori Ittehad (IJI) headed by Nawaz Sharif. The PPP government issued warrants to arrest him. However, Haji Ayub eluded arrest. He surfaced after the fall of the Benazir Bhutto government, pleaded innocence and accused the former PPP government of harassment. During the 1990 election campaign, the IJI openly sought his help to finance IJI candidates. The Haji reportedly purchased his own seat (NA–33, Khyber Agency), declaring that he would pay up to Rs 50,000 per vote. Haji Ayub Zakha Khel was and is deeply inter-connected in all the key institutions of power in Pakistan, including military intelligence, the presidency, and the ruling coalition.[23]

There is not enough knowledge of the activities and the connections of the powerful Khans of the low level Yusufzais and the Khattaks. Both groups are entrenched in the elite political, military and industrial circles of Pakistan. The majority of Pathans (recruited in Pakistan's army) belong to these two tribes. One of the sections of the Yusufzais who made it big was Lieutenant General Fazal Haq. One of General Zia's key protegees, he served as Zia's long-term Governor of NWFP and key adviser on the Afghanistan conflict. In 1990, he allied with Nawaz Sharif and won a seat to the Provincial Assembly. Throughout his career in the NWFP his name was linked with drug trafficking but the charge remained unproven. During his governorship, he led the government in its Khyber heroin war. Some say, however, that this war was between the Yusufzais and the Afridis over the control of the Frontier heroin trade.[24]

Other elites of these tribes reportedly involved in drug trafficking include Fazal Raziq, brother of Lieutenant General Haq and leader of the Madran narcotics group, and Anwar Khattak, a key figure in the Lahore-based Haji Iqbal consortium, reportedly related to the family of General (retd.) Habibullah Khan Khattak.

Baluchistan, one of the sparsely populated and far-flung areas of the world, is the largest province of Pakistan. The Baluchistan coast has been open to smuggling since days bygone while the land borders are also porous and extremely difficult to control.

It is believed by some that the former Governor of Baluchistan, Nawab Akbar Khan Bugti, Sardar of the powerful Bugti

[23]Ibid., p. 1609.
[24]Ibid., p. 1610.

tribe, is the real 'godfather' of Baluch heroin and uses his connections to the military, president and prime minister to deflect investigation and raids and to protect those who get caught. And that he gets a percentage of the profits in return.[25] The main tribe which he shelters are the Notezais. It has been reported that he lobbied with the Commandant of the Frontier Corps, the Chief of the Army Staff (COAS), and President Ghulam Ishaq Khan to get the FIR launched against Sakhi Dost Jan Notezai squashed or delayed. In April 1991, PNCB provided the Federal Cabinet with a list of 73 drug barons in Baluchistan. This list included a member of the National Assembly and four members of the Baluchistan Assembly as well as assorted Sardars and other notables.

Heroin is bought, sold, smuggled and used throughout much of Punjab, which is closest to the seat of power in the country. The first name related to Punjab's narco-trade which comes to mind is that of Haji Iqbal Beg, the owner of Plaza Cinema in Lahore. He is also known as the 'King of the Indian Route' for his control of heroin trafficking across the Indian border. He is believed to have links with the ISI in its plans to assist the Sikh insurgents. The Sikh rebels used to carry heroin to India in exchange for weapons and money. He also ran heroin into India across the border, further south in Cholistin and Tharparkar. His Indian allies in Mumbai and Delhi helped in moving it into international channels by sea and air.

Narco Barons-Politicians Nexus

The impact of narco money on the country's politics is more than evident. The nexus between narco barons and arm-runners has created a powerful vested interest in Pakistan that has permeated all stratas of political and social life in the country. In a report, the US Central Intelligence Agency had observed that Pakistan's drug-runners had established firm contracts with 'higher political circles in the country.'[26] What is more disturbing is that druglords financed political parties, bought enough votes for them to win seats in the National Assembly and thereby gained access to the highest

---

[25]Ibid.
[26]Ibid., p. 1595.

dignitaries in the land. Not only do they have close links with the big-wigs of the country, they have turned themselves into politicians. Various prominent leaders like the former Prime Minister Benazir Bhutto, Nawaz Sharif, the late President General Zia-ul-Haq and the former President Ghulam Ishaq Khan, have been linked with one drug syndicate or the other.

Known drug lords and narcotics traffickers sit in the National Assembly and the Provincial Assemblies of NWFP, Punjab and Baluchistan. In Sindh, the Assembly is full of *Patharidars* (influentials), landlords who protect bandit gangs involved in kidnapping, narcotics and illegal weapons. One Frontier drug chieftain, who was a member of the National Assembly, had access to the President House. A key figure in the drug trade in Punjab not only sat in the inner political councils of the former Prime Minister Nawaz Sharif, but was married into his cousin's family.[27] Moreover, the army of the drug lords who have procured the sophisticated weapons, supplied to the *Mujahideens* by the US government, are now equipped to handle any kind of military adventure by the government. These syndicates are virtually out of the control of the government.[28]

General Zia's involvement in drug trafficking came to light only after his death when the Minister of State for Narcotics, Mian Muzaffar Shah, revealed that Pakistani drug syndicates grew under the patronage of General Zia Raza Qureshi, a Pakistan drug trafficker who was arrested by the Norwegian Police at Oslo's Fornebu Airport in 1984, and exposed Zia's drug connection. The Norwegian Police disclosed three names of Pakistani nationals—Tahir Bhatt, Munawar Hussain and Hamid Hussain—patronised by General Zia.[29] The Norwegian Police visited Islamabad to investigate the matter and indicted these three for drug crimes. But the Pakistan government did not arrest them because of their political connections.

The most startling revelation that confirmed Zia's drug connection was the case of one of his ADCs, whose name was not disclosed. The ADC concealed heroin in 100 precious lamps to be gifted by General Zia to the delegates at a special session of the UN

---

[27]Ibid.

[28]Narcotics Control Strategy Report, the US Department of the State, p. 175.

[29]Iqramul Haq, *Pakistan: From Hash to Heroin* (Lahore: Anoor Publishers, 1991), p. 35.

General Assembly. General Zia suddenly changed his programme to travel via Iran and Iraq. In the process of shifting his baggage one of the lamps broke spreading heroin at New York Airport. Apparently the customs official checked all the lamps which were filled with heroin and seized them.[30]

One of the culprits, Hamid Hussain, was not only the vice president of the Government-owned Habib Bank, but was as close as a son to General Zia's wife. He handled Zia's accounts and used banking channels to launder the drug proceeds.

The former Chief Minister and Governor of NWFP, Lieutenant General Fazle Haque was another important drug baron who dominated Pakistani drug syndicates. Popularly known as Noriega of Pakistan, Haque was responsible for promoting the growth of the drug industry in the Swat Valley of NWFP. He successfully organized transshipment of heroin from Pakistan to the international market through his business contacts.

It is apparent that during Zia's tenure drugs played an important role in decision-making. After his demise in an air-crash in 1988, Ghulam Ishaq Khan, a close associate of Zia, took over as acting president. An Ismaili Pathan from NWFP civil services, he rose to prominence during Zia's time. His involvement in narcotics started after he joined the provincial civil services of NWFP and became a close associate of General Zia. He and the COAS General Aslam Beg worked together for the growth of the drug industry at the Pak-Afghan border. His drug connection was revealed during the investigation of the biggest bank fraud in the world, namely, the Bank of Credit and Commerce International (BCCI). Aslam Beg and Ishaq Khan became very close and strongly advocated the idea of Pakistan's decision to join the race for nuclear power. In the name of an Islamic Bomb they generated money from Arab countries and got away with the drug money laundered by the BCCI. It is significant to note that they founded an institute called Ghulam Ishaq Institute of Engineering, Science and Technology, which was the main recipient of funds from BCCI. In the name of funds for a nuclear bomb, the duo promoted the growth of narcotic drugs in the Golden Crescent.

---

[30]Nemisharan Mittal, *World Famous Drug Mafia* (New Delhi: Family Books, 1990), p. 103.

In 1988, with the restoration of democracy, Benazir came to power. However, the situation did not change. She referred to General Zia as having created 'a constituency of drug dealers, smugglers and corrupt elements in society.'[31] She exposed General Zia because it suited her political agenda. Her husband, Asif Ali Zardari, is infamous for his criminal connections. Besides, the members of the Pakistan People's Party (PPP) were directly involved in the drug trade.[32]

Hazi Iqbal Beg is another important drug dealer with powerful political contacts. Among his closest political allies is Malik Meraj Khalid, a founder member of the PPP. Khalid has served as Chief Minister of Punjab and in 1988 was elected to the National Assembly on the PPP ticket where he served as Speaker. It has been reported that Beg financed Malik Meraj Khalid's election campaigns. In his turn Khalid never abandoned him and was the negotiator for his bail after Beg was arrested on drug trafficking charges by the PPP government in 1990. Haji Iqbal Beg naturally denies the charge.

Another key figure belonging to the Kashmiri Syndicate is Sohail Zia Butt. Sohail Zia started his drug smuggling business under the guidance of Haji Iqbal Beg. He is also related by marriage to the former Prime Minister of Pakistan, Nawaz Sharif. In 1990, Sohail won successfully on the IJI ticket in the Punjab Assembly. Nawaz Sharif maintained close associations with Beg and allowed him to acquire denationalized industrial units including the Muslim Commercial Bank where Sharif was a *benami* partner.[33]

It is believed that in the 1990 election, the IJI was financed by hidden contributors from the Beg cartel. The rapid expansion of the family-owned Ittefaq industries in less than a decade had also been ascribed by some to the use of drug money. The narco experts also believe that Nawaz Sharif used drug money to buy off the top army generals to keep himself in power.[34]

---

[31]David Philip, 'Ghulam the Grim', *Economic and Political Weekly*, 21 December 1996.

[32]Christina Lamb, *Waiting for Allah* (New Delhi: Viking, 1991), p. 99; Kshitij Prabha, 'Narco Terrorism and India's Security', *Strategic Analysis*, Vol. XXIV, No. 10 (January 2001), p. 1881.

[33]*New York Times* (New York), December 1994.

[34]K. Subrahmanyam, 'Heroin Connection: Role of Drug Money in Pakistan Politics', *Times of India* (New Delhi), 19 December 1994, p. 13.

It is relevant to note that Beg continued to nurture his ties with the premier Nawaz Sharif and simultaneously funded the elections of Mehraj Khalid of PPP who later became the Chief Minister of Punjab. Beg thus remained loyal to both Sharif and Benazir. After the fall of Benazir's government he was charged-sheeted for narcotic drugs smuggling. However, his close association with Sharif got him released on bail.

Waris Khan Zakha Khel made no secret of his pro-PPP sympathies and was appointed by Prime Minister Benazir Bhutto to her cabinet as Minister of State for Tribal Affairs. During the celebrated no-confidence vote in the PPP government, tabled in the National Assembly by Nawaz Sharif in late 1989, Malik Waris Khan reportedly mobilised drug money to enable the PPP to buy the votes of wavering members of the National Assembly.[35]

Most of the alleged drug barons have refuted the charges levelled against them, while the prominent political leaders have denied connection with the drug lords. In fact, in the 1993 election campaign, the rival parties had used the CIA report for mud-slinging against each other. Nawaz Sharif accused Benazir Bhutto of running politics on drug money. And that 'the illegal money was made available to her by a leading drug baron, Senator Gulzar Ahmad.'[36] In reply, the PPP leader, Masroor Ahsan, said that the man who has accused PPP co-chairperson, Benazir Bhutto, of using drug money for elections, is himself a product of a system wherein elections were manipulated on the strength of the heroin dollars made by him. And that he had connections with Ayub Afridi.[37]

These are some of the many instances of the drug syndicate's control over Pakistan politics. There are hundreds of political leaders in the drug business in Pakistan. Since political leaders are beneficiaries of the international drug trade, it is not possible to keep intelligence and army away from the scene especially in the light of the fact that these two play an important role in Pakistan politics. In sum, the drug mafiosi have grown so powerful that they control certain parts of the state. The basic violation of state sovereignty has carved an illegitimate quasi-state within the state. The

---

[35]CIA Report on 'Heroin in Pakistan: Sowing the Wind', p. 1607.
[36]*The News*, 26 July 1993.
[37]*Frontier Post* (Lahore), 29 July 1993.

drug lords have generated enormous resources and have thus acquired the capacity to strike against the state.

Narcotics, Military, and ISI Axis

The military is significantly involved in narcotics. During the eight year period of martial law under General Zia-ul-Haq (1977–1985), a number of officers did become involved in narcotics. These were mostly majors who headed martial law courts and started by taking bribes from those accused in narcotics cases. In the early 1980s, the army charged 13 majors and 2 brigadiers in narcotics corruption cases. Some of these men—Major Afridi, Major Javed, Major Zahar—escaped from custody and became more deeply involved as traffickers connected to the Frontier Mafias.[38]

Many observers believe the cases involving the majors and brigadiers formed only the tip of the iceberg and that corruption in the military related to narcotics and the commission on weapon sales, etc. was more extensive. Lieutenant General Fazle Haq, a powerful member of General Zia's military junta once referred to as the richest General, also came to be widely associated with NWFP-based cartels.[39] Major Farooq Hamid, General Zia's ex-pilot who was found involved in a heroin smuggling case, was also arrested.[40] In 1986, a member of late Prime Minister Mohammad Khan Junejo's cabinet admitted on the floor of the National Assembly that as many as 18 Brigadiers and some Pakistan Air Force officers had been sentenced to various terms in jail on drug charges abroad.[41]

Besides, the individual army officers caught for drug smuggling and some military institutions, were also alleged to have been involved in the drug trade. 'Vehicles of army controlled National Logistics Cell (NLC), and those used to supply arms to the *Mujahideen* have also been used as drug carriers.'[42] Another instance of the NLC's role in drug trafficking is that of a 10 ton heroin

---

[38] *The News*, 23 September 1994.
[39] Ibid.
[40] *Newsline*, December 1989.
[41] *The News*, 23 September 1994.
[42] *Newsline*, December 1989.

consignment from Karachi, intercepted in January 1993 by Turkish authorities on a tip off from the USA. 'The consignment duly packed in shipping containers in Peshawar, was reportedly brought to Karachi on NLC trucks and loaded onto the ship on deep sea.'[43]

It was reported that the previous corps Commander at Lahore (IV Corps), Lieutenant General Mahsud Alam Jan, made a lot of money by facilitating the movement of narcotics from the Frontier to Lahore and on to India. Certainly, the substantial number of officers living well beyond their means has been noted for well over a decade.

Some other instances which came to light also exemplifies the penetration of the illegal narcotic traders' influence into the armed forces. According to media reports in Pakistan, Squadron Leader Qasim Bhatti of the Pakistani Air Force used to carry drugs as a part of the cargo in the military aircraft to the US and sell them directly to US military personnel.[44]

The ISI which holds political clout and ran the covert Afghan war, is also reported to have been involved in drug trade. Its former chief Lieutenant General Hamid Gul, was reported to be implicated in a drug trafficking case.[45] The drug money helped in the growth of the ISI from its modest origins to become an extensive intelligence network with global operations in less than a decade's time. The drug connection of the army and intelligence services came to light when at the instance of Robert Oakley, the US Ambassador to Pakistan, Benazir ordered investigation into the BCCI bungling. The entire exercise turned eye wash when Mirza Iqbal Beg was released on bail despite ample evidence of his involvement. Selig Harrison aptly remarked that Pakistan has 10 Noriegas very high up in the military and it was very difficult to disclose their names.[46] The genesis of this unholy nexus of narcotics drugs, army and ISI goes back to 1979 when the US government launched its combat mission against the Soviet invasion of Afghanistan. The US deliberately ignored the problem of narco-terrorism in this region. They were

---

[43] *The News*, 23 September 1994.

[44] Sreedhar and T. Srinivas, 'The Illegal Drug Trade: Asian Experience', *Strategic Analysis*, Vol. XX, No. 5 (August 1997), p. 723.

[45] Aabha Dixit, 'Narco-Power: Threatening the Very Roots of Pak Society', *Strategic Analysis*, Vol. XIII, No. 15 (May 1991), p. 191.

[46] Cited in David Philip, 'Ghulam The Grim', *Economic and Political Weekly*, 21 December 1996.

the first to use it against Soviet expansionism during the 1970s and 1980s. In fact, the US encouraged drug trafficking to raise funds for the *Mujahideen* fighting against the Soviets. The CIA was in full command of the region and purposely allowed the illegal trade to flourish.

Nawaz Sharif, in an interview to *Washington Post* published on 12 September 1994, disclosed that 'Pakistan's Army Chief, Gen. Aslam Beg and its Central Intelligence Chief, Durrani had sought his approval in 1991 for a detailed "blue print" to sell heroin to pay for covert military operations.' According to this paper, 'both Gen. Beg and Gen. Durrani insisted that Pakistan's name would not be cited at any place because the whole operation would be carried out by trustworthy third parties.'[47]

In this context, it may be recalled that Yunas Habib, the head of the notorious Mehran Bank, had disclosed that he had donated Rs 10 million to General Beg. This was a startling disclosure. A number of politicians demanded persecution of the retired General for illegal gratification. The General admitted that he had received this donation but he said that a part of it went to the ISI. He said that the President was informed of this and that it was not the first instance. The intelligence agency used to get such donations from a number of persons in Pakistan as well as other countries. A few days after this statement, Yunas Habib explained that the amount was not donated out of the funds of Mehran Bank. In fact, he had collected it from a Memon businessman living in Karachi. Significantly, Yunas Habib is also a Memon. It is clear that a large amount was contributed by Memon smugglers. This was clearly tainted money.[48]

Parallel Drug Economy

The Pakistani drug syndicates run a parallel economy in connivance with political and military establishments.[49] According to a UNDCP

---

[47] *The News*, 13 September 1994.

[48] Jamna Das Akhtar, 'Pakistan–Narcotics–Terrorism: The Linkages', *Strategic Analysis*, Vol. XVII, No. 9 (December 1994), p. 1133.

[49] For a detailed account of the drug economy, consult Iqramul Haq, *Pakistan: From Hash to Heroin*.

Report Pakistan's heroin industry in terms of turnover is estimated at approximately Rs 74 billion, i.e., 5 per cent of its GDP in 1992–1993, which is 20–25 per cent of the total estimated shadow economy. It also reports that Pakistan earned US $1.5 billion from the export of heroin in 1992.[50]

The damage caused by the drug mafia to the country's economy is still being calculated. The World Bank says over 50 per cent of the national economy could be illegal.[51] This black economy is controlled entirely by smugglers and drug barons. 'They have fuelled speculation in real estate, taken over vast chunks of transport business, enlarged the illicit arms market, greatly disrupted normal trading practices, created a parallel change market and given rise to a host of malpractices.'[52]

Narcotics drug money today forms a major chunk of the national economy, particularly in the informal sector. 'Some economists believe that the informal sector now accounts for over 60 per cent of the GDP, which is very large by any standard.'[53] Many of the country's industrialists and businessmen are reported to have made their fortunes mainly through narcotics. A new breed of industrialists, contractors and businessmen who were totally obscure 10 years ago, are now dominating the investment scene.

Although the source of their wealth may not always be substantiated, it is common knowledge that narcotics has had a great deal to do with their sudden rise to the top. Sadruddin Ghanchi, a well-known businessman and a former director of the Sheraton Hotel, Karachi, served a long stint in Germany for carrying heroin. Others are more sophisticated in their approach, using couriers for the purpose. Several of these nouveau riche businessmen have gone to construction, creating a respectable cover for their operations.

The enormous money involved in narcotics can be assessed from the fact that the world's drug economy is estimated to be in the region of over 300 billion dollars. As a major heroin source, Pakistan gets a substantial part of this revenue. One analyst puts the figure at 30 per cent. By this estimate, 90 billion dollars worth

---

[50] *Times of India* (Mumbai), 19 December 1994, also see Mary Cooper's *Business in Drug.*
[51] *The Nation* (editorial), 30 April 1989.
[52] *The Pakistan Times* (Lahore), 5 May 1989.
[53] *Newsline*, December 1989, p. 17.

of narcotics from Pakistan annually finds its way into the world market. But other economists believe that this figure is unrealistic, maintaining that it is not more than 8 to 10 billion dollars. Even this conservative estimate makes the narcotics revenue far higher than the country's annual budget and almost one-fourth of the country's annual GDP at 40 billion dollars.[54] Set against the labour, capital outlay and risks involved, the profit margins are enormous.[55]

In Pakistan, however, only a fraction of drug money comes back to the country. According to one estimate, only 5 per cent of the revenue is channelized through different means into the economy, which nonetheless adds up to a huge amount. The major impact of this has been the unprecedented growth of the black economy which forms a major portion of the informal sector. Most of the money has gone into real estate, construction and to some extent transport. Real estate has been the most risky and lucrative investment.[56] The boom in real estate prices in Karachi, Lahore and some other cities in the 1980s is attributed largely to the influx of drug money. Many economists believe that the construction industry has also absorbed a substantial amount of this money. Drug money has created its own protected sectors and transport is one of them. This narcotics underworld provides not only finances but also protection to people in the business.[57] On a lower level the private transport system, particularly in Karachi, has also been financed by drug revenues. A parallel credit system in operation finances individual transporters. However, the greater part of drug revenue goes into unbridled consumption and extravagant living, which in turn fuels inflation. But traffickers are the major beneficiaries of this

---

[54]Zahid Hussain, 'Narco Power: Pakistan's Parallel Government', *Strategic Digest*, Vol. XX, No. 6 (June 1990), p. 2496.

[55]One kilogram of heroin purchased for 4,000 pounds sterling on the Pakistan-Afghan border may be sold in Britain for 20,000 to 25,000 pounds. If sold in separate sources one kilogram can fetch 28,000 to 42,000 pounds sterling. However, according to the Narcotics Control Bureau, Government of India, the price for heroin originating from the Golden Crescent that costs approximately one lakh rupees in South Asia fetches nearly a crore in rupees in the US market. The figures varies from place to place.

[56]Radhakrishna Rao, 'Narco-Terrorism: Pakistan's Thriving Business: But it Can Prove the Country's Nemesis', *PTI Feature*, Vol. XIII, No. 43 (12 June 1993), p. 424.

[57]Zahid Hussain, 'Narco Power: Pakistan's Parallel Government', p. 2496.

illicit revenue, the poor poppy growers receive just a tiny fraction of this wealth.

Besides, other related issues like corruption has serious ramifications. Narcotics related corruption has the capacity to purchase the various functionaries of the state, including the top echelons. It is one of the reasons for the erosion of state sovereignty.

The drug barons have powerful lobbies to protect their business interests. Included among them are politicians, members of the armed forces, customs and police officials, businessmen and big industrialists. And since they control over 50 per cent of the national economy, no government can afford to annoy them. In sum, drug money has corrupted the nation and the culture of Kalashnikov and drugs has shattered the entire fabric of the social and economic order.

Money Laundering

An illicit drug trade is highly lucrative and a short cut route to acquire wealth and affluence. It was easy to make money, but difficult to move the funds to their destination. The drug traffickers had to face major problems in the transaction of the drug proceeds. Therefore, innumerable channels were explored and created by drug syndicates. Their unorganized but systematic method of monetary transaction is popularly known as money laundering.

Money laundering is defined as use of money derived from illegal activity by concealing the identity of the individuals who obtained the money and conversion of it to assets that appear to have come from a legitimate source.[58]

The cash accumulated from narcotic drugs trafficking is laundered into illicit money through investments in foreign banks, real estate, hotels, transport and entertainment business.[59]

The best instance of money laundering through legitimate financial institutions is the case of BCCI and Pakistan's Habib Bank.

---

[58]Robert Powis, *The Money Launderer* (Chicago: Probus Publishing, 1992), pp. 191–236.
[59]K. Subrahmanyam, *Security in Changing World* (Delhi: B. R. Publishing Company, 1990).

The BCCI's involvement in money laundering was to such an extent that it was nicknamed Bank of Crooks and Criminals.

Pakistan Sponsored Narco-Terrorism

Narco-terrorism refers to the nexus between narcotics and terrorism. Narco-terrorism is a mutually beneficial alliance between narco-barons and terrorists. Each takes advantage of the experience, equipment, and contacts of the other to promote their respective interests. India sandwiched between the two major drug producing region of the world, i.e., the Golden Triangle and the Golden Crescent has been a victim of Pakistan sponsored narco-terrorism for the last two decades.

A close scrutiny of the evolution of militancy in Jammu and Kashmir and Punjab indicate that it had covert/overt linkages with narcotics smuggling. The drug-syndicates are providing them financial assistance and offer small arms to raise the level of activities of these movements. Export and promotion of illicit narcotics and terrorists suit Pakistan's foreign policy aspirations in this region. According to one study, the amount Pakistan spends on sponsoring terrorism in India is nearly the same as it generates from illicit narcotics trade i.e., approximately US$ 2 billion.[60] It could be a valid argument that it is narcotics that sustain Pakistan's determination to keep India engaged in countering cross-border terrorism. Islamabad aims to weaken India's political and economic will. By pumping the hard money currency generated from its illicit narcotic drugs trade, Pakistan plans to disturb the local money market and make a dent in the Indian economy. The drug money is being floated in an unorganized but systematic manner into the Indian money market thereby damaging financial institutions. Therefore, the illicit drug trafficking from Afghanistan and Pakistan threatens both the polity and economy of India.

It is an established fact that the Pakistan government in collaboration with the ISI uses drug money and small arms trade to fund terrorism in India. Pakistan also seeks to create ethnic divisions

---

[60]Iqramul Haq, *Pakistan: From Hash to Heroin*, p. 17.

in the social fabric of the country by exploiting the religious sentiments and economic backwardness of Muslims in the bordering
states of Jammu and Kashmir, the Punjab, Rajasthan, Assam,
Nagaland, Manipur and other states. This was substantiated by the
disclosure of the former Prime Minister Nawaz Sharif and numerous
reports point out that military intelligence (The Inter-Services
Intelligence Directorate—ISID) used illegal but lucrative heroin profits
to help finance the war in Afghanistan[61] and has developed similar
arrangements with Sikh militants and Kashmir insurgents in India to
support their political designs across the border.

The ISI, the army and the Pakistan government are together
in 'operation terrorism'. In the bordering states of Kashmir, the Punjab
and Assam, Pakistan directly or indirectly sponsors mercenary forces to
destabilize India. All such activities cost money. A rough estimate,
according to one study, for expenses could be within the range of 100
to 150 crore a month.[62] *The North East Times* reports that the United
Liberation Front of Assam (ULFA) spends nearly 4 to 6 crore a
month.[63]

Narcotics drugs are the main source for funding terrorist
activities in the Punjab and Kashmir where the Pakistan government
overtly sponsors terrorism. There is no authentic estimate available
for assessment of expenses incurred by Pakistan for creating the
spectre of terrorism in India. According to one estimate Pakistan
spends approximately 20 to 30 crore a month on payment to militants alone. Besides weapons and logistics, ISI pays Rs 15 to 20 lakh
to militant leaders per month, 3 to 5 lakh to Afghan *Mujahideens* on
contract basis and 15 to 20 thousand to new recruits from both sides
of Kashmir.[64]

There have been regular reports from the late 1980s
onwards that narcotics cultivation on the Pakistan-Afghanistan
border is on the increase as compared to the earlier decade, i.e.,
1975–1985. For inexplicable reasons, even after the Soviet military
withdrawal from Kabul, no stable government was allowed to come
into existence in Kabul. The Afghan watchers feel that the warring

---

[61]A. Marvin G. Weinbaum, 'War and Peace in Afghanistan: The Pakistani Role',
Middle East Journal, Vol. XXXXV, No. 1 (Winter, 1991), p. 76.
[62]Kshitij Prabha, 'Narco-Terrorism and India's Security', p. 1885.
[63]*North East Times* (Jorhat), 23 October 1988, p. 4.
[64]Kshitij Prabha, 'Narco-Terrorism and India's Security', p. 1886.

factions in Afghanistan are made to fight by the narcotics lords to keep the trade going.

In fact, the richest and strongest among these factions, the Taliban, which made a dramatic appearance on the Afghan scene in late 1994 and acquired a high profile from 1996 onwards, is a typical example of what drug money can do. There were regular reports in the international media saying that narcotics crops in the Taliban controlled area in Afghanistan have registered an increase. According to knowledgeable people, drug syndicates' financial support to the Taliban is as high as 75–80 percent.[65]

The ISI is deeply involved with the Sikh and Kashmiri militants, who use Pakistan as sanctuary and use dirty money earned by rogue drug operations to fund their arms purchases. Most of the pro-Pakistan militant groups, such as Hizb-ul-Mujahideen, Lashkar-e-Toiba, Harkat-ul-Mujahideen, and Sipah-e-Mohammad Pakistan are funded and trained by the ISI. Pakistani involvement is further corroborated by the fact that Haji Iqbal Beg, a well-known Pakistani drug lord cooperated with the ISI in its programme to assist anti-India Sikh insurgents in their violent rebellion against New Delhi. Also, 'Sikh rebels became the mules in the cross-border heroin trade, carrying heroin into India in return for money and weapons.'[66] Further, it has been reported that Chaudhury Shaukat Ali Bhatti who was elected to the Punjab Assembly on the IJI ticket in 1990, and an important member of the Asian mafia, brokered a Rs 9 million (US$ 357,000) arms deal between Darra Adam Khel arms merchants and Sikh militants.[67]

According to Haron-al-Rashid, the late General Akhtar Abdul Rahman, Director General of the ISI, had spread the tentacles of his spies throughout India. He organized a separate wing that helped Khalistanis in East Punjab and terrorists in Kashmir.[68] He and the late President General Zia were of the view that with the liberation of Kashmir and Afghanistan and creation of Khalistan, the balance of power in this part of Asia would tilt in favour of Pakistan.

---

[65]Sreedhar and T. Srinivas, 'The Illegal Drug Trade: Asian Experience', p. 724.
[66]US Central Intelligence Agency Report on, 'Heroin in Pakistan: Sowing the Wind'.
[67]Ibid.
[68]Sreedhar and T. Srinivas, 'The Illegal Drug Trade: Asian Experience'. pp. 714–25.

The report from Netherlands asserts that the ISI has spread its network in Europe and other parts of the world. These networks are headed by Pakistani nationals. The Pakistani ring leaders are operating as part of operation K-2/TOPAC, conducted by the ISI.

The ISI has set up about 40 Muslim fundamentalist groups in Kashmir, as well as the Islamic Supreme Command Council base in Pakistan and helped recruit Algerian, Tunisian, Moroccan and Egyptian fundamentalists to the cause.[69] However, to seek legitimacy for 'operation terrorism' the ISI and the terrorists have unhesitatingly used the name of Islam, *Jihad* as they call it as a shield for their illegal activities. Counter-insurgency experts feel that militant outfits are getting money to acquire weapons from a variety of sources and a substantial portion of the money is coming from narcotic smuggling.[70] It has been shown that this strategy has been financed by a significant increase in heroin shipment from Karachi to Cairo, and from Lahore and Karachi to Europe. Sources in the Netherlands believe that money laundering networks established in Lahore, Sialkot and Faisalabad might be using Pakistan's largest Bank, Habib Bank Limited, to conduct these operations. According to Dutch authorities, the master-minds behind the networks are Iqbal Seth from Sialkot, Ahmed Tanvir and Humeir Bakht from Rawalpindi, Shahid Hussain Ghulam from Gujeranwala, Chaudhuri Bashir, Jan Mohammad Chaudhuri and Javad Khan from Jalalabad, in neighbouring Islamabad.[71]

International arms suppliers are increasingly becoming suspicious that the weapons bought by Pakistan's military is partly paid from the secret accounts maintained abroad, which are funded with profits from the heroin trade. This is substantiated by the mismatching budgetary provisions disclosed to the Parliament.[72]

Pakistan's ISI has used huge narcotics funds for establishing bases in Myanmar, Bangladesh and Nepal. Also some insurgent groups in the northeast of India have longstanding links with the groups based in Bangladesh, Burma and Nepal where tribal ties quite often spill over borders. Indian Intelligence officials assert

---

[69]Mark A. R. Kleiman, *Against Excess* (New York: Harper Collins Publishers International, 1992), p. 131 and 'ISI Plans for Fuelling Terrorism Busted', *The Observer* (London), 16 March 1994.

[70]Jamna Das Akhtar, 'Pakistan–Narcotics–Terrorism: The Linkage,' p. 1143.

[71]N. C. Menon, 'Peril of Pakistan Heroin', *The Hindustan Times* (New Delhi), 24 September 1994.

[72]'Pak Peddles Drugs for Arms', *The Hindustan Times*, 1 January 1994.

that the ISI has built upon some of these ties.[73] The deadly chain of bomb blasts in Bombay in 1993, exposed the strong link between Bombay's underworld and the narco-terrorist network of Pakistan patronized by its ISI.[74] The hijacking of the Indian Airbus flight IC–814 also reveals that Nepal is a convenient base for the ISI's nefarious activities against India.

The ISI of Pakistan is proliferating firearms in Bombay, Bihar, Uttar Pradesh and the North Eastern states of India. It has been admitted that it has the potential and adequate fire power to destabilise India.[75] Moreover, Pakistan's clandestine nuclear weapons programme based on purchase of equipments and materials illegally from western markets has been almost entirely financed by drug money.[76] Noted defence analyst K. Subrahmanyam, comments that Pakistan's drug activities and its weapons acquisition occurred under the benign watch of the Central Intelligence Agency of the US.[77]

Besides providing training to the militants in training camps, the ISI often allures the poverty-ridden populations of Jammu and Kashmir, the Punjab, Rajasthan, Assam, Nagaland and Manipur, at times others as well, into illicit narcotic drugs trade to fund terrorist activities in India. This is because terrorism incurs heavy expenditure and Pakistan is not economically sound enough to siphon huge amounts from the state exchequer.

There is already evidence that drug addiction is increasing in the Punjab, and in the North Eastern states and drug related cooperation among the security personnel is also rising. Many Indians in Kashmir are addicted to the drugs supplied by the ISI of Pakistan and they are instructed to recruit others, if they want more drugs. Dr Zeenat Naquqtee, a prominent human rights activist, says that narco-terrorism has become a 'fact of life' in Kashmir with

---

[73]J. Sarkar and A. Rashid, 'Proxy War', *Far Eastern Economic Review*, 20 October 1994.

[74]*The Times of India*, 27 August 1994, p. 6.

[75]Kishore Gandhi, 'Kashmir—A Holistic Approach', *The Hindustan Times*, 18 October 1994, p. 11.

[76]M. K. Dhar, 'Pak Nuclear Plan Financed by Drug Money', *The Hindustan Times*, 18 October 1994, p. 1.

[77]K. Subrahmanyam, 'Zia Used Drug Money to Run State, Says Pak Weekly', *The Economic Times* (New Delhi), 21 October 1994, p. 8.

militants distributing drugs to get new recruits.[78] The ISI is also trying to wreck the economy by circulating fake currency notes.

Narcotics and the Civil Society

The Pakistan government fails to understand that the trap it had laid for India, namely the net of terrorists and drug smugglers, has boomeranged on it and proved fatal for the civil society in Pakistan.

Growing Menace of Addiction

Drug trafficking has spread like cancer in Pakistani society, sowing the seeds for spiralling addiction. Until 1980, drug addiction was confined to a microscopic minority of urban elite, whereas now it has become pervasive in all sections of society. The evolution of drug culture in Pakistan reads like a horror story. There has been an exponential rise in the number of drug addicts in the country. 'From every 15 minutes in 1987, a drug addict is now born every 10 minutes in Pakistan.'[79] The UNDCP report confirms that there were 1.5 to 1.9 million drug addicts in Pakistan in 1993.[80] Today, according to an official estimate, four million people in Pakistan have become hard-core addicts whereas according to unofficial sources, about one-third of the population has come under the vice-like grip of drugs. The heroin drug has no barriers, no geographical boundaries. It has hit almost every section of Pakistan's society—students, young professionals, taxi drivers, petty vendors, crafts-men and even public servants. And it is equally rampant in Karachi, Lahore, Peshawar, Rawalpindi, Multan and Quetta. Pakistan now has a drug addiction rate higher than that of the United States.

Perhaps the hardest hit by this heroin onslaught are the Pakistani youth. Most of the male heroin addicts are in the age-group of 14–40 years and female addicts in the 17–30 year age

---

[78]'Narco-Terrorism Grips Kashmir', *The Hindustan Times*, 27 May 1994.
[79]'Fighting Drug Abuse', *The Muslim* (Islamabad), 16 May 1989.
[80]For details see UNDCP report, 1994.

group,[81] which means that the flower of the country's youth is being destroyed. And so is its future. Every ninth male in Karachi is hooked on the deadly heroin.[82] This is because there were large heroin dens in Karachi, such as those in Sohrab Goth. By 1987 about 40 drug outlets were doing a roaring business in the city which by that time housed half the country's heroin addicts.[83]

The same is the case with the second largest city, Lahore, where heroin worth Rs 5,00,000 is sold every day.[84] As admitted by the provincial authorities there are one million drug addicts in the Punjab, the largest province which consumes a million grams of heroin every day.[85] And not to be left behind are the women. It is surprising that in a conservative country like Pakistan, there are 150,000 female drug addicts, half of them again in Karachi.[86]

The drug culture is leaving a deep imprint on the society. It is damaging the social fabric of Pakistan. The abuse of drugs in a society creates social imbalance, moral decay and reduces productivity. The fallout of this spiralling addiction rate as well as trafficking in narcotics has woven a web of despair for the people of this country.[87]

But no action was taken against the rising menace of drug trafficking and drug addiction. This was part of the price Pakistan had to pay for the Afghan war. And Washington willingly swept the issue under the carpet because its primary objective was to get the Soviets out of Afghanistan by funding the *Mujahideen* war. Both Washington and Islamabad became so preoccupied with the Afghan war that they easily ignored the 'heroinisation' of Pakistan and its harrowing consequences.

---

[81] *The Muslim*, 16 May 1989.
[82] Editorial, 'Growing Menace of Addiction', *Dawn* (Karachi), 2 November 1987. For details see also survey conducted by PNCB, 1987.
[83] For details see *The Muslim*, 12 December 1987.
[84] *The Muslim*, 16 May 1989.
[85] *Dawn*, 14 March 1989.
[86] *Dawn*, 6 November 1988.
[87] See, Khalid Mahmood Malik, 'Drug Menace in South Asia', *Regional Studies*, Vol. VIII, No. 3 (Summer, 1990), p. 39.

Narcotics, Terrorism and Ethnic Violence

In addition to it the drugs and arms linkage has torn the social fabric of the society. Millions of unlicensed Kalashnikov rifles in Pakistan are in the hands of armed gangs organized by the drug mafia. There are an estimated one lakh Kalashnikovs in Karachi alone. Afghanistan has almost 10 million illegal weapons of all kinds. Many of them are sold in Peshawar for use in Karachi and other parts of Pakistan. The extent of arms proliferation in Pakistan is evident from the fact that university students, both boys and girls, carry AK-47s in their hostels. As a result, violence has become a way of life in Karachi and Kalashnikov a household name. Since its introduction to heroin culture, Karachi has witnessed daily bouts of delirium and there seems no end to this exercise in insanity. It has divided the society on ethnic lines thanks to the clever manipulation of drug barons, and the city has been at war with itself for more than a decade now.

The threats to the security of the Pakistan state and civil society are exacerbated by linkages of weapon proliferation with drug trafficking. The advent of drugs ushered in the Kalashnikov culture which is an enduring legacy of General Zia's Afghan policy. The drug barons soon developed a nexus with the arms dealers. The easy availability of arms increased criminalization which has fuelled ethnic violence in Pakistan.[88] The induction of large quantities of deadly arms in Pakistani society inevitably undermined law and order and led to serious long-term social and political repercussions.[89] The increasing criminalization of society in Pakistan has been the fallout of the funnelling of arms for the Afghan war, with Pakistan acting as a conduit. Vast quantities of small arms were supplied to the *Mujahideen*. 'They ranged from Kalashnikov assault rifles, powerful machine guns and rocket launchers, grenades and explosives, landmines, shoulder fired surface-to-air missiles (SAMs) like Stringers, Strella and Blowpipes.'[90] Arms reached the battlefield through the CIA's secret arms pipeline to the *Mujahideen*. This pipeline was riddled with

---

[88]Sumita Kumar, 'Drug Trafficking in Pakistan', *Asian Strategic Review 1994–95* (New Delhi: Institute for Defence Studies and Analysis, 1995), pp. 211–17.

[89]Consult Pervez Iqbal Cheema, 'Impact of the Afghan War on Pakistan', *Pakistan Horizon*, Vol. XXXI (1988), p. 32.

[90]Jasjit Singh, 'India's Strategic Environment in Southern Asia', p. 10.

opportunities for corruptions.[91] 'It is reported that 40 per cent of the total arms aid entering through Pakistan was siphoned off along the way by corrupt officials, Afghan leaders and *Mujahideens.*'[92] It is alleged that both Pakistani officials as well as Afghan political leaders peddled weapons for personal profit. A large number of such arms found their way into the underground network of drug lords and arms bazaars.[93] Four main arms bazaars namely, Landi Kotal, Jamrud, Bara Bazaar and Darra Adam Khel, have been functioning in the NWFP area, all of which deal in a range of narcotics as well. With the Afghan war Baluchistan turned into a great drug and arms bazaar and Sindh became the regional headquarter of the drug and arms mafia. Sindh in general and Karachi in particular have become a dumping ground for weapons and drugs. These arms have terribly disruptive consequences for Pakistan as demonstrated in Sindh and Punjab. Armed with sophisticated fire arms, the sectarian zealots have held the city hostage. All this has led to the brutalization of the society.

Curbing the Drug Menace

The drug phenomenon has exerted a serious strain on the country's social, economic and political stability and its future developments. Besides, Pakistan's increasing role in drug trafficking and gun-running is threatening the socio-economic stability of West Asia, North America and parts of Europe. There are two views on how to curb drug trafficking.[94] On the one side there are those who argue that the trade should be legalized. Others suggest such harsh measures as death penalty for traffickers, ban on poppy cultivation and strict enforcement of anti-drug laws.

---

[91]Brig. Mohammad Yousaf and Major Mark Adlkin, 'The Bear Trap: Afghanistan's Untold Story', *Jang* (Lahore, 1992), p. 97. Also see Chris Smith, *The Diffusion of Small Arms and Light Weapons in Pakistan and Northern India* (London: Brassey's), p. 12.

[92]*The Nation* (Lahore), 31 July 1987.

[93]A. K. M. Abdus Sabur, 'Pakistan: Ethnic Conflict and the Question of National Integration', *BIISS Journal*, Vol. XI, No. 4 (1990), p. 508.

[94]For drug control measures, consult Mohammad Riaz, 'Drug Control on Priority', *Pakistan and Gulf Economist*, Vol. VIII, No. 13 (7 April 1989), pp. 10–18.

Those who favour the forcible destruction of poppy crop cannot see the wood for the trees. Just as alcoholism cannot be curbed by dismantling breweries and cigarette factories cannot be destroyed to reduce smoking, drug trafficking cannot be curbed by destroying the poppy crop. It is just like finding a military solution to a political problem and is tantamount to curing the symptoms instead of eliminating the causes. Prohibition, too, is no solution. The US outlawed trade in alcoholic drinks in the 1920s but it did not work. Ultimately the ban was lifted.

Legalizing this trade will have some advantages. It will fetch the government a lot of revenue and will also help in the classification of drugs so that the user is aware of their ill-effects.

But there are obvious disadvantages too. Legalizing the trade would be as risky as prohibition, the easy availability of drugs would lead to 'an explosion of abuse', as observed by the International Narcotics Control Board of the UN in its annual report of 1989.[95]

To curtail narcotics production and trafficking, the government has announced several measures including a separate narcotics ministry and formation of an elite force under the PNCB. The actions taken by the Pakistan government against drug traffickers like the freezing of assets of some infamous drug lords was long overdue. Efforts against drug trafficking were made by the Benazir government in 1989. However, the anti-drug campaign by the government, under US pressure, soon fizzled out. Her efforts were undermined by the considerable influence wielded by the drug lords. It is an unfortunate reflection on the commitment of governments in Pakistan to fight against the drug menace that the ordinance promulgated by Moeen Qureshi's government in 1993 prescribing capital punishment for confirmed drug traffickers was allowed to lapse.

Although the government claims that it has succeeded in destroying a substantial number of labs in the Khyber and Mohammad agencies, there is no concrete evidence of any substantial reduction in heroin production. Despite reported claims of reduced poppy production in Pakistan, heroin manufacturing has not been affected. While a crackdown on drug factories and smuggling routes is of paramount importance, this is not an easy task. The porous

---

[95] *The Frontier Post* (Lahore), 12 January 1992.

Afghan border not only permits traffickers to slip across to escape detention, it even enables them to shift production facilities to across the border. Success in combating drug production is substantially linked to the resolution of the Afghan problem.

Pakistan declared its first war on drugs in December 1986 and lost as the drug barons, who were forced to leave Sohrab Goth, Karachi, interpreted the police raid as an attack on one ethnic group. The resulting tension and rioting later became a feature of Karachi's social life.

The second war was launched in December 1988. As the government began its crackdown on narcotics, the drug barons and their armed gangs issued death threats to anti-narcotics officials.[96] And they did carry out the threat in one case at least, in the wake of the government campaign. An official of the PNCB was killed in Karachi a day after he announced the seizure of a huge amount of heroin.[97]

The government in 1989 prepared a list of 35 notorious smugglers and vowed to deal with them with an iron hand. Two of them Haji Ayub of Khyber Agency and Haji Iqbal Baig of Lahore, were issued legal notices by the newly created Narcotics Division. While the former's arrest was claimed to be a major success, he was later released for lack of evidence against him. This shows how influential they are and how difficult it is to initiate proceedings against them.

A sustained effort coupled with a sense of strong commitment is required on the part of the government to uproot the multi-billion dollar narcotic industry. There has to be an immeasurably strong political will to break the deep-rooted unholy alliance between the drug barons and various political groups. A strong consensus and campaign will have to be evolved if the war against the narco mafia is to be waged with any effect.

But given the enormity and international dimension of the problem, these measures seem inadequate. The major issue at the moment is not only to plug the sources but also counter the strong and influential mafia. The drug-mafia already have become powerful enough, especially in Pakistan, to foil any attempt to challenge its economic and political activity. As experience of Colombia has

---

[96] *Time*, 7 August 1989, p. 13.
[97] For details see *Newsline*, November 1984, p. 91.

shown, it is quite difficult for an individual state to fight this war on its own. A global effort, therefore, is needed for this purpose. The drug syndicates are so deeply entrenched in the country's political and economic system that the government alone cannot tackle it.

To prevent its economy with its poor industrial base and modest agricultural activity from collapsing, the country may, in the circumstances, find itself forced into intensifying its narco-terrorist activities. The prevailing high levels of corruption, lawlessness and criminalization of society would appear to be set to give further boost to narco-terrorism, a situation which could spell the doom of this ethnically divided country created just five decades ago.

And finally, there is a need to change public attitude towards this trade. As long as the notion of 'trading for development' remains socially accepted, all efforts to eradicate the drug menace will end in smoke.

Chapter VII

Restoration of Democracy and Crisis of Governability: 1988–1999

The restoration of democracy in Pakistan in the last quarter of 1988—after the seemingly unending 11 year long brutal reign of General Zia-ul-Haq, which ended suddenly and unexpectedly with his demise in a mysterious air-crash—ushered a new era of significance in the political history of that country. Benazir Bhutto's appointment as the Prime Minister of Pakistan was considered more than a mere change of government—it heralded a change of regime. The euphoria, however, could not last for long. And it was replaced by disillusionment and cynicism in the nation. Since 1988, Pakistan had gone through four general elections. Both Pakistan People's Party (PPP) leader Benazir and Pakistan Muslim League (PML) leader Nawaz Sharif had two terms each. But no political consolidation took place during the 11 years of democratic rule.

The restoration of democracy had coincided with a steady decay of political institutions, social conflict and economic mismanagement. As a perceptive scholar Seyyed Vali Reza Nasr aptly remarks, a crisis of governability had emerged as a concomitant of the democratization process because of a combination of low legitimacy and low effectiveness of the country's political leadership.[1] To define with Atul

---

[1] Seyyed Vali Reza Nasr, 'Democracy and the Crisis of Governability in Pakistan', *Asian Survey*, Vol. XXXII, No. 6 (June 1992), p. 521.

Kohli, a crisis of governability identifies the failure of rulers to 'maintain coalitional support, initiate solutions to problems perceived to be important, and resolve political conflicts without force or violence.'[2] In these three areas, during 1988–1999 Pakistan was doing worse than it did 11 years ago. It is true that democracy was restored in 1988 but the legacy of Zia-ul-Haq's 11 year long autocratic rule was difficult to be disposed. The legacy of Zia-ul-Haq's rule in terms of the Eighth Amendment had overshadowed the political process throughout 1988–1999. The Eighth Amendment had been intended by General Zia mainly to provide immunity to the army for its actions during the martial law period and also to provide the military-bureaucratic establishment a veto against an elected government. After the restoration of democracy, three governments (Benazir twice and Sharif once) had been casualties of the Eighth Amendment. After 11 years of democracy, Pakistan once again witnessed a dramatic change of government, democracy to military in October 1999. This once again has raised a fundamental question that has haunted Pakistan ever since its creation in 1947, whether democracy has a future in Pakistan. Most of Pakistan's energy gets dissipated in working out who really should govern Pakistan.

This chapter seeks to highlight the evident erosion and decay of political institutions in Pakistan during 1988–1999 by taking into account those variables that have had a negative impact on the democratic processes in that country. The chapter also aims to identify the causal relations between key variables with a view to analyze and explain the dialectic of the democratization process in Pakistan.

Restoration of Democracy Under Benazir: 1988–1990

A close scrutiny of the political situation in Pakistan reveals that Benazir Bhutto came to the office circumscribed constitutionally, politically, economically and structurally. The circumstances in which

---

[2]Atul Kohli, *Democracy and Discontent: India's Growing Crisis of Governability* (New York: Cambridge University Press, 1990), p. 383.

Benazir came to power, coupled with the organizational weakness of the PPP, created problems for the ruling party and subsequent democratic processes in Pakistan. The major constraint stemmed from the fact that the government was one element in the 'troika' of power that also comprised the president (non-PPP) and the army chief. While attempting to evaluate the functioning of the Benazir government, one must keep in mind the inner dynamics and structure of politics in the last 40 years' history of Pakistan. The military-bureaucratic alliance has played a predominant role in Pakistan's politics for a considerably long period. The question arises: how did the military-bureaucratic junta allow the formation of a civilian government in Pakistan? In fact, a set of unanticipated factors left little room for any other political manoeuvre to keep the democratic forces out. The military-bureaucratic alliance permitted the restoration of democracy, essentially to fill the vacuum in the structure of state power in Pakistan caused by the sudden departure of Zia and felt that this was not the appropriate time for the armed forces to act. Their strategy was to provide some political space to the democratic forces without disturbing, in any serious manner, its basic and long-term stakes in power. The forging of the Islamic Democratic Alliance (IDA)[3] was a significant move in this direction. It is evident that the military-bureaucratic junta had staged a tactical retreat and its cooption of the democratic component of the Pakistani polity in its structure of state power was tactical. It was looking forward to rediscovering its political role at the suitable moment.[4]

It is noteworthy that accidentally the indecisive and ambiguous verdict of the November 1988 elections amply suited the overall interest and strategy of the military-bureaucratic junta. The PPP led by Benazir Bhutto emerged only a truncated winner—short of absolute majority at the centre. In the provincial assemblies, the PPP could

---

[3]It is an open secret in Pakistan that the IDA was put together by the Military's Inter-Services Intelligence, which brokered a deal between an array of right-of-centre and Islamic parties to prevent a PPP sweep at the polls. In IDA's coalitional arrangement, the Muslim League Party was the chief component and a few smaller parties, including the Muhajir Quami Movement (MQM), Awami National Party (ANP), and the Niazi group of the Jamiatul Ulema-i-Pakistan (JUP), were its partners.

[4]S. D. Muni, 'Internal Political Problems', *World Focus*, No. 115 (July 1986), pp. 7–8. Also see Veena Kukreja, 'Restoration of Democracy in Pakistan: One Year of Benazir's Rule', *Strategic Analysis*, Vol. XII, No. 11 (February 1990), pp. 1163–74.

boast of a complete sway in Sindh; but there too, it was battered in the urban areas by the Muhajir Quami Movement (MQM). Benazir's power was circumscribed as the IDA snatched control of the biggest province, the Punjab, which is the bastion of the military-bureaucratic power and influence. In the other two provinces, the NWFP and Baluchistan, the PPP was nowhere near forming a government of its own.

Furthermore, PPP's organizational weakness had strong negative bearing on the functioning of the democratic process as it prevented Benazir government from promoting mass support, maintaining its coalition arrangement in parliament, and guarding off challenges to its authority by the president and the army. The PPP has never been a strong party since its inception.

Since Z. A. Bhutto's execution in 1979, the PPP has remained a shell and its organizational abilities have eroded. Benazir Bhutto, as the new leader of the PPP led the efforts to mobilize popular support for the restoration of democracy in Pakistan in the early 1980s but showed no enthusiasm for the reorganization of the party. The lack of cadre and dedicated organizers in the party, the inexperience of Benazir, and her poor rapport with PPP's old guards resulted in converting the PPP and the Movement for the Restoration of Democracy (MRD) into extensions of her personal struggle for power. Benazir gave another set-back to the PPP by giving election tickets to her new allies or loyal 'Yes men', many of whom had been Zia's men; and several of those who joined the PPP cabinet in 1988 had also served in the Muslim League government in 1985–1988. All this made a mockery of the PPP and had negative repercussions on the morale of dedicated PPP activists and partymen.[5]

The 'Troika System' of Power Sharing

Benazir had to strike political compromises with the military-bureaucratic junta to get into power because of her weak electoral strength. She had, from the beginning, tactically come to terms with the military by giving it an important say in everything that matters to it—the defence expenditure, the conduct of foreign policy

---

[5]Reza Nasr, 'Democracy and the Crisis of Governability in Pakistan', p. 523.

and autonomy in its own affairs.[6] Thus, the military made it amply clear that it desired to share power and not transfer power.

The bureaucracy component of the military-bureaucratic oligarchy represented the then acting President Ghulam Ishaq Khan. To him, Benazir promised her support in his election as the president of the country. She also agreed to work in close consultation with the president in the matters of key appointments and policies.

The price that Benazir had to pay for her compromises with the military-bureaucratic alliance was obvious and evident. For example, she had to follow the American line on the Afghanistan question and had to accept Sahibzada Yaqub Khan as her foreign minister imposed by the army, and also to adopt a go-slow gesture towards the warm Soviet incentives and moves for improving overall relations with Pakistan.

She was obviously hoping that she would be able to change the terms of the deal struck by her with President Ishaq Khan and the Chief of the Army Staff, General Mirza Aslam Beg, once she consolidated her power. This did not happen. In fact, she had less room for manoeuvre because the Zia loyalists, operating through the IDA, had been able to enlist the support of other significant political actors.

Rifts in the 'Troika'

Although on the surface, in the beginning, one might find areas of mutual and temporary convergence between the political interests of Benazir with the military-bureaucratic junta, yet one could discern that the overall relationship of the former with the latter remained uneasy. This was quite apparent when one views the triangular tussle between the prime minister and the president, the centre and the Punjab, and the combined opposition party and the PPP.[7]

The tension between the prime minister and the president gets reflected in routine matters as also on those issues whose

---

[6]S. D. Muni, 'Internal Political Problems', p. 7. Also see Rasual B. Rais, 'Pakistan in 1988: From Command to Conciliation Politics', *Asian Survey*, Vol. XXIX, No. 2 (February 1989), pp. 199–206.

[7]Ibid., pp. 1163–66.

political fallout is quite important. Among the controversies, one pertained to the president's undue delay in inviting Benazir to take over as prime minister and the other was the dissolution of the Baluchistan Assembly, which many presumed, was done with his prior knowledge, if not concurrence. Besides, in the controversy regarding the continuation of Admiral Iftikhar Ahmed Sirohey as the Chairman of Joint Chiefs of Staff Committee (JCSC) beyond August 14, the all-powerful President Ghulam Ishaq Khan prevailed over Ms Bhutto. Moreover, the president had also not looked with favour on the prime minister's attempts to rehabilitate those civil servants who were persecuted during the Zia period. Even in the conflict between the centre and the opposition-ruled Punjab, on the question of the appointment of federal civil servants in the Punjab against the wishes of the IDA chief minister, and Benazir's formidable political foe, Mian Nawaz Sharif, the president reportedly tried to moderate the prime minister's position to make her accommodate Nawaz Sharif. There are so many other examples of crossing swords on similar small but important issues.[8]

However, the undercurrent tension between the prime minister and the president stemmed from the mischievous Eighth Amendment which was introduced by Zia and gave tremendous powers to the president.[9] Aware of the constitutional prerogative of the president to dismiss the prime minister and dissolve the National Assembly, Benazir wanted to repeal this Eighth Amendment. However, the PPP lacked the requisite two-thirds majority in the National Assembly, besides having a Muslim League controlled hostile Senate. Moreover, the IDA's vehement opposition to doing away with the amendment, which would make the prime minister more powerful, had further reduced its chances of being repealed.

Besides the president, the army also wielded considerable power in the new set-up. Benazir could not take decisions on her own on defence and nuclear policy matters. This is why the stand she was taking on the nuclear issue prior to the election was not guiding her actions now. Benazir did not want to take any chances.

---

[8]Mushahid Hussain, 'Pakistan President Plays Key Political Role', *The Times of India* (New Delhi), 18 July 1989, p. 6. Also see Dilip Mukherjee, 'Ms. Bhutto's Predicament: Sharing Power to Survive', *The Times of India*, 4 May 1990, p. 6.
[9]For details of the powers of the president, consult the text of Revival of Constitutional Order of 1985.

This was clear from her answer to a question on defence expenditure. As *Newsweek* put it in a post-election round up, 'Asked whether it was possible to cut the military's massive budget,' she casually replied 'Surely ... if you want to invite martial law.' In Benazir's own words, 'Realistically speaking, given the present situation, it would be very difficult for any government to survive without the critical backing of the armed forces.'[10] This also marked a significant departure from the stand she took during the election campaign.

In the summer of 1989, things were beginning to fall apart, but Benazir did not see the signs. On the contrary, she felt it was time to assert herself. The *Mujahideen* thrust against Jalalabad had failed and Benazir started off by spreading rumours that the army was responsible for the failure of the Afghan policy. At the same time, she openly blamed the president's obstructiveness for her inability to change things in the Frontier Province. More foolhardy were her attempts to get at the army.

She first had the Inter-Services Intelligence (ISI) Chief, Hamid Gul, transferred as Commander of the Strike Corps in Multan. Next, she appointed a committee under one of her buddies, Air Marshal Zulfiqar Khan, to see how the country's intelligence agencies could be reformed. Between April and October 1989, she tried her best to retire the Joint Chief of Staff, Admiral Iftikhar Ahmed Sirohey. Her intention was to kick the army supremo General Mirza Aslam Beg to Sirohey's position and install an army chief of her choice. This was a loud attack and it completely alienated her from the armed forces. The other case that widened the gulf between the prime minister and the military was the Pucca Qila incident in May 1990.[11] Besides, Benazir tried to influence the working of the army's selection board, seeking to extend the term of Lieutenant General, Alam Jan Mehsud, Corps Commander in Lahore. This led the military top brass to conclude that Benazir was not upholding the military and was interfering in their professional domain.

So far as the government's relationship with the bureaucracy was concerned, the PPP alienated it by maintaining an unusually

---

[10] *Newsweek* (New York), 16 December 1989.
[11] For details consult, Saeed Shafqat, *Civil–Military Relations in Pakistan: From Z. A. Bhutto to Benazir Bhutto* (Boulder: Westview Press, 1979), pp. 229.

large roster of government servants as Officers on Special Duty, a designation denoting the absence of a regular posting for an indefinite period. Therefore, the bureaucracy felt ignored and mistrusted by the PPP. In another move, she completely bypassed the Pakistan Public Services Commission and opened an employment exchange in her own office. Through this expedient, she unabashedly appointed party workers and posted them at all levels of the federal and provincial bureaucracies.

Centre-Province Confrontation

Another major constraint in the system had been introduced by the electoral verdict: confrontation between the centre and the Punjab, a state comparable with Uttar Pradesh in India. The opposition provincial government in the Punjab was virtually operating a 'state within a state'. The Centre-Punjab rift began from day one, when Nawaz Sharif of the IDA staked his claim to form the government. Since then, the two warring parties have been engaged actively in a political battle to checkmate each other.[12] There was no aspect of political competition and meanness that had been left untouched in the conflict.[13] The IDA, which represented the hardcore interests of the military-bureaucratic alliance, had resorted to public accusation on foreign policy issues (such as the Afghanistan question, nuclear proliferation and Pakistan's relations with India), the appointment of the State Chief Secretary by the centre, the police raid at the Secretariat in the Punjab and the consequent transfer of the state's Inspector General of Police, and so on. The IDA's efforts in widening the PPP's rift with the provincial forces like the Awami National Party (ANP) and Baluchistan National Alliance and even the MQM intensified the political war between the PPP and the IDA, as also between the federal and Punjab governments. The centre, on its part, was equally active in exposing the IDA supporters. With both sides eager to topple the other, horse-trading took priority over administration.

---

[12]Christina Lamb, 'Power Struggle Paralysis', *Financial Times* (London), 3 July 1989.
[13]See Mushahid Hussain, 'A Counter Offensive by the PPP', *The Times of India*, 14 September 1986, p. 6.

Benazir, instead of winning friends and influencing people, was steadily antagonising every power-centre in Pakistan. She went hammer and tongs to destabilize the opposition governments in the Punjab and Sindh. In the context of centre-state relations, it is worth noting that the imprudent attitude of the federal government on the issue of provincial autonomy was equally responsible for its tense relationship with the governments of the Punjab and Baluchistan. She introduced the discredited People's Works Programme (PWP), a Pakistani version of the Congress (I) Jawahar Rozgar Yojana, under which her party workers were empowered to implement federally-funded projects in the provinces. Opposition parties feared that the programme would weaken them at the grassroots levels and strengthen the PPP, which was using its district level workers for implementation. The PWP was a major factor which led to the breaking of the PPP's accord with the ANP in the NWFP.

The attitude of Nawaz Sharif as Chief Minister of Punjab was certainly confrontational but Benazir also did little to promote a politics of accommodation and her inability to control or seek conciliation with the Punjabi leadership further weakened her position. Both Benazir and Sharif were not able to dislodge the other, but in the process centre-province confrontation intensified, tarnishing Benazir's image and weakening her government's ability to evolve meaningful relations with the provinces.

The severest political challenge to her 11-month-old regime was posed by the Opposition United Front on 23 October 1989, in terms of the tabling of the motion of no-confidence. She won the round on 1 November, but with the barest of margins and was temporarily chastened. Besides, some shine had worn off from Benazir's rather glossy international image since the motion for no-confidence exemplified a yawning chasm that existed between her performance in foreign affairs and that of her government at home.[14]

---

[14]Mushahid Hussain, 'Benazir's Goal is Consolidation Now', *The Times of India*, 4 November 1989, p. 6. Also see Lawrence Ziring, 'Pakistan in 1989: The Politics of Stalemate', *Asian Survey*, Vol. XXX, No. 2 (February 1990), pp. 129–34.

Managing the Economy

On the economic front, Benazir adopted a two fold policy to spur an economic rejuvenation. First, the PPP abandoned its socialist goals and she sought to bring the private sector back to the centre of economic activity. She tried to reassure the private sector by allowing non-government investment in industry. Her administration also streamlined the process of granting industrial licences by setting up an investment bureau in the prime minister's office. The second element of the prime minister's programme, akin to Ayub Khan's economic programme in the 1960s, provided the private sector with easy access to investment funds from government controlled banks.[15] But the prime minister received more blame than credit for her economic policies, since there was widespread feeling that her investment bureau had favoured her political allies, relatives and friends. Moreover, the economic decision-making was centralized in Benazir's hands. Unemployment, inflation and stagnation in industrial enterprises, particularly in the public sector, demanded immediate attention and policy action, which the Benazir government did not seem to be able to provide. The government's failure in managing the economy in terms of corruption, the misuse of government authority in allocating licences for establishing new industries, granting cheap credit from state-owned commercial and investment banks by the prominent members of PPP, as also Benazir's husband Asif Ali Zardari's reputation as 'Mr. Ten Percent' all eroded the legitimacy of her government.

Managing the Ethnic Conflicts

In Sindh, the endemic strife between ethnic groups was another area of concern with implications for its internal stability for Benazir's government.[16] Proliferation of illicit arms and their easy accessibility, compounded by extensive drug cultivation and trade had led to the brutalization of society.

---

[15]Shahid Javed Burki, 'Pakistan's Cautious Democratic Course', *Current History*, Vol. LXXXXI, No. 563 (March 1992), p. 119.
[16]See Reza Nasr, 'Democracy and the Crisis of Governability in Pakistan', p. 521.

With the escalation of ethnic violence in Sindh, the army was called in. She had herself sought the easy way out in Sindh by trying to use the army for her political ends, thereby eschewing the more difficult political path of a dialogue leading to some sort of reconciliation with the other side in Sindh's growing political divide. This was a sad return of what her father attempted in Baluchistan with disastrous results for democracy.

While Sindh burned, her failure to pressure India on the Kashmir issue fuelled the opposition's propaganda against her. By this time, her opponents were up in arms—determined to bring about a final showdown. The early part of 1990 marked the beginning of her downfall. President Ishaq Khan opposed her budget and succeeded in amending it according to his desire. The Senate picked up the Shariat Bill and passed it. The army forced her to approve its list of transfers and appointments. Besides, Benazir Bhutto again was at odds with General Beg. The main point at issue was the Benazir government's refusal to confer on the army the powers needed to enable the soldiers to deal with terrorism and lawlessness in Sindh 'firmly and fairly'. This had touched off a virtual slanging match between some PPP leaders and the all-powerful General Headquarters. In the wake of these problems, her opponents began planning another no-confidence motion.

Aware of the fact that the ground was slipping under her, Benazir started her own political campaign. In mid-July 1990, the intelligence agencies reported to the president that this time too Benazir was likely to return with a formidable majority if mid-term elections were held. Once the military-bureaucratic alliance got wind of the news that she was secretly preparing for elections, it was time to act. Benazir Bhutto had to be stopped.

The Bhutto government was dismissed on 6 August 1990, by President Ghulam Ishaq Khan on charges of corruption and mismanagement. He dissolved the National Assembly and appointed the combined opposition leader Ghulam Mustafa Jataoi (once an ardent follower of Zulfiqar Ali Bhutto and who had deserted Benazir some years ago) as the care-taker prime minister. The president also announced elections on 24 October 1990.

Nawaz Sharif at the Helm: 1990–1993

The 1990 election marked a watershed in Pakistan's politics. The Zia proteges were back, in triumph, under the banner of the IDA, winning a clear majority. Nawaz Sharif's government became the first in Pakistan's history to enjoy more than a two-thirds majority in the National Assembly. It was also the first time, as one might point out, that the same party was in power in all the four provinces. Nawaz Sharif's government had two advantages over Benazir. He enjoyed an absolute majority in the National Assembly, together with total control over the Punjab, Pakistan's heart in every sense of the term, something which Benazir lacked and which turned out to be her major handicap in effective governance. Besides, the IDA controlled the effective exercise of power in Karachi through the MQM. Above all, Sharif had the overriding merit of having an excellent rapport with the two mighty pillars of the ruling establishment, President Ishaq Khan, with his discretionary constitutional power, and the army, indisputably the final arbiter of things in Pakistan.[17] But even though he started with such advantages, Nawaz Sharif witnessed a continuing decline in stature quite rapidly. Ethnic violence escalated, policy-making at the centre and local levels became confused.[18]

The Political Scene

However, after just over four months, the once 'ideal troika' was ridden with conflicts. Its three components were pulling in different directions.[19] Nawaz Sharif was evidently facing a worsening in his relations with President Ishaq Khan, on account of the latter's constitutional prerogative that he derived from the mischievous

---

[17]For details, see Veena Kukreja, 'Politics in Pakistan: Nawaz Sharif at the Helm', *Strategic Analysis*, Vol. XXX, No. 6 (September 1991), p. 665.

[18]Mushahid Hussain, 'Important Gains for Pakistani Democracy', *The Times of India*, 9 November 1990, p. 6.

[19]See Veena Kukreja, 'Restoration of Democracy and Crisis of Governability in Pakistan: 1988–92', in, Subrata Mukherjee and Sushila Ramaswamy (eds), *Political Science Annual 1993* (New Delhi: Deep and Deep, 1994), pp. 198–212.

Eighth Amendment, promulgated by Zia-ul-Haq in 1985, and which invested tremendous powers in the office of the president. During the two years, President Ishaq Khan had steadily become an alternative centre of power at the prime minister's cost. The president had taken *de facto* charge of Pakistan's foreign policy. He played a leading role on the nuclear issue. In the domestic arena, he had been inclined to treat Sindh as his personal fiefdom with his son-in-law playing a high profile role in the province's administration. These interventions led to the enormous expansion of presidential powers.

In this context, it is important to note that the IDA's controversial electoral victory in 1990 convinced the IDA's rank and file of the need for the president's support (and thus for the Eighth Amendment) in the drive against the PPP. In practical terms, this restrained Nawaz Sharif's ability to draw upon the absolute loyalty of his party-men in the National Assembly. As an eminent scholar Mohammad Waseem aptly remarked,

'He faces an anomalous situation; on the one hand, the existing constitutional framework has rendered his position to one of proxy for extra-parliamentary forces symbolized by the President, thus costing him in terms of legitimacy as an elected leader in his own rights. On the other hand, it continues to restrain him from following a course of action that would promote a policy of accommodation with the PPP opposition and establish a working relationship with it.'[20]

So far as Sharif's relationship with the Army Headquarters was concerned, it had been somewhat less than satisfactory. During the Gulf War, General Aslam Beg, the COAS, took a position that was opposed to the official policy. The government supported the coalition building efforts of the United States against Iraq, while the COAS supported Iraq—this embarrassed the government and the prime minister. Similarly in June 1992, when General Asif Nawaz Janjua started operation clean-up in Sindh it struck at the very roots of PML(N)–MQM alliance.

On the political front, Sharif pursued the policy of containing and suppressing the PPP to establish the dominance of the PML(N).

---

[20]Mohammad Waseem, 'Pakistan's Lingering Crisis of Dyarchy', *Asian Survey*, Vol. XXXII, No. 7 (July 1992), reproduced in *Strategic Digest*, Vol. XXII, No.12 (December 1992), pp. 1592–93.

His government pursued this vigorously by encouraging court cases against Benazir, her husband Zardari, and other PPP stalwarts. In Sindh, Sharif skillfully expanded and consolidated a partnership with MQM and ventured to build a support base in rural Sindh. In the NWFP, he forged an alliance with the Awami National Party (ANP). By building an alliance with MQM and ANP, Sharif succeeded in containing the PPP. His alliance with the ANP evoked disapproval from the Jamaat-i-Islami and eventually contributed towards the break up of the IDA.

However, in due course of time, Sharif's troubles began with the political and ideological sections of the IDA. The IDA of Sharif was cobbled together, consisting of right-of-centre and Islamic parties by the notorious Inter-Services Intelligence on the eve of the 1988 election with the avowed purpose of defeating the PPP. The IDA coalition had eroded its edge further by the withdrawal of support by the MQM.[21]

To cap it all was the law and order situation in Sindh; violence became *prima ratio* and replaced the normal channels of problem solving in the country. In May 1992, the army launched 'operation clean up'. Though it was supposed to be against gangsters, its target was the MQM. As a result, the MQMs, MNAs and MPAs submitted their resignation and went underground.

State of the Economy

Turning his attention to the economy, Sharif had moved to base the economy on the free market mechanism, aimed at rebuilding confidence in the private sector and to attract foreign capital. A series of reforms was carried out to accelerate the pace of economic growth through deregulation and privatization. However, there was severe criticism of the way the government went about it. Besides, such factors as suspension of US aid to Pakistan, drying remittances from the Gulf, decline of national income from managing the Afghan *Jihad* and rampant corruption in the country's ruling circles had played a

---

[21]Dilip Mukherjee, 'Sharif on Sticky Wicket: Frailty of Pakistan's Democracy', *The Times of India*, 16 October 1992, p. 8. Also see Lawrence Ziring, 'Dilemma and Challenge in Nawaz Sharif's Pakistan', in Charles H. Kennedy (ed.), *Pakistan: 1992* (Boulder: Westview, 1993), pp. 1–18.

significant role in preventing the government in enduring the stalemate at the economic front. Nawaz Sharif's involvement in some shady financial deals, including the alleged sell-out of the Muslim Commercial Bank and the bankruptcy of certain cooperatives of the IDA ministries and leaders had seriously eroded the credibility of the government. The regime initiated grandiose projects like Motorway and Yellow Cab Scheme, during which normal procedures were set aside. Since Pakistan's economy and finances was being managed by the president during the Zia years, this situation evoked heavy criticism from him.

Opposition's Strategy

Booted out of power, Benazir assuming the role of the opposition leader in the parliament, demonstrated greater resilience, imagination and manipulative capacity to mobilize the masses. She made efforts to mend relations with the army, create a wedge between the president and the prime minister and exploited shrewdly, the differences between the two and both of them sought her support. Under siege from either side by the president and the opposition, Sharif resorted to draconian measures to prevent the opposition from capturing the capital through street action. The 'long march' by the opposition failed to deliver the goods but the IDA government's harsh actions allowed Ishaq Khan to issue veiled threats to Sharif by making known his 'displeasure' at the government's trampling of the people's democratic rights.

In sum, the ongoing discussion presents a 'skewed pattern of authority'[22] in Pakistan. The four leading actors on the political scene of Pakistan in 1992 were President Ishaq Khan, the military, Prime Minister Nawaz Sharif and the People's Democratic Alliance (PDA) led by Benazir. The dyarchical arrangement for sharing power between the parliamentary and non-parliamentary forces represented a situation characterized by limited policy choices and an inherently unstable relationship between the permanent state

---

[22]Mohammad Waseem, 'Pakistan's Lingering Crisis of Dyarchy', p. 1600–1602.

apparatus, on the one hand, and political leaders and parties who participate in electoral politics, on the other.[23]

Epic Struggle between the President and the Prime Minister

The dyarchical pattern of power sharing initiated a proxy war between President Ishaq Khan and Prime Minister Nawaz Sharif. The power struggle between the president and the prime minister began when Nawaz Sharif publicly suggested a reduction in the president's powers, including abolition of the National Assembly. Nawaz Sharif's first attempt to curtail the president's power was made through the Shariat Bill and the Thirteenth Amendment, both enactments widely seen as a concession to the po'itico-religious lobby in the country. But both enactments had a sting in them in that they curtailed, to a limited extent, the presidential powers.[24] Ishaq Khan saw through Sharif's game plan and put his foot down.

Relations between the president and the prime minister reached the lowest ebb on the appointment of an army chief after the death of General Asif Nawaz Janjua in January. Ishaq Khan exercised his discretionary powers under the Eighth Amendment to appoint General Abdul Waheed Kakar, a fellow Pathan, superseding six senior generals in the process.

This move prompted Sharif to come out openly against the Eighth Amendment and he appointed a Cabinet Committee to took into the issue of repealing it. At the same time, he maintained an equivocal silence on the issue of giving Ishaq Khan a second term as president.

Realizing that a presidential re-election would allow Ishaq Khan another five years to dominate him, Sharif obviously viewed the current political situation as favourable. The President, he hoped, could

---

[23]Rais Ahmed Khan, 'Pakistan in 1992: Waiting for Change', *Asian Survey*, Vol. XXXVIII, No. 2 (February 1993), pp. 129–40. Also see Tahir Amin, 'Pakistan in 1993: Some Democratic Change', *Asian Survey*, Vol. XXXIV, No. 2 (February 1994), pp. 191–99.

[24]*The Times of India*, 22 February 1993. Also see *The News* (Lahore), 1 March 1993; M. B. Naqvi, 'Survival of the Wiliest', *Sunday Times of India*, 11 April 1993.

be neutralized by repealing the Eighth Amendment. In this endeavour, he had hoped to get Benazir Bhutto's support, as together they had the necessary two-thirds electoral strength to repeal the infamous controversial amendment. By taking à line diametrically opposite to that of the President, Sharif set the agenda for the future course of the power struggle.

But Sharif's targeting of the Eighth Amendment brought a stiff response from the president who went on record to state that it was his duty to defend every Article of the Constitution and he would prevent any subversion of it.[25] In a bid to build counter pressure upon Sharif, Ishaq Khan began activating his 'men' in most political parties, pushing Sharif into a corner. The distrust between Sharif and Benazir had failed to bring them into any rock-solid alliance and the only option left for Sharif was to back out and suggest the nomination of the president for a second term.

But the tussle between the president and the prime minister heightened; it was not resolved even after the government officially decided to field Ishaq Khan as its nominee for the president's post. The president was in no mood to relent.

The return of Benazir had complicated the picture further—by seizing the chance to re-enter the establishment's good books, she met the president for the first time since her dismissal. She demanded the dissolution of the National Assembly.[26] Her role was opportunistic and aiming to maximize her gains by aligning with the winning candidate.

There was a difference of opinion in Pakistan even within the PPP ranks over the wisdom of abandoning the Eighth Amendment. It was felt that repealing this provision could result in an over ambitious person like Sharif keeping all powers for the prime minister. Even Ishaq Khan warned that the Eighth Amendment 'serves as a safety valve against imposition of martial law'[27] which is a reference to the 1977 Zia inspired coup.

The hostility between the president and the prime minister became open once Sharif made a strong speech on television on 17

---

[25]Aabha Dixit, 'Focus on Pakistan's Army', *The Times of India*, 24 Apri 1993, p. 14.

[26]M. B. Naqvi, 'Brightest Star on Pakistan's Firmament Under Cloud', *The Times of India*, 27 June 1993, p.12. Also see his 'Ishaq Khan–Machiavelli in Pakistan Politics', *The Times of India*, 2 June 1993.

[27]V. K. Dethe, 'Pakistan: Power Play: Of Leaders and the President's Prime Ministers', *The Times of India*, 20 April 1993, p. 21.

April 1993, attacking the intrigues' and 'conspiracies' hatched by the presidency. While the bold gambit by the prime minister was apparently timed to stop the steady stream of resignations by pro-Ishaq men from the Federal Cabinet and government, it ended only in hastening his departure.

Nawaz Sharif Sacked

Ishaq Khan, the Machiavelli of Pakistan, responded quickly—dissolving the National Assembly and sacking the prime minister on 18 April 1993, on charges of corruption and incompetence, and announced elections in July. Nawaz Sharif challenged the decision of the president in the Supreme Court, and the Chief Justice, Nasim Hasan Shah, in an unprecedented decision demonstrating the independence of judiciary, issued a verdict saying Ishaq Khan had exceeded his powers, and restored the National Assembly.[28] The hopes that the Supreme Court verdict would curb Ishaq Khan's authoritarian style of functioning were belied as he took the political battle to the provincial level. The presidentially appointed Governor of Punjab dissolved the assembly which was on the brink of throwing its weight behind Sharif.[29] The Lahore High Court on 8 June restored the Punjab Assembly in an interim order, sending the country's politics into a tail spin once again.[30]

Army Brokers a Deal

In the wake of a constitutional breakdown, the opposition announced a long march on Islamabad to force the prime minister to call for new elections, but on 15 July, the march was called off on the army's appeal.[31]

---

[28]See *Muslim* (Islamabad), 18 April 1993. Also see H. K. Dua, 'Pakistan: Politics of Intrigue', *The Hindustan Times* (New Delhi), 22 April 1993, p. 13.

[29]See *Dawn* (Karachi), 27 May 1993. Also see Samina Yasmeen, 'Democracy in Pakistan: The Third Dismissal', *Asian Survey*, Vol. XXXIV, No. 6 (June 1994), pp. 572–86.

[30]*Muslim*, 1 July 1993 and *The Times of India*, 1 July 1993, p. 8.

[31]Praful Bidwai, 'Lahore Verdict Opens New Phase in Pakistan', *The Times of India*, 11 June 1993. Also see *The Times of India*, 9 June 1993.

In the wake of talks about a military takeover,[32] in a deal brokered by the Army Chief, General Abdul Waheed Kakar, Ishaq Khan and Sharif agreed to resign to end the nearly five-month-long struggle between the prime minister and the president that had made Pakistan virtually ungovernable, paving the way for fresh elections.[33] It was also a tribute to the powers of the army that the two antagonists, Nawaz Sharif and Ishaq Khan, proclaimed that they quit voluntarily to save the nation and democracy. It exemplifies the army's continuing clout in the political affairs of Pakistan.

Benazir's Second Term: 1993–1996

The 1993 elections held under the supervision of the military brought Benazir Bhutto and her party, the PPP, to power once again after 40 months in the wilderness. This time too Benazir's PPP could not get a clear majority in the National Assembly and had to form the government with the help of its ally the PML (Junejo) and the minority members, smaller parties and some independents. Resuming the prime ministership, Benazir Bhutto made appointments that showed much more experience and skill in retaining, building and sustaining not only the coalition government in the Punjab but also relations with important national leaders and political parties. In the opening spell of Benazir's second term in office, she tried to be non-controversial and moved with great caution in strengthening her position within the establishment. In this context, Mahmood Monshipouri and Amjad Samuel rightly observe, 'she appeared intent on developing her own links with the army, confirming its role in Pakistani politics but making it indirect.'[34]

---

[32]See *The Times of India*, 1 July 1993, p. 8.

[33]M. B. Naqvi, 'Army May Step in as Crisis Builds in Pakistan', *The Times of India*, 3 July 1993.

[34]Mahmood Monshipouri and Amjad Samuel, 'Development and Democracy in Pakistan', *Asian Survey*, Vol. XXXV, No. 11 (November 1995), p. 984. Also see, Kanti Bajpai and Sumit Ganguly, 'Transition to Democracy in Pakistan', *In Depth*, Vol. III, No. 2 (Spring, 1993), pp. 59–86.

Relations with the Military Establishment

By forging cordial relations with the establishment, Benazir protected herself and preferred to toe their line on several issues, including the Kashmir question, the Afghanistan issue and regular increase in defence spending. Compared to her first government, Benazir, in her second term, was prudent in dealing with the military, avoiding interference in army affairs. For example, the retirement of JCSC Chairman, General Shamim Ahmad was managed smoothly and efficiently, unlike the Sirohey affair. Similarly, the selection of the chiefs of air staff and the naval staff were made without causing any ripples. On 12 January 1996, General Jehangir Karamat took over the command of the Pakistan army upon the completion of term of General Abdul Waheed, the first time that the senior-most general had become COAS.

Benazir also carefully protected the corporate interests of the military by vigorously campaigning to procure arms from different sources, but especially from the US. The Brown Amendment was trumpeted as a victory for her government. Despite pressures from the International Monetary Fund (IMF), the World Bank, and her own government's public pronouncements on increasing funds for health, housing, education and population welfare, she resisted decrease in defence allocation, and in 1993–1994 and 1994–1995, defence expenditures stood at 26 per cent of the entire budget. Thus, the civilian regime was constrained and chose to pursue vigorously a security agenda defined by the military. In sum, the Benazir government was careful not to antagonize the military. On Kashmir, her government made concerted efforts but without sufficient homework to present the Kashmir issue on various international forums and United Nations but won little support from the international community on Pakistan's position.

Benazir and the President

Within a few months of coming into power, Benazir was able to get her confidant Sardar Farooq Ahmed Leghari as the President. This had substantially changed the power structure in Bhutto's favour.

However, after a few months, Benazir's relations with the loyalist President Farooq Ahmed Leghari became strained. During the initial period, after being installed as president, Leghari demonstrated his proximity to the prime minister. But later, he tended to distance himself from Benazir on numerous key issues. The differences between the president and the prime minister became public for the first time on the issue of the selection of the new COAS. Leghari voted in favour of the military's choice i.e., Jehangir Karamat instead of Benazir's candidate for the COAS. Besides, Leghari prescribed a moderate course of action in Karachi, which sharply varied with the government's determination to find a military solution for the problem. Similarly, Leghari preferred to side with the armed forces on several other issues concerning Afghanistan and Kashmir.[35] After sharing a comfortable relationship with the former Army Chief, General Abdul Waheed, Benazir was not on easy term with the new COAS, General Jehangir Karamat.

Political Institution-Building

The political institutions in the country remained weak. The National Assembly and the Provincial Assemblies became the arenas for unprincipled horse-trading, rather than a forum for constructive debates on major political and socio-economic issues. The two major political parties, the PPP led by Benazir and the PML led by Sharif respectively were not well knit, cohesive, grassroots political organizations. From top to bottom both the parties had nominated leadership whomsoever sat on the top. Besides, every party was riven with factions. A split occurred within the PPP. Murtaza Bhutto, who returned to the country after 16 years of exile, regarded himself as the true heir of his father. To prevent Nusrat's bid to declare Murtaza her successor in the PPP, Benazir expelled her mother from the party's co-chairmanship. This intensified the power struggle within the Bhutto family. The PML was no better than the PPP. One of the factions of the League, which broke away from the parent party, had joined hands with the PPP in 1993 to form the government in the Punjab.

---

[35]Aabha Dixit, 'Developments in Pakistan', *Strategic Analysis*, Vol. XIX, No. 4 (July 1996), p. 623.

Benazir used patronage in its various forms to secure allegiances and reward the party loyalist. To ensure that judicial decisions do not disturb the politics, the government had filled the judiciary with men who supported the PPP. Top positions in the civil services had also come under political scrutiny.

The PPP retained the characteristics of a mass movement rather than a disciplined political party. The PPP was dominated by Benazir alongwith her few chosen advisors. 'The Prime Minister's secretariat', according to LaPorte, 'rather than the federal cabinet, played institutional role in policy-making, and Bhutto's personality was the dominating factor.'[36] Given the loss of its prominent ideological dimension in the 1970s and its anti-establishment rhetoric of the 1980s, 'There was', as Wilder observes, 'now little to differentiate the PPP and the PML(N) as they showed virtually the same manifestos, many of the same members of the National Assembly, and the same sole objective of winning and hold on to power at all costs.'[37]

Nawaz Sharif, when he was in power, was not any better than Benazir. He also took decisions without consulting his cabinet or the National Assembly. An intense confrontation between the PPP government led by Benazir Bhutto and the opposition PML(N) led by Nawaz Sharif dominated Pakistani politics during 1993–1996. Neither the government nor the PML(N) showed any tolerance towards each other, with the former pursuing vengeful policies, while the latter indulged in ceaseless agitation.[38] Both the government and the opposition remained locked in bitter confrontation politics. And each was the mirror image of the other. The PPP government behaved in a manner similar to the way the PML(N) had behaved when it was in power (1991–1993), and the PML(N) emulated the same agitational tactics that the PPP had used against it. As one observer aptly remarks, 'the sanctity of the institutions—president, judiciary and administration—suffered badly as a consequence, unintentionally increasing

---

[36]Robert LaPorte, Jr. 'Pakistan in 1995: The Continuing Crisis', *Asian Survey*, Vol. XXXVI, No. 2 (February 1996), p. 180.

[37]Andrew R. Wilder, 'Changing Patterns of Punjab Politics in Pakistan: National Assembly Election Results 1988 and 1993', *Asian Survey*, Vol. XXXV, No. 4 (April 1995), p. 343.

[38]See Tahir Amin, 'Pakistan in 1994: The Politics of Confrontation', *Asian Survey*, Vol. XXXV, No. 2 (February 1995), pp. 140–46.

dependence of the political process on the military in the familiar pattern that had led to coups in the past.'[39]

During 1989–1990, Nawaz Sharif seemed to work the wheels within the establishment to prevent Benazir from functioning. During her second term, Benazir had improved her relationship with the establishment. As a result, there was a qualitative change in the PML(N) political strategies. In a bid to undercut Benazir's support bases, Sharif had spent most of his time in the rural areas.

Sharif believed that the most effective strategy of putting pressure on Benazir came through street action—by paralyzing the functioning of her government. While attempting to strike a posture of reasonableness in public, Benazir was working within the parliament to undercut Sharif through a series of disclosures about financial irregularities committed during his term in office. The Mehran Bank scandal exposed the widespread level of financial corruption pervading the body politic. The image of many politicians were tarnished in the scandal involving Rs 600 crore.

Sharif revived the earlier bogey of Asif Ali Zardari representing the corrupt face of the PPP government, dubbing him as 'Mr. Twenty Five percent.' The replacement of the PML(N)-ANP coalition government in the NWFP by the PPP government set the ball of agitational politics rolling.

Benazir remained vulnerable to the pressure from the opposition, because of the wafer-thin majority that the PPP had managed. While the value of a strong opposition cannot be underestimated in a democracy, the struggle for power between Benazir and Sharif led to a very personalized, acrimonious kind of politics, where neither was willing to give an inch to the other. Benazir and Sharif—two ambitious, driven, arch rivals—instead of accepting each other as long-term rivals within a democratic modus vivendi, followed the path of a vicious zero-sum game.[40]

---

[39]Ibid., p. 141. Also see Robert LaPorte, Jr., 'Pakistan in 1996', *Asian Survey*, Vol. XXXVII, No. 2 (February 1997), pp. 119–20.
[40]Veena Kukreja, 'Pakistan's 1993 Election: Back to Square One', *Strategic Analysis*, Vol. XVI, No. 10 (January 1994), pp. 1363–64.

Ethnic Strife

So far as ethnic strife is concerned, Karachi became the sore point as the Benazir government had failed to curtail ethnic violence. The near anarchy situation in Karachi was the result of several years of urban civil war. The conflict and rise in violence had various dimensions, such as, ethnicity (Sindhis, *Muhajirs*, Pathans, Afghans and Biharis pitted against each other), sectarianism, Islamic fundamentalism, economics, the struggle for power and absence of power sharing, and drug trafficking. The situation became worse by the easy availability of weapons. The reported crime in Karachi increased by 10.2 per cent in November 1995 as compared to 1994, and murder for the same period increased by 49 per cent.[41]

Since regaining power, Benazir had found herself battling with the MQM in Karachi, where sectarian violence had grown enormously and residents expressed frustration with the government and wanted it to end the violence. In late 1994, the MQM-government tension in Sindh province intensified and led to a spiral of violence. Instead of finding a political solution to the *Muhajir* problem, the government permitted the security agencies to unleash an unprecedented wave of terror against the *Muhajirs* in Sindh and against other ethnic groups elsewhere in the country.

In Sindh, in the absence of an agreement on power-sharing between the MQM and the PPP, internecine civil war between the two factions of the MQM broke out. It was further fuelled by the covert role of civil and military intelligence agencies, and sectarian conflict between extremist Shia and Sunni organizations. This created, according to Tahir Amin, 'a proverbial Hobbesian condition of "war of all against all" in Karachi.'[42] This resulted in violence.

It appears that the PPP had learned little from its past mistakes vis-à-vis its policies in Karachi. The MQM, which had supported the PPP's presidential candidate unconditionally, became increasingly alienated because of lack of accommodation in the power structure at the provincial level. The PPP sought to rely on the military to maintain law and order in Karachi, which in turn, generated feelings of public resentment against the army in the urban areas of Sindh. The frequent breakdown of law and order in Karachi, Pakistan's largest city, had a

---

[41]Robert LaPorte, Jr. 'Pakistan in 1995: The Continuing Crisis', pp. 162–83.
[42]Tahir Amin, 'Pakistan in 1994: The Politics of Confrontation', p. 144.

crippling effect on its commercial life. The conviction of self-exiled MQM leader, Altaf Hussain in absentia, and the persecution of the other leading MQM activists strengthened the demand for the division of Sindh along linguistic lines. The repressive political climate under Benazir led to human rights violations. Benazir's handling of the *Muhajir* alienation in Sindh epitomized gross incompetence.

The Benazir government used the sectarian card to crush *Muhajir* unity. Imambaras and mosques became the principal targets, and some of the most gruesome killings resulted from sectarian tensions. Benazir failed to control the escalating sectarian violence, particularly between the Sunni and Shia militant organizations. These sectarian groups mushroomed during the Zia period and had private armies. These radical groups had been involved in mass killings of the members of the other sects, particularly in mosques during prayers. There was no initiative from the government to involve the saner elements of the sects to curb the growing menace to the common citizens. The sectarian problems related to the theological controversies, which have marked the history of Islam, had to be tackled tactfully rather than as a mere law and order problem.[43]

Economic Crisis

The severe economic crisis, however, proved the last straw on the camel's back which led the Pakistani establishment to dismiss Benazir. The deepening economic crisis was exposed with the budget for the 1996–1997 year. The budget had imposed a heavy burden on the people in order to meet the burgeoning deficit. As the country was living beyond its means for so many years, it had accumulated such a huge amount of public debt that annual interest charged had come to account for 45 per cent of the current expenditure of the federal government. The spectre of a financial crash had started looming large because of the extremely tight position of the country.

---

[43]Kalim Bahadur, *Democracy in Pakistan: Crises and Conflict* (New Delhi: Har-Anand Pvt. Ltd., 1998), p. 49.

The IMF refused to help Pakistan out of the present jam. The IMF wanted Pakistan to put its fiscal and financial house in order.[44]

Some of the conditions that the IMF laid in front of the Pakistan government included: (1) the fiscal deficit to be brought down to 4 per cent of the GDP; (2) taxation of agricultural incomes be undertaken to widen the tax base and enlargement of revenue receipts; (3) expenditure on defence and public administration to be cut down drastically to restore fiscal balance; and (4) overhauling of the tax collecting system with a view to plugging widespread tax leakage and evasion.[45]

However, the Benazir government found itself incapable of implementing the desired structural adjustment reforms. This was not so much due to lack of political will on the part of government as to the existing power structure of the country. The ruling elite of the country consists of big landlords of Sindh and Punjab, the defence establishment, and the civil-bureaucracy who rejected these reforms. In the wake of this economic mess, the opposition parties launched nationwide campaign and rallies calling for Benazir's resignation.

Benazir Bhutto, by her arrogance, unconcern for democratic norms and the interests of the people, had herself struck a blow against democracy and threw the country into a serious political and economic mess.

In sum, Pakistan's political system suffered from institutional decay, widespread economic crisis and rampant corruption, spiraling ethnic violence and bloodshed leading to near anarchic conditions in certain parts of the country. The military, because of its institutional interest had chosen to support the government despite an open invitation from opposition politician to intervene.[46]

In the wake of this economic and political mess the government was in a state of paralysis.[47] Power was slipping out of the government's hands. In addition to the killing of Murtaza Bhutto in a shoot out with Karachi Police on 20 September 1996, accusations in the court against Zardari further destroyed Bhutto's credibility and vital political card in the home province Sindh. Murtaza's widow

---

[44]Ahmed Rashid, 'Bhutto's Burden: Pakistan in Deep Economic Crisis', *The Times of India*, 23 September 1996, p. 13.

[45]B. M. Bhatia, 'Near the Brink', *The Hindustan Times*, 25 October 1996, p. 10.

[46]Tahir Amin, 'Pakistan in 1994: The Politics of Confrontation', p. 140.

[47]Ahmed Rashid's News Analysis, *The Nation*, 5 November 1996.

had openly implicated Asif Zardari in her husband's murder. Murtaza's murder signalled that Bhutto's government had all but ceased to exist. The announcement of her dismissal by the president was only a matter of formality.

On 5 November 1996, President Farooq Leghari issued a Dissolution Order that dismissed the government of Prime Minister Benazir Bhutto, following months of domestic turmoil and a dismal performance of the economy. In her second term from 1993–1996, the Bhutto government had succeeded in alienating the president, the military, the judiciary, the international assistance community, the business community and the public at large.

Nawaz Sharif's Second Term: 1997–1999

Nawaz Sharif stormed back to power for a second term with an un-precedented and astounding victory in the election held on 3 February 1997. Nawaz Sharif's PML commanded a decisive mandate—the largest ever majority in the country's political history winning two-thirds majority in the National Assembly. And PML, with its allies, formed the government in three of the four provinces in the country. Benazir's PPP witnessed an eclipse and ended with less than 20 seats in the house of 217. The PPP also suffered a humiliating defeat in the Punjab, once the citadel of the party's strength. But the tremendous goodwill that Sharif enjoyed when he returned to power evaporated too quickly. Nawaz Sharif's lust for absolute power did not take him long to expose his phony commitment to democracy.

The Political Scene

To spare himself from the sword of Democles, i.e., sudden dismissal by the president, Nawaz Sharif moved quickly to repeal the notorious Eighth Amendment [Article 58–2(b)]. This step was necessary for Sharif's own political survival. He had been the casuality of the Eighth Amendment during his first tenure in office. Therefore, the 13th Amendment was the only way for the survival of the Sharif government in case of confrontation with the president, which was inevitable. The 13th Amendment was appreciated by the political circles though there were some reservations. The resultant restoration of parliamentary sovereignty may have been the best thing that could happen to Pakistan's democracy. But according to Sharif's critics, the development meant little more to him than consolidating his personal authority.[48] Some observers suspected that given Sharif's proneness to authoritarian functioning, he would have no checks hereafter.[49]

The confrontation between Pakistan's executive and judiciary threatened Sharif's rule when the Supreme Court initiated contempt of court proceeding against him in November 1997.[50] The Pakistan polity remained involved in a three way struggle for power among the president, allied with the chief justice, the prime minister with a large majority in parliament, and a judiciary divided roughly into two equal factions. After several weeks of high constitutional drama, in which all the three branches of government were locked in mortal combat with one another, the prime minister appeared to have emerged victorious. President Farooq Leghari resigned and Chief Justice Sajjad Ali Shah of the Pakistani Supreme Court was ousted. Sharif's handling of the judicial crisis in late 1997 was totally undemocratic, when he authorized PML workers to storm the Supreme Court. Leghari's resignation was prompted by threat of impeachment. Thus, Nawaz Sharif weakened the democratic institution and strengthened the rule by his family.

The humiliation and removal of the chief justice and the president in their confrontation with the prime minister led to a gradual concentration of power in the hands of the latter, making him a 'democratic despot'. Nomination of a known Islamic conservative Rafiq Tarar for the election of president, caused disappointment among the party leaders as Sharif had ignored the claims of many senior party leaders of the PML. It was for the first time in the history of Pakistan that all the important positions in the country were held by Punjabis. The decision on putting up Rafiq Tarar was taken by the prime minister and a small coterie.

---

[48]Zaffar Abbas, 'Full Circle', *The Herald*, November 1999 reproduced in *Strategic Digest*, Vol. XXIX, No. 12 (December 1999), p. 1793.

[49]Kalim Bahadur, *Democracy in Pakistan: Crises and Conflict*, p. 169.

[50]For details see Answar H. Syed, 'Pakistan in 1997: Nawaz Sharif's Second Chance to Govern', *Asian Survey*, Vol. XXXVIII, No. 2 (February 1998), pp. 119–20.

Nawaz Sharif weakened political institutions in his lust for power. He turned into an autocrat by converting the parliament into a rubber stamp. In fact, Nawaz Sharif had gone further than General Zia in quashing his legislators. His parliament did not even know if a constitutional amendment bill was in the offing. Sharif had forced his assembly to muzzle its own mouth by getting it to pass an anti-dissent law. The cabinet hardly met.[51] He trusted only his family members. His kitchen cabinet, headed by his illustrious father, had indirectly elected senators. In this context, a perceptive scholar, Tariq Ali, has aptly remarked, 'Nawaz Sharif, his brother Shahbaz and their father Muhammad, strong believers in globalization and neo-liberal economics, helped in creating an enterprise culture in which they genuinely believed that everything was for sale, including politicians, civil servants and yes generals.'[52]

If one looks at the nature of the PML, one finds that ᴛ.ᴇ post-1985 PML has never acted as a political party in the conventional sense. It was either a conglomerate of political elements who were either close to the military establishment, or were known as Bhutto-haters.

After Sharif took over the reins of the government for the second time in his political career, the party began to split. Some senior members started to complain about being ignored in the decision-making process while others felt that Sharif had become too autocratic. It soon became apparent that the only factor that was keeping the party intact was the fact that it was in power. Differences between ordinary legislators and Sharif's inner circle continued to grow—a case in point being Sharif's tensions with Eiazul Huq but they could never quite surface in the form of any organized protest. However, 'When Sharif introduced the Shariat Bill in the National Assembly in August 1999 without consulting his own party, it almost led to a mini-rebellion.'[53]

---

[51]Zohra Yusuf, 'The Year in Democracy', *The Herald,* Annual (Karachi), January 1998, pp. 89–90; Aamer Ahmed Khan, 'The New Face of Nawaz Sharif', *The Herald,* Annual, Vol. XXIX, No. 1 (January 1998), p. 89.
[52]Quoted from *The Pioneer* (Delhi), 7 April 2000, p. 7.
[53]Zaffar Abbas, 'Future Uncertain', *The Herald,* November 1999, reproduced in *Strategic Analysis,* p. 1817.

Ethnic and Sectarian Strife

Another major concern for Nawaz Sharif was the continuing ethnic and sectarian strife in various parts of the country which had gone out of hand without the government having any clue as to how to resolve it. The already complicated scene in the Sindh province was wrecked by violence. Thousands of innocent people had fallen victim to the sectarian fanaticism of armed militias. Many observers saw the Sunni-Shia conflicts as a 'proxy war', between Saudi Arabia and Iran waged on the soil of Pakistan. No measures were taken to curb the tide of rising violence and bloodshed. This was particularly apparent in Karachi.

The PML and the MQM had hated each other but their common hatred of the PPP had brought them together to keep Benazir's PPP out of power. However, this relationship soon ran into difficulties. The MQM periodically organized protest marches and strikes in order to press the government for the implementation of the agreement of cooperation that they had signed in February 1997. The MQM complained that its representatives were excluded from policy-making on important provincial affairs. In August, its ministries resigned from the federal and provincial cabinets and the party demanded an investigation by the United Nations into the killings of its workers by the state security agencies. The federal government managed to woo the MQM back but they soon developed sharp differences on the escalating violence in Karachi. The federal government accused the MQM hard core of involvement in these incidents and imposed Governor's Rule in Sindh on 30 October as the first step in a massive security operation. NWFP, Wali Khan's Awami National Party (ANP) and the Baluchistan people were all angry with the all pervasive Punjabi dominance symbolized by the Sharif brothers, the prime minister and Shahbaz, the Chief Minister of Punjab. The ANP, which had been supporting the PML(N) for the previous eight years, dropped out when the federal government refused to rename the NWFP as Pakhtunkhwa. The ANP alleged that Sharif and his associates had backed out of an earlier commitment for this change.

Besides the federal government's unilateral decision in June to revive the Kala Bagh hydro-electric dam project at the river Indus in NWFP, caused a serious and dangerous polarization on the lines of federal government/Punjab versus other provinces.[54] The polarization sharpened when the Sharif government unveiled its plan to introduce a constitutional Amendment (15th) to amass more powers at the expense of the parliament, the judiciary and the provinces, under the pretext of introducing *Sharia* (Islamic laws) and mobilize orthodox Islamic groups to counterbalance his political adversaries.

State of Economy

As far as the state of the economy was concerned, it was in dire straits. The faltering economy constituted the most serious threat to the polity. The government was unable to muster enough political will and institutional capacity to cope with the culture of tax evasion, rampant corruption and extravagant government expenditure. The business community, the traditional stronghold of Sharif, twice foiled the government's attempts to impose 'a general sales tax. Similarly, agriculturalists were not prepared to pay more than nominal taxes. Naturally the shortfall in revenue collection accentuated the existing resource gap and forced the federal government to cut back on the revenue share of the provinces.[55]

The major public sector enterprises like the Water and Power Development Authority, Karachi Electricity Supply Company, Pakistan International Air Lines, Pakistan Steel and Railways continued to face acute financial crises. Another intricate problem was the non-payment of outstanding bank loans held by political influentials, including the Sharif family.

The major international financial institutions including the IMF, the World Bank, and the Asian Development Bank suspended economic assistance to Pakistan as a punitive measure for going nu-

---

[54]The ethno-nationalist groups and parties from Baluchistan, NWFP, and Sindh vowed to protect their provincial rights and autonomy. Some demanded both that Pakistan should be declared a 'multinational state' and that a new constitution should be framed by a new Constituent Assembly that would have equal representation from all the provinces. Twenty-eight ethno-nationalist groups and parties established the Pakistan Oppressed Nations Movement in October demanding the establishment of a loose federation of autonomous and sovereign Punjabi, Sindhi, Baluchi, Pakhtoon and Siraiki 'nation'. See *Muslim* (Islamabad), 3 October 1998.

[55]Hasan Askari Rizvi, 'Pakistan in 1998: A Polity Under Pressure', *Asian Survey,* Vol. XXXIX, No. 1 (January–February 1999), pp. 181–82.

clear. This created the spectre of Pakistani failure to service its foreign debts, which exceeded $32 billion in September.

Pakistan was facing a gloomy future as macro-economic fundamentals remained in a precarious position and recession continued to grip the country. Moreover, Pakistan's nuclear explosions in May 1998 and aggression in Kargil brought the country to the brink of economic and political bankruptcy.[56]

Pakistan's sinking economy stifled under the weight of international sanctions imposed after its tit for tat response to India's nuclear tests of May 1998. Besides, there were allegations that the Sharif family was amassing wealth through unfair means.

Civil-Military Relations

The Sharif government's narrow-based and personalized decision-making led to strains in civil-military relations. The Army Chief, General Jehangir Karamat, made a host of statements on the growing threats to the polity, and talked about the adverse implications of the current economic deterioration and internal stability and external security. He also proposed the establishment of a National Security Council backed by a 'team of credible advisors and a think tank of experts' in order to 'institutionalize decision-making.'[57]

When Sharif expressed his displeasure with the statement, General Karamat decided to step down three months ahead of his retirement rather than withdraw his remarks. He was replaced with Pervez Musharraf, an Urdu-speaking *Muhajir* from Karachi, superseding two senior Pakhtoon and Punjabi generals. Sharif hoped that a *Muhajir* army chief presiding over a predominantly Punjabi-Pakhtun high command would be weak and thus not able to build pressure on the government.[58]

Sharif's relations with General Musharraf reached the lowest ebb in the wake of the Kargil misadventure. Sharif made the grave mistake of attempting to place the blame for the Kargil fiasco on the

---

[56]Sanjaya Baru, 'War and Economic Pakistan's Road to Ruin', *The Times of India*, 14 January 1999, p. 16.
[57]Kamran Khan, 'PM's Bolt From the Blue Actions Cause Army's NSC Move', *The News* (Lahore), 7 October 1998.
[58]Hasan Askari Rizvi, 'Pakistan in 1998: A Polity Under Pressure', p. 181.

military, hoping to mollify public criticism of the unconditional Pakistan withdrawal which had adversely affected the internal coherence, morale and credibility of the armed forces. It was inevitable that Sharif and his Army Chief Musharraf would fall out over the apportionment of blame on Kargil.[59]

Meanwhile, having made up his mind to get rid of the army chief, Sharif set about trying to divide the army's top command. The ISI, which was effectively under the prime minister's control, was now employed to serve the ends he desired. But the army chief's own intelligence network was briefing him on the prime minister's moves. On the advice of the ISI chief, Lieutenant General Ziauddin, who was eyeing the top slot despite being from the Engineers Corps, Sharif decided to sack General Musharraf and appoint General Ziauddin as the new army chief—only to realize a few hours later that it was the biggest blunder he could ever have committed. In the end, despite having been elected with a huge mandate, Sharif not only managed to bring his own government down but also ensured that in the process, Pakistan's brief phase of parliamentary democracy also breathed its last.[60]

In 1997, as the head of a powerful government, Sharif could have tried to forge a democratic compact and equip society to support it. In any case his political culture was in line with authoritarian tradition. But democracy is more complex than parliamentary majorities, supporters in important posts and constitutional amendments. These are only the trappings.[61]

In sum, during the 11 years of democratic restoration there were four elected governments which took office and all of them were removed arbitrarily. There have been executive-judiciary confrontations, disposition of the chief justice of the Supreme Court and an imminent military takeover, leading to the persistence of a military hegemonic system.

---

[59]Samina Ahmed, 'A Friend for All Seasons', *Newsline* (Karachi), October 1999 reproduced in *Strategic Digest*, Vol. XXIX, No. 12 (December 1999), p. 1850.

[60]Zaffar Abbas, 'Full Circle', p. 1794.

[61]Syed Ali Dayan Hasan, 'Requirement for the Third Pakistani Republic', *The Herald*, November 1999, reproduced in *Strategic Digest*, Vol. XXIX, No. 12 (December 1999), p. 1830.

Chapter VIII

Persistent Praetorianism: Pakistan's Fourth Military Regime

Events in Pakistan have come full circle with the military's return to power in October 1999 as the final arbiter of country's destiny. After long speculations of the possibility of a military coup in Pakistan, the removal of Prime Minister Nawaz Sharif by the Chief of Army Staff (COAS), General Pervez Musharraf, has flung Pakistan's nascent democracy into turmoil and uncertainty. After the death of General Zia in 1988, the military-bureaucratic junta had permitted the restoration of democracy, essentially to fill the vacuum in the structure of state power in Pakistan caused by the sudden demise of Zia. Benazir Bhutto had to make compromises with the army as the price for assuming the office of the prime minister. As a result, even after the restoration of democracy, the army continued to remain the supreme arbitrator in Pakistan, although its style appeared to have undergone a distinct change. Now, the military drove the government from the back seat instead of being on the steering wheel. Under the system which came to be known as 'Troika', the military became one of the pillars of power structure, the other two being the president and the prime minister. It has been widely acknowledged that the army played a role in bringing down the governments in power in Pakistan in 1990 (Benazir Bhutto), 1993 (Nawaz Sharif) and 1996 (Benazir Bhutto). Yet, restoration of democracy, however partial, was a major advance in Pakistan's political evolution. This hope seemed to acquire certainty with the advent of Nawaz Sharif's government with two-thirds majority in 1997. However, Musharraf's coup revealed the fragility of Pakistan's experiment with democracy.

The present chapter seeks to describe the phenomenon of October 1999 coup of General Pervez Musharraf, highlighting the political ethos and the deep rooted contradictions and motivations which have led to a military takeover in Pakistan. An attempt is made to analyze the nature of conflictual relationship between the prime minister and the COAS. The chapter also takes into account the nature and modality of the coup and internal and international responses to the coup. In the final section, Musharraf's efforts to legitimize his regime and prospects of the present regime are discussed.

Background of Musharraf's Coup

The military has broken an 11 year old taboo of directly intervening in national politics by dismissing Nawaz Sharif on 12 October 1999 in a bloodless coup. General Pervez Musharraf took over the government after the prime minister had dismissed his services as COAS while he was away in Sri Lanka and appointed Lieutenant General Khawaja Ziauddin Ahmed, the Director General (DG) of the Inter-Services Intelligence (ISI) Directorate in his place. Prime Minister Nawaz Sharif, his brother and Punjab Chief Minister, Shahbaz Sharif, and the ISI Chief, General Khwaja Ziauddin, were taken into 'protective custody' of the army. In a televised address to the nation (on October 13), General Musharraf said that the armed forces had moved in as a last resort to prevent any further destabilization but did not spell out what kind of government would be installed. General Musharraf named himself the chief executive and suspended the constitution and National Assembly and declared a state of emergency in Pakistan. Though the term 'martial law' has not been used, that is effectively what all this amounts to. In a nationally televised address, General Musharraf accused Sharif's government of 'systematically destroying' state institutions and driving the economy towards collapse. He is reported to have stated,

You are all aware of the kind of turmoil and uncertainty that our country has gone through in recent times. Not only have all the institutions been played around with and systematically destroyed, the economy too is in a state of collapse.[1]

General Musharraf also blamed Nawaz Sharif for trying to weaken the army. He said:

All my efforts and counsel to the government it seems were of no avail. Instead they now turned their attention on the army itself. Despite all my advices (sic), they tried to interfere with the armed forces, the last remaining viable institution—our concerns were conveyed, in no uncertain terms, but the government of Nawaz Sharif chose to ignore all these and tried to politicize the army, destabilize it and tried to create dissension in the ranks.[2]

Autocratic Civilian Rule

Nawaz Sharif had won an unprecedented landslide victory in the election in 1997. Using that brute majority, he was able to get the constitution amended to strip the president of his powers to dismiss the prime minister. He managed to get rid of an inconvenient and interfering chief justice by arranging his overthrow by his fellow judges. With the army chief on his side, he had a showdown with the president who had to resign. He got his family lawyer elevated to the presidency. The large province, Punjab, was controlled by his brother as the chief minister. He got the leader of the opposition, and his arch rival, Benazir Bhutto, convicted for corruption and made sure that she exiled herself from Pakistan. Finally, he got the army chief, General Jehangir Karamat to resign for an impropriety. He too, like Z. A. Bhutto, felt that he was unchallengeable. He superseded two senior officers to select General Musharraf as the army chief on the presumption that as a *Muhajir* he had no local constituency. His regime was marked by pervasive corruption, sectarian strife and economic chaos. After systematically undermining the civil institution, Sharif shackled the press and opted for religious laws to strengthen his hold on the country. Nawaz Sharif's

---

[1] *Asian Recorder* (New Delhi), 1999, p. 28552.
[2] Ibid., p. 28553.

authoritarianism resulted in a struggle between autocratic civilian rule and benign military dictatorship. The civil-military relationship in Pakistan was plagued by this recurrent conflict: civilian rulers wishing to assert primacy by reining in the army. This impasse was demonstrated in Kargil operation.

Strains in Civil-Military Relations

The origin of the political crisis could be traced to the departure of General Karamat in October 1998, which was the initial manifestation of tension between the army and the political leadership. The former COAS was the chairman of the Joint Chiefs of Staff Committee (CJCSC), the apex military body. The CJCSC comprises the three military chiefs, wherein the seniormost four-star general, air chief marshal or admiral among them by rotation becomes its chairman. The fact that the prime minister kept the position of CJCSC vacant for five full months from November 1998 to March 1999 indicates strains in the political-military relationship since then. Sharif's other act of commission, after Karamat's resignation, to antagonize the army was the appointment of Lieutenant General Ziauddin as the DG, ISI Directorate, reportedly without consulting General Musharraf.[3]

The DG, ISI reports directly to the prime minister and therefore the two tend to develop a close working relationship. In a sense, the DG, ISI, apart from providing the government both external and internal intelligence inputs, also functions informally as a political advisor to the prime minister. He probably did not trust Musharraf completely. Sharif's strained relationship with Musharraf became evident from the fact that the latter was reluctantly appointed the CJCSC only in April 1999. The reports suggested that there was a possibility that the CJCSC would be made the operational head of the nuclear command and authority for Pakistan and the appointment would be upgraded from a three-star Lieutenant General to that of a four-star full General on par with the COAS. If this scheme were implemented, Lieutenant General Ziauddin might have been made the new COAS and General Musharraf appointed as the CJCSC. Thereafter probably

---

[3]Bidanda M. Chengappa, 'Pakistan's Fourth Military Takeover', *Strategic Analysis*, Vol. XXIII, No. 9 (December 1999), p. 1437.

the army's abortive attack on Kargil was bound to have exacerbated tensions between the prime minister and the COAS.[4]

The antagonism between Nawaz Sharif and General Musharraf, originating in the fiasco of Kargil, increased on account of the government's decision to withdraw from Kargil. Nawaz Sharif started to distance himself from Musharraf thinking that a militarily discredited Musharraf will not have the support in the command structure of the Pakistani army. This resulted in some nascent intentions to organize a coup against Sharif on the part of Musharraf between end July and mid-September 1999.

As soon as Sharif learned about Musharraf's intention, he sent his brother Shahbaz Sharif and then Chief of the ISI, Lieutenant General Ziauddin to the US to persuade Washington to counter possible moves by Musharraf. The US warned the Pakistani military establishment against a military coup, which was given calculated publicity. Despite the cautionary warnings from the US, Musharraf remained committed to his plan but postponed its implementation. Given his apprehensions about Musharraf, Sharif assumed that inner difference in the upper echelons of the army high command coupled with US opposition to any coup will neutralize Musharraf.

However, Nawaz Sharif's calculations proved wrong because whatever the inner differences, the higher command of the armed forces remained united and loyal and committed to its chief. More significantly, the armed forces were antagonized by Nawaz's deliberate moves aimed at tarnishing their image and eroding their power. It was evident from the resignations of General Jahangir Karamat and Admiral Bukhari, which were manifestation of Sharif's differences with the armed forces. Besides, the military establishment suffered collectively from a sense of acute resentment at the way Nawaz Sharif had betrayed it by agreeing to pull out from Kargil. The military was of the view that the army would have succeeded in Kargil had it not been pressurized to withdraw. Nawaz Sharif also did not realize that despite his overwhelming majority in the parliament, the public was disillusioned with his increasingly autocratic rule.

The underhand manner in which he tried to get rid of General Musharraf when he was out of the country, robbed his decision of the virtues of self-confidence and boldness in asserting civilian authority.

---

[4]Ibid., p. 1438. Also see Chengappa, 'Pakistan's Fourth Coup, *The Hindustan Times* (New Delhi), 21 October 1999, p. 9.

To compound all this, he replaced Musharraf by an officer Lieutenant General Ziauddin, who belonged to the Engineering Branch with no credibility as a combat general.

Nature and Modality of the Military Coup

General Musharraf's coup was in the true tradition of a bloodless coup. The transfer of power took place easily and smoothly without violence. The troops quickly moved through the main cities, many Pakistanis, danced in the streets and waved flags celebrating the ouster of a prime minister who had become dictator.

Musharraf's coup against Nawaz Sharif seems to repeat the similar chain of events of what happened on 5 July 1977. This time the coup was triggered by Sharif's adventurist decision of sacking General Musharraf. According to print media reports, the Chief of the General Staff and a Musharraf loyalist, General Aziz, got to know about General Musharraf's dismissing orders on the morning of October 12. This gave him enough time to activate the contingency plans to topple the government by the time. He played the same role for Musharraf—what General Chisti played for Zia-ul-Haq.

Presumably, contingency plans for a coup were part of regular planning of the Pakistani General Staff. The Pakistani army chief, ably supported by his chief of general staff (CGS), was able to preempt the prime minister and flouted his plans to have an army chief of his choice.

Zia's coup of July 1977 seems analogous to Musharraf's. Bhutto had made up his mind to sack his Army Chief General Zia (whom he had appointed COAS by superseding half a dozen seniors), as he suspected him of being close to the opposition political alliance namely the Pakistan National Alliance. On the night of 4 July 1977, Bhutto mentioned to some of his close confidantes that he would issue the orders the next morning. It would appear that one of those confidantes tipped off Zia-ul-Haq. The army chief struck back a little after midnight before Bhutto could issue his orders.

Both Bhutto and Sharif accumulated dictatorial powers in their hands. Both appointed Army Chief Zia and Musharraf respectively by superseding a number of their successors. In both cases, the prime ministers found that the officers they thought would be pliable proved to be their nemesis.[5]

In Janowitz's classification of the typology of coups, Pakistan's fourth military regime could be cited as an example of 'reactive militarism'. In this case, the army did not seek political power but was compelled to react to the moves of the political leadership which were aimed at destroying its institutional existence.[6] The military high command was no doubt incensed at the governments' attempt to gain US sympathy at their cost. Sharif's decision to send ISI Chief, Lieutenant General Ziauddin to the US according to Samina Ahmed, 'encroached on the military's jealously guarded internal autonomy, threatening its corporate interest and damaging its external credibility.'[7]

But it is only a partial interpretation of the modality of the October 1999 military takeover. According to the intelligence community, the smooth and swift military takeover could not have been possible without elaborate planning. The precision with which the coup was carried out clearly indicated that the blueprint was ready well in advance. Musharraf's coup was partly a 'designed coup' because it was a result of collective resentment among the military top brass against Sharif's withdrawal from Kargil. Besides there has been increasing influence of Islamic fundamentalists over the Pakistani armed forces. Nawaz Sharif, in a manner akin to Bhutto (who laid the blame for the break-up of Pakistan in 1971 squarely at the military's door), tried to make a scapegoat of the army chief for the Kargil fiasco. Moreover, the military took the reigns of power not in the interest of the country, but to defend the crown of their chief. They have conquered their own country for the fourth time.

---

[5] K. Subrahmanyam, 'Battle Fatigues: Predictable Replay in Pakistan', *The Times of India* (New Delhi), 18 October 1999, p. 14.
[6] Chengappa, 'Pakistan's Fourth Military Takeover', p. 1442.
[7] Samina Ahmed, 'A Friend for All Seasons', *Strategic Digest*, Vol. XXIX, No. 12 (December 1999), p. 1850.

National and International Responses to Musharraf's Coup

Ironically, the dismissal of Nawaz Sharif's government seemed to be welcomed by several quarters in the country. Under the cover of a crushing two-thirds majority, Nawaz Sharif had tended to accumulate power for himself by molesting institutions, rules and conventions. The people had a feeling of relief at the end of his 31 months of chaotic rule. Almost all the political parties welcomed the military intervention.

The exiled opposition leader, Benazir Bhutto, accused Sharif of antagonizing and provoking the military against his own government. She said that Nawaz Sharif had sought to politicize the army and dismantle democracy. She is reported to have said in an interview with Sky TV that 'The people believe that that man is violating every rule of law and there is no one to stop him. The armed forces had to protect themselves as an institution.'[8] Benazir defended the army in the hope that the army would allow her to return home. However, the military regime rejected her plea for safe passage.

The Muhajir Quami Movement (MQM) also welcomed the coup. The MQM supporter and leaders held Sharif's government responsible for what happened. The people on the streets distributed sweets, and played pro-MQM songs.

As far as the response of the Grand Democratic Alliance (which included the Pakistan People's Party, the Movement for Justice of Imran Khan and MQM) is concerned, it welcomed the dismissal of Nawaz Sharif's regime and backed the seven-point agenda of Pervez Musharraf.

An exception to the general welcome accorded to the military coup was the right wing fundamentalist party Jamaat-i-Islami. In a statement issued on October 15, the Jamaat, while urging the armed forces to give priority to making corrupt rulers accountable, criticized Musharraf's decision to declare a state of emergency and stated that it could not support the martial law and the suspension of fundamental

---

[8] *Asian Recorder*, 1999, p. 28554.

rights. It also pointed out that whatever is happening in the country is because it never had a chance to have a real Islamic system.[9]

The reaction of even the Pakistan Muslim League (PML) headed by Nawaz Sharif was not as violently critical of the military takeover as would have been expected. The PML, in a statement issued on 21 October, demanded the immediate release of Nawaz Sharif as well as the restoration of democracy. But the PML avoided a policy of confrontation with the army and refrained from condemning the army's action. Soon the party found itself in disarray with leaders failing to determine the next course of action in terms of strategy.

What explains the low-key criticism and condemnation of the strangulation of democracy in Pakistan, not to speak of organized violent demonstrations and protests? It could not be merely the fear of the strong hand of the army in a country which had fought a bold, all-party struggle for the restoration of democracy during Zia's time. According to one analyst,

> In the context of Pakistan's history, the nation as a whole had got immunized to the choice between democracy and dictatorship. Even the best of democratic leadership elected with overwhelming electoral support had behaved as the worst dictators, such was the grip of deeply feudal mindset over the behaviour of the Pakistani political class. For the people of Pakistan therefore, the choice was not between democracy and dictatorship in the institutional sense, but between bad governance and good governance, whosoever delivered it.[10]

International reaction to the Musharraf coup has, predictably, been negative. Military coups are not fashionable in the post-Cold War era as the world community's revulsion towards coups is now unequivocal. As far as the response of the US is concerned, it no longer favours military takeovers. As the army chief announced the dismissal of the Sharif government, the Clinton administration immediately called for the earliest possible restoration of democracy. The US warned that a military coup would make it impossible to carry on business as usual. The Commonwealth moved swiftly to suspend Pakistan and the European Union has been tougher than the US in demanding

---

[9]Ibid.
[10]Sumita Kumar, 'Sharif vs. Musharraf: The Future of Democracy in Pakistan', *Strategic Analysis*, Vol. XXIV, No. 10 (January 2001), p. 1867.

restoration of democracy. The UN Secretary General had deplored it, and the International Monetary Fund director had declared that loans to Pakistan will be suspended until democracy is restored. Ministers from the eight nations Commonwealth ministerial action group took the decision at a meeting, saying the suspension would be effective 'forthwith' and would remain pending till the restoration of democracy in the country. However, in practical terms it means very little. Since no sanction or trade bars are involved, Pakistan's suspension only means a moral sermon. It will certainly not pinch Pakistan.

Musharraf's Search for Legitimacy

While capturing power is relatively easy for the military, it is much more difficult for it to govern. As for all other ruling groups, it is imperative for them to convert power into authority and legitimacy. Only then can they ensure their survival.

In the early stages of their tenure, for the goal of aggregating their power they seek legitimacy through the propagation of their self-image as a set of missionary, progressive, neutral and patriotic guardians of the nation. However, the popular will expects performance rather than platitudes. Aware that military solutions to social problems are counter-productive and guided by practical common sense, they seek a 'creative relationship with the civilian political groups.' But sooner or later they have to think about civilianizing their rule and or evolving a political framework for the future. This makes it imperative for them to cultivate political groups so that at least the policies initiated by them are not reversed and their corporate personal interests are adequately protected.

Civil-Military Partnership

As has been emphasized by Henry Bienen, 'military regime' is a misnomer as all 'military regimes' have large civilian components.[11] First,

---

[11]Henry Bienen, 'Military Rule and Political Process: Nigerian Example', *Comparative Politics*, Vol. X, No. 2 (January 1978), pp. 205–25.

because the military leaders want to give a degree of civilian colour to the new regime. Second, confronted with the practical task of running the government, as military leaders lack the requisite political and administrative skills, they are forced to recruit appropriate talent from the civilian sector. Both the civil and military bureaucracies in Pakistan shared the same social class and identical interests and outlook.

Like the military regime of Ayub Khan, the new military government kept army personnel in the background and ran the administration through civilian institutions and officials, described as the 'civil-military combine' by the military rulers. The military rulers establish monitoring cells at different levels to oversee and supervise the working of the civilian institutions.

Musharraf's regime seems to opt for institutionalized technocratic politics, building on the models of both Ayub and Zia. General Musharraf, notwithstanding his professed admiration for Turkey's Kemal Ataturk, seemed to emulate General Zia by appointing the National Security Council. The inclusion of Sharifuddin Pirzada, the late Zia's attorney-general during the martial law and Atiya Inayatullah, another associate of Zia, tend to suggest that General Musharraf is looking more to Zia as a role model than to the great Turkish reformer and modernizer. Instead of the Turkish model, Pakistan seems closer to the Sudanese model with a Turaibi-like figure from Jamaat-i-Islami as an ideologue.

The military has been working on cobbling together a government of technocrats with the primary task of putting the economy back on track. General Musharraf has announced his plans to set up a two-tier system to run the country: a national security council comprising the chiefs of the armed forces and civilian members of the government, which will work as a supreme administrative body, assisted by a group of advisors to help in running the country's day to day affairs.[12]

Measures Against Political Parties

The handling of the dissenting political parties by military rulers exemplified a Machiavellian streak, which surprised the politicians

---

[12]Zahid Hussain, 'Day of the Generals', *Newsline* (Karachi), October 1999.

who allowed themselves to be manipulated. General Musharraf's military government has initiated a series of measures that were largely perceived to be vindictive against popular leaders of the main parties. These include the so-called accountability drive, under which several prominent leaders have been booked for their alleged acts of omissions and commissions, and the controversial amendment to the Political Parties Act (on 9 August 2000), barring individuals convicted on charges of corruption from holding party posts. The legislation, in effect, dethroned or nearly eliminated the political future of the two former prime ministers, Nawaz Sharif and Benazir Bhutto, as leaders of their parties.

With the ousted Prime Minister Nawaz Sharif in jail and the opposition PPP leader Benazir Bhutto out of the country, Musharraf had little to worry on the political front. Sharif's wife Kulsoom Nawaz was the only one taking on the army and asking it to return to the barracks. But she too faced problems from sections within the PML that were unwilling to accept her leadership.

To eliminate Sharif from Musharraf's political path, the case was finally framed on 10 November. Nawaz Sharif and four others were charged with attempted murder, hijacking and criminal conspiracy. The military regime, to convict Sharif, got the former chairman of the Civil Aviation Authority, Aminullah Chaudhry to turn approver. Chaudhry stated that Nawaz Sharif had ordered him to deny permission to the plane carrying Musharraf and other passengers to land at Karachi on 12 October 1999. Chaudhry, in return, asked for pardon under the code of criminal procedure.

The next significant step taken by the military regime was to amend the Anti-Terrorism Act of 1997 on 2 December 1999. Under this amendment, the Anti-Terrorism Court would henceforth be able to hear cases under several additional sections of the Pakistan Penal Code, bringing under its purview jurisdiction offences like hijacking and criminal conspiracy. The court was also enabled to award death sentence for abetment if there was no express provision for its punishment.

The chargesheet filed against Sharif was submitted in the Court of Justice Shabir Ahmed of the Sindh High Court who was appointed to a special Anti-Terrorist Court to hear the case against Sharif and his associates.

On the other side of the legal battle, PML(N) filed a suit in the Supreme Court on 22 November 1999 challenging the military intervention and demanding the reinstatement of the elected government. The petition maintained the 'constitutional deviation' of 12 October was totally contrary to the constitution and the principles of democracy.[13] It is notable that the ruling was given by the judges of the Supreme Court who pleaded allegiance to the military regime in January 2000.

The noose was tightened around the deposed Prime Minister Nawaz Sharif, as expected. He was found guilty of hijacking and terrorism by an Anti-Terrorist Court at Karachi on 6 April. In an uncanny run of events, almost 21 years to a day after Zulfikar Ali Bhutto was sentenced to death, Sharif was sentenced to two life imprisonments. The judge, Rehmat Hussain Jaffery, who pronounced the judgement also ordered seizure of all the assets and property of Nawaz Sharif. His two concurrent life sentences mean he can expect upto 25 years behind bars. For each charge, he was also fined Rs 5 lakh, ordered to pay Rs 20 lakh as compensation to the passengers of the Pakistan International Airlines (PIA) plane PK 805.

In the run-up to the verdict, General Musharraf faced mounting international pressure not to put the former premier to death. In fact, the six other persons accused along with Sharif, including his brother Shahbaz Sharif, had been acquitted of all charges. The regime needed to send a message across that the verdict was fair and had not been dictated by the ruling junta. This move of the regime had underminded global confidence in Pakistan's judiciary. The refusal by Justice Shabhir Ahmed of the Sindh High Court to continue hearing the case on the ground that the large presence of plain clothes policemen in the court precluded a fair trial, had raised further questions, as had been the gunning down of Sharif's defence lawyer Iqbal Radh, on 10 March. Moreover, the government has imposed a ban on public rallies and meetings and warned activists of Sharif's PML against holding street protests after the verdict was announced.

In sum, Pakistan's military did not seem to finish with the Sharif family. Sharif's double life sentence was only the beginning of a long legal battle as a dozen more cases were pending against him. Two corruption cases have already been lodged against the former

---

[13] *Asian Recorder*, 2000, p. 12.

prime minister for defaulting on a business loan and evading tax on the purchase of a Russian MI–8 helicopter. The military regime, not satisfied with the so-called lenient sentence awarded to Sharif, filed an appeal in the Sindh High Court on 18 April seeking death penalty for Sharif, as Sharif filed an appeal in the same court pleading for acquittal.

With the court finding Sharif guilty of hijacking and terrorism, his PML, which he nurtured to become the largest party in the country, was facing the prospect of yet another split. The possibility of a split became real due to the serious differences in the party ranks on the issue of leadership and its future policy. Cracks have begun to appear in the PML, as soon as the military overthrew Sharif's government on 12 October and seized power; but Sharif's opponents within the party decided to adopt a wait-and-watch policy because they felt that any hasty decision might ruin their political future as well.

Sharif's loyalists in the PML wanted his wife Kulsoom to take over the reins of the party because they felt that only she could keep the party and its vote bank united. The group, which was dependent on the charisma of the Sharif family for its own political survival, had taken her from town to town to introduce her to the local and regional party leaders.

But many in the party, including senior party leaders and the former ministers, were opposed to handing over the party to a woman from the Sharif family because they thought this would perpetuate another political dynasty like the Bhuttos and the Nehrus and Gandhis. There were also serious differences within the PML on the question of launching an agitation against the military rulers. Even staunch Sharif supporters were not in favour of crossing swords with the army. In sum, the dissidents and the pro-Nawaz groups had been jockeying for supremacy in the Punjab, and holding parliamentary and counter-parliamentary meetings.

Formation of Alliance for the Restoration of Democracy

A significant development took place in terms of a formation of 15 party alliance namely the Alliance for the Restoration of Democracy

(ARD). The former arch-rivals Benazir and Sharif came together under one umbrella organization, under the leadership of Nawabzada Nasrullah Khan, for a common cause against the military regime. On 6 August 2000, an All Party Conference (APC) was held in Lahore to present a united front against the military rule. It was attended by senior leaders from the PML(N), the PPP, the Awami National Party (ANP), the Jamaat-i-Islami and almost all the provinces. The APC demanded the immediate restoration of political activities and rejected any changes whatsoever in the constitution, thus even blocking the proposed reversal of the Thirteenth and Fourteenth Amendments enacted by Nawaz Sharif.[14]

The group of expatriate rebels in London have also started consolidating their protest movement against the military regime. At a well-attended conference on 1 September 2000, Altaf Hussain, the MQM leader, Ataullah Mengal, the convenor of the Pakistan Oppressed Nations Movement, and Mehmood Khan Achakzai of Pakhtoonkhwa Milli Awami Party, demanded of the army to return to the barracks and hand-over the country's governance to the duly elected representatives.[15]

In the political scenario, with two leading political figures, Benazir Bhutto and Nawaz Sharif, both in exile, Musharraf appeared to have won himself some room for manoeuvre. There is a view that Sharif's exile was hastened because the new alliance had brought the PPP and PML together on the same platform. A recent formal split in the PML(N) can now enable Musharraf to create a constitutional package that would, in the long run, favour the army. Having divided the opposition, Musharraf can now appoint his own politicians. However, sending Sharif into exile may only exacerbate Musharraf's problems. The Sharif deal has lost Musharraf the last vestiges of credibility and he might lose even more. The exile has made Musharraf look like a man susceptible to bribes of foreign powers and who has the audacity to subvert the judicial process.

At the same time, the leader of the Jamaat-i-Islami, Qazi Hussain Ahmed, continues to remain defiant. He has embarked on an agenda to bring the Islamic groups into a separate anti-army alliance. The only element that continues to provide some reprieve

---

[14]Ziagham Khan, 'Blundering on Blasphemy', *The Herald* (Karachi), June 2000, p. 541.
[15]Ibid., p. 604.

to the military junta is a faction of the PML led by the so-called dissidents. People of divergent views and backgrounds, such as Ejazul Haq, Begum Abida Hussain, Mian Azhar and even Chaudhry Shujaat Hussain, have joined hands to try and hijack Sharif's PML by trying to create the impression that the military regime may soon restore the parliament. Interestingly, Ejazul Haq even managed to get stories published in a couple of American newspapers that he may well be the next prime minister.[16]

Coup Against the Judiciary

General Musharraf resorted to the shocking but not surprising move of clipping the wings of a constitutional authority that was showing visible signs of challenging his legitimacy—the country's Supreme Court. The sacking of 16 judges upon their refusal to take a fresh oath swearing allegiance to the military regime, only confirmed the deep-rootedness of martial rule in Pakistan. It is obvious that once they had affirmed loyalty to the military dictator, these judges could not have declared the regime unconstitutional when the issue of its legitimacy came up for the consideration. The judges had before them the infamous precedents of the earlier Supreme Courts of 1958 and 1977 to justify the military usurpation under the 'doctrine of necessity'. The sack order exemplifies that democracy will not return in a hurry in Pakistan. As expected, the Supreme Court has held the dismissal of General Musharraf by Nawaz Sharif as illegal and upheld the military coup as the principle of 'doctrine of necessity.'

The shake-up of the judiciary hardly comes as a surprise considering that all the military predecessors of Musharraf had acted similarly and assumed absolute control of the judiciary in order to neutralize any constitutional challenge to their authority.

The story of the struggle for power in Pakistan was unfolding exactly according to the script written by General Pervez Musharraf. He seemed to have had enough reasons to be satisfied with the verdict of the Anti-Terrorist Court. The Supreme Court ruling on 12 May 2000 that the military takeover in October 1999

---

[16]'Army Under Pressure', *The Herald* (Karachi), October 2000, reproduced in *Strategic Digest*, Vol. XXXI, No. 1 (January 2001), p. 18.

was justified under the 'doctrine of necessity' further strengthened his position. The court gave the army a three year deadline to restore democracy. In a decision akin to the one handed over when Zia regime was challenged, the supreme court while justifying the military coup under the 'doctrine of necessity' said that 'sufficient evidence of corruption of the former government was presented by the state.'[17] Moreover, in a separate judgement delivered on 22 July 2000, the accountability court sentenced Sharif to 14 years imprisonment and barred him from holding public office for 21 years in a corruption case.[18]

On 10 December 2000, General Musharraf surprised the world by permitting Nawaz Sharif and his family to go into exile in Saudi Arabia, after a meeting with the corps commanders. The federal cabinet endorsed the decision at a later date. It was obvious that Musharraf could not have got away with an option like execution of Nawaz Sharif, taking into account international opinion as well as the fact that Sharif enjoyed immense support of the Punjabi elite (one of the core groups in Pakistan). On the other hand, Musharraf probably hoped that such a decision would keep the doors open for the flow of Saudi money or investment into the country. However, at the same time, Sharif's release has brought a big question mark on the military regime's process of accountability and seems to highlight its failure in that sector as well.

Reviving the Economy

After finally entrenching themselves in power, Pakistan's new military junta faced the daunting task of pulling back the economy from the verge of a total collapse. Most political analysts foresee a regional fragmentation and the Lebanonisation of Pakistan if the present military regime fails to arrest the economic downslide.

Most economists agree there is no quick-fix solution to Pakistan's grave economic problems. The coup leaders will have to take some very painful measures to resuscitate a near-dead economy.

---

[17]*Asian Recorder*, 2000, p. 379. Also see Idress Bakhtar, 'The Return of State Necessity', *The Herald* (June 2000).
[18]For details refer Mubashir Zaidi, 'Day of Judgement', *The Herald* (August 2000), pp. 68–69.

Tax increases, raising electricity and gas tariffs, as well as petroleum prices will just be the beginning of any meaningful economic reforms.

Cleaning up the Economic Mess

As part of its populistic programme for an economic revival, the military junta has launched a crackdown on corrupt politicians and intensified efforts to recover unpaid loans owned to state-owned commercial banks and it has also moved against tax evaders. A major challenge before the new Pakistan rulers is to force the rich to pay taxes.

The massive crackdown on corruption and loan defaulters has put out of action not just Nawaz Sharif and Benazir Bhutto, representing the two major political centres in Pakistan, but also almost the entire upper crust. For General Musharraf, it was vital that he kept his promise to clean up the loot, for that was about the only way he could remain popular, besides earning for the military regime a measure of legitimacy. The list of people arrested and declared fugitive includes the best known names in politics, business and even some senior ex-servicemen, Benazir and her husband, the Sharif brothers and key figures from Sharif and Benazir governments.

General Musharraf promised to clean up Pakistan's corrupt elite, rebuild national confidence and morale, revive the economy, strengthen the crumbling bonds between the four provinces that make up the country, and cleanse institutions to install 'real democracy' before the army relinquishes power. 'Cleansing the system' is the standard exercise which all armies use to justify a coup. Their claim invariably is that they reluctantly stepped in to save the country from the corrupt civilians and that they would hand back power to an elected government the moment some semblance of order is restored. Just as putschists elsewhere in the world will not do, Pakistan's military rulers have always promised a clean government, economic growth and the restoration of true democracy. Low growth, rising poverty and an increasingly onerous debt burden have been features of the Pakistani economy for at least a decade. The military government blamed Sharif for the economic collapse. However, the military junta prioritised accountability over economic revival.

Without the introduction of economic and structural reforms, the securing of the IMF package in the coming months will not mean that Pakistan's downturn economy will be out of the wood soon. The government is required to be committed to the tough decision of economic reforms.

Those optimistic about the ability of General Musharraf's team to give the country's faltering economy a desperately needed boost seem to be the most disappointed. Instead of creating an atmosphere conducive to foreign investment, they argue, the rulers have only exacerbated the problem of Pakistan's diplomatic isolation. In fact, many leading businessmen share the politician's perception that the country stands more isolated than ever before.

What the country needs is a crusade against wrong doing without the fear that it is going to be an unpopular move. For instance, almost one-third of the economy—agriculture—is outside the tax net. This government should be bold enough to attack this fundamental issue.

That Pakistan is a nation of tax evaders rather than tax payers is a reality. At present, not more than 1.5 million out of a population of 140 million pay taxes in Pakistan. There is an inbuilt resistance, at the national level, to pay taxes that is rooted in the people's complete and utter lack of faith and credibility in the system of tax collection and assessment.[19]

While widening the tax base and eradicating the inherent inequalities in the taxation is a major aspect of economic reform, it must run parallel with curtailing expenditure. Both government and military expenditure must be questioned for their cost effectiveness. With people's aspirations rising higher and the ruling elite not making any effort to meet them, Pakistan's economy looks gloomy.

Last year the junta regime had talked a lot about poverty alleviation. And, seemingly, there has been plenty of action on this regard. Some Rs 21 billion were allocated for poverty alleviation in the 2000–2001 budget. The components of this programme are the creation of a micro-credit bank, a food support programme as well as public works, and poverty alleviation is said to be high-priority on the government.

---

[19]Samina Ibrahim, 'A Nation of Tax Evaders', *Newsline* (Karachi), May 2000, reproduced in *Strategic Digest*, Vol. XXX, No. 7 (July 2000), pp. 887–990.

However, reality is different from the slogan and reveals a different picture. The government's own figures demonstrate that roughly 44 million individuals are living below the poverty line in Pakistan. If this Rs 21 billion were to be distributed amongst the poor, simple back-of-an-envelope calculation show that each person would get merely Rs 39.70 per month.[20]

So far as the repercussions of 9/11 on the Pakistan's economy are concerned, it is a popular belief that the terrorist attacks on the US have in certain ways benefited Pakistan's economy as the former has promised millions of dollars in assistance, waived sanctions and granted loans to the latter as a reward for its support to the war against terrorism. However, it is a misperception to think that Pakistan has been very clever in managing the Osama bin Laden affair to its economic advantage. On the contrary, it is merely getting some compensation for the economic mess it has been pushed into by US action.

Legitimization Through Civilianization

In a bid to legitimize his rule, like Ayub Khan and Zia-ul-Haq, Pakistan's military ruler Pervez Musharraf had floated an idea of holding partyless elections.

Devolution Plan and Partyless Election

Unlike General Zia, who had announced his intention of holding elections within 90 days of seizing power in 1977, Musharraf did not make any promise on 12 October 1999. On 29 October 1999, when he met a fact-finding team of the visiting Commonwealth foreign ministers, he told them that he could not give any assurance when democracy would return to the country.

However, the regime has been under tremendous international pressure regarding the demand for restoration of democracy and was criticized strongly for overthrowing a democratic govern-

---

[20]Asad Sayeed, 'Behind the Facade of Economic Revival, *The Herald*, November 2000, reproduced in *Strategic Digest*, Vol. XXXI, No. 1 (January 2000), pp. 24–25.

ment, both by the Commonwealth and the South Asian Association for Regional Cooperation (SAARC). Two days before the visit of President Bill Clinton, on 23 March 2000, Musharraf announced that he would hold elections in the local bodies later in the year throughout the country, as the first step towards the return to 'real' democracy. Later, the Chief Executive, General Musharraf, in a special address to the nation on 14 August 2000 coinciding with the Independence Day, announced the devolution plan and the scheme of partyless elections scheduled to begin in December 2000 and likely to be completed by May 2001. A second round of local elections—at the district level were to be held in July 2001, effectively putting municipal governments back in power.[21] In order to justify his decision, the Chief Executive maintained, 'Democracy starts here at the district and local governments. From here, we will move up step by step to provincial and federal elections in due course.'[22] The Supreme Court of Pakistan had fixed October 2002 as the deadline for the military government to hand over power to the civilian institutions.

General Musharraf's plan of restoring 'real' democracy via the local elections was seen by many as a ploy to consolidate his personal power and perpetuate his rule. Musharraf's local bodies plan seems clearly designed to create a new power base for the military regime. This plan for the devolution of power may, in fact, lead to the centralization of more powers with the central government at the expense of provincial autonomy.[23] Besides, the devolution plan was considered 'a blue print for the destruction of politics.'[24]

The political parties termed the devolution scheme 'old wine in a new bottle' and linked it to the 'Basic Democracy' propounded by the military regime under General Ayub Khan in the 1960s. The political parties felt it would only help perpetuate the feudal order in society.

---

[21]For detailed analysis of the Local Government 2000 Plan consult Idress Bakhtiar, 'Localizing Sovereignty', *The Herald* (September 2000), pp. 46–50.

[22]*Asian Recorder*, 2000, pp. 267–68.

[23]Zahid Hussain, 'Empowering the Khakis?' *Newsline* (September 2000), pp. 50–53.

[24]Aamer Ahmed Khan, 'Devolution Destruction', *The Herald* (September 2000), pp. 50–51.

The Pakistan Muslim League and the Pakistan People's Party, who have ruled Pakistan for much of the time, came out strongly against the scheme. They believed that General Musharraf could use the office bearers of the local bodies as an electoral college for future Provincial Assembly elections.

In short, they suspected the motives of the military regime. In their view, the devolution plan could be a gimmick to institutionalize martial rule. Their worry was compounded by the contempt shown by General Musharraf towards politicians and political parties. Building a democratic society at the grassroots level without the involvement of political parties is not possible. That would further depoliticize the people and strengthen the influence of *biradaris* (endogamous group of families) and tribes and promote the already entrenched feudal, economic and social mafias in society.

The PPP leader, Khalid Kharal, said that the new scheme was unclear and unworkable. Devolution of the prevalent local government would prove dangerous for the country and make it difficult for redressal of public problems and grievances. In sum, the devolution plan was largely denounced as illogical and unworkable.

It has been reported that Pakistan's military ruler General Musharraf may assume the office of president as Muhammad Rafiq Tarar is likely to step down. He seems likely to emulate General Zia-ul-Haq to end the criticism that he is a military dictator. He may assume the constitutional office and retain the all-powerful post of the army chief, while running the administration, through hand-picked civilians.

In sum, it seems that Musharraf will resort to a carefully planned transition to 'civilianization' through constitutional and political engineering and cooption of political leaders. He may not have a grand vision for the future, but he is expected to institute changes in the constitutional arrangement to ensure checks and balances among key institutions and officials, as well as create an institutional framework for the formal participation of the military in decision-making. The pace of transition to democracy depends on the dynamics of domestic policies, the disposition and policy choices of the senior commanders and interaction between the military regime and the political forces.

Musharraf's Self-Elevation to the Presidency

On 20 June 2001, General Pervez Musharraf, in a master stroke, assumed the office of president, ousting the figurehead namely Rafiq Tarar. The self-elevation of Musharraf to the presidency is a bid to legitimize his position. The rehabilitation of Musharraf—who overthrew the then Prime Minister Nawaz Sharif in October 1999 and subsequently exiled him to Saudi Arabia—was complete. While Musharraf's accession to the presidency was more or less expected, its timing was not lost on his countrymen. The Agra Summit may have been one of the factors in Musharraf's hasty decision. Admittedly, the general seized the highest office in an undemocratic manner anointing himself president unconstitutionally. Arguably, the general required political legitimacy at home before he set foot on Indian soil for negotiations.

Not all countries reacted as charitably to the new president, who also dissolved the national legislative and four provincial assemblies. The US criticized the 'second coup' and the United Kingdom was equally sharp. In Pakistan itself, there were protests from Benazir Bhutto's PPP and Sharif's PML.

Just what was on the general's mind? In October 2002, after all, he is committed as per a Supreme Court ruling to restoring civilian rule in Pakistan. A clue to Musharraf's plan may lie in the Provisional Constitutional Order that accompanied his swearing in as president. In a move unusual for a military dictator, Musharraf decided that the Chief Justice of the Supreme Court would officiate as president should the man who wears three hats—army chief, chief executive and head of state—be travelling or be indisposed.

This stipulation has been opposed by some of Musharraf's otherwise supportive subordinates. They feel the *de facto* vice-president should also be a man in uniform. Musharraf seems to be sticking to his guns and on the verge of experimenting with his own version of guided democracy.

Army Backed Quasi-Democracy

It seems Musharraf wants an army-backed quasi-democracy. It is believed that he will seek a permanent constitutional political role for the army and make it the guarantor of a quasi-democratic system by 2002. Musharraf, like his predecessors, does not believe in transferring power but in sharing it with elected civilian representatives.

Musharraf plans to amend the constitution, so that effective power lies not with the democratically elected prime minister and parliament, but in a military dominated National Security Council that he proposes to head. He has laid the foundation for a houseful of lackeys in the provincial and national assemblies through local body election of nazims, who will operate with the blessings and directions of corps commanders.

From the contours of the new constitutional package, it is amply clear that NSC will be constitutionalized as a super body, armed with the powers over and above the prime minister and his cabinet. All the services chiefs will sit on this all-powerful forum to be headed by the president. The National Security Council is likely to be empowered to advice the president on the sacking of the prime minister. General Musharraf will retain his office of president as Zia had done and later got validation from parliament through the Eighth Amendment.

While Musharraf has succeeded in splitting the Pakistan Muslim League, his proteges have not done well in the non-party elections to local councils (held in July 2001). It is well-known that Musharraf's corps commanders, popularly known as 'Crore Commanders' in Pakistan, spared no effort to compel legislators to elect only those considered 'suitable' to hold important offices wielding government patronage.

Musharraf and Islamic Fundamentalists

The liberals who expected General Musharraf to curb or at least control the political clout of religious fundamentalists have been disappointed as the general buckled under the pressures of the Islamists on issues like blasphemy laws. The leader of the Jamaat-i-Islami, Qazi Hussain Ahmed, has embarked on an agenda to create an alliance of anti-army Islamic groups. Musharraf's policy of appeasement towards religious fundamentalists can be guaged from the fact that on 15 July 2000 he issued a decree reviving the Islamic provision of the country's suspended constitution. It was the second time within two months that Musharraf had met the demands of the fundamentalist clergies. In May, he had withdrawn a proposed change to the application of the blasphemy law that human rights groups said was often used to target non-Muslim religious minorities. The decree was considered necessary 'to re-affirm the continuity and enforcement of the Islamic provisions'[25] of Pakistan's constitution which Musharraf had suspended after the coup. Among other things, these provisions prohibit any law that conflicts with Islamic principles.

General Musharraf seems in no position to control the fundamentalist Islamic terrorist organizations like the Lashkar-e-Toiba (LeT), Jaish-e-Mohammad (JeM) and Harkat-ul-Mujahideen (HuM). It will be worthwhile to remember that his attempts to regulate the functioning of the *madrassas* through an Ordinance issued on 19 August last year came to nought and his crackdown on the fundamental Islamic militias like the JeM and LeT in the same month was called off almost immediately after it started. Similarly the government in Sindh province, which had banned the forcible collection of funds by Islamic terrorist organizations, has had to climb down pathetically following angry protests.

Musharraf continues to follow the policy of export of terror based on a military intelligence complex, which has varied global target. By doing so, like General Zia, General Musharraf seems to seek the support of the fundamentalist parties like Markaz Dawa-wal-Irshad, Lashkar-e-Toiba and other religious parties. These religious parties have private militias trained by the ISI, which are fighting for the so-called *Jihad* in Kashmir, Chechnaya, Philippines, Myanmar, Dagesthan and other countries. To save his skin, Musharraf has to obtain the support of the fundamentalist parties even at the cost of sanctions and pressures from the US and the western world. However, this could have dangerous implications, not only for Pakistan, but also for the South Asian region as a whole.

Musharraf's close links with the Islamic fundamentalist terrorist were clearly demonstrated by the manner in which the notorious Lashkar-e-Toiba held its annual congregation near Lahore from 3 to 5 November 1999 and called for a *Jihad* as a holywar

---

[25]Zaigham Khan, 'Blundering the Blasphemy', *The Herald* (June 2000).

against India and the US. Nor is it a mere coincidence that Pakistan's terrorist activities against India have increased steeply following the installation of a new regime. Having stoked the fire of fundamentalism and its fighters with gun culture, Pakistan may find it difficult to contain the monster. Musharraf is convinced that support for the Taliban does give Pakistan 'strategic depth', and bleeding India through a thousand wounds is a desirable policy.

According to Harrison, 'recent information makes clear that the newly installed Chief of Army Staff (COAS), General Pervez Musharraf, has long standing links with several Islamic fundamentalist groups.'[26] During the 1980s, he was picked up by General Zia-ul-Haq for advancement on account of his religious beliefs as a Deobandi. The fact that Musharraf was strongly recommended by the Jamaat-i-Islami no doubt weighed in heavily. Musharraf was put in charge of the training of *Mujahideen* groups[27] for fighting the Soviet military in Afghanistan where he also came in contact with Osama bin Laden.

Musharraf's Aggressive India Policy

The Pakistani Chief Executive has asserted that his country is committed to providing all diplomatic, moral and political support to the people of Kashmir in their 'just struggle for self-determination.' Musharraf's India policy is underpinned by an aggressive military stance. There has been a qualitative and quantitative increase in Pakistani subversive violence against India and its military activities across the Line of Control. The concerted attacks—as military camps and establishments, terrorist violence against civilian targets and infiltration of terrorists and weapons into India—have increased. The hijacking of flight IC–814, the large-scale attack against Indian posts in the Akhnoor-Chamb sector on 22–23 January and the Sikh massacre by militants in Chitthi-Singhpora in Anantnag on 20 March 2000 and the gunning down of 100 Amarnath pilgrims are major

---

[26]Seling Harrison, 'First Put Pressure on Pakistan to Pull Back', *International Herald Tribune* (London), 16 June 1999.
[27]Jasjit Singh, 'The Army in Pakistan', in Jasjit Singh (ed.), *Kargil 1999: Pakistan's Fourth War for Kashmir* (New Delhi: Knowledge World, 1999), pp. 43–44.

manifestations of Pakistan's policy of covert and overt confrontation. Moreover, he has occasionally used the tactics of nuclear blackmail.

Musharraf's approach is that the Kashmir issue has to be settled on Pakistani terms and conditions, otherwise proxy war and terrorism will be continued by him. He considers confidence building measures as a farce. He wants discussions on Kashmir *de novo*.[28]

The architect of Kargil aggression, General Pervez, is still not willing to learn the lesson of the setbacks Pakistan suffered in 1948, 1965, 1971 and 1999. Indeed, since General Musharraf is unlikely to succeed in setting things right domestically in Pakistan, his hope is to demonstrate some spectacular achievements in the proxy war in Kashmir. Its declaration of a public holiday on 5 February as a mark of solidarity with the mercenaries and terrorists fighting in Kashmir is a clear indication of the shape of things to come. In this context, Prem Shankar Jha aptly remarks

> annexing Kashmir is part of nationalist agenda in Pakistan. The keepers of this agenda are the armed forces. A military government is therefore the very last one that can be expected to give it up. Indeed it is an article of faith in the Pakistan armed forces that without the goal of annexing Kashmir, Pakistan could fall apart.[29]

Most significant of all are Pakistan's repeated threats that it would not hesitate to use nuclear weapons against India.

Both Ayub and Zia-ul-Haq had been in power for 8 and 11 years respectively and were facing growing pressure to democratize the polity when they launched their Kashmir ventures. Today, General Musharraf is similarly hardening his tone day by day as the economic and fiscal reforms he is trying to impose on Pakistan create their backlash of unrest.

The recent announcement of the unilateral *Ramzan* Ceasefire by New Delhi and its extension till May 2001 end, has not, for obvious reasons, received the response that was needed to push the process of peace talks forward. Islamabad has made no move to curb the terrorist groups based in Pakistan, which have been continuing violent attacks in Kashmir and other places. This reveals the fact that

---

[28]J. N. Dixit, 'In the General's Own Words', *The Hindustan Times* (New Delhi), 2 February 2000, p. 11.

[29]Prem Shankar Jha, 'Where Next With Pakistan', *The Hindustan Times*, 11 February 2000, p. 13.

Pakistan has no interest in creating a conducive environment for the commencement of an India–Pakistan Peace dialogue.[30]

Post-11 September Musharraf's Pakistan

The terrorist attacks on the World Trade Centre and Pentagon in the US on 11 September 2001 resulted a shift in all geo-political dynamics—international, regional, and local. The extraordinary situation in which it was placed forced the US to coopt Pakistan— the fountain head of terrorist activities—into its 'crusade' against global terrorism. Pakistan, once again, on account of dictates of geography, became a frontline state against Afghanistan for a second time in the last 10 years. For any operation inside Afghani- stan, the Americans sought their old ally: Pakistan's feared intelli- gence agency, the ISI. During the time of the Soviet war on Afghanistan, the CIA was utterly dependent on the ISI to pass on arms and training to the guerrillas in their struggle against the Russians.

Ironical as it may sound, the prime suspect of the terrorist attack on the US, Osama bin Laden, the most wanted man in the world and the perceived symbol of evil, received his first lessons in the art of clandestine operations and subterfuge from the CIA. Bin Laden, the legendary US ally of the 1980s, became a dreaded terrorist of the 1990s and the most privileged guest of the Taliban. The two converted Afghanistan into what a state Department Report on the 'Patterns of Global Terrorism' called the new epicentre of international terrorism.

Pakistan has created and nurtured the Taliban to acquire the much vaunted 'strategic depth' vis-à-vis India and Iran. The US was interested in the Taliban as a possible operational asset against Iran and as the facilitator of oil and gas pipelines from Turkmanistan to Pakistan through Afghanistan.

After the black Tuesday terrorist attacks, the military regime in Islamabad was caught in the biggest dilemma Pakistan has ever

---

[30]Kalim Bahadur, 'Pakistan Journey to Nowhere', *World Focus*, Vol. XXI, Nos. 10– 11–12 (October–November–December 2000), p. 32.

faced. In the context of a whole set of new international and regional priorities, General Musharraf was in a tight spot. On the one side, the world's most powerful nation, wounded and angry, was bluntly telling the general that if he did not act as a friend now he would be considered as the enemy. On the other were the Taliban leaders of the most brutish police state in the world and their hordes who threatened *Jihad* against the very country that had nurtured them. If the general sided with the Taliban zealots, there was little doubt that the US would reduce Pakistan to another failed state as it did in Iraq. If he played ball with America, he could unleash an Islamic storm that would swamp Pakistan.

In sum, terrorist attacks on the US has put Pakistan in the midst of a gathering storm of America-led global war against international terrorism. The military regime's options were limited to risking US punishment for supporting the Taliban, neutrality, or seeking strategic dividends by assisting the US. With a weak economy, a polarised polity, China backing Washington and the Islamic bloc a virtual non-factor, Pakistan was left with no choice. Fearing further global isolation, bankruptcy, and even a possible American attack on Pakistan's nuclear facilities, General Musharraf has decided to make a virtue of necessity and has proclaimed support for US moves to target Osama bin Laden and the Taliban leadership.

Pakistan has chosen to side with Washington by offering its unstinted cooperation'. Consequently, the fundamental assumption of Islamabad's extant policy, that the Taliban-controlled Afghanistan is the vital interest of Pakistan, has been discarded. However, the spin-offs of Pakistan's U-turn on its Afghan policy included financial dividends in terms of lifting of sanctions imposed on it in 1998 by the US, waiver of loans, fresh dose of economic aid plus a more sympathetic view of its position on Kashmir.

General Musharraf seemed eager to persuade his compatriots, especially, the critics, that he faced a virtual Hobson's choice in deciding to go along with the US in the latter's war against terrorism. He utilized a televised addressed to portray his US friendly act as a 'strategic decision', that was designed to prevent a proactive India from isolating Pakistan on the international scene in the aftermath of the world's worst episode of terrorism. He also specified Pakistan's professed concerns for cooperation with the US namely Pakistan's integrity, the state of economy, the sustainability of its strategic assets of nuclear weapons and missiles, besides the Kashmir issue.

However, Musharraf's decision of both distancing himself from the Taliban ruled Afghanistan and also agreeing to provide help to Washington in such key areas as 'intelligence and information exchange', use of Pakistan's 'air space' and 'logistical support' involved tremendous risks. These were related to the survival of the present regime in the face of pro-Taliban sentiments within Pakistan, deep societal split along the liberal/radical-right ideological divide and violent dissension within the Pakistan security establishment, especially along pro-American and vehemently anti-American/pro-Taliban feelings.

It was apparent that General Musharraf was in a difficult position torn between US demands for cooperation and demands by the Islamic clergy, and terrorist organizations like LeT, HuM, JeM and Al-Badr and others for rejecting the same. Flush with narco dollars, terrorist networks are fast shedding their dependence on state sponsors. The authors of Pakistan's Afghan policy must have been a worried lot today as Pakistan has now become a hostage to its Afghan Policy.

General Musharraf was haunted by the gathering anger of the fundamentalists of various hues and cries, *madrassas* students, the tribals of the NWFP and the Federally Administrated Tribal areas, the Afghan returnees in his army. A series of events across Pakistan has provided multiple jolts to the Musharraf government. The regime became a helpless spectator as hordes of armed tribesmen blocked for over a week the arterial Karakoram highway, on the fabled silk route. Their demand was that Pakistan should reconsider its support to the US military campaign.

However, on the economic and diplomatic front the impact of the events of 9/11 on Pakistan reminiscent of the Soviet military intervention in Afghanistan in 1979 is especially conspicuous. The United States' 'War Against Terror' has changed Pakistan's destiny once again. All the sanctions related to the nuclear tests have been lifted and aid has started to flow, inconvenient facts about cross-border terrorism have been brushed under the carpet. Moreover, Pakistan's profile in the eyes of the West, and particularly the Americans, has changed completely. General Musharraf had been courted and flattered by world leaders as the defender of the faith of the civilized world.

Operation Enduring Freedom in Afghanistan has made little dent in curbing cross-border terrorism in Jammu and Kashmir. In

India those who expected that Pakistan, source of cross-border terrorism, would be a prime target of the US war against terror have been disappointed. Large scale terrorist attacks in the Jammu and Kashmir continued. Moreover, the brutal attack on the Jammu and Kashmir Assembly complex by a suicide squad of JeM was launched on 1 October 2001, even as analysts were predicting a period of relative peace for the state consequent to the forces shifting to Afghanistan. This attack had a direct linkage with Pakistan's volatile situation emanating from *Jihadi* violent demonstrations against Pakistan's decision to make common cause with US against the Taliban. Having joined the US in its fight against terrorism, General Musharraf needed as rarely before to pacify the *Jihadis* and demonstrate his commitment to Kashmir. Implicit in the attack was a warning to India about joining any global war against terrorism.

In the context of Pakistan supported cross-border terrorism in Jammu and Kashmir, the US did nothing more than listing the LeT and the JeM as 'foreign terrorist organizations'. In fact, General Pervez Musharraf is considered by the US and his other Western allies as an important bulwark in the anti-terrorist fight, a moderate who needs to be supported and fortified.

As the war against terrorism in Afghanistan progressed, it became clear that Musharraf was not prepared to forsake the Taliban entirely. This was evident from his advocacy of a major political role in Afghanistan for some so called 'moderate Taliban'.

Pakistan was playing a double game—helping the US offensive while trying to ensure that their old Taliban allies have a prominent role in post-war government. General Musharraf has opposed US support to the Northern Alliance. Sections of the US media felt that Pakistan was not a reliable ally. The CIA has accused the ISI of playing a double-game of pretending to help yet allowing the flow of weapons into Afghanistan. Wary of the ISI, the US pressurized Musharraf to remove the ISI Chief Mahmud Ahmed and co. via sweeping changes in the army on 8 October 2001, in the hope of getting credible intelligence on Taliban.

After lying to the world about the links that his army establishment had with the Taliban, Musharraf was confronted with a rather difficult and embarrassing situation when the American bombing started in Kunduz, Afghanistan, where Pakistan army officers who have been fighting alongwith Taliban got trapped.

According to a story published by Seymour Hersh in the New Yorker, the Americans allowed Pakistan to evacuate thousands of its army officers and personnel trapped in Kunduz before it fell to the forces of Northern Alliance on 25 November 2001. Pakistan evacuated not only its personnel but also members of Al-Qaida and Taliban cadres. The Bush administration caved in to Musharraf's request for evacuation primarily because they felt that the killing or surrender of a large number of officers of the Pakistan army would embarrass and weaken Musharraf. This is, however, a strategic blunder that Bush administration is going to regret.[31]

Strangely enough, even after destroying all the suspected hideouts of Taliban–Al-Qaida the leadership of neither of the two organizations were to be seen anywhere. They were neither captured nor killed. When the speculation started that they might have been smuggled into Pakistan by their sympathizers in the bordering provinces of Baluchistan and NWFP, General Musharraf suddenly announced on 21 December 2001 about Osama bin Laden. He told a Chinese television network that 'Osama is not in Pakistan' and that he suspects that he is killed in the US bombing. This shrewd ploy saved him not only from any possible US wrath of its failed mission but also from the possible backlash effect of the Pakhtuns and projected him as a man who bailed out the Pakhtun-dominated Taliban leadership.

But there is another side to the story. Pakistan's Afghanistan policy has proved to be a disastrous failure. The fall of Kabul to the Northern Alliance is the Pakistani military strategists' worst nightmare come true. As far as India is concerned, the destruction of the Taliban, and its terrorist networks in Afghanistan is a plus point. Pakistan has lost a client state, which it had as long as Afghanistan was under the control of the Taliban. The Northern Alliance's victory over Kabul has certainly put Musharraf under immense pressure. General Musharraf is subjected to severe criticism both within and outside the military. The crux of this criticism is that the general's decision to support the US in its war against Afghanistan has not resulted in any strategic gain.

The image boost General Musharraf received after 11 September proved transitory. Today Musharraf is frantically scrambling

---

[31]G. Parthasarathy, 'Osama, ISI, Taliban: The Disappearing Act', *The Pioneer* (New Delhi), 3 January 2002, p. 6.

amid the rubble of his Afghan policy. Pakistan now faces the grim prospect of isolation abroad and violent convulsions at home. Its notion of acquiring strategic depth in Afghanistan has proved to be a mirage.

In the post-Taliban scenario, General Musharraf has only the Kashmir issue to build domestic support in his favour and divert attention from the foreign policy failures. The Thursday (13 December 2001) terrorist attack by JeM on the Indian parliament, located at the heart of the capital's high security zone, substantiates this view. The attack was well-planned, carefully crafted and timed with precise intelligence inputs. The timing of the blast indicates its purpose. It was to convey two strident messages on behalf of Pakistan's Musharraf regime. The first was that despite the success of the United States-led coalition in the Afghan war, terrorism is alive and well. It had become imperative to send it to raise the morale of terrorists in India and Pakistan which had sunk to their boots following the collapse of the Taliban regime. The second message was that the attack was a proof of the fact that the Musharraf regime had not sold out to the US, and its alliance with the latter was meant to safeguard Pakistan's nuclear arsenal and prevent the US from including its cross-border terrorism against India in its anti-terrorist agenda. It was addressed principally to fundamentalist Islamic militias like the LeT, HuM and JeM as well as other *Jihadi* groups in Pakistan which are fuming over what they consider to be the Musharraf regimes' betrayal of the Taliban and Osama bin Laden.

In the post-Taliban scenario, one finds that the evidence of close ties Islamabad has had with the Taliban, Osama bin Laden and the Al-Qaida, and these three had with terrorist militias like the LeT, JeM and HuM directly and through Pakistan's ISI, had destroyed its credibility with the US and other Western countries. They are now convinced that their war against terrorism will not be completed without squelching militias like the LeT, JeM and HuM which pose a threat to them as well. Hence, Pakistan was under intense pressure to clamp down on these and reform the country into a moderate Islamic state.

Pakistan is an ally of the US in the war against terrorism and Musharraf has agreed publicly in his 12 January speech to wage the war domestically and make the choice which the US and the democratic world wants him to make. Going by the reaction to his 12

January speech, the whole world seems to be in a mood to give the general a standing ovation for his bold and visionary approach to tackle terrorism.

However, General Musharraf even while renouncing terrorism for the Kashmir cause, has repeated his usual formula on the Kashmir issue. He talks of Kashmir as being a part of every Pakistani's blood.

The actions Pakistan has taken against various terrorist outfits so far are superficial. The leaders of the JeM, and LeT were arrested only after they had nominated their deputies, the bank accounts of both were frozen in a manner that had enabled them to withdraw a bulk of funds in advance. By all accounts, Pakistan seems to be going through the motions of acting against them without hurting them. The aim seems to ward off pressure for their dismantling and preserve their basic infrastructure and to revive them once the US pressure eases. There are reports that the Taliban, the Al-Qaida, the Jaish and members of the Pakistan military and ISI have now regrouped in Pakistan and renamed themselves.

More than a month has passed since the speech. Beyond arresting a couple of thousands of terrorists—of whom we do not know now how many have been released—Musharraf has done nothing. On the other hand, a US journalist Daniel Pearl had been taken hostage by Omar Sheikh who was released in return for the hijacked passengers of the IA Plane IC–814. He has confessed that he was responsible for the attack on the Jammu and Kashmir Assembly, the Indian parliament and the American Centre in Kolkata. This cast doubts about the Pakistani leader's effectiveness or even willingness to control terrorism and transform Pakistan into a moderate Islamic state. Besides, the brutal murder of Daniel Pearl exemplifies the fact that Pakistan continues to be the epicentre of terrorism.

Two questions predominate in the post-12 January scenario. First, did the general really mean it when he roundly denounced religious fundamentalism and terrorism as instruments of state policy? Second, is he willing and able to deliver on his brave promises and abjure both? He cannot deliver on his promise. But what he did was run rings round the US in his 'historic' speech. He as an astute painter has painted on a wide canvas with very broad strokes. He announced his intentions of drastically cleansing Pakistani society and polity of religious fundamentalism, violence and terrorism. It is humanly impossible for one man, working under heightened personal security and thus at considerable remove from the masses, to bring about social revolution and that too in a society that is deeply mired in illiteracy, poverty, religious extremism and exclusiveness, and social conservatism. Thus, Musharraf is incapable of bringing about a qualitative change in Pakistani societal structures and making it democratic, plural, secular and terrorism free.[32] In normal circumstances, a change can come only if there is a strong popular urge for it. The situation in Pakistan has not reached such a point.[33]

In sum, at this present phase, the war against terrorism is focused on the scourge within Pakistan. Even though he has willingly accepted all the US directions, it remains to be seen whether General Musharraf can translate them into reality on the ground. But the US has made it clear that it will stay in Pakistan till it is cleansed of terrorism. The US will support Musharraf as long as he plays the role Washington wants.[34] Pakistan's fate, once again, is in the hands of three 'A's'—America, Army and Allah. The very future of Pakistan and General Musharraf's political survival are at stake. This is a period of immense uncertainty for the Pakistani ruler, the army and society.

---

[32]Ajoy Bagchi, 'The General Just Cannot Deliver', *The Pioneer* (New Delhi), 26 January 2002, p. 8.
[33]Muchkund Dubey, 'Transforming Pakistan', *The Hindu*, 1 February 2002, p. 8.
[34]K. Subrahmanyam, 'Washington's Waiting: Islamabad's Tokenism will not Work', *The Times of India*, 11 February 2002, p. 14.

Chapter IX

Authoritarianism, Democracy and Development

Fifty years of Pakistan's traumatic political history unveils a long drawn-out battle between military hegemony/authoritarianism and democracy/constitutionalism or an imbalanced and uneasy relationship between the state structure and civic institutions intent upon establishing an accountable polity and equitable socio-economic order. Authority, stipulating state structure both in the historic and political sense, is strictly anchored on bureaucratic and military axis with the coopted elite from the landed aristocracy. At the same time, Pakistani polity represents

> an enduring ideological conflict among the triumvirate forces of state-led Muslim nationalism, regional particularism, and ethnic pluralism. The internecine conflict among contending sectarianism and ethnic groups exemplifies the fragile state of Pakistani political processes and their dependence upon the army.[1]

Besides, today a turbulent Pakistan wounded with frequent onslaughts of military rule, rising tide of religious fundamentalism, terrorism, violent sectarianism, Jihadism, and collapsing economy can be a

---

[1] Iftikhar H. Malik, 'The State and Civil Society in Pakistan: From Crisis to Crisis', *Asian Survey*, Vol. XXVI, No. 7 (July 1996), p. 675.

source of tremendous instability for the whole South Asian region, leave alone Pakistan.

Search for a Viable Political System

The failure of democracy to take root in Pakistan lies in the entire political process on which the state and successive governments have based themselves. An overview of Pakistan's political history suggests that state construction and consolidation of Pakistan has been on a conflicting course with the social dynamics underlying the political processes. Pakistan, due to the absence of a well-developed political party organization, has been unable to integrate its provinces or distribute resource equitably between the pre-dominant Punjab and the subordinate provinces of Sindh, the North-West Frontier Province and Baluchistan as well as between the diverse linguistic groups within them. Like other post-colonial states, where the unfolding of political processes has been hampered, Pakistan too has relied on its civil service—the steel-frame of the Raj—and ultimately, on the army to maintain the continuities of government.[2]

Pakistan came into being in extremely difficult conditions and faced serious domestic problems of its own making coupled with a sense of insecurity vis-à-vis India. State survival became the primary concern of the rulers of Pakistan, who equated it with a powerful central government, strong defence posture, high defence allocations and an emphasis on monolithic nationalism. The imperative of a strong state apparatus was given priority over the need to create participatory political institutions and processes.

The initial problems, especially the urgent need to set up an effective government that could save the new state from collapsing, led to making civil servants and military the main instruments for state formation. Pakistan shaped up as a centralized administrative polity which stifled the growth of autonomous and viable political institutions and processes. The problems of religious leaders have been accentuated by the widening ethnic, regional and religious-sectarian cleavages, proliferation of weapons, and brutalization of society by

---

[2]Ayesha Jalal, *The State of Martial Law: The Origins of Pakistan's Political Economy of Defence* (Cambridge: Cambridge University Press, 1990), p. 1.

civic violence. The absence of consensus among the political leaders led the military to expand its role in the political process. Gradually the top commanders along with the bureaucracy expanded their role in the political arena.

Since her birth, Pakistan has been according very high priority to defence and spending disproportionately on the military at the cost of the social sector: Pakistan's identity crisis, coupled with its obsession to attain parity with India in military terms, pushed the military into the centre of the decision-making arena, allowing the defence establishment to play a more decisive role in internal and external politics. Pakistan's continued confrontation with India, coupled with its military and strategic connections with the US, helped to rationalize the centralist state structure, besides the growing expenditure on defence.

In due course of time, the bureaucracy monopolized power from the grassroots to the top echelons. It manipulated the political institutions in the country by coopting the army. The military and the bureaucracy both continued to share the pre-partition tradition of Punjabi-domination. The military and civil services as part and parcel of the same colonial bureaucratic set-up, shared a common antipathy towards accountable, reasonably representative and full-fledged mandated institutions. The bureaucratic-military elite played havoc with national institutions and used authoritarian elected governments and hampered the democratic process.

In the post-Cold War era, despite trends towards democracy and civilian rule, the military in Pakistan is the most formidable and autonomous political actor, capable of influencing the nature and direction of political change. Pakistan's half a century old search for a viable political system has produced the military-hegemonic regime which promoted the interests of the military-bureaucratic elites, consolidated the financial industrial groups, co-opted a feudal class, and followed *laissez faire* economic growth and development model. Its basic objective was to curb participatory politics and to subordinate the political parties and other autonomous interest groups to military hegemony. At the same time, through political control and political exclusion, the regime promoted centralization and authoritarianism, delegitimized political parties and leaders and depoliticized the masses. This was exemplified in the military hegemonic regimes of Ayub Khan, Yahya Khan, and Zia-ul-Haq. The present military regime of General Musharraf is also working on the same lines.

However, the post-military democratic experiences in Pakistan under Z. A. Bhutto, Benazir Bhutto and Nawaz Sharif respectively failed to subordinate the military-bureaucratic elites to civilian-led party dominance, and to build an alternative to the military rule. An analysis of the functioning of these civilian regimes suggests that the limitations and constraints of a successor civilian regime in the post-military hegemonic systems present a paradox. On the one hand, a party dominance system emerges as a response to the military-hegemonic system, while on the other hand, the functioning and development of the former is conditioned by the latter. The dynamics of this relationship are adversarial and competitive to the extent that each seeks control over the resources of the society. Both inhibit the growth and development of autonomous groups and political parties. Consequently, party-building, associational activity, and competitive party politics remain low priorities. Socialization of democratic norms and values remain weak and authoritarian and hegemonic tendencies persist.

Ironically both transitions, i.e., in 1971 and 1988, from military-hegemonic to civilian rule were burdened with divisiveness, rather than consensus. Transitions that occur in the context of social and political cleavages and divisiveness were bound to be fragile, violence prone and inherently unstable. Thus, Pakistan embarked on a path of restoration of democracy, which was conflict ridden, divided and tentative.[3]

It is worth noting that the long years of direct rule have allowed the military to penetrate so widely into the government, the economy and society that its clout and influence no longer depend on controlling the levers of power. It is derived from its pervasive presence in all sectors of government and society. The military, therefore, after Zia-ul-Haq's death, preferred to pursue its interests from the sidelines. However, the military elites orchestrated the restoration of democracy in a manner that on the one hand, enabled them to impose checks on the newly installed Pakistan People's Party (PPP) government, while on the other hand, pushing the military backed Islamic Democratic Alliance (IDA) to confront the ruling party, particularly in Punjab. Consequently, the military's hegemony

---

[3]Refer, Gerald E. Heeger, 'Politics in the Post-Military State: Some Reflections on the Pakistani Experience', *World Politics*, Vol. XXIV, No. 2 (January 1977), pp. 242–62.

in politics could not be reduced and it assumed the role of an arbitrator and a referee between the ruling PPP and the opposition IDA. Musharraf's coup was an institutional response to what senior commanders perceived as a threat to the professional and corporate interests of the army.

The development of the Pakistani state suggests that a well-entrenched military-bureaucratic establishment, the bedrock of Pakistani state structure, constitutes a thinly based edifice. These monopolist power elites have too often opposed measures such as democratization, decentralization, accountability, media freedom, land reforms and independence of the judiciary. A number of civil and military intelligence agencies have masterminded political alliances and counter alliances known as the 'secret hand' or 'invisible government'. They do not allow the maturing of political processes and democratic institutions.[4]

In sum, the Pakistani state

...in a rigorous sense, is anchored on the uncontested primacy of bureaucracy and the military, which has become solidified over the years through a legacy of elitism and authoritarianism. Its opportunistic dallying with the feudal forces and religious-spiritual leaders have not allowed meaningful decentralization and democratization in a plural society like Pakistan.[5]

In addition, the governments, usually led by a bureaucratic-military and feudal axis, have emphasized on depolitization. Civil society was scorned as it would have meant strengthening political institutions and decentralization of power and egalitarian power sharing—all anathema to the Pakistan ruling elite.

The all pervasive and arbitrary role of the army and the monopolization of power by the bureaucracy made the civil institutions mere 'appendages of a state' which suffered from a dual crisis in mandate and legitimacy. The way in which civil society was gradually beleaguered can be understood in terms of the administrative and economic priorities of the state as reflected in the annual budgetary

---

[4]Iftikhar H. Malik, *State and Civil Society in Pakistan: Politics of Authority, Ideology and Ethnicity* (New York: St. Martin's Press Inc., 1999), chapter 5, pp. 94–114.
[5]Ibid., p. 10.

allocation which led to a crumbling/diminishing of institutional civic foundation.[6]

The governments usually led by bureaucracy, military and feudal axis, has exhibited an ethnic discreetness and oligarchic manner which has added to the disenchantment of centrifugal forces. The overpowering elitist oligarchies monopolized the Pakistani polity and dominated the decision-making process, preferred self-preservation over national prerogatives, and opted for executive-administrative personality measures rather than political/constitutional solutions. Their personality-centred and manipulative strategies have done irreparable damage to the country and the institutions essential for national cohesion. According to one scholar,

> The Pakistani state has appeared blind to the societal pluralism and the dictates of civil society like political culture, civic institutions.... The non-representative elites, with no mandate or legitimacy in a wider national context, have adopted a neo-colonial role to usher Pakistan into the modern era assuming the absolutist role of pre-democratic European oligarchies.[7]

Legitimacy has been sought by non-representative elites through a politics of cooption with intermediaries and dependence on Islamic ideology. Pakistani polity is rooted in the colonial tradition of patronage, with the landed aristocracy frequently acting as a willing partner and a coopted elite. All the regimes have used Islam to legitimize their authority and to avoid elected politics. However, the ideological groups, suffering from internal splits and undefined quest for identity, have been unable to provide any tangible alternative other than rhetoric. The military bureaucratic elite carried on the political, geographical, economic and demographic imbalances that existed in the polity since the Raj.

In terms of socio-economic stratification or class formation, Pakistan is still a predominantly agrarian rural and feudalist society. The four provinces that form Pakistan comprise overwhelmingly of a feudal political leadership. And these are inherently incapable of leading a democratic country. Feudalism is anti-democratic. The feudals have been totally integrated with the military-bureaucratic establishment either through marriage or lineage. The feudals have not only

---

[6]Ibid., p. 115.
[7]Ibid., p. 40.

created a socio-economic situation in society that is to their benefit, they have also influenced politics and the political psyche of Pakistan.

The feudals use popular slogan mongering to win support from the people only for their own purposes. Simultaneously, they ensure that the people do not organize around any known agenda or manifesto. The urban politicians and the feudals have a tactical understanding that the social and economic structures will not be changed at all and that the status quo will remain. This aspect of politicians has remained unchanged throughout Pakistan's history. The balance between the bureaucracy and the armed forces on the one hand and the political set-up on the other, and the repeated imposition of martial law have tilted the balance against democratic political set-up.

The breaking down of existing islands of power, namely, the tribal and feudal power, is a prerequisite for the establishment of democracy in Pakistan. To change the social structure and eliminate the feudals, the need is to organize the people governed and controlled by the feudals themselves. To pave the way for a liberal democratic system, it is imperative to bring land reforms without which it is not possible to have a proper democratic dispension in this country.

Pakistan urgently needs land reforms so as to balance land ownership and to create an equitable and efficient system guaranteeing improvement of the peasant's sore conditions, providing finances to the government through agricultural tax, etc. However, it still remains an utopia. Such reforms would not only eradicate politico-economic injustice at both the local and national levels, they would also furnish tangible incentives for productive farming. This would go a long way towards abolishing poverty and strengthening civic institutions in the country. This would pave the way for making the entire political structure more participatory, viable and responsive to the needs of the masses rather than pampering a few thousand people at the top.[8]

In 1959 and 1972, there were two half-hearted efforts to bring about some change in this direction. The Ayub regime could not afford to alienate the landed aristocracy and so the land reforms were timid in nature. Similarly, Z. A. Bhutto's land reforms provided only window dressing to an age-old malady.

During the Zia era, the land-tenure system remained intact and unchallenged. The stagnation of the agriculture sector led to

---

[8]Ibid., p. 90.

exodus to urban areas and the Gulf. Due to good harvests and influx of foreign remittances, the economy remained stable but poverty remained pervasive. In its quest for legitimacy, the military regime spared the landed aristocracy from reforms or agricultural tax. The landed elites reaped all sorts of political, economic and managerial benefits for lending support to the system. Their heavy representation in the *Majlis-i-Shoora* (consultative council), Local Bodies, Provincial Assemblies, the National Assembly and the Senate has guaranteed the perpetuation in the state structure.

In sum, during all the regimes, whether civilian or military,

both the state and the propertied elites have already established a dependency relationship which is both exclusive and partisan. It operates as the vehicle for the continued disenfranchisement of the masses and intermediate class, who, in dispensation, turn parochial or sectarian. The multiple nature of this elitist oligarchy hampers the growth of a responsible, egalitarian and dynamic civil society which may eventually result in the devolution of powers.[9]

There are a variety of other factors as well. The religious dogma the people has been taught and which the religious outfits in the country continue to dish out to the people is also anti-democracy. It is not religion that is anti-democracy but religious dogma. It is also anti-liberal because it does not accept new ideas or modern thinking. This is an impediment in the way of the development of a modern democratic polity.

State and the Civil Society

As far as the relation between the state and the civil society is concerned, the state is an important prerequisite for any civil society and more so in the case of post-colonial societies, but centralization, monopolistic elitism and unrepresentative institutions only erode nationhood. As a perceptive scholar comments,

Ideologically and organizationally weak political parties in Pakistan have remained vulnerable to official manipulation, and the central-

---

[9]Ibid., pp. 92–93.

ized organs of the state routinely accuse them of impotence and corruption. Rather than consolidating political and constitutional norms, through dialogue and consensus, Pakistani politicians frivolously consume their energies on internecine dissensions, occasionally resorting to populist political appeals for street agitation or succumbing to horse-trading and trespassing all the parliamentary norms. Such behaviour suits the centralist forces within the state and is amply used to discredit both politicians and democracy itself.[10]

The narrow nature of the state has constantly politicized ethnicity, finding momentum both from primordial and institutional factors. Given the disparate nature of the former West and East Pakistan and the eventual separation of East Pakistan, successive Pakistani regimes have been apprehensive of ethnic heterogeneity and cultural pluralism in the country. The usual official aversion to democracy and constitutionalism has not allowed various regional and ethnic forces to enter mainstream politico-economic institutions. Instead of opting for logical and egalitarian policies based on consensus, the regimes have sought to carve out an overarching Pakistani identity at the expense of ethnic pluralism. The state itself, confronted by a resurgence in regionalist identities, instead of initiating appropriate constitutional and politico-economic measures for their cooption, sought an easy refuge in Islamic symbols. Vigorous attempts at Islamization were made from the mid-1970s but such attempts only sharpened the internal conflicts and contradictions of Pakistan.

The dilemma of state and civil society not only hinges on the feudalization of politics and bureaucratization of the polity, it is also manifested in the ethnic arena, which is still largely undefined despite its centrality in Pakistan's national experience. In Pakistan, ethnic pluralism is usually treated by the policy-makers as a mere law and order problem. The ethnic multiplicity in Sindh, its comprehension and appropriate responses to it through tangible measures poses a significant challenge to the state and civil society. It signals the urgency of considerably long overdue reforms in the politico-administrative, and economic system, on the one hand and decentralization and de-bureaucratization on the other.

---

[10]Malik, 'The State and Civil Society in Pakistan: From Crisis to Crisis', p. 681.

An overview of various sectors which have become non-priority areas as a result of official policies may illustrate the failure of civil society in Pakistan to check the monopolistic, centralist and elitist preferences that harm its own citizens. The persistence of poverty, basic inequalities within the society, high defence expenditure, the marginalization of the social sector including vital areas like education and health, the exclusion of women from many aspects of national life, the muzzling of the press, an extremely narrow tax base and the evasion of overdue measures like agricultural tax and land reforms—all these point to the failure to establish an enduring and plural civil society. Such a scenario does not suit non-representative regimes which thrive on non-accountability. The awakening of civic institutions, namely, an empowered parliament, a free press and public opinion, an independent judiciary and energetic non-governmental organizations, provides institutional restraints on a growing oligarchic or elitist state and adds to the forces of despair or defection in various cross-sections of the society.[11]

Correlation between Democracy and Development

Although the term 'development' is generally used to indicate the economic status of a country, it also involves levels of social and political development, which produces mechanisms for change and provides a platform of basic civil and political rights. In Pakistan, economic development has been viewed as a process that is initiated and controlled by the state to improve the economy, and the state and the elite groups have been the major beneficiaries of this development.

Samuel P. Huntington has hypothesized that economic development, incremental or decremental, has a positive influence on the process of democratization. He maintains that when nations reach a given development threshold as defined by their GNP, they are highly likely to become democracies. Slow development, he believes, will result in slow transition to democracy, whereas rapid development creates tensions in a society that often unseat or force liberalization on

---

[11]Ibid.

the authoritarian regimes and, hence, lead to broader political, participation.[12] Broadly speaking, two opposing views have characterized the correlation between regime types and development. Some theorists contend that a non-democratic government is best for development on the grounds that unrestrained democracy leads to indiscipline and inefficiency and thus is antagonistic to development. Others, while arguing that development promotes democracy, maintain that democratic regimes enhance economic and political freedom created for stable and credible development in the long run. As such, democracy-development trade-offs are vehemently refuted. The proponents of this view maintain that far from restraining development, democracy furthers it. But in the case of Pakistan, economic growth has been successfully achieved under authoritarian regimes, thus growth has never reinforced or fostered democracy there. No clear pattern has emerged showing the relationship between development and democracy in the country's brief history. The 'lack of such a correlation indicates that economic growth without the expansion of civil and political rights is unlikely to lead to democracy in Pakistan.'[13] Although Huntington's broad thesis is true in most cases, no single approach can be used to quantify the prospects for democratization in countries with diverse social, political, cultural and economic systems as Pakistan.

Economic growth has failed to produce a strong, large middle-class in Pakistan; instead, it has created and strengthened only the elite groups. Significant foreign interest and interference has culminated in external manipulation of the nation's policies. These considerations have affected Pakistan in ways not taken into account by Huntington's economic analysis. Pakistan has had governments that were authoritarian and produced good economic results but failed to promote sustainable democracy. 'Rapid growth created some tension as Huntington predicts, but the response to the tension never progressed to the establishment of democratic values. The economic, political and social dimensions of Pakistan's history reflect fluctuations between authoritarian and more democratic regimes, and the activities

---

[12]Samuel P. Huntington, *The Third Wave: Democratization in the Late Twentieth Century* (Norman, Okla: University of Oklahoma Press, 1991), pp. 60–61, 69, 271 and 361.
[13]Mahmood Monshipouri and Amjad Samuel, 'Development and Democracy in Pakistan: Tenuous or Plausible Nexus?', *Asian Survey*, Vol. XXXV, No. 11 (November 1995), p. 975.

of each have created tension between socio-political development and economic development.'[14]

Various Regime Types and Their Economic Performance: A Comparative View

Pakistan's first experiment with democracy from 1947–1958 was labelled as the decade of stagnation. The first few years were spent in struggling with post-partition problems rather than in the formulation of long-term programmes for economic growth. Strained relations with India and Afghanistan led to high defence spending and neglect of social sector. Most individuals in Pakistan consider Ayub Khan's decade as Pakistan's 'best', in terms of economic development with General Zia's a close second. In contrast, the democratic regimes of Z. A. Bhutto, his daughter, Benazir Bhutto, and Nawaz Sharif reveal only the worst economic performance. Yet, these statistical figures reveal only half the picture.

Ayub Khan's decade of development represents a period of miraculous economic growth. In the 1960s, Pakistan's economy grew by 6.8 per cent a year, no mean achievement for a country that began with very little. General Zia's 11 years between 1977–1988 were equally impressive with the economy growing by about 6.5 per cent annually, agriculture by 5.4 per cent and industry by 8.2 per cent. Moreover, for the period 1980–1988, Pakistan's GDP growth rate was recognized by the World Bank as the fourth highest in the world. In contrast, in the five and a half years under Z. A. Bhutto (1971–1977) the economy grew on an average by 4.4 per cent per annum, with both agriculture and industry growing by a mere 2 per cent on an average. Inflation too averaged 14 per cent in this period. Worse still has been the performance of the economy in the post–1988 period of democracy, easily labelled as the worst decade in Pakistan's history. Gross growth rates, however, do not explain the dark and scarred side of the picture.[15]

Ayub Khan's period was truly impressive in terms of statistical numbers, although much of the explanation for this growth is to be

---

[14]Ibid., p. 976.
[15]S. Akbar Zaidi, 'Democracy, Dictatorship and Development', *The Herald* (November 1990), reproduced in *Strategic Digest*, Vol. XXIX, No. 12 (December 1999), pp. 1835–36.

found in the colonial economic and political exploitation of East Pakistan, whereby its resources were drained to West Pakistan. Without the ample use of foreign exchange earned from jute towards industrial investment in West Pakistan, it is improbable that the latter would have registered such high rates of growth. The two main factors responsible for General Zia's great achievements were: remittances worth 23 billion dollars being sent to Pakistan from the Gulf States and following the Soviet military intervention in Afghanistan, huge quantities of military and economic aid from the West which fuelled growth in the services and industrial sectors. While the economic growth was impressive, Zia was oppressive and favoured a feudal order.

This is not to suggest that democracy has done any better, as Z. A. Bhutto's period has shown. The socio-economic reforms that the Bhutto regime carried out could only register mild gains leaving the masses at large disenchanted. The socio-economic reforms were motivated more by political conditions than by the professed ideals of social justice. Similarly, while corruption, mismanagement and bad governance have played a seminal role between 1988–1999 in the worst decade since independence—consensus amongst economists points to the adherence, if not capitulation to the International Monetary Fund's and World Bank's structural adjustment programme since 1988 as being significantly more important.

A brief review of Pakistan's economic history suggests that very special conditions led to high growth under military dictators and that this correlation is not a natural law. All those who have high hopes of a revival of the economy by the Musharraf regime should take into account the changing realities. In 1958, as well as in 1977, it was far easier to manage Pakistan's economy than it is today. Since the nature of Pakistani society is critically different from what it was even 24 years ago, new sets of rules to govern society will be needed. Moreover, many of the gains made by civil society over the 11 years (1988–1999), are unlikely to be pushed aside very easily. That the global and regional situation is fundamentally different from both 1958 and 1977 has important implications for Pakistan's polity as well.[16]

---

[16]Ibid., pp. 1836–37.

Various Regime Types and Socio-Economic Equality: A Comparative View

All Pakistani governments have failed to consolidate democracy significantly and attain socio-economic equality. A survey of the regimes in Pakistan's history shows that authoritarian regimes have generally provided good economic growth but this has not paved the way for socio-political equality or democratic practices. During Ayub's period, regional and class disparities increased. Zia's regime strengthened anti-democratic measures. Sharif's civilian regime neither weakened the foundations of a semi-authoritarian government nor projected a transition towards democracy.

During the Ayub era, economic growth was commendable but it was neither accompanied by structural changes nor social justice. Economic wealth of the country got concentrated in a few hands. The land reforms of 1959 did not bring any substantial change to the feudal structure of the country. Moreover, the uneven impact of the Green Revolution on the different stratas of rural population sharply widened the disparities among all rural stratas and regions. The landlords benefited from the mechanization of agriculture under the Green Revolution as the peasants felt uprooted and looked for employment centres. The benefits of the Green Revolution remained confined to the big and medium sized farmers of Punjab. The small farmers felt that the initial programme of the Green Revolution worked against them and that large-scale agri-business farming threatened their survival. As a result, Ayub's development model, which was based on the doctrine of 'functional inequality', widened the income inequalities between East and West Pakistan and urban and rural areas of the respective wings of the country, and later on culminated into anti-Ayub agitations.

Z. A. Bhutto claimed to build a socialist political economy. However,

> his nationalization measures only consolidated the unchallengeable transcendency of the state over vital financial institutions and led to added stagnation. The land reforms were largely cosmetic and failed to alter the traditional land-holding pattern given the feudal vetoing power in the PPP regime.[17]

---

[17]Malik, *State and Civil Society in Pakistan*, p. 121.

According to one estimate, 'barely 1 per cent of the landless tenants and small owners benefited from the 1972 land reforms.'[18] Ever since, according to one noted scholar,

> successive regimes have been held to ransom by vested interests in order to ward off any basic economic structural changes. The imposition of the agricultural tax has been resisted by feudal groups on the plea that, given the low agricultural income, realization of such a tax would be difficult.[19]

Notwithstanding this argument, 'it is used as a tax shelter by the rich. This has seriously eroded the tax base and contributed to the regressive nature of the tax system in Pakistan.'[20]

The Zia-ul-Haq period, even though it produced impressive economic growth, also produced unprecedented schisms and tensions in society in terms of ethnic and sectarian violence raging across the country. Zia's short-sighted policies led to the emergence of the 'Kalashnikov and heroin' culture and a parallel black economy which began to undermine the real economy. A scrutiny of developments in Karachi reveals a close relation with Pakistan's Afghan policy. The Afghan refugees brought with them any number of small arms inside Pakistan, and these gun-loving militants later on started making a living by mercenary activities, especially in Karachi. Ethno-centralism, sub-nationalism and Islamic sectarian violence—the three major threats confronting Pakistani polity today—to a large extent, can be attributed to Pakistan's policies towards the former Soviet Union's invasion of Afghanistan. Besides, Zia introduced certain Islamic principles in the economic arena which justified the feudal and capitalist interests. In fact an exploitative and oppressive order alienated the masses.

In addition to all these, the Zia regime failed to check escalating inequalities and to formulate appropriate policies for equitable distribution of resources. The regime's emphasis was more on economic efficiencies and growth for the eradication of persisting regional economic disparities rather than on distributive policies.[21]

---

[18]Omar Noman, *Pakistan: A Political and Economic History Since 1947* (London: Kegan Paul, 1988), p. 75.

[19]Malik, *State and Civil Society in Pakistan*, p. 121.

[20]Asian Development Bank, *Strategies for Economic Growth and Development: The Bank's Role in Pakistan* (Manila, 1985), p. 117.

[21]Wolfgang Peter Zingel, 'Some Economic and Social Problems of Pakistan in 1980's', in Wolfgang Peter Zingel and Stephanie Lallemant Zingel (eds.), *Pakistan in the 1980s:*

Moreover, the growth which took place was not accompanied by equitable distribution, as the 1985–86 budget, according to critics, exemplified a recipe for profiteering by the super rich.[22]

With the restoration of democracy in 1988, Benazir Bhutto came into power. On the economic front, unlike her father's policies of nationalization and public sector expansion, she attempted to bring the private sector to the forefront of economic activity in Pakistan but the economy remained stagnant. During her second term she continued the economic liberalization process of her predecessor, but there has also been a rise in domestic political violence and militancy in Karachi. But the end of the 1980s got caught in the classical 'debt trap' scenario. Nawaz Sharif stimulated the economy with his intense privatization but his social policies were too coercive. Decline in US aid, high spending on military and 'debt trap' all resulted in a total economic mess in Pakistan.

Table 9.1
Comparative Military Expenditure as Percentage of GDP, 1990–1998

Year	Pakistan	India	Nepal	Bangladesh	Sri Lanka
1990	5.7	2.9	0.8	1.4	2.1
1991	5.8	2.6	0.7	1.5	2.8
1992	6.1	2.5	0.8	1.7	3.0
1993	5.7	2.4	0.8	1.7	3.1
1994	5.2	2.2	0.8	1.5	3.4
1995	5.2	2.1	0.8	1.5	5.3
1996	5.1	2.0	0.7	1.5	5.0
1997	4.6	2.2	0.8	1.6	4.2
1998	4.2	2.1	0.9	1.6	4.2

Source: *SIPRI Yearbook 2000, Armaments, Disarmament and International Security* (London: Oxford University Press in collaboration with SIPRI, 2000), p. 278.

The consistent pattern that runs through all the governments is a negative correlation between the economic growth rate and socio-political liberalization and related democratic consolidation.

Ideology, Regionalism, Economy, Foreign Policy (Lahore: Vanguard Books, 1985). See A. R. Kemal, 'Income Distribution in Pakistan: A Review', *Research Report Series* No. CXXIII (Islamabad: Pakistan Institute of Development Economics, 1981).

[22]'The State of Economy 1984–88', *Pakistan Progressive*, Vol. VII, No. 2 (Fall 1985), p. 6.

No government has thus far been able to combine significant economic growth with social justice and a stable political order. The tension between social change and those seeking economic growth mirrors the country's uneven distribution of wealth and the prevailing elitist politics. On the one hand, Pakistan has been suffering from poverty and basic inequalities within the society, on the other, from uneven development, rural–urban differences, feudatory land-holding patterns, narrow tax base and huge non-development expenditure. Despite the impressive growth rates during the Ayub and Zia periods and substantial increases in domestic productivity, the social sector of Pakistan has remained grossly neglected and underdeveloped (see Table 9.1).

Various sectors of civil society, including social welfare, education and health, have been the direct casualties of monopolist, narrowly based statist elitism, with the administration ignoring priorities to the development sector. Pakistan spends considerably less per capita on education, health facilities and public utilities than many other Third World countries and is very far from achieving a balanced development of economic sectors, geographic regions and social classes. Moreover, economic growth has been less egalitarian, given the almost matching increases in population and defence expenditures in a conflict-ridden region like South Asia. Defence, the servicing of foreign loans and upkeep of the bureaucracy and administration take almost three-quarters of the national budget, with little left over for the social sector (see Table 9.2). Ever increasing government expenditure and additional loans have been consuming the limited foreign exchange reserves along with a vertical increase in the national debt and annual deficit. Table 9.3 depicts that the Pakistan government's resource allocation policies are biased in favour of defence spending as against social development. The combined expenditure on the two important social sectors, namely, health and education is much less than the military spending.

On the question of education and health, which are the basis of any civil society, Pakistan's record has been poor. Rationalized by a constant security threat, defence spending and the resultant increasing expenditure have been eating away scarce resources that would otherwise be available for development. In spite of a persistent increase in population, there has been a reduction in funds for education and health.

Table 9.2
Comparative Military Expenditure and Social Sectors (Education and Health), 1960 and 1994

Country	HUMAN RESOURCES Population	Armed Forces (thousands)	Teachers (thousands)	Physicians (thousands)	PUBLIC EXPENDITURES Military million 875	Military % of GNP	Military % of GNP	Education million 875	Education % of GNP	Education % of GNP	Health million 875	Health % of GNP	Health % of GNP
	1994	1994	1993	1993	1994	1994	1960	1993	1993	1960	1963	1960	1963
South Asia	1,216,035	2,174	5,544	439.9	13,077	2.9	2.2	14,770	3.5	2.2	5,089	0.5	1.2
Afghanistan	18,879	45	35	2.4	...	...	2.2	...	...	0.9	...	...	...
Bangladesh	117,767	116	369	22.1	388	1.7	...	509	2.3	0.6	111	...	0.5
India	913,600	1,265	4,239	353.4	9,060	2.5	2.0	12,665	3.7	2.4	3,995	0.5	1.2
Nepal	21,360	35	110	1.3	45	1.1	0.4	116	2.9	0.4	32	0.2	0.8
Pakistan	126,284	587	615	60.3	3,220	6.8	5.4	1,206	2.6	1.1	827	0.3	1.8
Sri Lanka	18,125	126	176	3.4	364	4.0	1.0	273	3.1	3.8	124	2.0	1.4

Source: Ruth Leger Sivard, *World Military and Social Expenditure, 1996* (Washington, DC: Library of Congress, 1996). p. 46.

Table 9.3

Pakistan: Defence versus Development (1990–1999)

FY	Health % of GNP	Education % of GNP	Defence % of GNP
1990–91	0.7	2.1	3.0
1991–92	0.7	2.2	6.2
1992–93	0.7	2.2	6.5
1993–94	0.7	2.2	5.8
1994–95	0.6	2.4	5.3
1995–96	0.6	2.4	5.4
1996–97	0.8	2.5	5.4
1997–98	0.7	2.3	4.9
1998–99	0.7	2.2	4.8

Source: *Pakistan Economic Survey, 1998–99* (Islamabad: Govt. of Pakistan), Military Balance (International Institute of Strategic Studies) 1995–1996, 1996–1997, 1997–1998, 1999–2000, and Pervaiz Iqbal Cheema and Jasjit Singh, Defence Expenditure in South Asia, RCSS Policy Studies 10 (Colombo: Regional Centre for Strategic Studies, 2000) pp. 53–54.

It is also evident that Pakistan has continued to allocate resources for military purposes at the cost of its economic security. Such a high level of expenditure naturally shows an adverse impact on economic growth and development. Since the 1990s, Pakistan's economy has been in a severe crisis. Pakistan's foreign debt has reached the astronomical figure of US$ 38 billion. Ever since the nuclear tests in 1998, Pakistan has been on the verge of bankruptcy. Pakistan's education, medical services and social welfare programmes have totally collapsed.

As far as military expenditure is concerned, it is the most sacred of this country's sacred cows. It continues to consume almost half of the total revenues of the country and it is unrealistic to expect any military government, quasi or civilian, to cut down on defence expenditure, particularly in the shadow of the Kargil fiasco. The US, by pumping in 30 billion dollars into the Pakistani military during the Ayub and Zia era, created a 'monster with a huge appetite'. The question is, can the country afford to feed it now when outside support has dried up? And at what cost to a nation with an official literacy rate of 33 per cent, a nation where the majority of the population has no access to clean drinking water or basic health care facilities? In addition, Pakistan fails to realize the folly of attempting to compete with India and overlooks the high risks involved in imitating the erstwhile Soviet Union which broke down competing with the defence efforts of the much stronger and richer United States. The present military regime has highlighted the reduction in the recent defence budget, in fact it had been raised by 10 per cent in real terms. The continuing proxy war against India and international terrorism too have their costs in economic and political terms both internationally and domestically. However, Pakistan fails to understand it and ignores the dire need for economic reforms to save the country from an economic collapse.

Pakistan's economic performance under various regimes suggests that market-oriented economic policies without the establishment of social justice or corresponding liberalizing social policies have resulted in class and regional disparities and polarization of the society. These disparities are especially harsh in Pakistan, where a dominant elite class operates in a patron-client system. Pakistan's political history, as mentioned above, reflects the tension between economic development and the expansion of civil society. The power elite emphasizes economic development while the masses seek social and political change along with economic development. Since the expansion of civil society requires some degree of political liberalization and democratization, it is appropriate to describe this predicament as tension between economic development and political development. Economic development alone will not necessarily produce democracy. Likewise, democracy—the creation of a representative popular government wherein the will of the people is the final authority—may hinder economic development in a traditional society like Pakistan.

Prospects

The success of democracy in Pakistan has remained highly problematic, given the country's complex socio-political environment and the military's continued influence in national and regional politics. Pakistan's ruling elite has not been able to defuse interethnic conflicts, subnational loyalties and identities, and rampant regional disparities by authoritarian practices. The causal relationship between economics and democracy, as outlined by Huntington, cannot be demonstrated in the case of Pakistan. The nature of relations between regime types and development defies the established finding that economic growth fosters progress toward democratic performance. Under Pakistan's unique circumstances, the relationship between development (as measured in terms of per capita GNP) and democracy is vague and indeterminate. It reinforces the argument that economic growth alone cannot thrust a nation into steady democratization. For the latter to happen, economic growth must be accompanied by a measured political liberalization.

Elections and other democratic institutions do not create democracy in the absence of social and political consensus. They have plunged Pakistan into paralyzing cycles of polarization and confrontation, reversals of economic policy, and constitutional crises. Pakistan's fickle, fractious and short-lived experiments in restoration of democracy (1988–1999) has established 'the need for policies that link gradual social and political change to broad economic improvement. With the simultaneous expansion of civil society, economic growth by itself cannot be counted on to bring about democracy in Pakistan.'[23] The restoration of democracy began in 1988 had little contend itself for, yet it has a process that reflected and articulated the concerns, needs and aspirations of certain economic and social groups and classes. Perhaps the main feature of this period has been the rise of a large middle class, which has found democracy quite lucrative. Nevertheless, while a middle class may have consolidated itself economically in terms of the development of its politics, it still has far to go.

At the same time, the late 1980s witnessed the emergence of a civil society from an abysmal state struggling to redefine itself. As a major feature of this transforming civil society, the press, the judiciary, and numerous non-governmental organizations have begun to assert themselves forcefully, challenging the earlier conformist traditions. These vital elements of the civil society are striving to establish basic human rights and duly expose the endemic corruption. During the 11 years of democratic experiment, the print media has mushroomed and, despite a long period of suffocation of oppression, has rediscovered its potential as the journalists are engaged in investigative journalism. However, Nawaz Sharif's bout with Maleeha Lodhi, the editor of *The Nation*, and Najam Sethi, the editor of *The Friday Times*, only established professional solidarity among journalists across

---

[23]Mahmood Monshipouri and Amjad Samuel, 'Development and Democracy in Pakistan: Tenuous or Plausible Nexus?', p. 989.

the country as he was compelled to withdraw his punitive action. In sum, Pakistan has apparently found new catalysts of change and accountability in the press and is emerging vigorous vigilante of a nascent civil society in exposing the unsavoury side of society. Besides, the Pakistan Human Rights Commission and other non-governmental organizations of concerned citizens have become active in their roles as watch-dogs though all of them have a long way to go before establishing a civil society with a restraining influence on the powerful institutions of the state and its coopted intermediaries.[24]

The children of the post-partition generation or the younger generation in Pakistan are critical of the military-bureaucratic axis as well as dynastic elitism and are clamouring for an accountable and efficient government. The efforts of its political activists (alongwith the support of politicized masses and ordinary citizens) to establish a moderate and forward looking political system, based on popular participation, guaranteeing basic rights and curbing coercion and corruption, raises hopes of more positive developments in the near future.

However, the military coup by General Musharraf in 1999, has once again raised the question about the future of civil society and democracy in Pakistan. The military coup also revealed the fragility of Pakistan's experiment with the restoration of democracy. Apart from weak political institutions and persistent feudal structure throughout its turbulent and uncertain history, Pakistan has been unable to develop a consensus-based culture facilitating national integration. Due to the long list of failures, Pakistan has in the last few years been often described as a 'failed state' or 'failing state' by foreign and Pakistani observers. Some analysts have even used a much stronger term like 'anarchic state' and predicted its disintegration in the near future. In my view, to call Pakistan a 'failed' or 'anarchic' state is rather a harsh judgement as it could be applicable to many other developing countries in Asia and Africa also. The very survival of Pakistan as a country despite the odds, has amazed observers. From the backwaters of the British empire, Pakistan has reached the threshold of a middle-income country. Pakistanis withstood a radical shift in the regional balance of power in the 1970s, following a military defeat and India's nuclear explosion in the 1974, resisted temptations and coercion from a global power and re-established the nation's creditability, resilience, and re-

---

[24]Malik, *State and Civil Society in Pakistan*, p. 167.

gional pre-eminence.[25] In the 1990s, it attained nuclear parity with India. Though it cost Pakistan immensely, the country came of age. In sum, for a state as large and resourceful, and endowed with a sense of history and ideology as Pakistan, it is not likely to 'fail' in modern time. Nor does the international system normally permit a strategically significant state like Pakistan to collapse easily. Another reason why the international community would probably ensure Pakistan's survival is due to its nuclear weapons capability.

Pakistan has to choose between a healthy democratic polity, economic growth and prosperity for its people on the one hand, and an exaggerated self-perception of its strategic importance and power on the other. General Pervez Musharraf has thus far shown neither the wisdom nor the sagacity to understand and accept this reality.

The recent history of Pakistan demonstrates just how difficult it is to reverse the phenomenon of military authoritarianism. The interplay of domestic, regional and global factors during the Cold War era, which established the fact of military predominance in Pakistan, cast the state structure into an enduring mould. These factors combined again in the late 1970s and 1990s to reaffirm institutional imbalances in Pakistan. The military-bureaucratic state utilized their powers of patronage to coopt significant segments of dominant socio-economic elites and to localize political horizons in a manner reminiscent to the colonial state. Political processes in Pakistan remain hostage to highly inequitable state structure. Continuing imbalances within the state structures and also between them and civil society foreclose the possibility of a significant reapproaching of political power and economic resources in the very near future.[26]

As far as the prospects of democracy in Pakistan are concerned, democracy, defined in terms of a political system which permits sustained and full political participation of the people, has yet to strike roots in Pakistan. The roots of democracy lie in egalitarian socio-economic structures, a modernizing entrepreneurial elite and a large middle class. It also needs an expansion of civil society, namely, an independent judiciary, free press and rule of law. An emerging nascent civil society has a long way to go before attaining a curbing influence on the powerful institutions of the state. It would be incorrect to say

---

[25]Ibid., p. 259.

[26]Ayesha Jalal, *Democracy and Authoritarianism in South Asia: A Comparative and Political Perspective* (Cambridge: Cambridge University Press, 1995), pp. 120–21.

that democracy has no future in Pakistan, but one can certainly say that it would be quite a few decades before democracy obtains unshakeable roots in Pakistan. The future of democracy in Pakistan, therefore, is clouded by uncertainty. Unless the military voluntarily decides to withdraw from politics or is forced to withdraw by a mass movement, democracy is unlikely to take roots in the country.

The only solution to get rid of the cycle of coups in Pakistan lies in the development of civilian institutions which will function smoothly, negating the necessity for a military takeover. Only then will the military take its proper place by playing a constructive role in the protection and strengthening of the nation–state, within the range of its legitimate institutional pressure–group role. But the task of civilian institution-building can be undertaken only by the return to civilian rule through a strong, national, grassroots, mass-based political party led by a skilful political leadership.

What will emerge in Pakistan remains to be seen but it is quite clear that until Pakistan's institutional poverty—especially the weaker political party base, leadership norms, evolving socio-economic structure, security considerations, psychological barriers and mindset against India manifested in terms of military and strategic ties with other countries—remains the same, the military will continue to walk in the corridors of power in Pakistan.

In the post-Taliban scenario, General Musharraf has announced his project of restructuring Pakistani society under immense US pressure. Indeed, it is as much India's dream, as General Musharraf's vision that Pakistan emerges as a 'moderate Islamic welfare state' with a sound political and economic agenda at the earliest.

Obviously Pakistan cannot prove itself to be a moderate Islamic state without giving up its espousal to the clash of civilization thesis in form of the two-nation theory, *Shariah* constitutional provisions, blasphemy laws, Hadood punishments and closing down the *madrassas*.

Reality, however, pens a less optimistic script for the General's avowed intentions. The reforms announced by Musharraf at best can be characterized as 'strategic reversal' not policy change. Musharraf has not delivered on his promise yet and he cannot deliver. In Pakistan there is no widespread and strong popular urge for societal transformation. Neither the military-bureaucratic oligarchy nor the elite outside it reveal any awareness for a change.

Therefore, Pakistan in the near foreseeable future, is not likely to transform itself into a moderate Islamic democratic society. At least in the near future, democracy in Pakistan, if and when it is restored, will remain a puppet democracy. General Musharraf has asserted in an unambiguous manner that notwithstanding the promised October 2002 ballot activity, he is not walking away into the sunset. On the contrary, he plans continue in office till 2007. In sum, the military will continue to remain central to the power structure of the country.

Glossary

Ahmadis	followers of Mirza Ghulam Ahmed Qadiani; a religious minority in Pakistan
Alim	religious scholar
Amir	a person holding authority, a ruler, head of an organization
Amir-ul-Momineen	leader of Muslims
Biradari	endogamous groups of families
Brelavi	belonging to the Indian town Bareilly, and to the religious sect which adheres to the doctrine of Ahmad Raza of Bareilly; a conservative sect
Deobandi	belonging to the Muslim religious seminary of Deoband, India; an orthodox sect which abhors superstitions attributed to the Brelavi sect
Fatwa	a ruling by a jurist on the legality or otherwise of an action
fidayeen	an action suicide
Fiqh	literally, the exercise of one's intelligence to understand a matter, used for Islamic jurisprudence
Fiqhi Islam	interpretations for *Quran* and *Ahadith* as contained in the *fiqh* (jurisprudence) of medieval times
Hari	landless peasant in Sindh
Hudood	plural of *hadd*, punishments under Islamic Law
Imam	faith

Ishtmaal-i-arazi	land consolidation scheme
Islami Moswat	Islamic equality
Islamiat	Islamic religious studies
Jihad	struggle in the name of Islam
Jihad-fi-Sibilillah	holy war in the name of God
Kafir	one who refuses to believe in the unity of God, infidel
Katchi abadis	rural and tribal areas
Lashkars	armies
Madrassas	religious schools
Majlis-i-Shoora	consultative council
Malik	Pushtun tribal chieftain
Mashaikh	spiritual leaders
Muswat-e-Mohammadi	the equality of the followers of Mohammad
Maulvi	Muslim theologian
Mudraraba	profit-sharing
Muhajir	Muslim migrant
Muhalla	a small section of a town or city
Mujahid	one who participates in *Jihad*
Mujahideen	plural of *mujahid*
Muzaraa	share-cropping
Nizam-e-Mustafa	the pattern of government the holy prophet had given under his auspices to the state of Medina
Pakhtun or *Pushtun*	people of the Afghan race inhabiting mostly the North-West Frontier Province in Pakistan
Patharidars	influentials
Pir	spiritual leader
Qadianis	see Ahmadis
Qazi	a judge; judge of a Shariah Court
Quaid-i-Awam	the leader of the people
Quaid-i-Azam	the great leader, a title used for the founder of Pakistan, Mohammad Ali Jinnah
Raj	British rule in India
Riba	usury, interest, unearned income
Sajjada Nashin	the successor to a spiritual leader
Salat	prayer
Sardar	chieftain, usually in Baluchistan and South-Western Punjab

Shariat	Islamic Law
Shoora	advisory body
Sunnah	tradition of the prophet
Taqwa	piety and abstinence
Ulama	learned authorities on Islam
Ummah	community
Ushr	tithe (tax at the ratio of one-tenth)
Wadera	Sindhi landlord
Zakat	charity at the ratio of 2.5 per cent
Zamindar	landowner

Select Bibliography

PRIMARY SOURCES

Government Documents

Indian Statutory Commission, *Report of the Indian Statutory Commission*, Vol. 2 (survey CMD 3568) (London: His Majesty's Stationery Office, 1930).

Government of Pakistan, *Quaid-i-Azam Mohammad Ali Jinnah: Speeches as Governor-General, 1947–48* (Karachi, 1948).

Government of Pakistan, *Constituent Assembly of Pakistan Debates, 1949*, Vol. V (Karachi, 1949).

Government of Pakistan, *Report of Court of Inquiry Constituted Under Punjab Act II of 1954 to Enquire into Punjab Disturbances of 1953, The Munir Report.*

Government of Pakistan, Constituent Assembly of Pakistan. *Debates*, Vol. I, No. 4, 19 March 1956.

Government of Pakistan, *Report of the Land Reform Commission for West Pakistan, 1959* (Lahore, 1959).

Supplement to the Composite Report of President's Committee to Study the United States Military Assistance Program, Vol. 2 (Washington, DC: US Government Printing Office, 1959).

Martial Law Regulations and Orders issued by Supreme Commander and Chief Martial Law Administrator, 1960.

Principles of Foreign Economic Assistance (Washington, DC: US AID, 1963).

Government of Pakistan, Planning Commission, *Second Five Year Plan 1960–65* (Karachi, 1968).

Government of Pakistan, Planning Commission, *The Mid Plan Review of the Third Five Year Plan 1965–70* (Karachi, 1968).

Government of Pakistan, *A New Beginning: Reforms Introduced by the*

People's Government of Pakistan (Islamabad: Printing Corporation of Pakistan Press, 1972).

Government of Pakistan, Z. A. *Bhutto, President of Pakistan, Speeches and Statements: 20 December 1971 – 31 March 1972* (Karachi: The Department of Films and Publications, 1972).

Government of Pakistan, *4th Triennial Census Central Government Employees* (Islamabad, 1973).

Government of Pakistan, *The Constitution of Islamic Republic of Pakistan 1956.*

Government of Pakistan, *The Constitution of Islamic Republic of Pakistan 1973.*

White Paper on Baluchistan (Islamabad: Printing Corporation of Pakistan Press, 1976).

White Paper on the Conduct of the General Election in March 1977 (Islamabad: Printing Corporation of Pakistan Press, 1978).

White Paper on the Performance of the Bhutto Regime (Islamabad, 1979).

US Government, Department of State (authored by Stephen P. Cohen) 'Security Decision-Making in Pakistan'. Report Prepared for the Office of the External Research, Department of State, September 1980.

Pakistan: Human Rights Violations and the Decline of the Rule of Law (London: Amnesty International Publication, 1982).

Government of Pakistan, *Main Findings of the 1981 Population Census, Statistical Division, Population Census Organization* (Islamabad, 1983).

Amnesty International Report 1985 (London: Amnesty International, 1985).

Government of Pakistan, Economic Advisory Wing, *Economic Survey: 1993–94* (Islamabad: Finance Division, June 1994).

US House, *Mutual Development and Cooperation Act of 1973, Hearings.* 93rd Congress, 1st Session.

Special Reports

The Asian Bank, *Strategies for Economic Growth and Development: The Bank's Role in Pakistan* (Manila, 1985).

International Commission of Jurists, *The Events in East Pakistan* (Geneva, 1971).

International Institute for Strategic Studies, *Military Balance, 1992–93 to 1999–2000* (London, 1999).

The World Bank, *World Development Report: 1990–2000* (Oxford, 1990–2000).

United Nations Development Programme, *Human Development Report (1990–98)* (Oxford, 1998).

US Central Intelligence Agency, *Report on Heroin in Pakistan: Sowing the Wind* (September 1992).

World Armaments and Disarmaments, *SIPRI Year Book* (Oxford, 1974 to 2000).

SECONDARY SOURCES

Books

Afzal, M. Rafique, *Political Parties in Pakistan, 1947–1958* (Islamabad: National Commission on Historical and Cultural Research, 1976).

Ahmad, Khurshid (ed.), *Studies in Islamic Economics* (Leicesur: The Islamic Foundation, 1981).

Ahmad, Zia ul Din, et. al. *Money and Banking in Islam* (Islamabad: Institute of Policy Studies, 1983).

Ahmed, Akbar S., *Pakistan Society: Islam, Ethnicity and Leadership in South Asia* (Delhi: Oxford University Press, 1988).

Ahmed, Aziz, *Islamic Modernism in India and Pakistan 1957–1964* (London: Oxford University Press, 1967).

Ahmed, Ishtiaq, *The Concept of an Islamic State in Pakistan* (Lahore: Vanguard, 1991).

Ahmed, Kamruddin, *The Social History of East Pakistan* (Dacca: Crescent Book Store, 1967).

Ahmed, Mohammad, *My Chief* (Lahore: Longmans, Green and Company, 1960).

Ali, Muazzan (ed.), *Islamic Banks and Strategy of Economic Cooperation* (London: New Century Publishers, 1982).

Ali, Tariq, *Can Pakistan Survive: The Death of a State* (Harmondsworth: Penguin, 1983).

Ali, Tariq, *Pakistan: Military Rule or People's Power* (London: Jonathan Cape, 1970).

Amin, Tahir, *Ethno-National Movements of Pakistan* (Islamabad: Institute of Policy Studies, 1988).

Bahadur, Kalim, *Democracy in Pakistan: Crises and Conflict* (New Delhi: Har-Anand Private Pvt. Ltd., 1998).

Banuazizi, Ali and Weiner, Myron (eds), *The State, Religion and Ethnic Politics: Pakistan, Iran and Afghanistan* (Lahore: Anguard Publishers, 1987).

Bhutto, Zulfikar Ali, *If I am Assassinated* (New Delhi: Vikas Publishing House, 1979).

Blackburn, Robin, (ed.), *Explosion in a Sub-continent* (Harmondsworth: Penguin, 1973).

Brown, Michael E. and **Ganguly, Sumit** (eds), *Government Policies and Ethnic Relations in Asia and the Pacific* (Cambridge, Mass: The MIT Press, 1997).

Burki, Shahid Javed and **Baxter, Craig,** *Pakistan Under the Military: Eleven Years of Zia-ul-Haq* (Boulder, Colo: Westview Press, 1991).

Burki, Shahid Javed, *Pakistan Under Bhutto: 1971–77* (London: Macmillan Press Ltd., 1980).

Campbell-Johnson, Allen, *Mission With Mountbatten* (London: Robert Hale, 1951).

Chaudhri, Muhammad Ali, *The Emergence of Pakistan* (New York: Columbia University Press, 1967).

Cheema, P. I., *Pakistan's Defence Policy, 1947–58* (London: Macmillan, 1990).

Chisti, General Faiz Ali, *Betrayals of Another Kind: Islam, Democracy and the Army in Pakistan* (Cincinnati, Oh: Asia Publishing House, 1990).

Chowdhury, G. W., *The Last Days of United Nation* (London: Macmillan, 1974).

Cohen, Stephen P., *The Pakistan Army* (New Delhi: Himalayan Books, 1984).

Cooper, Mary H., *The Business of Drugs* (Bombay: Popular Prakashan Ltd., 1993).

Coupland, Reginald, *India: A Restatement* (London: Oxford University Press, 1945).

Dixit, Aabha, *Ethno-Nationalism in Pakistan* Delhi Papers 3 (Delhi: Institute for Defence Studies and Analyses, January 1996).

Dixit, J. N., *Anatomy of a Flawed Inheritance: Indo–Pakistan Relations: 1970–94* (New Delhi: Konark Publishers Pvt. Ltd., 1995).

Doorn, Jacques Van (ed.), *Armed Forces and Society* (Mouton: The Hague, 1968).

Easton, David, *The Political System: An Inquiry into the State of Political Science* (New York: Alfred A. Knopf, 1953).

Esposito, John L. (ed.), *Islam in Asia: Religion, Politics and Society* (Oxford: Oxford University Press, 1987).

Feldman, Herbert, *Revolution in Pakistan* (London: Oxford University Press, 1967).

Freemantle, Brian, *The Fix* (London: Michael Joseph, 1985).

Gardezi, Hassan and **Rashid, Jamil** (eds), *Pakistan: The Roots of Dictatorship: The Political Economy of a Praetorian State* (Delhi: Oxford University Press, 1984).

Gardezi, Hassan, *A Reexamination of the Social Political History of Pakistan: Reproduction of Class Relations and Ideology* (New York: The Edwin Mellen Press, 1991).

Gough, Kathleen and **Sharma, Hari P.** (eds), *Imperialism and Revolution in South Asia* (New Delhi: Monthly Review Press, 1973).

Haq, Iqramul, *Pakistan: From Hash to Heroin* (Lahore: Anoor Publishers, 1991).

Haq, Mahbubul, *The Strategy of Economic Planning: The Case of Pakistan* (Lahore: Oxford University Press, 1963).

Harrison, Seling S., *In Afghanistan Shadow: Baluch Nationalism and Soviet Temptation* (Washington, 1981).

Harrison, Seling, Kreisberg, Paul and Kux, Dennis, *India and Pakistan: The First Fifty Years* (New York: Cambridge University Press, 1999).

Huntington, Samuel P., *The Third Wave: Democratization in the Late Twentieth Century* (Norman, Okla: University of Oklahoma Press, 1991).

Hussain, Asaf, *Elite Politics in an Ideological State* (Folkestone: Dawson, 1979).

Islam, Nural, *Development Strategy of Bangladesh* (Oxford, 1978).

Jahan, Rounaq, *Pakistan: Failure in National Integration* (New York: Columbia University Press, 1972).

Jahani, Carina, *Standardization and Orthography in Balochi Language* (Upsalla, Sweden: Almquist and Wikeseth International, 1989).

Jalal, Ayesha, *Democracy and Authoritarianism in South Asia: A Comparative and Political Perspective* (Cambridge: Cambridge University Press, 1995).

Jalal, Ayesha, *The Sole Spokesman: Jinnah, The Muslim League and the Demand for Pakistan* (Cambridge: Cambridge University Press, 1983).

Jalal, Ayesha, *The State of Martial Law: The Origins of Pakistan's Political Economy of Defence* (Cambridge: Cambridge University Press, 1990).

Kennedy, Charles H. (ed.), *Pakistan: 1992* (Boulder: Westview, 1993).

Khan, Mohammad Asghar, *Generals in Politics 1958–1982* (New Delhi: Vikas Publishing House, 1983).

Khan, Mohammad Asghar (ed.), *Islam, Politics and The State: The Pakistan Experience* (London: Zed Press, 1985).

Khan, Muhammad Ayub, *Friends Not Masters: A Political Autobiography* (London, Oxford University Press, 1967).

Khan Lt. Gen. Gul Hassan, *Memoires of Lt. Gen. Gul Hassan Khan* (Karachi: Oxford University Press, 1993).

Khan, Major General Fazal Muqeem, *The Story of the Pakistan Army* (Karachi: Oxford University Press, 1963).

Kleiman, Mark A. R., *Against Excess* (New York: Harper Collins Publishers International, 1992).

Kochanek, Stanley A., *Interest Groups and Development: Business and Politics in Pakistan* (New Delhi: Oxford University Press, 1983).

Kohli, Atul, *Democracy and Discontent: India's Growing Crisis of Governability* (New York: Cambridge University Press, 1990).

Kolodziej, Edward A. and Harkavy, Robert E. (eds), *Security Policies of Developing Countries* (Lexington: Lexington Books, 1982).

Kukreja, Veena, *Civil-Military Relations in South Asia: Pakistan, Bangladesh and India* (New Delhi: Sage Publications, 1991).

Kukreja, Veena, *Military Intervention in Politics: A Case Study of Pakistan* (New Delhi: NBO, 1985).

Kumar, Satish, *The New Pakistan* (New Delhi: Vikas Publishing House, 1978).

Lamb, Christina, *Waiting for Allah* (New Delhi: Viking, 1991).

Laxmi, Y., *Trends in India's Defence Expenditure* (New Delhi: ABC, 1988).

Loshak, David, *Pakistan Crises* (London: Heinemann, 1977).

Malik, Brig. S. K., *The Quranic Concept of War* (Lahore: Wajidalis, 1979).

Malik, Iftikhar H., *State and Civil Society in Pakistan: Politics of Authority, Ideology and Ethnicity* (New York: St. Martin's Press Inc., 1997).

McGrath, Allen, *The Destruction of Pakistan's Economy* (Karachi: Oxford University Press, 1996).

Mittal, Nemisharan, *World Famous Drug Mafia* (New Delhi: Family Books, 1990).

Munir, Muhammad, *From Jinnah to Zia: A Study of Ideological Convulsion* (Lahore: Vanguard Books, 1980).

Myrdal, Gunnar, *Asian Drama: An Inquiry into the Poverty of Nations* (New York: Pantheon, 1968).

Nayak, Pandav (ed.), *Pakistan: Society and Politics* (New Delhi: South Asian Publishers, 1984).

Nayak, Pandav (ed.), *Pakistan: Dilemmas of a Developing State* (Jaipur: Aalekh Publishers, 1985).

Noman, Omar, *Pakistan: A Political and Economic History Since 1947* (London: Kegan Paul International Ltd., 1988).

Noman, Omar, *The Political Economy of Pakistan 1947–85* (London: Routledge and Kegan Paul, 1988).

Pai Panandiker, V. A. (ed.), *Problems of Governance in South Asia* (New Delhi: Konark Publishers Pvt. Ltd., 2000).

Papanek, Gustav F., *Pakistan's Development: Social Goals and Private Incentives* (Cambridge: Harvard University Press, 1968).

Phadnis, Urmila, *Ethnicity and Nation-Building in South Asia* (New Delhi: Sage, 1990).

Powis, Robert, *The Money Launderer* (Chicago: Probus Publishing, 1992).

Rahman, Ataur, *Pakistan and America: Dependency Relations* (New Delhi: Young Asia Publications, 1982).

Rizvi, Hasan Askari, *The Military in Politics in Pakistan* (Lahore: Progressive Publishers, 1976).

Rizvi, Hasan Askari, *Military, State and Society in Pakistan* (London: Milton Press Ltd., 2000).

Roy, Asim, *Islam in South Asia: A Regional Perspective* (New Delhi: South Asian Publishers, 1996).

Rupesingha, Kumar and Mumtaz, Khawar (eds), *Internal Conflicts in South Asia* (London: Sage Publications, 1996).

Sayeed, Khalid Bin, *Politics in Pakistan: The Nature and Direction of Change* (New York: Praeger Publishers, 1980).

Sayeed, Khalid Bin, *The Political System of Pakistan* (Boston: Houghton Mifflin Co., 1967).

Sayeed, Khalid Bin, *Pakistan: The Formative Phase 1857–1948* (Karachi: Pakistan Publishing House, 1968).

Shafqat, Saeed, *Civil-Military Relations in Pakistan: From Zulfikar Ali Bhutto to Benazir Bhutto* (Boulder: Westview Press, 1997).

Siddiqi, A. R., *The Military in Pakistan: Image and Reality* (Lahore: Vanguard, 1996).

Singh, Jasjit (ed.), *Kargil 1999: Pakistan's Fourth War for Kashmir* (New Delhi: Knowledge World, 1999).

Sivard, Ruth Leager, *World Military and Social Expenditure 1977* (Lessburg, Virginia: WMSE Publications, 1977).

Smith, Chris, *The Diffusion of Small Arms and Light Weapons in Pakistan and Northern India* (London: Brassey's, 1993).

Subrahmanyam, K., *Security in Changing World* (Delhi: B.R. Publishing Company, 1990).

Sutton, John L., *Arms to Developing Countries, 1945–1965* (London: Institute of Strategic Studies, 1966).

Syed, Anwar H., *The Discourses and Politics of Zulfikar Ali Bhutto* (New Delhi: St. Martin's Press, 1992).

Syed, Anwar Hussain, *Pakistan—Islam, Politics and National Solidarity* (New York: Praeger, 1982).

Syed, G. M., *Struggle for a New Sind: A Brief Narrative of Working of Provincial Autonomy in Sind During the Decade (1937–1947)* (Karachi: 1949).

Tahir-Kheli, Shirin, *The United States and Pakistan: The Evolution of an Influence Relationship* (New York: Praeger Special Studies, 1982).

Taseer, Salman, *Bhutto: A Political Biography* (New Delhi: Vikas Publishing House, 1980).

Varma, S. P. and Narain, V. (eds), *Pakistan Political System in Crisis: Emergence of Bangladesh* (Jaipur: University of Rajasthan, 1972).

Wander, Thomas, Arnett, Eric and Bracken, Paul (eds), *The Diffusion of Advanced Weaponry: Technologies, Regional Implications and Responses* (Washington, DC: American Association for Advancement of Science, 1994).

Waseem, Mohammad, *Politics and State in Pakistan* (Islamabad: National Institute of Historical and Cultural Research, 1994).

White, Lawrence J., *Industrial Concentration and Economic Power in Pakistan* (Prince: Princeton University Press, 1974).
Zaidi, A. M. (ed.), *Evolution of Muslim Political Thought in India*, Vol. I (New Delhi: Michiko and Panjathan, n.d.).
Zaidi, Akbar S. (ed.), *Regional Tribalances and Regional Questions in Pakistan* (Lahore: Vanguard Books, 1992).
Zingel, Wolfgang Peter and Zingel, Stephanie Lallemant (eds), *Pakistan in the 1980s: Ideology, Regionalism, Economy, Foreign Policy* (Lahore: Vanguard Books, 1985).
Ziring, Lawrence (ed.), *The Sub-Continent in World Politics* (New York: 1975).

Articles, Journals

Abbas, Zaffar, 'Sindh: Falling Apart?', *The Herald* (Karachi), May 1989.
Abbas, Zaffar, 'Full Circle', *The Herald*, November 1999 reproduced in *Strategic Digest*, Vol. XXIX, No. 12 (December 1999), p. 1793.
Ahmad, Eqbal, 'Pakistan: Sign-Posts to a Police State', *Journal of Contemporary Asia*, Vol. IV, No. 4 (1974).
Ahmad, Kamaluddin, 'Six-Point Movement and the Emergence of Bangladesh', *South Asian Studies*, Vol. 13 (July–December 1978).
Ahmar, Moonis, 'Ethnicity and State Power in Pakistan: The Karachi Crisis', *Asian Survey*, Vol. XXXVI, No. 10 (October 1996).
Ahmed, Feroz, 'Ethnicity and Politics: The Rise of Muhajir Separatism', *South Asia Bulletin*, Vol. 8 (1988).
Ahmed, Feroz, 'Ethnicity, Class and State in Pakistan', *Economic and Political Weekly*, 23 November 1996.
Ahmed, Feroz, 'The Rise of Muhajir in Pakistan', *Pakistan Progressive*, Vol. X, Nos. 2–3 (Summer-Fall, 1989).
Ahmed, Munir D., 'The Current International Constellation in Pakistan', *Journal of South Asian and Middle Eastern Studies*, Vol. VI, No. 4 (Summer, 1983).
Ahmed, Samina, 'A Friend for All Seasons', *Newsline*, (Karachi), October 1999 reproduced in *Strategic Digest*, Vol. XXIX, No. 12 (December 1999).
Akhtar, Jamna Das, 'Pakistan–Narcotics–Terrorism: The Linkages', *Strategic Analysis*, Vol. XVII, No. 9 (December 1994).
Alavi, H., 'Pakistan and Islam—Its Ethnicity and Ideology', *Mainstream*, 21 and 28 February 1987.
Alavi, H., 'US Aid to Pakistan: An Evaluation', *The Economic Weekly*, Special Number, July 1963.
Alavi, Hamza, 'Nationhood and the Nationalities in Pakistan', *Economic and Political Weekly*, Vol. XXIX (8 July 1989).

Ali Salamat, 'Baluchistan: An Upheaval in Forces or Forecast', *Far Eastern Economic Review*, 19 October 1979.

Amin, Tahir, 'Pakistan in 1993: Some Democratic Change', *Asian Survey*, Vol. XXXIV, No. 2 (February 1994).

Amin, Tahir, 'Pakistan in 1994: The Politics of Confrontation', *Asian Survey*, Vol. XXXV, No. 2 (February 1995).

Anand, Som, 'Islamism and Pakistan's Social Realities', *Man and Development*, Vol. II, No. 1 (March 1980).

Arif, Mohd, 'Sindh in the Midst of Crisis', *Strategic Analysis*, Vol. XXIII, No. 11 (February 2000).

Ayoob, Mohammad, 'Pakistan Comes Full Circle', *India Quarterly*, Vol. XXIV, No. 1 (January–March 1978).

Ayoob, Mohammad, 'Two Faces of Political Islam: Iran and Pakistan Compared', *Asian Survey*, Vol. XIX, No. 6 (January 1979).

Bagchi, Ajoy, 'The Gordian Knot', *The Pioneer*, New Delhi, 23 September 2000.

Bahadur, Kalim, 'Ethnic Problems in Pakistan', *World Focus*, Vol. XV, Nos. 4–5 (April–May 1994).

Bahadur, Kalim, 'Pakistan Journey to Nowhere', *World Focus*, Vol. XXI, Nos. 10–11–12 (October–November–December 2000).

Bajpai, Kanti and Ganguly, Sumit, 'Transition to Democracy in Pakistan', *In Depth*, 32 (Spring, 1993).

Bakhtar, Idress, 'The Return of State Necessity', *The Herald* (June 2000).

Bakhtiar, Idress, 'The Altaf Factor', *The Herald*, Karachi, January 1993.

Bakhtiar, Idress, 'Localizing Sovereignty', *The Herald*, September 2000.

Barnds, William J., 'Pakistan's Disintegration', *World Today*, Vol. XXVII, August 1971.

Baru, Sanjaya, 'War and Economic Pakistan's Road to Ruin', *The Times of India*, New Delhi, 14 January 1999.

Bhatia, B. M., 'Near the Brink', *The Hindustan Times*, 25 October 1996.

Bidwai, Praful, 'Lahore Verdict Opens New Phase in Pakistan', *The Times of India*, 11 June 1993.

Bienen, Henry, 'Military Rule and Political Process: Nigerian Example', *Comparative Politics*, Vol. X, No. 2 (January 1978).

Burki, Shahid Javed, 'Managing Pakistan's Present Economy: International Obligations vs. Internal Compulsions', *Pakistan Horizon*, (April–July 2000), reproduced in *Strategic Digest*, Vol. XXXI, No. 1 (January 2001).

Burki, Shahid Javed, 'Pakistan Under Zia, 1977–1988', *Asian Survey*, Vol. XXVIII, No. 10 (October 1988).

Burki, Shahid Javed, 'Pakistan's Cautious Democratic Course', *Current History*, Vol. LXXXXI, No. 563 (March 1992).

Chakravarty, Sukha Ranjan, 'The Paktoon National Movement', *Foreign Affairs Reports*, Vol. XXV, No. 1 (1976).

Changez, A. R., 'Political Parties Have No Place in an Islamic State', *The Pakistan Times,* 16 September 1977.

Cheema, Pervez Iqbal, 'Impact of the Afghan War on Pakistan', *Pakistan Horizon,* Vol. XXXI (1988).

Chengappa, Bidanda M., 'Pakistan's Fourth Coup', *The Hindustan Times,* (New Delhi), 21 October 1999.

Chengappa, Bidanda M., 'Pakistan's Fourth Military Takeover', *Strategic Analysis,* Vol. XXIII, No. 9 (December 1999).

Chopra, Surendra, 'Islamic Fundamentalism and Pakistan's Foreign Policy', *India Quarterly,* Vol. XLIX, Nos. 1–2 (January–June 1993).

Dayan Hasan, Syed Ali, 'Requirement for the Third Pakistani Republic', *The Herald,* November 1999, reproduced in *Strategic Digest,* Vol. XXIX, No. 12 (December 1999).

Dethe, V. K., 'Pakistan: Power Play: Of Leaders and the President's Prime Ministers', *The Times of India,* 20 April 1993.

Dhar, M. K., 'Pak Nuclear Plan Financed by Drug Money', *The Hindustan Times,* 18 October 1994.

Dixit, Aabha, 'Narco-Power: Threatening the Very Roots of Pak Society', *Strategic Analysis,* Vol. XIII, No. 15 (May 1991).

Dixit, Aabha, 'Developments in Pakistan', *Strategic Analysis,* Vol. XIX, No. 4 (July 1996).

Dixit, Aabha, 'Focus on Pakistan's Army', *The Times of India,* 24 April 1993.

Dixit, J. N., 'A Difficult Neighbour', *The Hindustan Times* (New Delhi), 27 October 1999.

Dixit, J. N., 'In the General's Own Words', *The Hindustan Times* (New Delhi), 2 February 2000.

Dua, H. K., 'Pakistan: Politics of Intrigue', *The Hindustan Times,* 22 April 1993.

Dupree, Louis, 'The Military is Dead! Long Live the Military', *American Universities Field Staff Report* (South Asian Series), Vol. XII, No. 3 (1969).

Engineer, Asghar Ali, 'Pakistan's Policy and its Viability', *The Hindu,* (Delhi), 14 October 2000.

Fazal, M. Abul, 'Feudalism', *The Nation,* 10 and 11 June 1997.

Galeotti, Mark, 'The Drugs War in Central Asia', *Jane's Intelligence Review,* (October 1994).

Gandhi, Kishore, 'Kashmir—A Holistic Approach', *The Hindustan Times,* 18 October 1994.

Griffith, Ivelaw L., 'From Cold War Geopolitics to Post-Cold War Geonarcotics', *International Journal,* Vol. XLIX, No. 1 (Winter, 1993–94).

Gutteridge, William, 'The Indianization of the Indian Army 1918–45: A Case Study', *Race,* Vol. IV, No. 2 (May 1963).

Haq, Farhat, 'Rise of the MQM in Pakistan: Politics of Ethnic Mobilization', *Asian Survey,* Vol. XXXV, No. 11 (November 1995).

Haroon, Assia, 'Prophetic Times','Newstime, No. 10 (April 1998).

Harrison, Selig, 'First Put Pressure on Pakistan to Pull Back', *International Herald Tribune*, London, 16 June 1999.

Hassan, Riaz, 'Islamization: An Analysis of Religious. , Political and Social Change in Pakistan', *Middle Eastern Studies*, Vol XXI, No. 3 (July 1983).

Heeger, Gerald A., 'Politics in the Post–Military State: Some Reflections on the Pakistani Experience', *World Politics*, Vol. XXIX, No. 4 (January 1977).

Housepain, Nubar, 'Pakistan in Crisis: An Interview with Eqbal Ahmad', *Race and Class*, Vol. XXII, No. 2 (Autumn, 1980).

Hurst, C. D., 'Pakistan's Ethnic Divide', *Studies in Conflict and Terrorism*, Vol. XIX (1996).

Hussain, Asaf, 'Ethnicity, National Identity and Praetorianism: The Case of Pakistan', *Asian Survey*, Vol. XVI, No. 10 (October 1976).

Hussain, Mushahid, 'A Counter Offensive by the PPP', *The Times of India*, 14 September 1986.

Hussain, Mushahid, 'Benazir's Goal is Consolidation Now', *The Times of India*, 4 November 1989.

Hussain, Mushahid, 'Important Gains for Pakistani Democracy', *The Times of India*, 9 November 1990, p. 6.

Hussain, Mushahid, 'Pakistan President Plays Key Political Role', *The Times of India*, 18 July 1989.

Hussain, Zahid, 'Day of the Generals', *Newsline* (Karachi), October 1999.

Hussain, Zahid, 'Empowering the Khakis?' *Newsline*, September 2000.

Hussain, Zahid, 'Narco Power: Pakistan's Parallel Government', *Strategic Digest*, Vol. XX, No. 6 (June 1990).

Hussain, Zahid, 'Three Major Drug Syndicates in Pakistan', *Newsline*, reproduced in *Strategic Digest*, Vol. XXIII, No. 10 (October 1993).

Ibrahim, Samina, 'A Nation of Tax Evaders', *Newsline*, Karachi, May 2000.

Iqbal, Anwar, 'Is the Tide Turning Against the MQM?' *The Muslim*, Islamabad, 17 May 1989.

Iqbal, Javid, 'Islamization in Pakistan', *Journal of South Asian and Middle Eastern Studies*, Vol. VIII, No. 5 (Spring, 1985).

Ishaque, Khalid M., 'The Islamic Approach to Economic Activity and Development', *Pakistan Economist*, Vol. XVII, No. 20 (July 1977).

Jalal, Ayesha, 'Inheriting the Raj: Jinnah and the Governor-Generalship Issue', *Modern Asian Studies*, Vol. XIX, No. 1 (1985).

Jha, Prem Shankar, 'Where Next With Pakistan', *The Hindustan Times*, 11 February 2000.

Jilani, Hina, 'Zia and the End of Civil Society', *The Herald* (Karachi), August 1999.

Kandar, Shahid, 'Can We Repay Our Debt?' *The Nation*, 21 December 1997.

Karim, Methab S., 'Karachi's Demographic Dilemma', *Dawn, Friday Magazine*, 27 February 1987.

Kemal, A. R., 'Income Distribution in Pakistan: A Review', *Research Report Series* no. 123 (Islamabad: Pakistan Institute of Development Economics, 1981).

Khalid, M., 'The Islamic Approach to Economic Activity and Development', *Pakistan Economist*, Vol. XII, No. 20 (July 1977).

Khan, Aamer Ahmed, 'Devolution Destruction', *The Herald*, September 2000.

Khan, Aamer Ahmed, 'The New Face of Nawaz Sharif', *The Herald*, Annual, Vol. XXIX, No. 1 (January 1998).

Khan, Aftab Ahmed, 'Massive Growth in Public Debt', *The News*, 28 July 1997.

Khan, Behroz, 'Sectarian Spill Over', *Newsline*, October 1999.

Khan, Kamran, 'PM's Bolt From the Blue Actions Cause Army's NSC Move', *The News*, (Lahore), 7 October 1998.

Khan, M. Asghar, 'Quaid-I-Azam on Soldiers and Politics', *Defence Journal*, Vol. IV, No. 11 (1978).

Khan, Rais Ahmed, 'Pakistan in 1992: Waiting for Change', *Asian Survey*, Vol. XXXVIII, No. 2 (February 1993).

Khan, Zaigham, 'Allah's Army', *The Herald*, January 1998.

Khan, Zaigham, 'Blundering the Blasphemy', *The Herald* (June 2000).

Korson, J. Henry, 'Islamization and Social Policy in Pakistan', *Journal of South Asian and Middle Eastern Studies*, Vol. VI, No. 2 (Winter, 1982).

Kukreja, Veena, 'Pakistan's 1993 Election: Back to square One', *Strategic Analysis*, Vol. XVI, No. 10 (January 1994).

Kukreja, Veena, 'Politics in Pakistan: Nawaz Sharif at the Helm', *Strategic Analysis*, Vol. XXX, No. 6 (September 1991).

Kukreja, Veena, 'Restoration of Democracy and Crisis of Governability in Pakistan: 1988–92', in Subrata Mukherjee and Sushila Ramaswamy (eds), *Political Science Annual 1993* (New Delhi: Deep and Deep, 1993).

Kukreja, Veena, 'Restoration of Democracy in Pakistan: One Year of Benazir's Rule', *Strategic Analysis*, Vol. XII, No. 11 (February 1990).

Kukreja, Veena, 'The Zia Regime: Legitimization Through Islamization', *Strategic Analysis*, Vol. XV, No. 3 (June 1992).

Kukreja, Veena, 'Civil-Military Relations in Developing Countries', *India Quarterly*, Vol. XLV, Nos. 2–3 (April–September 1989).

Kukreja, Veena, 'Pakistan's 1993 Election: Back to Square One', *Strategic Analysis*, Vol. XVI, No. 10 (January 1994).

Kumar, Satish, 'Militant Islam: The Nemesis of Pakistan', *Aakrosh*, Vol. III, No. 6 (January 2000), reproduced in *Strategic Digest*, Vol. XXX, No. 8 (August 2000).

Kumar, Sumita, 'Drug Trafficking in Pakistan', *Asian Strategic Review 1994–95* (New Delhi: Institute for Defence Studies and Analysis, 1995).

Kumar, Sumita, 'Pakistan's Jehadi Apparatus: Goals and Methods', *Strategic Analysis*, Vol. XXIX, No. 12 (March 2001).

Kumar, Sumita, 'Sharif vs. Musharraf: The Future of Democracy in Pakistan', *Strategic Analysis*, Vol. XXIV, No. 10 (January 2001).

Lamb, Christina, 'Power Struggle Paralysis', *Financial Times*, London, 3 July 1989.

LaPorte, Jr Robert, 'Pakistan in 1995: The Continuing Crisis', *Asian Survey*, Vol. XXXVI, No. 2 (February 1996).

LaPorte, Jr Robert, 'Pakistan in 1996', *Asian Survey*, Vol. XXXVII, No. 2 (February 1997).

Malik, Hafeez, 'The Afghan Crisis and Its Impact on Pakistan', *Journal of South Asian and Middle Eastern Studies*, Vol. V, No. 3 (Spring, 1982).

Malik, Iftikhar H., 'The State and Civil Society in Pakistan: From Crisis to Crisis', *Asian Survey*, Vol. XXVI, No. 7 (July 1996).

Malik, Khalid Mahmood, 'Drug Menace in South Asia', *Regional Studies*, Vol. VIII, No. 3 (Summer, 1990).

Maniruzzaman, Talukdar, 'Group Interest in Pakistan Politics 1947–58', *Pacific Affairs*, Vol. XXXIX (1966).

Masood, Talat, 'Lessons for the Military', *News*, 19 October 1995.

Menon, N. C., 'Peril of Pakistan Heroin', *The Hindustan Times* (New Delhi), 24 September 1994.

Mirza, Mohammad, 'The Question of Custodial Killings', *Friday Times* (Lahore), 19–25 October 1995.

Monshipouri, Mahmood and Samuel, Amjad, 'Development and Democracy in Pakistan: Tenuous or Plausible Nexus?', *Asian Survey*, Vol. XXXV, No. 11 (November 1995).

Mozaffar, Shaheen, 'The Politics of Cabinet Formation in Pakistan: A Study of Recruitment to the Central Cabinets—1947–77' (Ph.D. Dissertation, Miami University, Ohio, 1980).

Mukherjee, Dilip, 'Ms. Bhutto's Predicament: Sharing Power to Survive', *The Times of India*, 4 May 1990.

Mukherjee, Dilip, 'Sharif on Sticky Wicket: Frailty of Pakistan's Democracy', *The Times of India*, 16 October 1992.

Muni, S. D., 'Internal Political Problems', *World Focus*, No. 115 (July 1986).

Naqvi M. B., 'Ishaq Khan–Machiavelli in Pakistan Politics', *The Times of India*, 2 June 1993.

Naqvi, M. B., 'Army May Step in as Crisis Builds in Pakistan', *The Times of India*, 3 July 1993.

Naqvi, M. B., 'Brightest Star on Pakistan's Firmament Under Cloud', *The Times of India*, 27 June 1993.

Naqvi, M. B., 'Survival of the Wiliest', *Sunday Times of India*, 11 April 1993.

Nasr, Seyyed Vali Reza, 'Democracy and the Crisis of Governability in Pakistan', *Asian Survey*, Vol. XXXII, No. 6 (June 1992).

Newman, K. J., 'Pakistan's Preventive Autocracy and Its Causes', *Pacific Affairs*, Vol. XXXII, No. 1 (March 1959).

Newman, K. J., 'The Constitutional Evolution of Pakistan', *International Affairs*, Vol. XXXVIII, No. 3 (July 1962).

Nizami, Arif, 'A Balance Sheet in the Deficit', *The Nation*, 2 December 1989.

Osmani, Nisar, 'Presidential System More Suitable', *Dawn*, 28 March 1978.

Pattanaik, Smruti S., 'Pakistan's North-West Frontier: Under a New Name', *Strategic Analysis* (August 1998).

Pattanaik, Smruti S., 'Islam and the Ideology of Pakistan', *Strategic Analysis*, Vol. XXII, No. 9 (December 1998).

Philip, David, 'Ghulam The Grim', *Economic and Political Weekly*, 21 December 1996.

Prabha, Kshitij, 'Narco-Terrorism and India's Security', *Strategic Analysis*, Vol. XXIV, No. 10 (January 2001).

Qureshi, S. M. M., 'Pakhtunistan: The Frontier Dispute Between Afghanistan and Pakistan', *Pacific Affairs*, Vol. XXXIX, Nos. 1–2 (Spring–Summer, 1966).

Rahman, M. Anisur, 'East Pakistan: The Roots of Estrangement', *South Asian Review*, Vol. 3, No. 3 (April 1970).

Rahman, Tariq, 'Language and Politics in a Pakistan Province: The Sindhi Language Movement', *Asian Survey*, Vol. XXV, No. 11 (November 1995).

Rais, Rasual B., 'Pakistan in 1988: From Command to Conciliation Politics', *Asian Survey*, Vol. XXIX, No. 2 (February 1989).

Rao, Radhakrishna, 'Narco-Terrorism: Pakistan's Thriving Business: But it Can Prove the Country's Nemesis', *PTI Feature*, Vol. XIII, No. 43 (12 June 1993).

Rashid, Ahmed, 'Bhutto's Burden: Pakistan in Deep Economic Crisis', *The Times of India*, 23 September 1996.

Rashid, Ahmed, 'Pakistan's Coup: Planting the Seeds of Democracy', *Current History* (December 1999).

Rashid, Ahmed, 'Riches and Rubble: Karachi Collapse Rocks Bhutto Government', *Far Eastern Economic Review*, Vol. CLVIII, No. 2 (12 January 1998).

Rashid, Ahmed, 'The Taliban Exporting Extremism', *Foreign Affairs*, Vol. LXXVIII, No. 6 (November–December 1999).

Riaz, Mohammad, 'Drug Control on Priority', *Pakistan and Gulf Economist*, Vol. VIII, No. 13 (7 April 1989).

Richter, William L., 'Pakistan in 1984: Digging In', *Asian Survey*, Vol. XXV, No. 2 (February 1985).

Richter, William L., 'Persistent Praetorianism: Pakistan's Third Military Regime', *Pacific Affairs*, Vol. LI, No. 3 (Fall, 1978).

Richter, William L., 'The Political Dynamics of Islamic Resurgence in Pakistan', *Asian Survey*, Vol. XIX, No. 6 (June 1979).

Rizvi, Hasan Askari, 'Pakistan in 1998: A Polity Under Pressure', *Asian Survey,* Vol. XXXIX, No. 1 (January–February 1999).

Sabur, A. K. M. Abdus, 'Pakistan: Ethnic Conflict and the Question of National Integration', *BIISS Journal,* Vol. XI, No. 4 (1990).

Saleem, Farooq, 'Pakistan Under a Mountain Debt', *The News,* 16 March 1997.

Samina Ibrahim, 'A Nation of Tax Evaders', *Newsline,* Karachi, May 2000, reproduced in *Strategic Digest,* Vol. XXX, No. 7 (July 2000).

Sarkar, J. and Rashid, A., 'Proxy War', *FEER,* 20 October 1994.

Sayeed, Asad, 'Behind the Facade of Economic Revival', *The Herald,* Karachi, November 2000, reproduced in *Strategic Digest,* Vol. XXXI, No. 1 (January 2001).

Sayeed, Khalid Bin, 'Pakistan's Constitutional Autocracy', *Pacific Affairs,* Vol. XXVI, No. 4 (Winter, 1963–64).

Sayeed, Khalid Bin, 'Collapse of Parliamentary Democracy in Pakistan', *The Middle East Journal,* Vol. XIII, No. 4 (Autumn, 1959).

Shafqat, Saeed, 'Pakistan Under Benazir', *Asian Survey,* Vol. XXXVI, No. 2 (July 1996).

Siddiqi, A. R., 'Army: Chickens are Coming Home to Roost', *Nation,* 23 October 1995.

Siddiqui, Taimur, 'Operation Rescue?', *Newsline,* Karachi, May 2000, reproduced in *Strategic Digest,* Vol. XXX, No. 7 (July 2000).

Singh, Gajendra K., 'Uphill Task Ahead', *The Pioneer,* New Delhi, 25 November 1999.

Singh, Jasjit, 'India's Strategic Environment in Southern Asia', *Journal of Strategic Studies,* Vol. VII (1988).

Singh, Jasjit, 'Nothing Uniform About Them', *The Sunday Times of India,* New Delhi, 25 November 1999.

Singh, Jasjit, 'Pakistan's Nuclear Posturing: Hitching its Stars to India's Wagon', *The Times of India,* New Delhi, 13 November 1996.

Singh, Jasjit, 'The Army in the Power Structure of Pakistan', *Strategic Analysis,* Vol. XVII, No. 7 (October 1995).

Sobhan, Rehman, 'The Problem of Regional Imbalance in the Economic Development of Pakistan', *Asian Survey,* Vol. 2, No. 5 (July 1962).

Spain, James, 'Military Assistance to Pakistan', *American Political Science Review,* Vol. XLVIII, No. 3 (September 1959).

Sreedhar, and Srinivas, T., 'The Illegal Drug Trade: Asian Experience', *Strategic Analysis,* Vol. XX, No. 5 (August 1997).

Sreedhar, 'Pakistan's Economic Dilemma', *Strategic Analysis,* Vol. XXII, No. 3 (June 1998), p. 445.

Stern, Jessica, 'Pakistan's *Jihad* Culture', *Foreign Affairs,* Vol. LXXIX, No. 6 (November–December 2000).

Subrahmanyam, K., 'Battle Fatigues: Predictable Replay in Pakistan', *The Times of India,* 18 October 1999.

Subrahmanyam, K., 'Zia Used Money to Run State, Says Pak Weekly', *The Economic Times*, New Delhi, 21 October 1994.

Subrahmanyam, K., 'Pakistani Drug Disclosure', *The Economic Times*, 20 October 1994, p. 8.

Subrahmanyam, K., 'Heroin Connection: Role of Drug Money in Pakistan Politics', *The Times of India*, New Delhi, 19 December 1994.

Syed, Answar H., 'Pakistan in 1997: Nawaz Sharif's Second Chance to Govern', *Asian Survey*, Vol. XXXVIII, No. 2 (February 1998).

Tahir–Kheli, Shirin, 'The Military in Contemporary Pakistan', *Armed Forces and Society*, Vol. VI, No. 4 (Summer, 1980).

Turbiville, Graham H. Jr., 'Narcotics Trafficking in Central Asia: A New Columbia', *Military Review* (December 1992).

Waseem, Mohammad, 'Pakistan's Lingering Crisis of Dyarchy', *Asian Survey*, Vol. XXXII, No. 7 (July 1992), reproduced in *Strategic Digest*, Vol. XXII, No. 12 (December 1992).

Weibaum, Marvin G. and Cohen, Stephen P., 'Pakistan in 1982: Holding On', *Asian Survey*, Vol. XXIII, No. 2 (February 1983).

Weinbaum, A. Marvin, 'War and Peace in Afghanistan: The Pakistani Role', *Middle East Journal*, Vol. XXXXV, No. 1 (Winter, 1991).

Weinbaum, M. G., 'The March 1977 Elections in Pakistan: Where Everyone Lost', *Asian Survey*, Vol. XXII, No. 7 (July 1977).

Weiss, Anita M., 'Women's Position in Pakistan: Socio-Cultural Effects of Islamization', *Asian Survey*, Vol. XXIII, No. 2 (February 1983).

Whitaker, Raymond, 'Pakistan's Top Orator Divides Karachi Voters', *The Independent*, New York, 22 October 1990.

Wilder, Andrew R., 'Changing Patterns of Punjab Politics in Pakistan: National Assembly Election Results 1988 and 1993', *Asian Survey*, Vol. XXXV, No. 4 (April 1995).

Wright, Theodore P. Jr., 'Indian Muslim Refugees in the Politics of Pakistan', *Journal of Commonwealth and Comparative Politics*, July 1974.

Yasmeen, Samina, 'Democracy in Pakistan: The Third Dismissal', *Asian Survey*, Vol. XXXIV, No. 6 (June 1994).

Yousaf, Brig. Mohammad and Major Mark Adlkin, 'The Bear Trap: Afghanistan's Untold Story', *Jang*, Lahore, 1992.

Yusuf, Zohra, 'The Year in Democracy', *The Herald*, Annual, January 1998.

Yusufzai, Rahimullah, Exporting Jihad', *Newsline*, September 1998.

Zaidi, Mubashir, 'Day of Judgement', *The Herald* (August 2000).

Zaidi, S. Akbar, 'Democracy, Dictatorship and Development', *The Herald*, November 1990, reproduced in *Strategic Digest*, Vol. XXIX, No. 12 (December 1999).

Ziring, Lawrence, 'From Islamic Republic to Islamic State in Pakistan', *Asian Survey*, Vol. XXIV, No. 9 (September 1984).

Ziring, **Lawrence**, 'Pakistan in 1989: The Politics of Stalemate', *Asian Survey,* Vol. XXX, No. 2 (February 1990).

Magazines, News Weeklies and Journals

Asia Week (Hong Kong)
Defence Journal (Karachi)
Delhi Recorder (New Delhi)
Economic and Political Weekly (Mumbai)
Economic Weekly (Mumbai)
Economist (London)
Far Eastern Economic Review (Hong Kong)
Herald (Karachi)
India Today (New Delhi)
Newsline (Karachi)
Newsweek (New York)
Pakistan and Gulf Economist (Karachi)
Pakistan Economist (Karachi)
Pulse (Islamabad)
Time (Chicago)
View Point (Lahore)
World Focus (New Delhi)

Newspapers

The Dawn (Karachi)
The Financial Times (London)
The Frontier Post (Lahore)
The Hindu (Delhi)
The Hindustan Times (New Delhi)
The Indian Express (New Delhi)
The Jang (Karachi, Lahore and Rawalpindi)
The Khyber Mail (Peshawar)
The Muslim (Islamabad)
The Nation (Lahore, Islamabad and Rawalpindi)
The Nawa-i-Waqt (Lahore)
The New Statesman (London)
The New York Times (New York)
The News (Lahore and Islamabad)
The North East Times (Jorhat)
The Observer (London)

The Pakistan Economist (Karachi)
The Pakistan Times (Lahore)
The Pioneer (New Delhi)
The Economic Times (New Delhi)
The Friday Times (Lahore)
The Times (London)
The Times of India (New Delhi)
The Tribune (Chandigarh)
The Washington Post (Washington, DC)

Index

About the Author

Veena Kukreja is Associate Professor in the Department of Political Science, University of Delhi. Her previous books include *Military Intervention in Politics: A Case Study of Pakistan* and *Civil–Military Relations in South Asia: Pakistan, Bangladesh and India*. Dr Kukreja specializes in international politics and Pakistan studies and has published numerous articles in scholarly journals.